RouterOS by Example

Understanding MikroTik RouterOS Through
Real Life Applications

2nd Edition

Stephen R.W. Discher

2nd Edition Editor: Lauren J.A. Discher
1st Edition Editor: Carolyn Discher
1st Edition Illustrations: Phillip Crawford
Cover Design: Enrique Gonzales

Printed in the United States of America, first printing, 2011.

Printed in the United States of America, second edition, third printing, January 2017.

Printed in the United States of America, second edition, fourth printing, April 2018.

Stephen R.W. Discher

LearnMikroTik.com

10770 State Highway 30
Suite 200
College Station, Texas 77845

Table of Contents

INTRODUCTION

In *RouterOS by Example, Second Edition*, I have updated the book to include the new features and commands introduced by RouterOS Version 6. I have also incorporated information based on comments sent to me by readers of the First Edition. I have also added a chapter that is not part of the MikroTik MTCNA Training (for which this book is designed to target), specifically teaching the inner workings of the Cloud Router Switches or CRS series of managed switch/routers from MikroTik.

I have always been the type of person that learns through doing, not just reading or listening. Therefore, in my classes, I teach through examples and have attempted to do that in this book.

A few things have changed in RouterOS since I wrote the first book, so I have edited the original book to include those changes. I have learned more tips and tricks that I will also share with you in this second edition.

Who or What is MikroTik?

Located in Riga, Latvia, MikroTik was founded in 1995 to develop routers and wireless ISP systems. With more than one hundred employees at the time of this writing, MikroTik is a growing company with a full-featured router operating system, RouterOS. In 2002, MikroTik entered the hardware-manufacturing field with the brand RouterBOARD. RouterBOARD continues to develop new designs, targeting small companies, WISPS (Wireless Internet Service Providers) and wired ISP's (Internet Service Providers) looking for high performance, small footprint and a powerful feature set.

This book is based on version 6.42 using Winbox version 3.

What is RouterOS?

In simple terms, RouterOS is routing software that runs on a PC-based hardware platform. Whether it's a conventional X86-based PC, RouterBOARD embedded device, or virtual machine, RouterOS is an operating system that will make your device a dedicated router, bandwidth shaper, transparent packet filter, or wireless-enabled device. Have an old PC lying around? With RouterOS, it can be converted into a powerful router.

RouterOS can also be installed on a virtual machine, VMware/ESX environment, or parallels if you are using Mac. Most recently introduced is the CHR (Cloud Hosted Router), a version designed specifically for labs and training without the need for a license and the associated cost. From the MikroTik forums, Normis, a MikroTik employee writes, "It is a Virtual Machine image of RouterOS that has full functionality of RouterOS without any kind of conventional RouterOS license, with the limitation of 1Mbit per interface. In the future, we will offer unlimited speed with a paid subscription. This allows you to use RouterOS for training classes, testing, experimentation, etc., without the need for a 24-hour trial or Demo license. We provide a generic (RAW) format IMG that you can convert to other formats with Qemu or other tools. For your convenience, we have already pre-converted them to VMDK (VMware virtual disk image) and VDI (VirtualBox disk image). Those are not installers, but ready disk images."

RouterBOARD is a hardware platform manufactured by MikroTik. The product can range from a very small home router to a carrier class access concentrator.

RouterBOARD – The MikroTik Hardware Platform

As previously stated, you don't need a RouterBOARD to run RouterOS. It can be run on any X86-based personal computer; however, the RouterBOARD platform is a cost-effective series of devices, specifically designed to be powerful routers. A brief introduction to the product line will help you understand how to pick the correct device for your application.

RouterBOARD Product Designations

RouterBOARDs can be divided into two basic groups: Integrated devices, meaning a board in a finished case with a power supply, or possibly an antenna. RouterBOARDs are bare motherboards that require the user to add accessories like cases and power supplies. They are also designated by a product name that is descriptive of the product's physical capabilities.

The line of integrated devices includes the popular RB750 or the RB751U-2HnD.

RB750   **RB751U-2HnD**

These are SOHO or small office/home office routers, suitable for use as Internet gateways, firewalls, VPN concentrators, or wireless access points.

The model number tells you about the capabilities of a RouterBOARD device. For example, the RB designates it is a RouterBOARD, the 7 designates it is a 700 series device with respect to the base system design, and the 5 means 5 Ethernet ports. The 0 in RB750 means there is no provision for wireless interfaces, that is, no integrated wireless cards or mini PCI slots to accept a wireless card.

The RB751U-2HnD on the other hand, is a 700 series RouterBOARD with a 2 GHz wireless interfaces integrated within, including dual chain antennas (designated by the letter D), a USB port (designated by the letter U), and it is capable of high power operation on 802.11n (which includes 802.11b/g operation as well).

Prior to the creation of the Cloud Core Series, the top-level router was the RB1100 series, specifically the RB1100AHx2, a dual core router based on the PowerPC architecture, outfitted with 13 Gigabit ports.

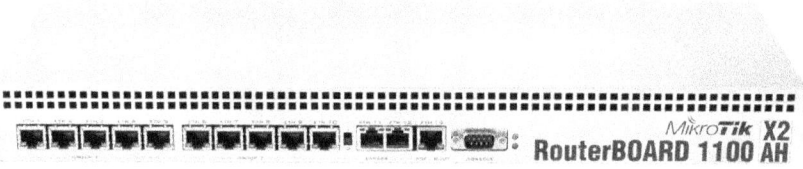

This device is suitable for use as an Internet router or firewall in a large office environment or as the gateway router for an ISP (Internet Service Provider).

After significant development and through a cooperative effort with processor chip manufacturer, Tilera, MikroTik has developed the CloudCore series of routers. It is the first truly affordable, multi-core (more than two) router with performance up to 51.5 million packets per second or 28-gigabit full wire speed. These top-of-the-line routers from MikroTik support one and ten gigabit SFP interfaces and feature up to 36 cores of processing power with a 72 core device in development at the time of the writing of this book, for carrier class compatibility and performance.

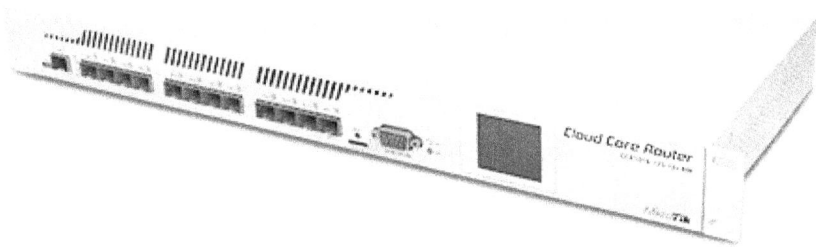

Custom RouterBOARD Solutions

If you need more of a custom solution, there is a complete line of RouterBOARDs that will allow you to configure a custom wireless or routing device. These can range from small CPE devices all the way up to the most powerful RouterBOARDs.

RB411   **RB800**

These devices can be outfitted with wireless mini PCI cards also built by MikroTik, and placed into indoor or outdoor cases.

MikroTik builds several styles of indoor cases for their boards. There are also several "Made for MikroTik" manufacturers that build indoor and outdoor cases ranging from rack-mounted cases to outdoor weatherproof cases for wireless access points. The options and combinations are endless, allowing a high level of flexibility with this product line. The cost for the bare boards ranges from $49 through $350 for the top-of-the-line RB800.

As previously explained, the product descriptor designates the capabilities of the product and at the time of this writing, they are (with minor exception for some legacy products) as follows:

First Letter – Model designation such as RB for RouterBOARD, CCR for Cloud Core Router, or CRS for Cloud Core Switch.

First Digit – Series number such as 4xx, 7xx, 8xx, 11xx, and 12xx.

Second Digit – Designates the number of Ethernet ports, such as 750, which means 5 Ethernet ports.

Letter Designators Following Model Numbers

- A - With respect to wireless capable devices, this device comes complete with a Level 4 license so it can be configured as an access point.
- U - Designates USB support and at least one USB port.
- H - Designates high power with respect to the CPU.
- A - Extra memory and usually a higher license level.
- 2 - Following a model number designates 2 GHz operation for the wireless interface.
- 5 - Following a model number designates 5 GHz operation for the wireless interface.
- N - Following a 2 or 5 designates 802.11n capability.
- H - For wireless devices, designates high RF power output.
- G - Designates Gigabit capability for the Ethernet ports.
- L - Designates low-cost or light edition.
- D - For wireless devices, designates dual chain 802.11n operation.
- P - Designates POE or Power over Ethernet output.
- EM - Extra memory.
- S - SFP Interface support.
- S+ - SFP plus interface support.
- e - PCIe interface support.
- MMCX - MMCX connector type.
- u.FL - u.FL connector type.
- BU - board unit (no enclosure) - for situation when board-only option is required, but main product already comes in the case
- RM - rack-mount enclosure
- IN - indoor enclosure
- OUT - outdoor enclosure
- SA - sector antenna enclosure
- HG - high-gain antenna enclosure
- EM - extended memory

As you can see, the product line is extensive, with more than 40 boards and interfaces available for a wide range of applications. With the availability of integrated, ready-to-use routers or components to allow you to custom-build a device to your specifications, the RouterBOARD product line is both versatile and powerful.

How This Book is Structured

I have written this book as a text for the MTCNA (MikroTik Certified Network Associate) training classes, which I conduct throughout the United States. Titled *RouterOS by Example*, I have taken the approach that simply describing features is pointless. What users really want is a simple guide to show them, step by step, through example, what they want to accomplish. They care less about minute details and more about best practice and getting things done.

This book is not a manual for the operating system, so it does not describe every feature in detail. If you are looking for a feature reference book, MikroTik offers the manual online and free of charge. That material will not be duplicated in this book.

Users need to understand the basic features and associated concepts, but without practical examples, they are left unequipped to solve network challenges. I want to give you applications, examples, and recommended practices, only describing the features you typically need and use. The lesser-used features and settings are in the free online manual located at http://wiki.mikrotik.com.

This book is meant to teach the basics using the subjects in the MTCNA syllabus written by MikroTik. They believe as well as I do that the MTCNA program contains all the features you will need to become proficient at a beginner or intermediate level. My goal for this book is to deliver that information to you according to the current syllabus on the date of this writing. I have followed the order of the syllabus as much as possible, but reordered some topics to present them in a more logical progression. I have strived to cover every single topic in the MTCNA syllabus in sufficient detail with examples.

Since the MTCNA is the first certification and considered the basic or foundation certification, I will not cover every single feature or detail available in RouterOS. You should, however, receive enough knowledge to use the system in powerful ways and through further experience, become quite proficient with the most complex setups.

Each bolded section is based on a concept and titled according to the feature that provides the concept. Most sections contain real-life applications presented through examples.

The Table of Contents will lead you to both concepts and examples. I have also included an Index of Terms in the back of the book. I approach indexes a little differently than some authors, in that I do not index every occurrence of a word. Instead, I index words based on the page in the book where the concept is best explained. Also included in the book is a Table of Figures. Screen shots are not included in that table because they are so numerous.

Chapter 1- First-Time Access

Whether you are installing RouterOS on a non-RouterBOARD
device or accessing a RouterBOARD with RouterOS already
installed, the basic method of access is the same. There are several
options to access the operating system, and they are WinBox (the
GUI, graphical user interface), Webfig (via HTTP and your web
browser), and command line via serial, telnet, or SSH. Additionally,
the RouterOS API provides yet another manner of accessing the
device that is far beyond the scope of this book.

WinBox

WinBox is a Microsoft Windows-based GUI that is by far the
simplest way to configure a RouterOS device. It is extremely
powerful and allows configuration of 99% of the feature set. WinBox
is a standalone executable, meaning it isn't necessary to install
anything on your PC. Just download the program by saving it to your
computer's desktop and double click it to start it. If you don't have
WinBox already, you can download it from MikroTik.com.

The first time you try to connect to your MikroTik device, it may or
may not have an IP address configured on it. One of the great
features of WinBox is the ability to get in without an actual IP
address, but a note of caution is needed here. Access using the MAC
address should only be used in order to configure an IP address on
the device. It is **not** a reliable way of accessing the router. I hesitate
to call it an unreliable method, but it's not the correct method and
sometimes you may get unexpected results (configuration pages that
don't properly populate or frequent disconnections). The feature is
meant to be used in the case of an emergency or for first-time access
to configure an IP address and log back into the device using the IP.

Version 3 of Winbox is a major rewrite, so if you are running
anything prior to version 3, these examples will not apply and you
should consider upgrading. After launching Winbox, click the
Neighbors tab to see any routers on your local area network.

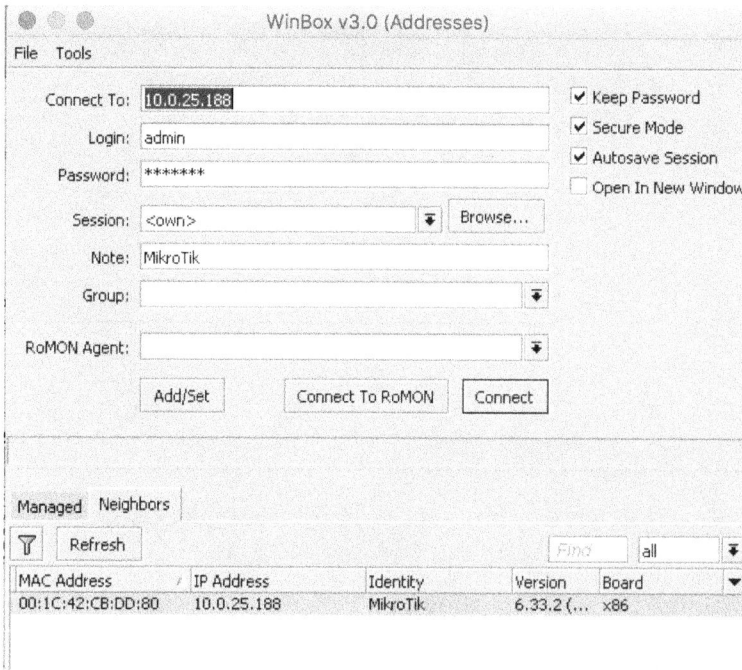

WinBox v3.0 (Addresses)

File Tools

Connect To:	10.0.25.188
Login:	admin
Password:	*******
Session:	<own> Browse...
Note:	MikroTik
Group:	
RoMON Agent:	

☑ Keep Password
☑ Secure Mode
☑ Autosave Session
☐ Open In New Window

Add/Set   Connect To RoMON   Connect

Managed Neighbors

🔍 Refresh   Find   all

MAC Address	IP Address	Identity	Version	Board
00:1C:42:CB:DD:80	10.0.25.188	MikroTik	6.33.2 (...	x86

Then, if you click on the MAC address of your device, it will be loaded into the "connect to" line. Conversely, if you click the IP address, it will load the IP address into the same line. Clicking the "Connect" button will then connect to the router. There are some new features Winbox Version 3 was specifically created to support, including Romon, which will be explained later in this book in Chapter 4.

Navigating WinBox

Navigating WinBox is straightforward. On the left side of the screen are "buttons" and clicking them either expands the menu selection provided by the button or it opens a "window".

Wireless	Wireless Tables	Interface <wlan1>	☒
Bridge	Interfaces	Nstreme Dual	General Wireless WDS Nstreme Status Traffic	OK
Mesh		Mode: ap bridge	Cancel
PPP	Name / Type	Band: 2.4GHz-B/G	Apply
IP	wlan1	Frequency: 2412 MHz	Enable
IPv6		SSID: abc	Comment
MPLS		Scan List:	
VPLS		Security Profile: default	Torch
Routing		Antenna Mode: antenna a	Scan...
System			Freq. Usage...
Queues		Default AP Tx Rate: bps	Align...
Files		Default Client Tx Rate: bps	Sniff...
Log			Snooper...
Radius		☑ Default Authenticate	
Tools		☑ Default Forward	Reset Configuration
New Terminal	1 item out of 5 (1 selected)	☐ Hide SSID	Advanced Mode
MetaROUTER			
Make Supout.rif			

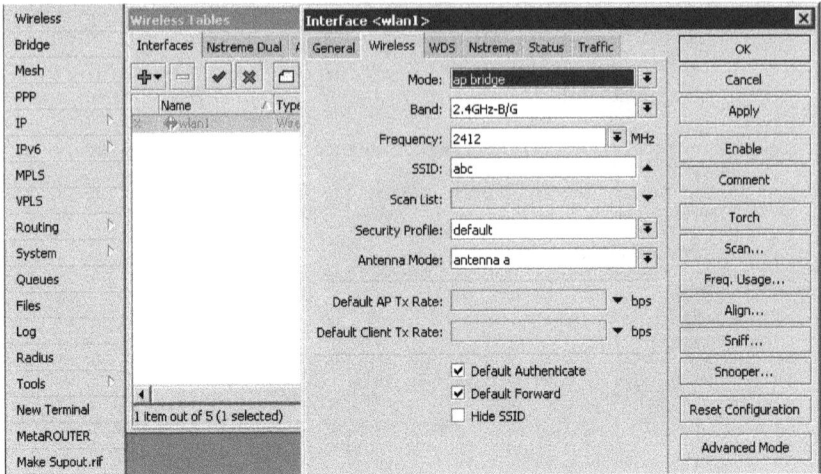

Buttons can also open sub-menus. In this example, clicking IP and then Addresses opens the Address List window.

Clicking the plus (+) sign allows you to create a new IP address.

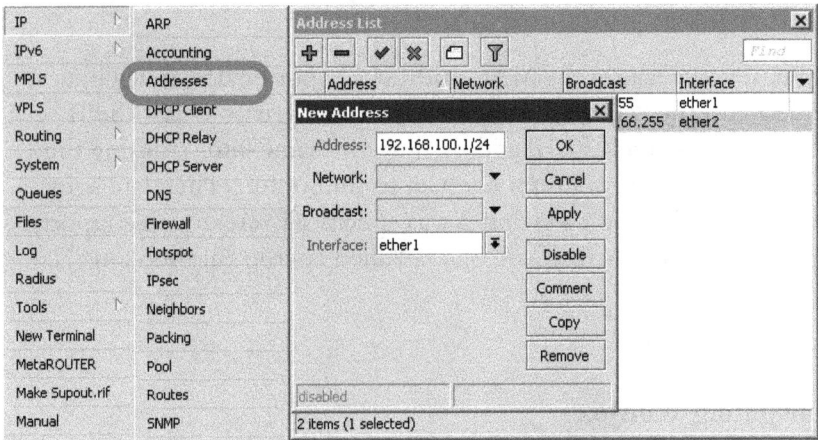

IP	ARP	Address List	☒
IPv6	Accounting		Find
MPLS	Addresses	Address / Network Broadcast Interface	
VPLS	DHCP Client	New Address	☒	55 ether1
Routing	DHCP Relay	Address: 192.168.100.1/24	OK	.66.255 ether2
System	DHCP Server	Network:	Cancel
Queues	DNS	Broadcast:	Apply
Files	Firewall	Interface: ether1	Disable
Log	Hotspot		Comment
Radius	IPsec		Copy
Tools	Neighbors		Remove
New Terminal	Packing		
MetaROUTER	Pool		
Make Supout.rif	Routes	disabled	
Manual	SNMP	2 items (1 selected)	

I will use the terms button, sub-menu, and window throughout the book to describe the process of navigating WinBox.

Inside WinBox

Within WinBox, each function or facility has common elements. These elements are:

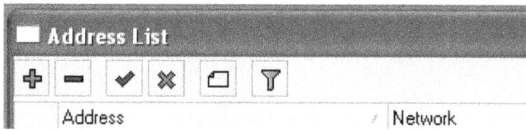

✚ Adds a new element to the list

━ Removes an element from the list

✔ Enables an element in the list

✖ Disables an element in the list

▢ Adds a comment to the list element

▽ Filters the list view

Colors are also used within WinBox to denote certain states of devices or options.

Red – If a rule or option is red, that denotes it is invalid. For instance, a DHCP Server configured on a physical interface will turn red if the interface is removed or added to a bridge, thereby making the server invalid. Another example is a firewall rule that has been created, but later the interface is removed. This rule will also turn red.

Blue – If there are two routes to the same destination, the active route will be black and the inactive route will be blue.

Bold – In the wireless interface, the **bold** entries are the standard channels for the regulatory domain that has been selected.

One more feature of WinBox that is worth mentioning and is a source of confusion for many users is the small square box that appears next to several configuration options. This box is often misunderstood to be a "check box" when in reality it is a "not" box. If you look closely at the following illustration, what you will see is that if you click inside the box, it produces an exclamation point instead of a check mark. The purpose of the box is to logically state "not". In the example, this firewall rule does not apply to 192.168.1.1 as a source address for the rule when the box is clicked. Be careful not to click that box unless you want to use it to mean "not" what is configured in the blank next to it.

Chain:	cnat
Src. Address: ☐	192.168.1.1

Chain:	srcnat
rc. Address: !	192.168.1.1

Safe Mode

In class, I always say, "safe mode is your friend", but what is safe mode? Safe mode is a mode where configuration changes are reversible. This means that typically when you apply a change or click OK, the change is immediate and is saved, so when the router is rebooted, the configuration is still there.

In safe mode, if you lose your connection to the router, all changes made after entering safe mode are reversed and it is as if they never happened. I recommend using safe mode when first learning RouterOS, however, you must exit safe mode for your changes to be saved. The process is: enter safe mode, make changes, if everything looks ok, exit safe mode. You can then enter it again, make more changes, and so on.

Use this example any time you are performing configurations that may cause you to lose connectivity to the router. Examples of these scenarios include adding or changing firewall rules, changing IP addresses or subnets, and making additions or changes to VLANs.

APPLICATION

Example – Entering Safe Mode

Safe mode can be entered inside WinBox in version 5 or later and from the command line.

From WinBox, click Safe Mode:

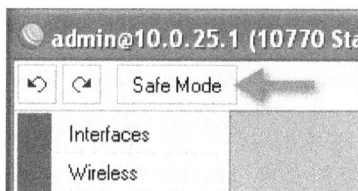

Alternative from the command line is to type the key combination ctrl-x. The prompt will change as follows:

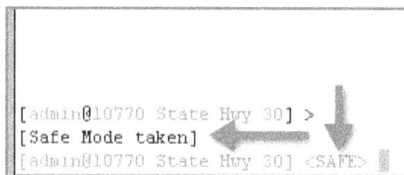

To exit safe mode, click the button to un-toggle it or type ctrl-x again.

If you are in safe mode and do not want your changes saved or to lose your ability to access the router, simply click the X to exit WinBox. If you are in a terminal window and still have connectivity to the router, type ctrl-d to exit safe mode and roll back changes.

Command Line Terminal Options

This section is included at this point in the book to keep in concert with the official MikroTik MTCNA course syllabus, however, these concepts are more advanced. You may wish to skip over the command line sections and come back here when you are more comfortable with RouterOS.

Telnet and SSH

Once the device has an IP address configured, telnet and SSH may be used to access the device. Once you are logged into the device, the command line commands parallel the WinBox command sequence for almost every function. In version 6.X there are still a few remaining functions that do not follow the command sequence displayed in WinBox. You will learn these exceptions as you become familiar with the command line.

Serial Terminal

Using a serial cable is the "back door" method to get into the router if all else fails. For example, if you accidentally disabled all of your Ethernet ports, you will no longer be able to get in through WinBox, telnet, or SSH, so serial is your last option.

If your computer does not have a serial port, you will need to purchase a USB to serial adapter at any computer store and install the drivers to use serial terminal. Few, except the high end and legacy RouterBOARD devices, have a serial port, so it is not always an option.

Use this example if you have forgotten or do not know the router password. You can use Netinstall if you have a router that has become damaged due to static discharge or other electrical event, an interrupted upgrade, lost password, or any time the router is not manageable by standard means. It can also be used to install RouterOS on an X86-based non-RouterBOARD device.

Example- Forgotten Password

If you have forgotten the user name or password (note that there is no password recovery routine), you will need to reset the board using the reset button. The procedure is tied to the board model, so always consult RouterBOARD.com for the product manual and correct procedure.

You can also re-flash the board using Netinstall and reset the router that way. Please understand that you will lose your configuration but there may be no other way to gain access to the device. There is no password recovery procedure.

Caution: Netinstall will destroy all configurations on the device if you do not check "keep old configuration" and in some cases, depending on the age of the device and the version you are running, may destroy the configuration even if you do check that option. Always make backups and document your passwords whenever possible.

The Netinstall process is accomplished as follows:

Download the Netinstall zip file from www.mikrotik.com and unzip it on your desktop.

Download the RouterOS file (the .npk package) from www.mikrotik.com and save on desktop.

Start your favorite serial terminal program (Hyperterm or Putty work fine).

These settings work with Putty for accessing a RouterBOARD. Putty will be used for purposes of this example. Putty.exe is a freely downloadable SSH/serial terminal client:

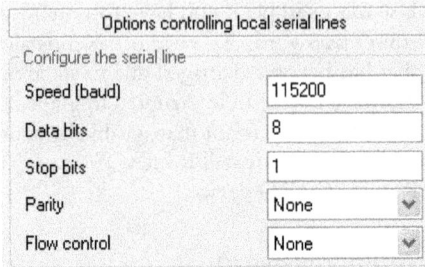

Options controlling local serial lines	
Configure the serial line	
Speed (baud)	115200
Data bits	8
Stop bits	1
Parity	None
Flow control	None

Set a static IP on your PC's Ethernet adapter, for example 192.168.1.1 with a netmask of 255.255.255.0.

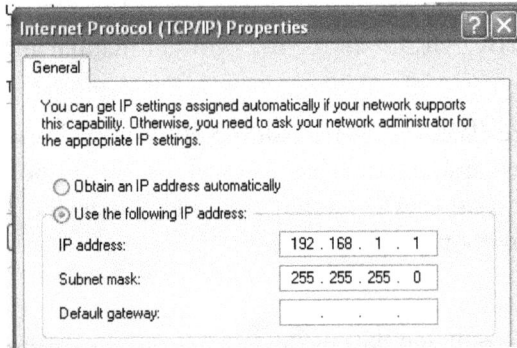

Internet Protocol (TCP/IP) Properties

General

You can get IP settings assigned automatically if your network supports this capability. Otherwise, you need to ask your network administrator for the appropriate IP settings.

○ Obtain an IP address automatically
⦿ Use the following IP address:

IP address:	192 . 168 . 1 . 1
Subnet mask:	255 . 255 . 255 . 0
Default gateway:	. . .

Start Netinstall on the PC. You should see a window like this:

(Continued on next page)

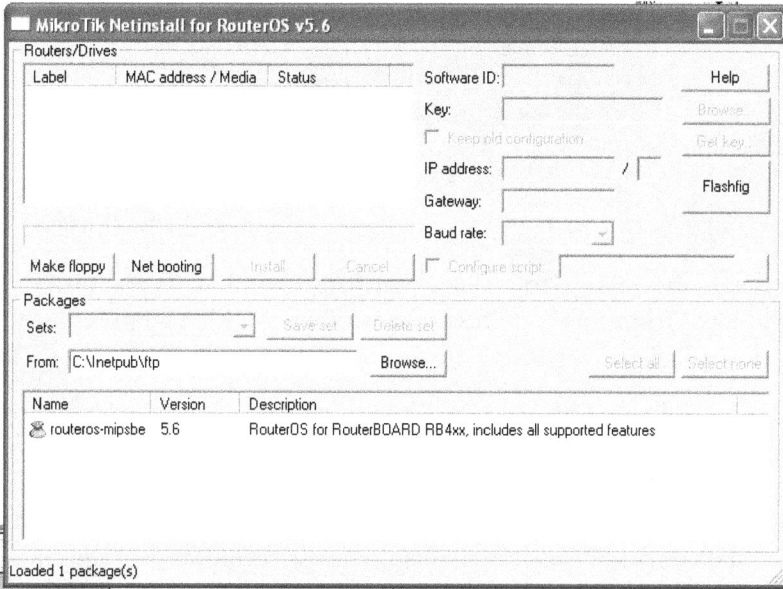

Click the Net Booting button and configure an IP address to give the board to be flashed on the same subnet as your PC. In this example, use 192.168.1.2 and check the box:

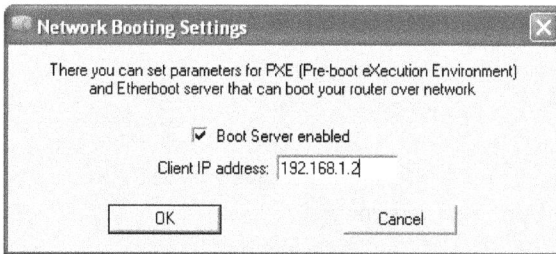

Click OK. Next, power up the board and watch the terminal on Putty. When the screen says, "Press any key within 2 seconds to enter setup", then press the enter key. Next type the letter "o", then "1", and then "x". Case of the commands is important.

The board should then boot from the Netinstall instance using the bootp protocol. Once booted you should see the router appear in the Router/Drives window:

(Continued on next page)

Select the version to install in the lower window. If you do not see a version there, try browsing to the .npk file you previously downloaded.

Note: The download page on www.mikrotik.com allows you to pick your hardware platform and the version you want to download, stable or legacy. It also allows you to download the "Main package" or "Extra package". Typically you will want the "Main package", as it contains the most common packages in a single file. If you need any optional packages, then the "Extra packages" zip file is your answer.

MikroTik has also changed their development cycle to accommodate several branches of development, which is one of the options on their download page.

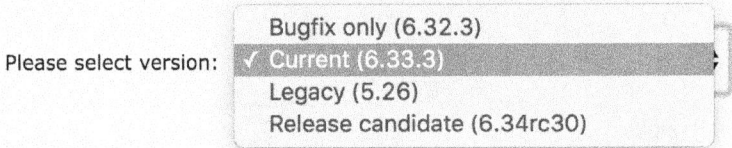

Figure 1 – RouterOS Version Selector at MikroTik.com

"Bugfix Only" will download a version that addresses any issues in the current stable version. "Current" is a version that will support bug fixes and new features, while "Release candidate" is the cutting-edge version, and "Legacy" is the last major stable version. Which do you choose? Well, that depends on your goal. Did you see a new feature that had been added that you want to take advantage of? Then you will need the "Current" version.

Looking for the most stable of all versions? Then "Bugfix only" is the right choice.

This graphic explains the process:

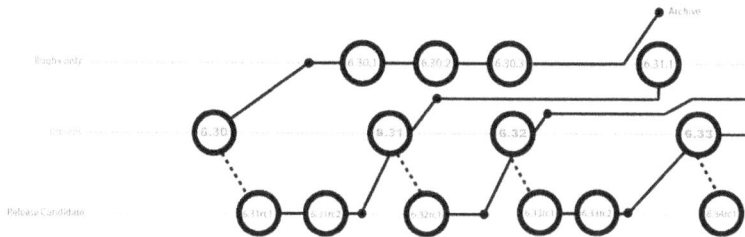

Figure 2 - Development Cycle 1

Click the Install button to install that version. Note: If you are attempting to recover a board for which you do not have the password, do not click the option "keep old configuration." It will also keep the password, thereby still rendering the board inaccessible.

Note: Netinstall can be used in the manner described above for recovering a board for which the password has been lost or for an initial install on a PXE bootable device, compact flash drive, hard drive, or most other non-volatile storage.

Working With a Simple Configuration

Due to the power of this device, even a basic configuration can be daunting. I will walk you through the creation of a basic configuration that will allow you to access this device easily until you are more experienced at configuring it. I will not explain the steps here, but instead will explain them in depth later in the book as we develop our explanations and examples of all of the different facilities provided by RouterOS.

When you first power up the device and connect to it using WinBox as described on page 22, provided the device has not been configured, you will see a window like this:

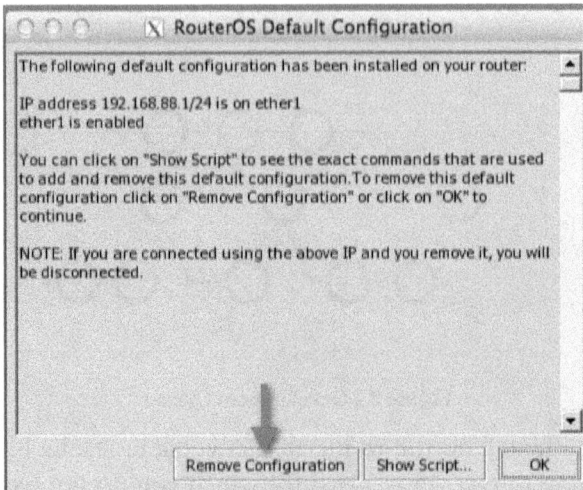

I recommend you use the default configuration at first, modifying it as you see fit. Once you are comfortable, remove the default configuration and start with a blank router. To achieve this, click System Reset Configuration and select No Default Configuration and Reset Configuration.

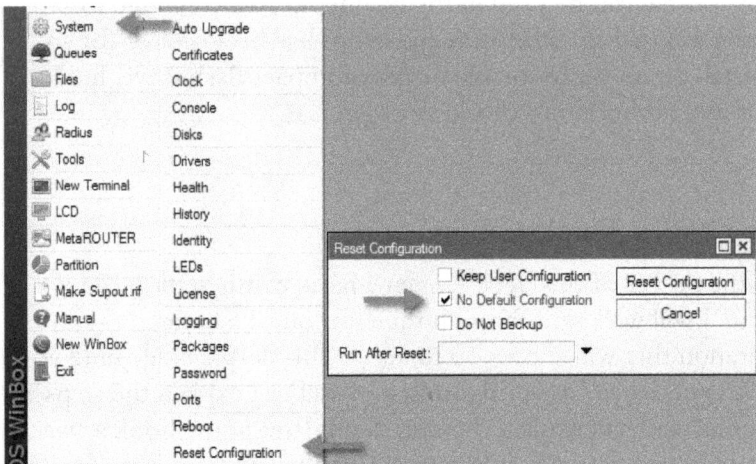

After reset, the router is blank. Note that you should be accessing the router via the MAC address as previously explained with WinBox any time there is no default configuration.

At this point, you will want to add an IP address or two, DHCP Server, and a few other configurations. To assist you, I have developed a script you can simply paste into the router and it will configure everything for you and get you started on the right track. You may download the script from my wiki site by searching for "scripts" at http://wiki.stevedischer.com.

Copy the text to your clipboard and then in WinBox, click the New Terminal button. Inside the terminal window, right click with your mouse and select paste and watch the script configure the necessities.

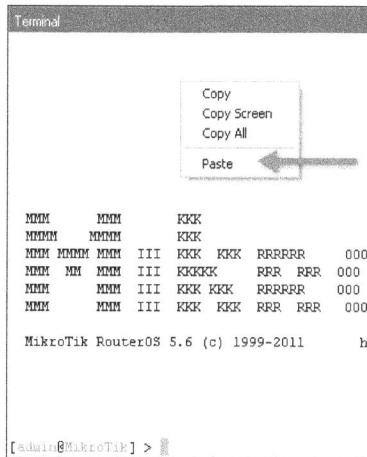

Now you should have a router with ether1 ready to connect to the Internet provider with the following assumptions:

Ether1 is the WAN port, it will expect a DHCP IP address from the provider.

Ether2 is the LAN port, it will give your computer a DHCP IP address.

If you have a wireless card, it will broadcast 2.4 GHz with the wireless network ID MikroTik. It will also pass out DHCP addresses.

You can connect with a cable to ether2 or wirelessly.

The system clock will be synchronized to NIST, the National Institute of Standards and Technology, and the clock will be set to US Central time.

The router will provide basic Internet access and has no admin password, no encryption, and no firewall. Please understand there is no security provided by this configuration! If you do not have Internet access and enjoy typing, you can type the commands on the following page into a terminal window instead of pasting.

```
/ip address
add address=192.168.1.1/24 disabled=no interface=ether2
add address=192.168.2.1/24 disabled=no interface=wlan1
/ip pool
add name=dhcp_pool1 ranges=192.168.1.2-192.168.1.254
add name=dhcp_pool2 ranges=192.168.2.2-192.168.2.254
/ip dhcp-server
add address-pool=dhcp_pool1 \
disabled=no interface=ether2 lease-time=3d name=dhcp1
add address-pool=dhcp_pool2 \
disabled=no interface=wlan1 lease-time=3d name=dhcp2
/ip dhcp-server config
set store-leases-disk=5m
/ip dhcp-server network
add address=192.168.1.0/24 dns-server=4.2.2.2 gateway=192.168.1.1
add address=192.168.2.0/24 dns-server=4.2.2.2 gateway=192.168.2.1
/system ntp client
set enabled=yes primary-ntp=50.19.122.125
/interface wireless
set 0 band=2ghz-b default-authentication=yes disabled=no\
wireless-protocol=802.11 mode=ap-bridge
/ip dhcp-client
add interface=ether1 disabled=no
/ip firewall nat
```

This basic configuration will get you started learning RouterOS.

Interfaces

Interfaces are the physical ports that allow input and output connections to the router. Interfaces are accessed from the Interfaces button. Interfaces can be renamed by double clicking on the interface name in the Interfaces list window and then setting their name on the General tab. This will help you identify them physically or logically and will assist you with troubleshooting.

I suggest using comments on interfaces rather than renaming them. My reason is that most enclosures are labeled with the same interface name as it appears in RouterOS and keeping them the same makes things simpler.

Use this example any time you need to add or make changes to an IP address.

Example – Add an IP Address

The first step in learning to configure this device is to gain access and configure an IP address. The assumption is made that you understand basic networking and subnetting and accept the fact that for two hosts to communicate on the same local area network or LAN, they must be on the same subnet or they will require the help of a router that has addresses on both subnets.

That being said, to add an IP address to a RouterOS device, it is first necessary to gain access through one of the methods previously described including WinBox through the MAC address, or through the serial terminal as outlined beginning on page 22. If WinBox does not see your router, try a different interface or use the serial terminal method.

1. Begin by clicking the IP button and then Addresses. Click the plus sign to add a new IP address to the desired interface.

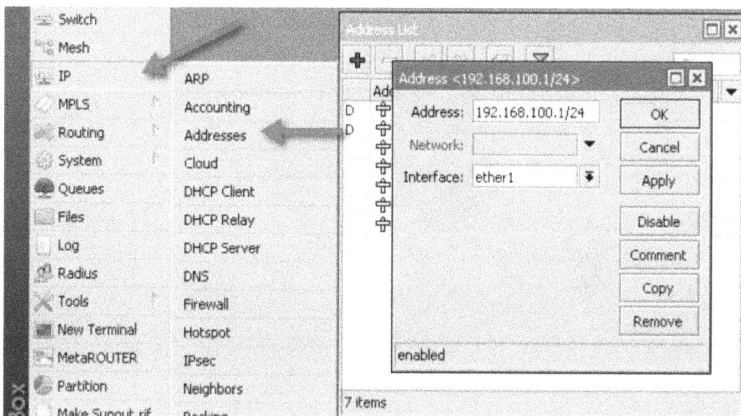

Note that RouterOS uses CIDR (Classless Inter-Domain Routing) or slash notation to determine the subnet and this must be included on the address line. The format for CIDR notation is 192.168.1.1/24 where the /24 determines the subnet. Do not fill in the Network address; it will be populated automatically when you click OK or Apply.

2. Click OK to save the address.

Chapter 2 – User Management

The title of this chapter is User Management, which should not be confused with UserManager. UserManager is a totally separate package distributed by MikroTik and is basically their implementation of Radius server. User Management is a function within RouterOS and should therefore not be confused with the UserManager optional package.

Users can be created with three different permission levels. By default, there exists a user named "admin" with permissions of full. By default the admin password is blank. Obviously for security purposes, changing the admin password to something a bit harder to guess than a blank password is prudent, however, you may wish to create several users with various levels of access.

Note: This task can be centralized and the administrative effort of controlling user access can be simplified by using a central authentication mechanism such as Radius or MikroTik's UserManager. More on that on page 41.

In WinBox, users are created by clicking the System button and then the Users menu item. The plus sign will add a user and allow you to set the password. Also selectable is the group and there are three by default. The group "full" has full read and write access to the router while "read" can only view the configuration and "write" can read and write the configuration. These three default example groups provide some demonstration of the granularity with the rights you can give each of them. Don't be confused by the group named "write". The write group isn't substantially different by design, it just has a different set of permissions as created by default. Typically, I recommend you create users with read access for anyone that doesn't need to change the configuration and full access for your trusted admins. Any deviation on this policy should be made on a case-by-case basis.

From the System Button, select Users.

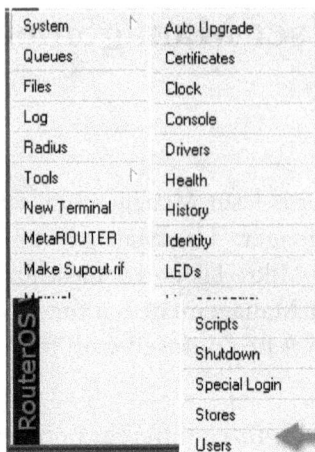

From the Groups tab, you can double click a group to see their details.

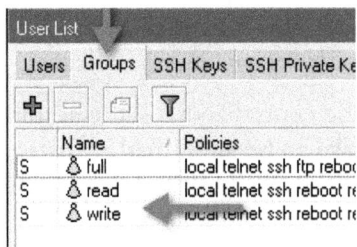

As you can see, there are a lot of possible combinations of group permissions available:

Your selections are dependent upon your individual circumstances.

Example - User and Group Assignments and Policy

User creation and group assignment is simple and self-explanatory, so instead of an example, a "best practice" might be more useful.

Here is an example of groups and access rights. You are considering using a consultant to provide network evaluation and possible configuration, but don't them to accidently cause an outage in your production network. Before giving anyone the "keys to the kingdom", I recommend creating for them a user with read access. This way, they are able to view your entire configuration without actually being able to make changes. Once you are comfortable with their abilities, then you can change their group to full.

For Further Study – UserManager

If you aren't ready to explore an advanced topic, you may skip this section and return to it later.

Imagine you are a network administrator with various levels of technicians and admins. You want a centralized approach to user management and various levels of access to ensure your ability to terminate network access for an employee quickly. The best and most scalable solution to this situation is MikroTik's UserManager.

The installation of UserManager goes beyond the scope of this book and the MTCNA certification, but a few instructions here can help steer you in the right direction. First, UserManager should be installed on a machine that is in a very stable part of your network with reliable power and connectivity. I suggest your NOC or data center as the ideal location. Since it is available as a package for RouterOS, it can be installed on a physical router or a virtual machine running the X86 version of RouterOS, the latter being my first choice. Typically, I put my Dude server and my UserManager on the same virtual machine since I run VMware in my data center. (The Dude is MikroTik's network monitoring program and is available for download at no charge on MikroTik's website.) UserManager creates a large quantity of log files and the availability of the extra disk space a virtual machine can provide is helpful.

Once UserManager is installed and working, you will install a radius client on each router to authenticate from UserManager. Next, you will check the box for "Use Radius" under the User's List through the AAA button. I recommend setting the local admin password on the router to something difficult to guess and only known to you or a trusted employee. This local user is always available to log into the device even if the UserManager server is unavailable. Then, create users within UserManager for each of your technicians with the appropriate User Group. If a technician is terminated, you simply remove their account in UserManager to disable their access to the entire network.

Obviously, there are many steps in-between the portions I have described and the MikroTik Wiki is a great place to go for a step-by-step process to deploy UserManager. Hopefully the pieces I have added here will fill in the remainder of the blanks and ensure a successful solution for centralized user management.

Chapter 3 – Upgrading and Downgrading the Operating System, Package Management

RouterBOARDs come from MikroTik preloaded with RouterOS. MikroTik recommends that you upgrade your board to the latest version of RouterOS before beginning any configuration.

The operating system is in constant development and new features or bug fixes are frequently available, sometimes as often as monthly. The decision to do an upgrade on a production system on the other hand, should be based on some basic logical reasoning such as:

1. Is there a feature I want to add to my device that the new OS will provide?

2. Is there a security vulnerability this version solves?

3. Is there a bug fix this version provides?

4. Do I need to upgrade to provide support for some new hardware?

All of these are valid reasons to upgrade your device. As a friend of mine says, "Every problem is the result of a previous solution." I think that holds true for upgrades. Another one I am sure you have heard is "if it isn't broken don't fix it". I think you get the point here. If the criteria expressed above doesn't apply, leave your router alone.

Use this example for routers that do not have internet access. You will need to download the upgrade package to a laptop with internet access and then connect to the router without internet access to upload the package and perform the upgrade.

Example – Upgrading the Operating System When the Router Does Not Have Internet Access

This is really not the preferred scenario because of the number of steps involved, but is your only choice when the router does not have internet access. An example of upgrading using the System Packages "Check for Updates" button will follow and is the preferred method for me.

1. First, you must download the upgrade package from MikroTik. After web browsing to the MikroTik site, locate the download section and select the platform you want to upgrade. See page 32 if you have any questions about which file to download.

2. Download the .npk package to your desktop. Typically, the package you want is the stable version, "Main Package". This single file contains the same features that are installed by default on the device.

3. Once the package is downloaded (typically around 12 megs), launch WinBox and access through the device's IP address, not through the MAC address. As stated before, the Layer 3 method is the best for all normal router management.

4. Inside WinBox, click the Files button. This will open the Files List showing all the visible files stored on the router.

(Continued on next page)

44

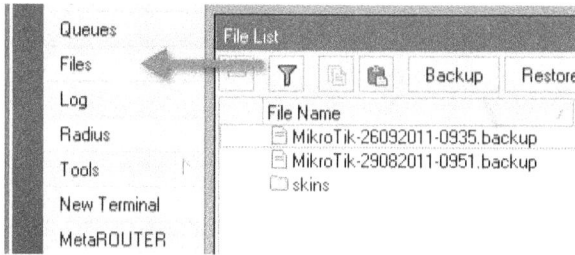

5. Next, drag the package from your desktop to the files window. This can be a bit tedious, depending on how the files are sorted in the files window. Dropping the file inside a folder will prevent the upgrade from taking place, so use care to get it at the top of the list. One trick here is to click the Backup button in the Files List. This will produce and save a backup file, which sorts to the top of the list and allows you a little space in which to drop the upgrade package. The npk file doesn't have to be the top file in the list, but make sure it isn't in a folder.

6. Dropping the file in the area identified by the red arrow will produce the desired result:

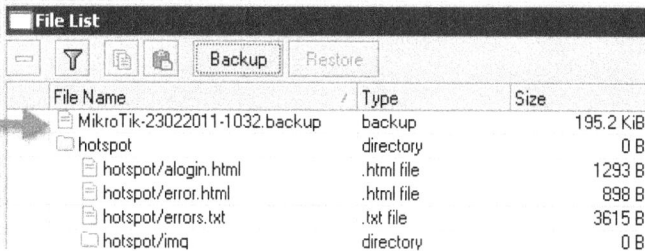

7. Once the file has completely uploaded, issue a reboot command by clicking System and Reboot.

Note: Pulling the power at this point will not upgrade the router. You must enter a graceful reboot using the reboot command due to the process RouterOS uses to update the device.

(Continued on next page)

System	Auto Upgrade
Queues	Certificates
Files	Clock
Exit	Logging
	Packages
	Password
	Ports
	Reboot

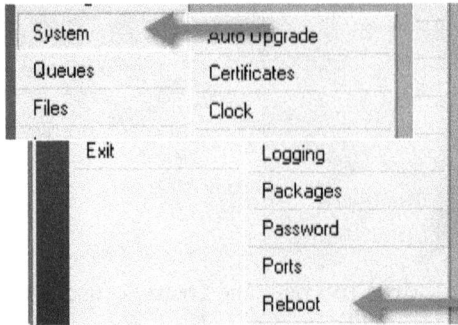

After a few minutes, your router will return to operation with the new version installed. You can confirm in several places, including WinBox and in the System Packages List.

Confirm in WinBox:

WinBox v4.16 on x86 (x86)

Interfaces
Bridge

And in the Package List:

Package List

Check For Updates | Enable | Disable | Uninstall | Unsch

Name	Version	Build Time	Scheduled
advanced-tools	6.33.2	Nov/27/2015 15:00:07	
dhcp	6.33.2	Nov/27/2015 15:00:07	
hotspot	6.33.2	Nov/27/2015 15:00:07	
mpls	6.33.2	Nov/27/2015 15:00:07	
ntp	6.33.2	Nov/27/2015 15:00:07	
ppp	6.33.2	Nov/27/2015 15:00:07	
routing	6.33.2	Nov/27/2015 15:00:07	
security	6.33.2	Nov/27/2015 15:00:07	
system	6.33.2	Nov/27/2015 15:00:07	
wireless	6.33.2	Nov/27/2015 15:00:07	
wireless-cm2	6.33.2	Nov/27/2015 15:00:07	
wireless-fp	6.33.2	Nov/27/2015 15:00:07	

Once the operating system has been upgraded, it is advisable to update the boot loader. This is done by clicking System RouterBOARD Upgrade.

(Continued on next page)

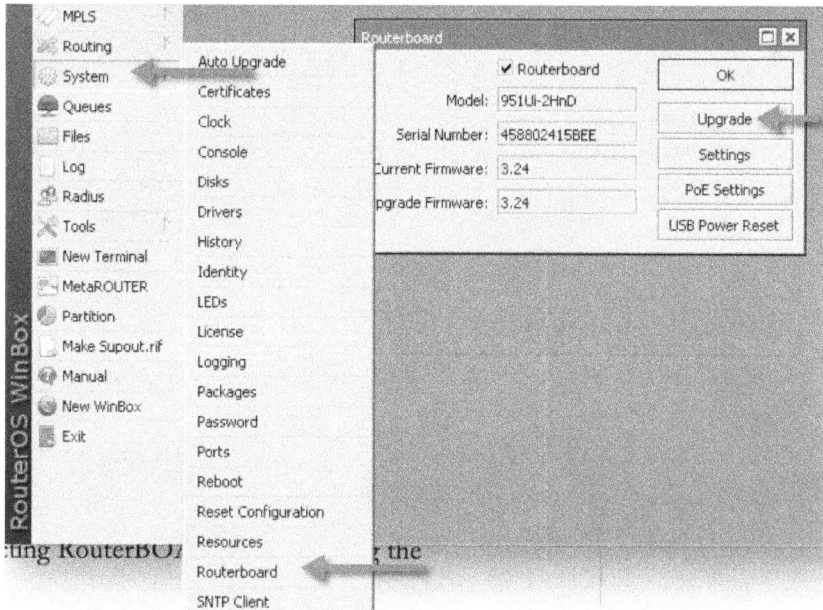

The system will ask for confirmation so answer "y". Then, reboot the system to upgrade the boot loader.

This two-step process will ensure that both the operating system and the boot loader are compatible versions. Upgrading the boot loader ensures the hardware is best able to communicate with the software and although not required, it is recommended. Upgrading the boot loader with an x86-based system is not possible or required.

Use this example when an upgrade causes some issue that did not exist prior to the upgrade. The net result will be to roll the router back to a previous software version.

Example – Downgrading the Operating System

Sometimes it is desired or necessary to downgrade the operating system.

1. This is performed in the same manner as upgrading, however, once the older package has been copied into the Files List, click the System button and select the Packages menu item.

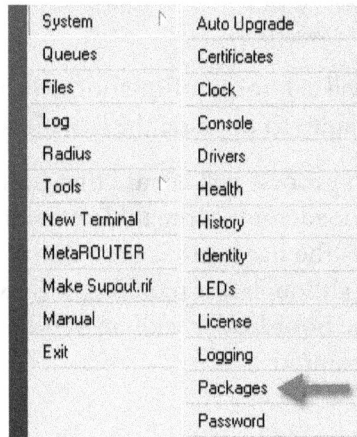

2. In the Packages List, select all of the packages and click the Downgrade button.

(Continued on next page)

Package List					
▽	Enable	Disable	Uninstall	Unschedule	Downgrade
Name	Version		Build Time		cheduled
🖥 routeros-mipsbe	5.6		Aug/02/2011 11:49:35		
🖥 advanced-t...	5.6		Aug/02/2011 11:46:59		
🖥 dhcp	5.6		Aug/02/2011 11:47:25		
🖥 hotspot	5.6		Aug/02/2011 11:47:58		
🖥 mpls	5.6		Aug/02/2011 11:47:44		
🖥 ppp	5.6		Aug/02/2011 11:47:36		
🖥 routerboard	5.6		Aug/02/2011 11:48:32		
🖥 routing	5.6		Aug/02/2011 11:47:38		
🖥 security	5.6		Aug/02/2011 11:47:23		
🖥 system	5.6		Aug/02/2011 11:46:55		
🖥 wireless	5.6		Aug/02/2011 11:48:21		

3. Reboot the router and the operating system will be downgraded.

Note: I do not recommend running different versions of packages unless you know what you are doing. To do so may be possible, but can produce unwanted results.

Use this example when you only have terminal access to the router. Winbox and http are easier choices for managing and upgrading, but sometimes FTP is necessary with Mac or Linux computers managing MikroTik routers.

APPLICATION

Example – Upgrading using FTP

If WinBox and the simple drag and drop method is not possible, you can use an FTP client to transfer the package to the router and then issue a reboot command. Simply FTP to the router and transfer the file to the root directory.

Use this example to upgrade any router with internet access, running a late version 5 build or any version 6 build. This method is always my first choice to do the upgrade.

Example – Upgrading When the Router Has Internet Access

If the router has Internet access, things are much simpler.

1. Click System, Packages, and the Check for Updates button.

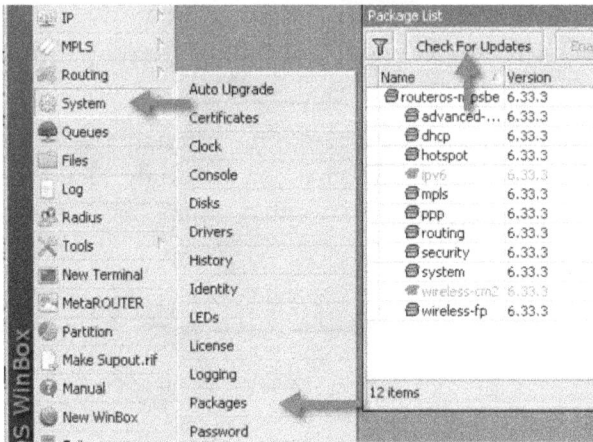

2. Choose the version you want to install using the criteria explained previously on page 38.

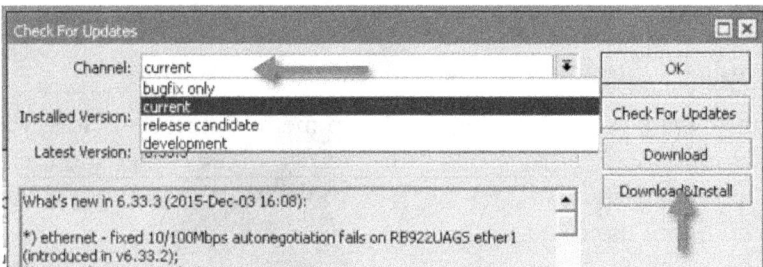

3. Clicking Download will download the file and allow you to reboot the router at a later time. Clicking Download & Install will download the file and immediately reboot the router so be prepared for that, as there is no confirmation asking, "Are you sure?"

Note that the "Check for Updates" dialog box also contains a textual explanation of the change log, which can be handy. Also, don't forget to upgrade the boot loader as described on page 46.

Use this example to add functionality provided by one of the packages that is not part of the default RouterOS package.

APPLICATION

Example – Adding a Package

Sometimes you find it necessary to add a package not already installed on the router. This may be true for adding a feature like UserManager, or if you accidently uninstalled a package that you now need. Packages not included in the combined package may be downloaded as a zip file from the same page on the MikroTik site where you downloaded the upgrade package.

To install a single package:

1. Download the "Extra Packages" and unzip on your desktop.

2. Drag the package to your Files List as you did previously for the system upgrade.

3. Reboot the router and the new package will be installed.

Use this example for all routers to ensure that the only services that are running are the ones you actually need. This is both a performance improvement and a security measure.

Example – Best Practice for Package Management

I also recommend uninstalling any packages you do not need or anticipate you will not need in the future. I also recommend disabling any packages you might need in the future, but don't need today. This will help secure your system, simplify the configuration, and reduce system resources.

I recommend the following packages be the minimum installed and enabled.

Chapter 4 – Router Identity & Remote Access

The identity of the router you are logged into is shown in several places in RouterOS. By default, the identity is MikroTik, which is obviously not very useful in your network, so it is a good idea to make setting the router identity part of your standard configuration routine. The convention you choose is entirely up to you, but I have found that using the physical address of the client is often helpful to troubleshoot at a later time. For example, setting the Router Identity to "103 Smith Street" is a good practice.

The router identity is found in several places. In WinBox, it appears on the title bar:

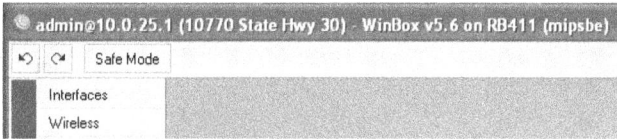

In the terminal window at the prompt:

And in the IP Neighbors List:

Interface	IP Address	MAC Address	Identity	Platform	Version	Board ...	IPv6
<l2tp-ISPV...		64:D1:54:66:5...	Jonathan	MikroTik	6.41.3 ...	RB952...	no
<l2tp-ISPV...		6C:3B:6B:C5:B...	Violeta...	MikroTik	6.41.1 ...	RB941-...	no
<l2tp-ISPV...		64:D1:54:47:2...	Pat-Ho...	MikroTik	6.40.6 ...	RB750r2	no
<l2tp-ISPV...		D4:CA:6D:96:4...	Sheren...	MikroTik	6.36.3 ...	RB951-2n	no
<l2tp-ISPV...	10.0.25.111	4C:5E:0C:A3:6...	Brad-H...	MikroTik	6.40.5 ...	CRS10...	no
ether6	10.252.252.2	D4:CA:6D:83:C...	10.0.0...	MikroTik	6.39.2 ...	RB2011...	no
ether12		00:0C:29:55:9...	10.0.0...	MikroTik	6.39.2 ...	x86	no
ether12	10.0.25.20	00:0C:29:6F:6...	UserMa...	MikroTik	6.39.2 ...	x86	no
ether12		4C:5E:0C:9D:E...	MikroTik	MikroTik	6.42 (s...	CRS12...	no
ether12	10.0.25.184	00:00:00:00:0...					no
sfp1	10.252.252.9	D4:CA:6D:83:C...	10.0.0...	MikroTik	6.39.2 ...	RB2011...	no
sfp1	10.253.253.2	D4:CA:6D:ED:...	ISP-Lab	MikroTik	6.38.1 ...	RB2011iL	no

Use this example for all routers. Setting the system identity makes routers easier to identify and reduces errors.

APPLICATION

Example – Setting the System Identity

The system identity is set using the commands System and Identity:

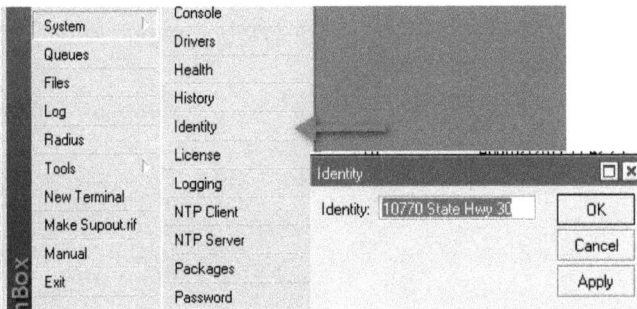

System	Console
Queues	Drivers
Files	Health
Log	History
Radius	Identity
Tools	License
New Terminal	Logging
Make Supout.rif	NTP Client
Manual	NTP Server
Exit	Packages
	Password

Identity: 10770 State Hwy 30

OK

Cancel

Apply

IP Cloud for Remote Access

Starting with RouterOS Version 6.14, IP Cloud has added the ability to remotely manage routers, even when they have a dynamic IP address, and without the use of problematic and complicated dynamic DNS scripting. The operation of IP Cloud is simple:

IP Cloud Operational Details[1]

- The router checks for an outgoing IP address change every 60 seconds.

- The router sends an update to the cloud server and waits for the cloud server response for up to 15 seconds.

- If "Update Time" is selected, the router will attempt to determine its time zone from MikroTik's IP address geolocation database and update the router's clock according to the MikroTik NTP server and the detected time zone.

After the router sends its IP address to the cloud server, it will stay on the server permanently. The DNS name (/ip cloud dns-name) will resolve to the last sent IP address. When the user sets /ip cloud set ddns-enabled=no, the router will send a message to the server to disable DNS name for this RouterBoard.

When enabled, IP Cloud will send encrypted UDP packets to port 15252 to the hosts that resolve from cloud.mikrotik.com. If you have connected a router and it has Internet access, you will see a DNS "A record" resolved for cloud.mikrotik.com in "/ip dns cache".

Once IP Cloud has been activated, your router will be reachable at a DNS name similar to:

634c0451d41d.sn.mynetname.net

This DNS name is unique to this one router and will never change.

One trick I like to use is to create a CNAME record in my domain's DNS for this name that is easier to understand. For example, I might create a DNS record in my DNS provider like this:

cams.myhouse.com CNAME 634c0451d41d.sn.mynetname.net

Obviously, "cams.myhouse.com" is much easier for me to remember and through my DNS provider points to

"634c0451d41d.sn.mynetname.net", thereby allowing remote access to some security cameras. IP Cloud takes the effort out of remote access when a site uses dynamic IP addresses.

Use this example for all routers that receive their address via dynamic addressing. Provided the WAN address is a public IP address, this will allow you to manage them remotely, even when the IP address changes frequently.

APPLICATION

Example – Setting Up IP Cloud

1. Click IP and Cloud and check the boxes as follows:

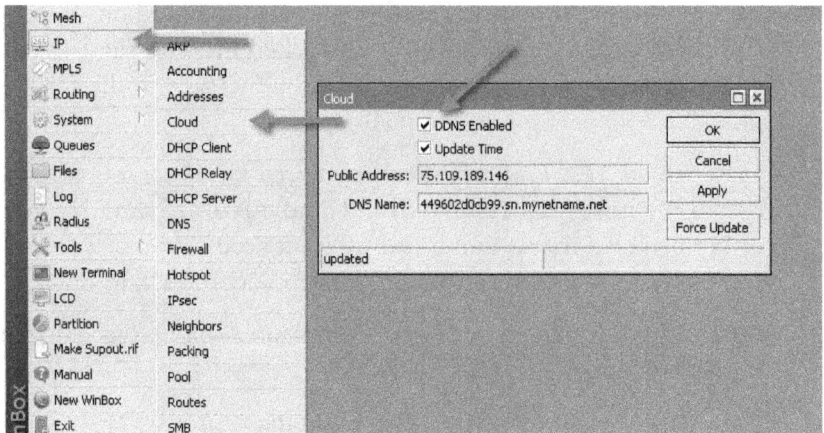

2. Click OK.

Take note of the DNS name; this is the name you will use in the future to access the router. You may also want to create a CNAME in your DNS server, but that is beyond the scope of this book.

Note: The "Update Time" box is good to check if you do not have SNTP set up. If it is set to "yes", then the router clock will be set to the time provided by the cloud server if there is no SNTP or NTP service enabled. Remember that you can also force an IP update at any time with the Force Update button.

RoMON

RoMON, or Remote Management Overlay Network, was added to RouterOS in Version 6.28. RoMON is helpful whenever you have routers you want to remotely administer, but they are located on another network, without individual public IP addresses.

Prior to RoMON, it was necessary to build tunnels to these remote networks and route traffic to them across the VPN tunnels. This is all quite doable with RouterOS, but requires additional effort and knowledge. RoMON makes this simple and easy.

To understand RoMON, let's begin with an example network ideal for RoMON:

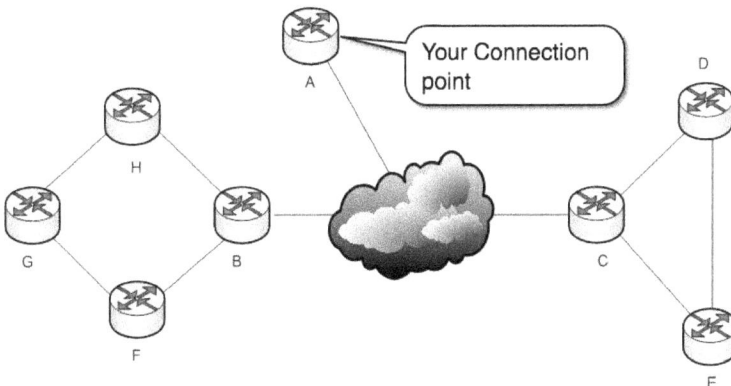

Figure 3 - RoMON Network Before Tunnels

Your connection point to this network is Router A. Your goal is to manage every router in each of the remote networks.

In simple terms, RoMON takes care of all the back-end tunneling for managing a RouterOS network. RoMON, coupled with the newer

Winbox Version 3, allows you to link your MikroTik devices together into a Layer2 management network. Then, by logging into one router, you can access all the other RoMON routers that are a part of the network.

With MikroTik RoMON, the requirements to participate in the RoMON network are simple:

1. They must be directly connected to another RoMON router that is on the same Layer 2 segment.

2. If they are not directly connected, they must be on the same "Ethernet Like" segment. Typically, this is an EoIP tunnel.

EoIP was "made for RoMON" and with the addition of IPSEC over EoIP automatically added in version 6.30, this is a single-step solution for managing a network.

To turn the example network into a RoMON network, simply create two EoIP tunnels, one between routers B and C, then one between routers A and B. We will cover all the steps in the example that follows. The result using EoIP will be something like this:

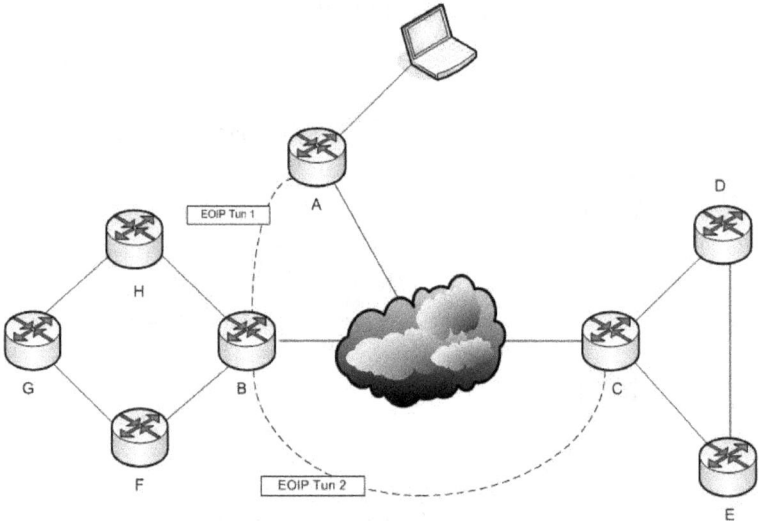

Figure 4 - RoMON Network After Tunnels

Now, as you can see in the diagram, Routers A-B-C all have Layer 2 adjacencies to each other via the EoIP tunnels and each has a Layer 2 adjacency to a router that also has Layer 2 interconnections to the remainder of the remote network. These EoIP tunnels satisfy the requirements of RoMON and do not need to be bridged or addressed.

Once RoMON is fully implemented using the following example, the laptop connected to Network A will be able to launch Winbox Version 3, connect to RoMON router A, and see in its Neighbors list, all routers A through H. It will thereby manage each individually through its MAC address.

Use this example to build a RoMON management network any time you need to manage routers that are on a private network(s) behind a public IP address without using NAT or port forwarding.

Example – Setting up a RoMON Network

First, we create EoIP tunnels between the routers that are separated by public networks. We will once again use this network as our example:

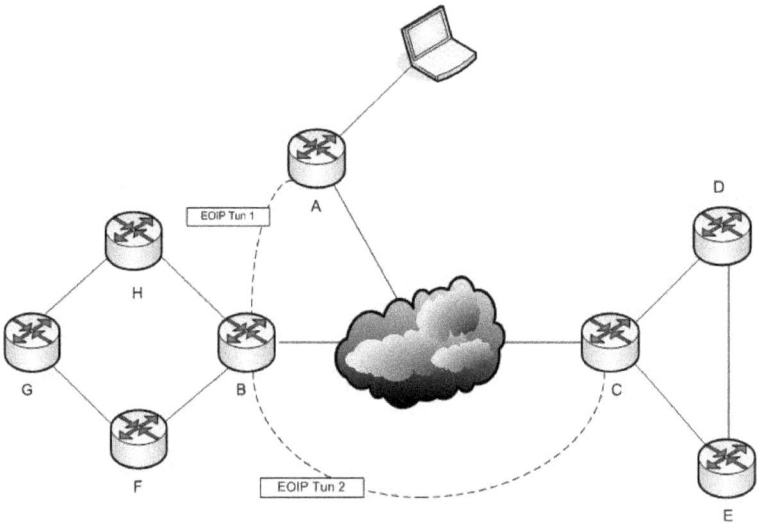

Figure 5 - RoMON Network After Tunnels With Example

1. Tunnel 1- In WinBox, click the Interfaces button and select a new EoIP tunnel interface. The only information that is mandatory is the Remote IP address of the other end of the tunnel. If tunneling across the Internet, this will be the public IP address of the remote host. The tunnel ID must be unique for every tunnel on the router, so use the default or change it when adding multiple tunnels.

(Continued on next page)

New Interface

General | Status | Traffic

Name: eoip-tunnel1
Type: EoIP Tunnel
MTU:
Actual MTU:
L2 MTU:
MAC Address: 02:9D:51:6A:67:5F
ARP: enabled

Local Address:
Remote Address: 66.76.13.10
Tunnel ID: 1

IPsec Secret:

Keepalive:

DSCP: inherit
Dont Fragment: no
☑ Clamp TCP MSS
☑ Allow Fast Path

OK
Cancel
Apply
Disable
Comment
Copy
Remove
Torch

enabled

2. Click OK.

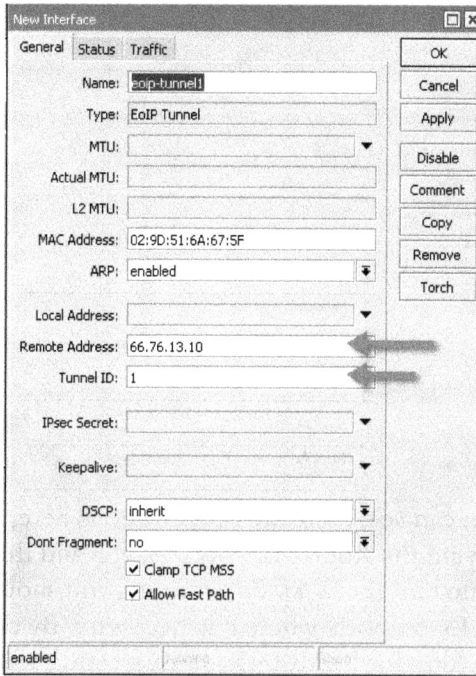

3. Repeat the process on the remote end of the tunnel,
    swapping the Remote IP address for the other end of the
    tunnel.

4. Repeat for Tunnel 2.

5. Ensure you have at least RouterOS version 6.29 on all
    routers, then enable RoMON like this:

(Continued on next page)

61

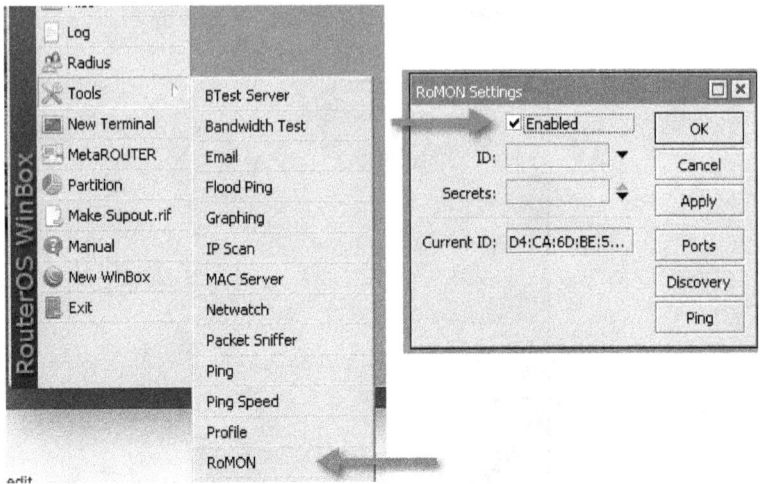

As you can see, there are other options here, such as specifying the Router ID, Secrets, etc. and these options are explained on the Wiki. For security, you should only enable RoMON on ports where it is necessary. By default, all ports are looking for RoMON routers, so you should forbid RoMON on any public interfaces.

You can also manipulate port cost to ensure the path that is used to get to the RoMON router is optimal for your architecture. The default cost is 100 and these costs have nothing to do with routing; they are only used for RoMON.

3. This process of enabling RoMON needs to be followed on all routers in the RoMON network that you want to be able to manage.

4. Once this is done, the last step is to ensure you have Winbox version 3 downloaded from the MikroTik.com web page. The RoMON-enabled version looks like this:

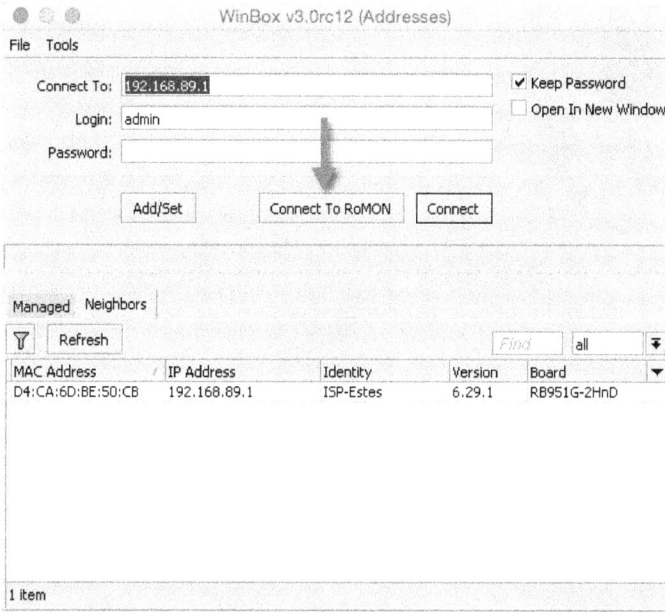

Once you click the button "Connect to RoMON", you get a new neighbors tab entitled RoMON Neighbors:

(Continued on next page)

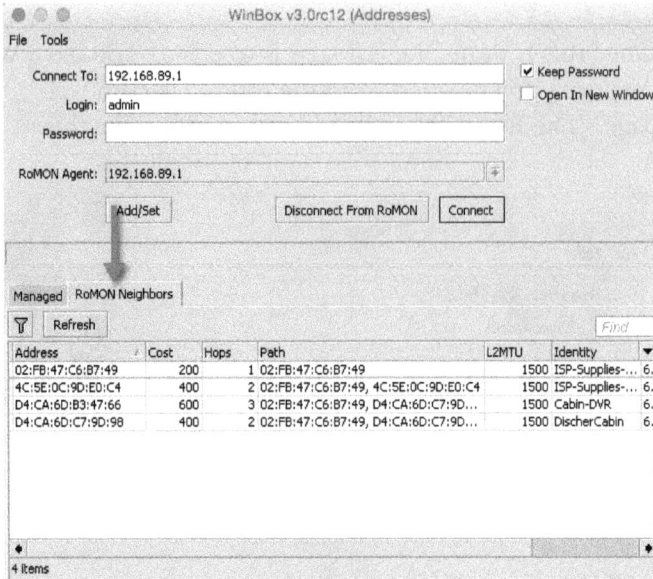

Click any MAC address in the list, then click Connect and you will immediately be logged into that RoMON router by traversing through Layer2 RoMON hops. Other great features I have noticed in Winbox are the ability to save layouts as sessions and to spawn a new Winbox session from Winbox.

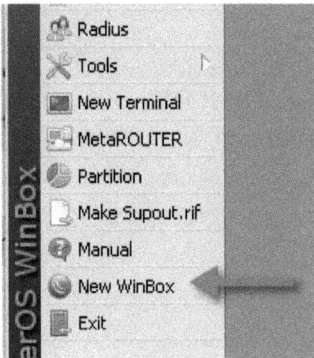

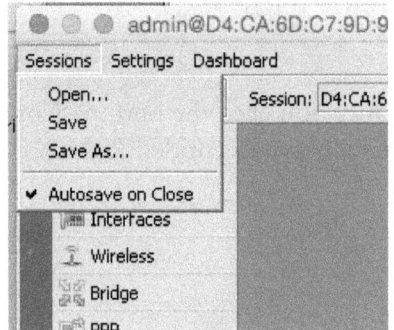

Some things to remember when building a RoMON network:

1. Only enable RoMON on interfaces facing other RoMON routers for security. Also, use a RoMON secret.

2. Use IPSEC on EoIP interfaces, as they are not secure by default. Version 6.30 and later make that easy.

3. Only use as many EoIP tunnels as you need to join dissimilar network segments.

4. Use port costs to ensure optimal routing, otherwise you may take a long or slow path unnecessarily.

Some other cool features are RoMON discovery (which shows you all your RoMON routers), RoMON Ping, and the ability to set the router ID used by RoMON (MAC address).

Chapter 5 – System Time and the NTP Protocol

NTP Client Setup

Having the system time set accurately is important for many purposes, especially logging and troubleshooting. Since RouterBOARDs do not have an onboard battery to keep the clock running, setting up the NTP client should be a part of your standard configuration.

The function of the NTP client is to query an NTP server, get the current time, and then set the local clock. The actual displayed time on the RouterBOARD system will be dependent on the local time setting on the device.

APPLICATION

Use this example for all routers to ensure the clock time matches local time. This ensures the logs are meaningful and readable, and is required for proper operation of certain dynamic protocols.

Example – Setting Up the NTP Client

1. The NTP client is part of the default packages, so there is no package that needs to be added. Simply select System and SNTP Client.
2. To have the device query a public Internet timeserver, set the Primary NTP Server to an IP address or leave them blank if using a DNS resolvable name. Recently added to the SNTP client is the ability to dynamically resolve DNS names for the timeserver. I suggest "us.pool.ntp.org" for U.S.-based systems. Adding a secondary NTP server is optional and you can consider one like pool.ntp.org. Fill them in as follows:

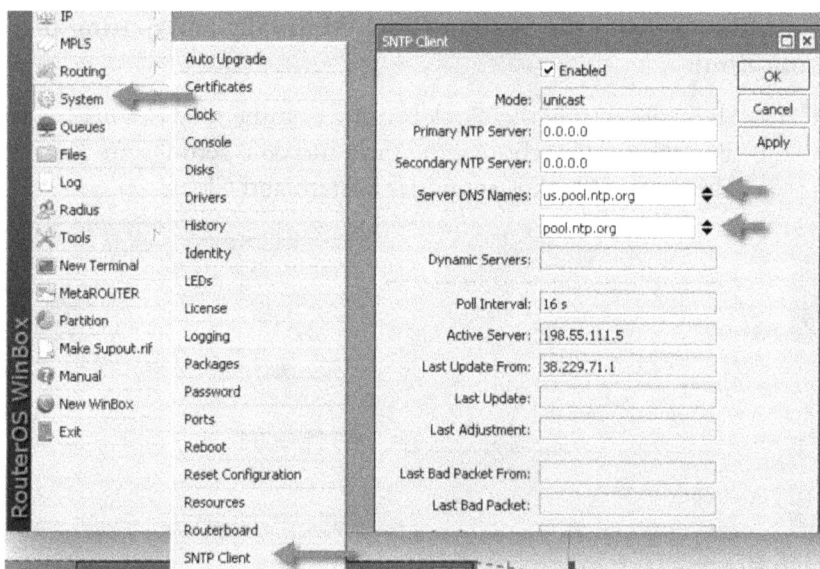

Using us.pool.ntp.org and more simply, pool.ntp.org, will typically yield two different NTP servers, but the router must have internet access and a working DNS server to resolve the DNS names. If the router is connected to the Internet, the NTP servers will be queried for the current date and time.

System Clock

Setting up the NTP client will not ensure that the local clock is accurate for local time, so you must set your time zone on the Clock setting to ensure your clock information is meaningful.

Use this example for all routers to ensure that the clock matches the local time zone.

APPLICATION

Example – Setting the System Clock Manually and Setting the Time Zone

1. Manually setting the clock is not recommended because every time the router reboots, the time and date settings are lost. The system clock is set under System and Clock:

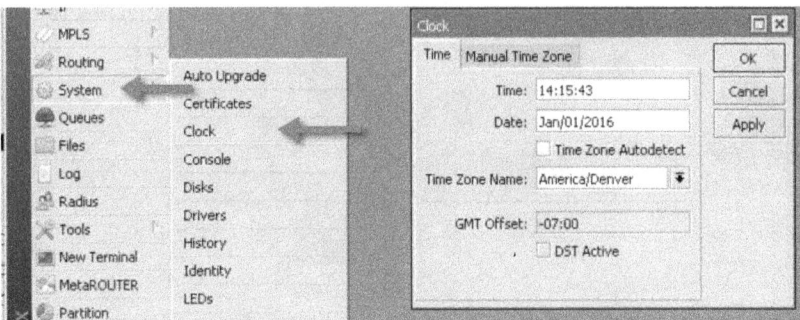

2. It is only necessary to select your local time zone from the pull-down list. The DST Active checkbox is a read-only indication of whether the standard settings dictate the current existence of Daylight Saving Time. It is only configurable on the Manual Time Zone tab by setting the beginning and ending dates for Daylight Saving Time.

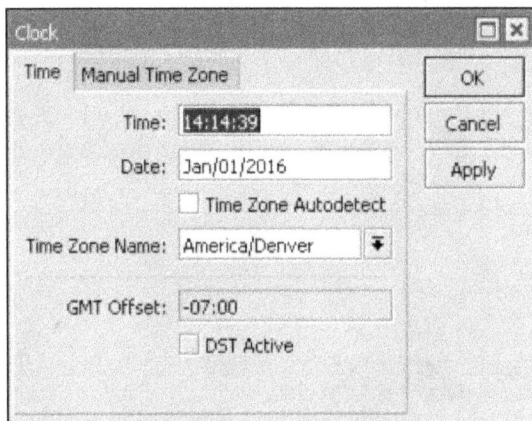

Advanced NTP Server Setup

This process is not needed for a basic setup. If you do not want to use an Internet-based time server or if you simply want to run your own, that is possible by adding the NTP Server optional package found in the package NTP. See Chapter 3 for instructions on Package Management.

Once the NTP package has been added and the router rebooted, the NTP server can be configured.

Use this example for any router in your network that needs to be able to act as an NTP server for other routers or devices.

Example – Enabling NTP Server

1. Download the "optional packages" zip file from mikrotik.com.

2. Unzip the package on your desktop.

3. Drag the NTP package into the files window.

4. Reboot the router. Once the router reboots, click the System button and then NTP Server and enable the NTP server for the protocol of your choice(s). Typically, checking "enabled" and "Broadcast" or the appropriate method you wish to use are the only settings required.

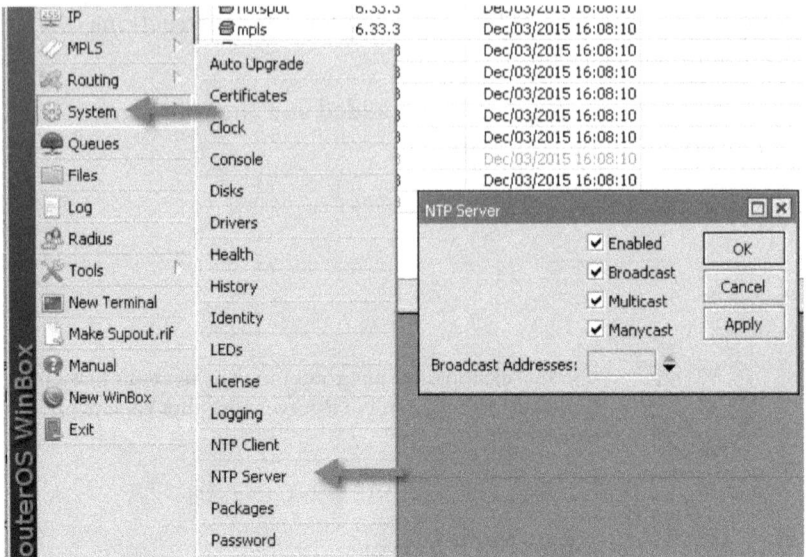

Other routers in your network will now be able to access this router as their NTP server.

Note: When you install the NTP package, another interesting feature is that the SNTP Client menu item changes to NTP Client and some of the new features recently added in version 6 (like using the DNS name for the NTP servers) simply go away.

This is a strange and often unfortunate consequence, so be aware before installing the NTP server. Possibly, this will be corrected in versions following 6.33. Here is the scaled down NTP client, which replaces the SNTP Client:

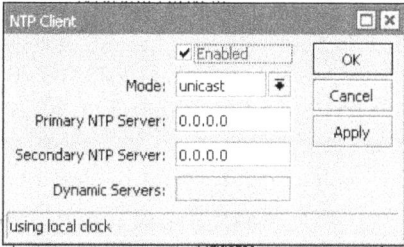

Chapter 6 – Backups

I once saw a sign that read, "Blessed is the pessimist for he hath made backups". I could not have said it better myself, as nothing is more difficult than trying to remember a configuration while screaming customers are down. Luckily, creating backups in RouterOS is quite easily done and can be automated as well to provide a high level of disaster recovery preparedness.

In summary, there are two types of backups – image backups and text-based backups. An image backups is not editable, but it is complete, simple to produce, and easy to restore. A text-based backup, on the other hand, is editable and can be restored to different hardware platforms by doing some simple editing with your favorite text editor such as Windows Notepad.

So, with two possible backup types, which do you choose? Well, my simple response to that is actually both. Each has its own unique value and by producing both, you have more flexibility when disaster strikes or if you simply need to upgrade a device.

An image backup is typically very simple to restore to the device it was created on. I like this method when trying something new on a router because I know I can roll back time to where I was prior to the changes. However, if you move that backup to another router, there are often strange consequences. For instance, if you restore a backup made on a RouterBOARD 450 to a RouterBOARD 433, the most obvious problem is a difference in the number of interfaces, thereby producing strange results. Also, MAC addresses are restored from the backup and overwritten on the new device, again causing issues. In this case, the text-based backup or "export" makes perfect sense and is usually my first choice for making an archive backup or cloning a router.

Use this example to create a backup that represents a snapshot in time. It is not optimal for cloning routers.

APPLICATION

Example – Creating an Image Backup

1. In WinBox, click on the Files button.

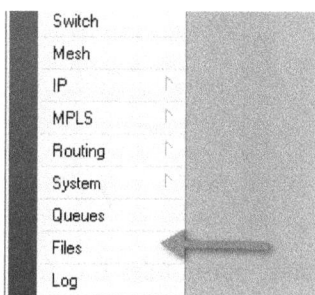

2. In the Files window, click the Backup button.

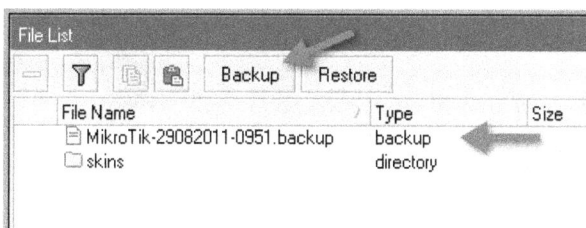

3. Once the backup file is created, it will appear in the Files List. Drag the file from the list to your local drive or desktop for safekeeping. It is also helpful to rename the file to something meaningful to you. For example, "main street access point 11-05-11.backup" or "gold standard AP 11-05-11.backup". It is also a good idea to include the date in all backup file names. If you don't do this, all the backups will start to look alike.

Use this example any time you need to go back in time to a point where the backup was made.

Example – Restoring an Image Backup

1. Click on the Files button.

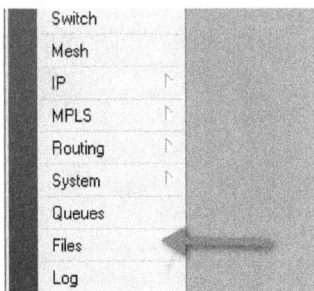

Switch	
Mesh	
IP	▶
MPLS	▶
Routing	▶
System	▶
Queues	
Files	
Log	

2. If the file is already in the Files List from a previous backup, click to highlight it, and then click the Restore button. The router will confirm the reboot. Once rebooted, the backup is restored.

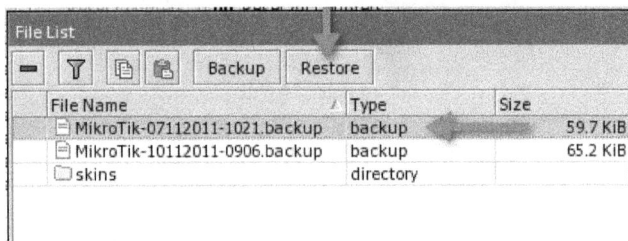

File List

	Backup	Restore		
File Name		Type	Size
MikroTik-07112011-1021.backup		backup	59.7 KiB
MikroTik-10112011-0906.backup		backup	65.2 KiB
skins		directory	

3. If the file to be restored is on your local drive, find it on your computer, drag it to the files window, and drop it at the top of the window. Click to highlight it and then click the Restore button. The router will confirm the reboot. Once rebooted, the backup is restored. When a backup is restored, you may need to enable the wireless interfaces.

Tip: Depending on the number and names of the files in your File List, sometimes it is difficult to drop the backup file where you want to drop it and it ends up in a folder, rather than the root directory. A good way to fix this is to create another backup using the process above, which will put the fresh backup at the top of your files list and create some space above any folders. Then, simply drag and drop in the new file and this operation is made much easier.

Text-Based Backups

My recommendation when restoring a text backup or "export" is to spend some time in your text editor cleaning up the configuration before importing it on the new hardware. In particular, do a word search for the phrase "MAC Address=". I recommend removing all those configuration segments, thereby making the restoration more universal. If you don't, when the import occurs, those lines will not be imported because the MAC address will not match the original hardware. Simply removing those configuration variables causes the file to load properly and usually without error.

Another use for the text backup is to establish a "gold standard" configuration. A gold standard is a configuration that is used on all your devices with general configuration options such as NTP client, clock settings, and SNMP (Simple Network Management Protocol) community strings. By configuring a single device with all the standard options you normally want, you can then produce a text export and edit it using a text editor, copying and pasting the appropriate sections into a new text file. Once you have all your configuration sections, test them on a new device and this file becomes your gold standard.

Use this example for making an editable backup or for cloning a router.

Example – Creating a Text Export (text backup)

The text export is created from the command line only.

1. Open a terminal window by clicking the New Terminal button.

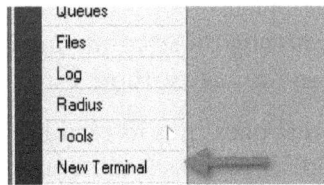

| Queues |
| Files |
| Log |
| Radius |
| Tools |
| New Terminal |

2. At the root prompt, type export file=[your file name here]. Of course, the square brackets are not actually typed, you should be naming your file in that field.

Example: export file=myconfig. It is not necessary to specify the file extension; the extension will be added automatically.

Producing the export will take 100% CPU for a few seconds, but will then produce a file in the Files List. From there you can drag and drop it to your desktop for renaming and further editing.

You can also omit the "files=" portion of the command and it will export the configuration to the terminal window. From there you can copy and paste parts of the file for use elsewhere.

Also note that the export is produced relative to the portion of the command tree you are in. For example, from the root of the command tree, you will export the entire configuration. By typing IP address and enter, you will then be inside the IP address menu branch and an export from there will only produce that portion of your configuration.

```
[admin@DudeServer] > ip address
[admin@DudeServer] /ip address> export
# mar/28/2011 09:24:11 by RouterOS 4.16
# software id = C80A-Q00P
#
/ip address
add address=216.81.36.   ; broadcast=216.81.36.   comment="" disabled=no \
    interface=ether1 network=216.81.36.`
[admin@DudeServer] /ip address>
```

Note that the default method of export is a compact export, meaning default configuration items are omitted, resulting in a very clean Config. If you want all the extra stuff (likely you don't, as it often causes issues), you can add a command line switch of "verbose" before "file=".

Use this example any time you want to apply a configuration you previously exported to a text file.

APPLICATION

Example – Importing a Text Backup

There are several methods of using the text backup you have created and edited. One way is to copy the text to your clipboard, right click inside a New Terminal window, and then paste. This way, the commands are executed "real time" so you can watch the effects as they occur. Another method is to import the file from the command line. One thing I have noticed is that the command syntax often changes "ever so slightly" between versions, so for the best experience, I suggest exporting and importing using the same exact versions. You can always upgrade the cloned router later, after you have configured it with the import.

1. In WinBox, click the New Terminal button to open a terminal window.

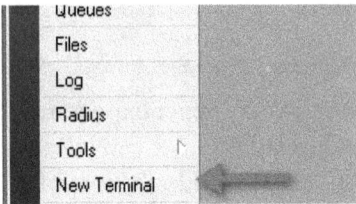

2. Drag the file to be imported into the File List root directory.

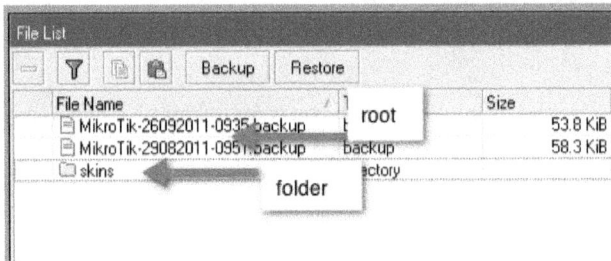

3. At the command line type import file=FileName.rsc.

A shortcut here is to type the command "import file=" and then hit the tab key to display all importable files. Typing a portion of the file name and hitting the tab key again will complete the name for you.

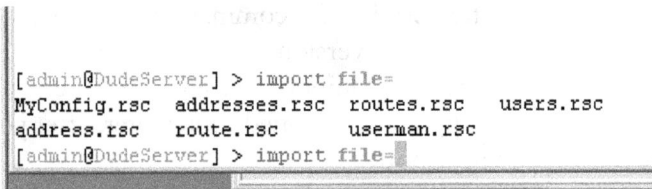

Chapter 7 – Licensing

One of the attributes of RouterOS that delivers the most value is the base feature set, which is consistent across the entire license range. While many manufacturers require additional fees to add even standard base features, MikroTik delivers all the features in all license levels and simply restricts the number of instances of certain devices. Licenses are included with RouterBOARDs and licensing is typically not an area where you will need to spend much time for basic setups. However, if you need to install RouterOS on a PC or turn a RouterBOARD designed as a client device into an access point, then this information is important.

For example, with a level 3 license, you can construct a point-to-point link with a single client, but to add multiple clients in ap-bridge mode, a level 4 license is required. On the other hand, MPLS, an advanced feature, is available across the entire license level spectrum.

The following chart displays the various license levels and their associated features:

Level	0	1	3	4	5	6
Price	no key	reg. required	volume only	$45	$95	$250
Upgradable To	-	no upgrades	ROS v5.x	ROS v5.x	ROS v6.x	ROS v6.x
Initial Config Support	-	-	-	15 days	30 days	30 days
Wireless AP	24h limit	-	-	yes	yes	yes
Wireless Client and Bridge	24h limit	-	yes	yes	yes	yes
Dynamic routing RIP, OSPF, BGP protocols	24h limit	-	yes(*)	yes	yes	yes
EoIP tunnels	24h limit	1	unlimited	unlimited	unlimited	unlimited

PPPoE tunnels	24h limit	1	200	200	500	unlimited
PPTP tunnels	24h limit	1	200	200	500	unlimited
L2TP tunnels	24h limit	1	200	200	500	unlimited
OVPN tunnels	24h limit	1	200	200	unlimited	unlimited
VLAN interfaces	24h limit	1	unlimited	unlimited	unlimited	unlimited
HotSpot active users	24h limit	1	1	200	500	unlimited
RADIUS client	24h limit	-	yes	yes	yes	yes
Queues	24h limit	1	unlimited	unlimited	unlimited	unlimited
Web proxy	24h limit	-	yes	yes	yes	yes
Synchr. interfaces	24h limit	-	-	yes	yes	yes
User Sessns.	24h limit	1	10	20	50	unlimited

(*) - BGP is included in License level 3 only for RouterBOARDs. For other devices you need level 4 or above to have BGP.

Figure 6 –RouterOS License Levels

Some additional things to know about licenses are: they never expire, level 4 and higher licenses include email support for up to 15 days after purchase, they can support an unlimited number of interfaces, and they can only be used for one installation.

All RouterBOARDs come complete with a license installed, the level of which is determined by the board's purpose. For example, if the board is intended to be a CPE (customer premise equipment) device, it comes with a level 3 license. Access point or AP boards come with at least a level 4 license, and so on.

Licenses cannot be upgraded, but they can be purchased and replaced. For example, if you own a device with a level 3 license, you can purchase a level 4 license and install it on the device, thereby turning it into an access point. Changing license levels is considered the equivalent of installing a new license, not an upgrade, so you have to pay the full cost of the level 4 license and not just an upgrade charge.

CHR – Cloud Hosted Router

A new feature added in 2015 by MikroTik, is the CHR or Cloud Hosted Router. CHR is a version of RouterOS meant to be hosted by a virtual machine. It supports the x86, 64-bit architecture and can be used on many popular hypervisors, such as VMWare, Hyper-V, VirtualBox, Amazon AWS, and others. The application for a CHR is any router for which you do not need physical network media access, in particular, VPN endpoints and Dude Monitoring servers. Running on even minimal hardware configurations, these devices can provide a high level of uptime for mission-critical applications at a very low cost of entry.

The method of installation of a CHR is covered in detail on the MikroTik Wiki, and changes based upon the hypervisor, so it is not covered here in detail. Generally, the steps are as follows:

Steps to install CHR

Step1: Download virtual disk image for your hypervisor.

Step2: Create a guest virtual machine.

Step3: Use previously downloaded image file as a virtual disk drive.

Step4: Start the guest CHR virtual machine.

Step5: Log in to your new CHR. Default user is "admin" without a password.

Images for all popular hypervisors can be found linked from the Wiki by searching for the phrase "CHR" in the manual section.

CHR Licensing

The CHR has 4 license levels, including "free", "p1", "p10", and "p-Unlimited". License levels refer to the maximum throughput of the router with -1 being 1 megabit and 10 being 10 megabit limit per interface. A 60-day free trial license is also available for all paid license levels. To get the free trial license, you have to have an account on MikroTik.com as all license management is done there.

The "P" refers to perpetual, meaning a lifetime license (buy once, use forever). It is possible to transfer a perpetual license to another CHR instance.

The following chart[1] demonstrates the licensing matrix and cost:

License	Speed limit	Price
Free	1Mbit	FREE
P1	1Gbit	$45
P10	10Gbit	$95
P-Unlimited	Unlimited	$250

All RouterOS licenses can be purchased by creating an account at mikrotik.com and entering the software ID as detailed in the examples that follow. Resellers and distributors are also a great place to buy licenses, as many of them provide license discounts.

Use this example to determine the license level of your router. If you don't have a certain feature, it is always best to ensure your license level supports it.

APPLICATION

Example – Determining Your License Level

To determine the level of license installed on your device, click on the System button and then License.

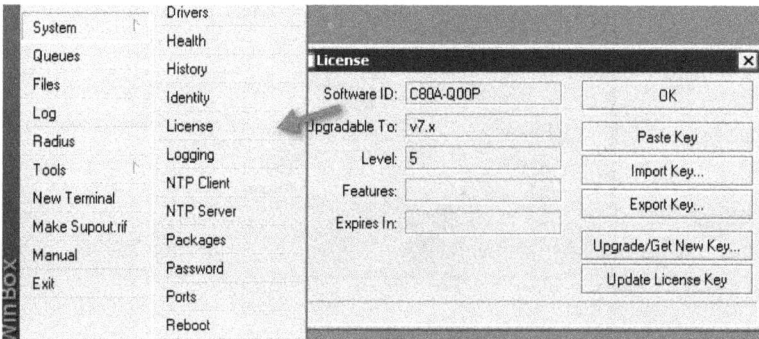

Use this example to install a license you purchased for a router.

Example – Install a License

1. To obtain a license key, repeat the procedure in the previous example and copy the Software ID to your clipboard. Create an account and log in at MikroTik.com. Purchase a new key using the Software ID and obtain the new key.

The key will look like this:

```
-----BEGIN MIKROTIK SOFTWARE KEY------------
K0x0Le06OWJ33lguQW2vD8wXydfkteJEdHeawpwbjsme
TE6KkvmF6gkFg3wl2bzIE/EAW8g0q+kGiTxCUpXJLA==
-----END MIKROTIK SOFTWARE KEY--------------
```

You can copy the key to your clipboard for installation. You should copy all of the text as follows including "-----BEGIN MIKROTIK SOFTWARE KEY: ------------" and "-----END MIKROTIK SOFTWARE KEY--------------". To paste the key into the router, select System License and click the Paste Key button.

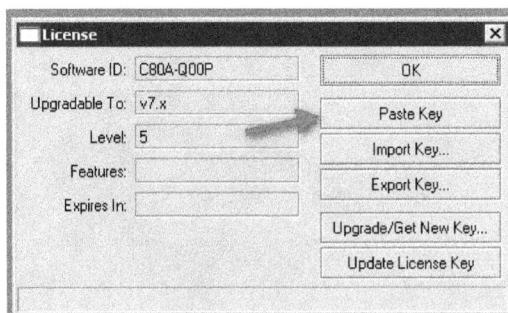

2. An alternate method is to use the .key file generated by MikroTik. Click the Import Key button and browse to the .key file to install it.

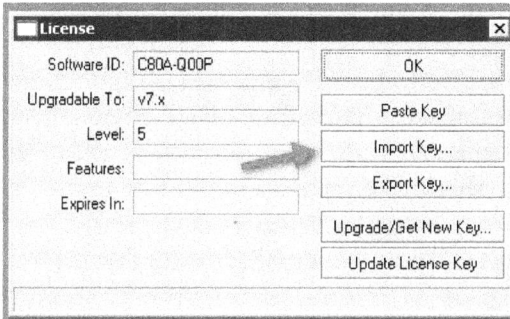

License	
Software ID: C80A-Q00P	OK
Upgradable To: v7.x	Paste Key
Level: 5	Import Key...
Features:	Export Key...
Expires In:	Upgrade/Get New Key...
	Update License Key

Note: The Update License Key button is used to update the key to the new format as presented when upgrading from version 3 to version 4 and requires the laptop to have Internet access in order to complete. There is no charge for this update.

Chapter 8 – Firewalls

Where there are options, there is power. Where there is power, there also can be complexity. Therefore, creating firewalls with RouterOS is often seen as an area of complexity where users fear to tread. As a result, many either make the decision to forego the firewall and hope for the best, or copy firewalls others have created online. This causes people not to realize the power that a properly created firewall can have and the protection it can offer their network or their network connected devices.

I have heard it said that the best way to protect a network is to put the hosts inside a vault, lock the door, post a guard, and never connect the network to a network. Although this is a bit extreme, the concept is basic and understandable: access to a network is the means by which a security breach or attack occurs. Remove the access and you remove the threat. Equally obvious is the fact that our networks need to be connected to the public Internet, so there is the application for firewalls.

By definition, firewalls should pass good traffic and block bad traffic. This good and bad traffic is passing either **to** our firewall, **from** our firewall, or **through** our firewall. In almost every circumstance, a firewall is also acting as a router, which doesn't really add any complexity, but is worth contrasting against what is typically termed a "passive" firewall or bridging firewall. In a passive or bridging firewall, the device is inserted into the network as a Layer 2 device, meaning it is not routing packets. It typically has an IP address, but only for the purpose of administration. Unlike a router, all packets that enter the passive firewall pass out of the firewall unless there are rules that specifically drop those packets. In this book, we will be covering routing firewalls, although passive firewalls are created in a similar manner.

Firewalls need rules to restrict traffic flow and fortunately, these rules are organized in chains. The purpose of the chains is to determine at what point in the progression of a packet into or through the firewall a set of rules is applied. The three default chains are input, forward, and output. There are also user-created chains for organizational and load-reducing purposes, but they rely on the three default chains. In summary, the user-defined chains do not see traffic or packets, unless the packets are sent there by one of the three default chains. I will cover that in detail later in this chapter.

Let's begin with the input chain. The input chain is designed to protect the router itself. Consider the following diagram:

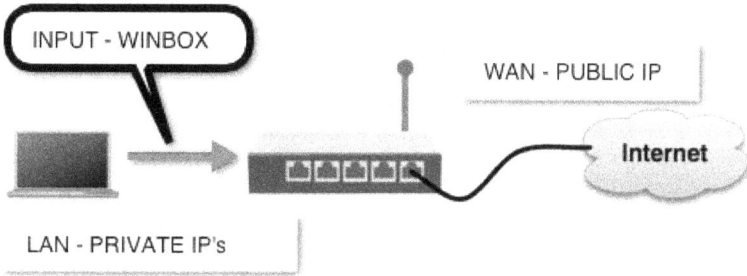

Figure 7 - IP Firewall Input Chain [1]

As you can see, this is a very typical placement of a firewall router at the gateway to the public Internet for a local area network. The Local Area Network or LAN uses private IP addresses, hidden from the public Internet, or WAN, behind the public address on the firewall/router's external or public IP address. Packets coming from the LAN or from the WAN destined for the router itself will pass to the input chain, so that is the logical location for rules to protect the router. This brings up an important detail about the operation of IP networks as it relates to the formation of packets.

I must digress from firewalls for just a moment and discuss packets. Packets are the messengers of the Internet, very similar to a letter you mail at the post office (but not nearly as slow). Every letter has a "to" address and a "from" or "return" address. The "to" address tells the post office where the letter should be routed and the "from" address tells them where to return the letter if it cannot be delivered. In the same way, packets have a "source" address (in this example the "from" or "return" address) and a "destination" address (in this example the "to" address). These are often abbreviated as dst for destination and src for source. When your computer sends a packet to Google, for example, it forms the packets with a dst address equal to the resolved IP for google.com and uses the PC's IP address as the src address. When Google gets the packets and wants to send it back with the information requested, it reverses the src and dst and you get what you requested. If something goes wrong along the way, upstream routers know what host to send the packets back to as "undeliverable" or "unreachable".

Now, back to our example of input chain rules. Typically, the only packets that should be going to our router are either packets from communications, connections our router has initiated (which we assume to be legitimate and safe), or packets representing us administering or configuring our routers. This greatly narrows down the list of safe host IP addresses and makes creation of firewall rules much simpler. The easiest scheme to use when creating firewall rules is to allow what you determine to be good or safe traffic and then use wildcards to drop all other traffic. You could try and do the opposite and drop all the bad traffic, one protocol and port combination at a time, but to do so would require thousands or millions of rules and you could never be sure that you covered every possible threat. Obviously, that is not a viable scheme, so we will allow the good and drop everything else.

So, what is "good" traffic to your firewall router? That's actually easy and can be found by thinking of two things:

1. What protocols and ports will you use to administer the router?

2. What services will your router provide to the network LAN or WAN?

These two questions will then define all the rules you will place in the "to" chain and everything else will then need to be dropped.

Before we move on, it is necessary to examine the way firewall rules in any chain work. Rules are simply packet matchers. They define certain criteria to identify packets, then they perform some action on those packets. Firewall rules work on an "if-then" principal. "If" a packet matches their criteria, "then" they perform the following action on them. The matchers assume that if something is specified, then it is identified, but if it isn't specified, it matches all packets.

The following is an example of a new firewall filter rule created in the input chain.

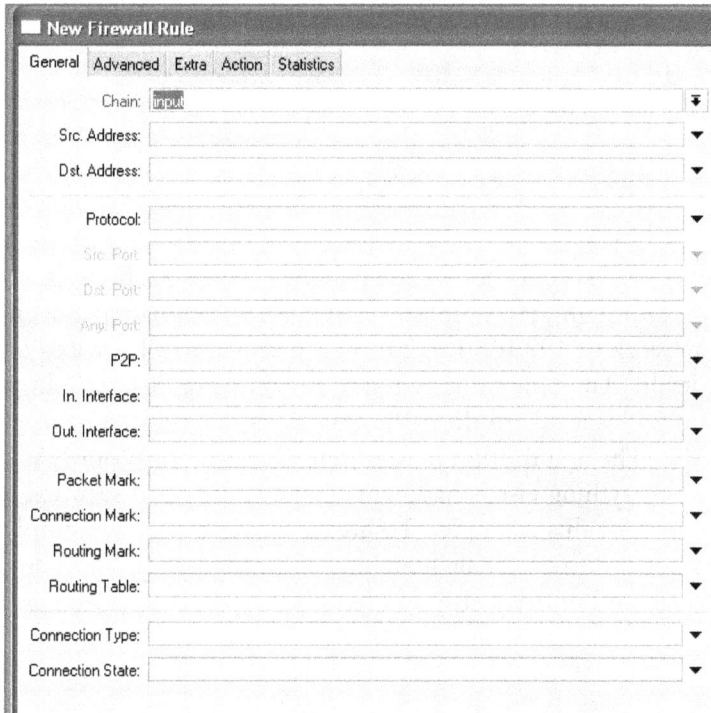

As you can see, nothing has yet been selected other than the chain. This rule then matches all packets going to the router. In the next illustration, we have begun the process of narrowing down the packet matching criteria:

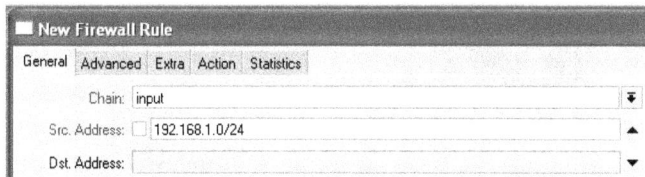

This rule now matches all types of packets, but only if they are coming from (src address) our private LAN. Adding additional criteria will further narrow down the scope of this rule. This is the "if" portion of the rule. Next, we must specify some action to be taken when a packet matches the rule. This is done on the Action tab.

In this illustration, we have selected the default action of "accept".

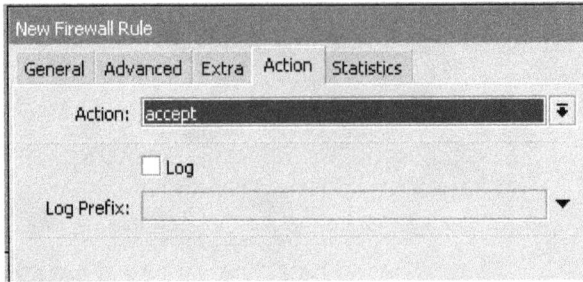

The action of "accept" allows the packet to enter the firewall. This one rule, although very simplistic in nature, will allow any host in our LAN network of 192.168.1.0/24 to have access to all services on the router itself. The only thing required to complete this very simple input firewall is a rule to drop all other traffic that doesn't come from our LAN. The assumption here is that all traffic from our LAN is safe and everything else is bad, which isn't really good security, but it is sufficient for this example. To create the drop rule, we simply create a second firewall rule matching all traffic by only selecting the input chain and nothing else on the General tab, then selecting an Action of drop.

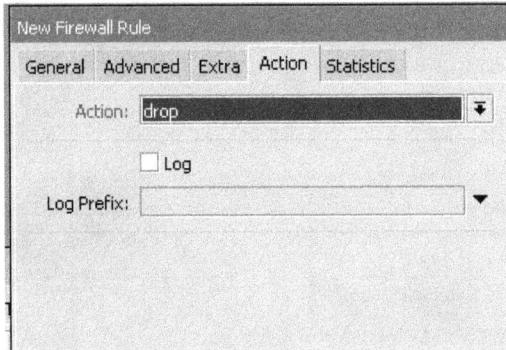

It is important to know that firewall rules, like almost all rules in RouterOS, are processed in order, top to bottom. Therefore, if your accept rule is before your drop rule, everything works as expected. If you put your drop rule first, you will lose access to your router.

In the previous example, we put an address from our LAN network on our laptop. With this IP we will be able to administer the router using SSH, WinBox, FTP, or HTTP. The router will not respond to pings from the public Internet and we will not be able to access the router from outside our LAN. This is the first building block of a firewall. A better "accept" would further narrow down the range of IP addresses to be allowed to administer the router to only our laptop or only the IP's used by the IT group, etc. In addition, it is advisable to only allow the protocols and ports you will actually use. This is the most secure type of input firewall.

If you follow the example above, you may notice that everything seems to work normally as it relates to accessing the router, however, this firewall will break other services the router provides to the LAN, such as DNS if you are using the DNS caching facilities of RouterOS. This is normal.

Learning firewalls can be very frustrating and complex unless you break them down into the building blocks that compose a firewall and learn these blocks in a progressive manner. I always tell my students in class to not be impatient as we step through this journey. Just learn one piece at a time, then we will put them all together, and things will work as expected. I had a guitar teacher that told me, "our goal is to *play* the song, not to *finish* the song." The same applies to learning firewalls.

Connections

Now we will bring in the next piece to the firewall puzzle, connections, but first let's discuss some basics. Communication in networks is conducted using ports. The device sending the packet sends the packet from a port (the source port) and the receiving device receives the packet on a port (the destination port). Protocols like TCP or UDP specifically are used, but let's restrict our discussion to ports for now. These combinations of source and destination port are held constant for each established connection between hosts. Our data will be transmitted across these connections. There are four types of connections: new, established, related, and invalid. Let's begin with new.

Generally, when a router receives a packet, and the source and destination IP address are not in the connection tracking table, it sees that as a new connection. Within a protocol like TCP, UDP or ICMP, there are some specific nuances, but generally the process is the same. For purposes of walking through an example, let's take a TCP connection. SYN packets are the first packet sent with a TCP 3-way handshake and their source and destination addresses and ports we can assume, are not in the router's connection tracking table. (Please note that we often abbreviate source as "src" and destination as "dst"). A connection is only new when it is initiated, and afterward, the packets that follow are called "established packets". So, what if a TCP packet arrives and its src/dst addresses and port combination are not in the connection-tracking table, but it is not a SYN packet? That would be an invalid packet. An invalid TCP packet is one that does not belong to any known connection, but does not create a new connection because it is not a SYN packet. In summary, invalid packets are not useful and therefore, should be dropped. They typically caused by a break in the network upstream.

In addition to new connections and established connections, there are also related connections. The easiest way to understand related connections is to think about them as what they are not. They are not new because they are created by a connection that has already been seen as new, they are not invalid, and they are not part of the established connection. They are simply "related" to an already established connection.

The rules to understand here and dedicate to memory are:

A connection is new when its src/dst/port combination is seen for the first time by either host participating in the communication.

A connection is established on the packets following the packet that creates the new connection. Without allowing a new connection to be opened, it can never be established or related. This is important - the new connections become the gatekeepers of established and related connections. Control the new connections and you control all other connections.

A connection can't be a related connection unless it is first a new connection. Related connections are not new or established, but are a part of an established connection.

Invalid connections aren't useful and should be dropped.

Firewall

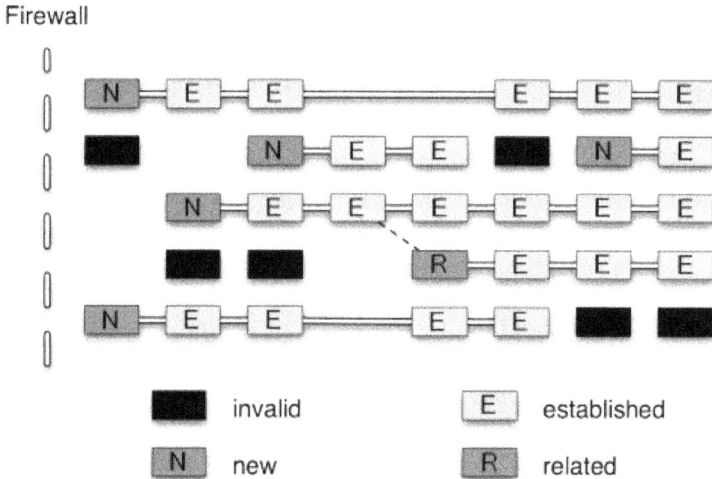

Figure 8 – Connections [1]

In the preceding diagram, you can see several states of connections and the combinations that are possible. Looking at a few we can see the following:

Beginning with the first line, the first packet begins the new connection. All packets following are a part of an established connection.

The second line begins with an invalid connection, not a part of any known connection, and not a new connection. Following it is a new connection, then an established connection.

The third line begins as the first line with a new connection, then an established connection, and then it spawns a related connection. We now have two parallel connections related to each other.

The fourth line begins as the first, but ends with two invalid connections, so can you guess what the next connection state would be? If you answered new, you now understand connection states.

Two Ways To Control Access

So far, we have discussed two ways to control access in the input chain. The first method is to simply filter every packet coming into the router. If it passes through our filter, it is allowed. If it doesn't pass, it is dropped.

The second method is to filter based on connection state. If the connection is in a certain state, accept it, if not we will drop it. In addition, if a connection is in the invalid state, we will simply drop it.

To understand how these two methods work together and are used by a RouterOS firewall, consider the first example I gave with two input rules. The first rule allowed all traffic from the LAN network. The second rule dropped everything else. If a host on the LAN tries to ping the router, it will get a reply. If the router tries to ping a host on the LAN, it will get a reply. But what if the router tries to ping a host on the WAN? If you try this, what you will find is that the ping times out. You may ask why that is, because we are not restricting the router from doing anything. The answer is that although the router creates and sends the ping packet, it can't get a reply, since we are blocking on the input chain. Effectively, the router doesn't know the host sending the reply packet, so it drops it.

Since the host you are pinging on the WAN isn't on the LAN network, and is therefore not allowed by the first rule, it is dropped by the second rule. One fix for this would be to write a new accept rule to accept ping packets from the WAN host you are pinging. This, however, would have to be done for every host you would ever want to ping from your router. Another option is to allow ICMP (Internet Control Message Protocol, the protocol ping uses) from all hosts, but again this isn't a good solution because it creates a security hole.

This is where connections state matchers can save the day. With connection state matchers, we can assume that if the router itself opens a connection, it is safe to allow return communications from that host for that one protocol and for that one connection. You can think about connections now as being a two-way street or a pipe. Traffic flows both directions once your router opens that pipe. This allows the ping to return from the host it was sent to.

It is not necessary to restrict new connections with firewall rules to the router because the only way a connection can be opened from the router is if we log into the router and generate a ping, open a telnet or SSH session, or use some other protocol that creates a new connection. Another scenario is if the router tries to do a DNS lookup on a DNS server on the WAN interface, it must open a new connection to that remote host. We can assume here that connections cannot be created from the router unless we initiate them or allow them to be initiated by using protocols that open connections like caching DNS. This is a safe assumption. The router opens the new connection and the return is handled using an established connection rule. Therefore, only one established connection rule is needed on the input chain for connections from anywhere to return to the router itself.

Now, back to the example with two firewall rules, one to allow packets from the LAN network and a second to drop everything else. By adding a third rule, we can allow our router to ping or do DNS lookups by allowing that return path through a connection state rule. This rule must be added above the drop rule and will allow a connection state of "established". Add one more rule like it for related packets and this solves the problem.

But now you might ask, "What about new connections? Don't we need a rule to allow them too?" In this scenario, new connections are only created when we do something like a ping from the router itself, so that becomes the control. The return connection when the ping packet reply arrives is now in the established state (remember, established connections are those that follow a new connection by virtue of their src/dst/port combinations), so our established connection state rule allows the return path. Obviously, a related connection state rule works the same way and is also needed. The result will be four rules on the input chain:

1. A rule to accept everything from the LAN network.

2. A rule to accept all established connections.

3. A rule to allow all related connections.

4. A rule to drop all other packets.

You could add a rule to drop invalid connections, but that would be redundant, since rule 4 above drops everything else, which includes invalid connections. The input firewall is now complete and you have thereby secured your router.

Forward Chain

As the input chain protects the router, the forward chain protects the clients. In this statement, I am referring to all hosts behind the firewall as the clients. Traffic to and from the hosts behind the firewall passes through the forward chain, so that is where we will place our rules.

Connection state matchers are ideally suited for this job. Consider the following scenario: You want to create filter rules to allow protocols to pass through your firewall and drop hacking attempts. If the only tool in your toolbox is firewall rules that match traffic based upon source IP and/or destination IP, you would actually need to write one rule for each host on the Internet you wanted to allow your customers to access and one rule for each return path! Obviously, this isn't feasible and port matchers help a little. For instance, you could allow all port 80 through the firewall and that would be a good start. Add port 110, 443, and some other common ports, and you are on your way. But what about protocols and ports you did not anticipate? What about the scenario when your client wants to use SSH on port 22 or some other new application? That is where connection matchers can once again save the day and that is why I teach the forward chain using connection matchers.

There are several assumptions here. First, that if a host on your local area network opens a connection to a host on the outside of the firewall, that was an intended operation and you, by default, are allowing them to do that. Second, remember that once the connection is opened, it is a two-way pipe. The host can now send data to the external host and the reverse flow will also be allowed. So far, none of these caveats create any extra work for me as a system administrator.

By understanding the connection states we discussed previously, we can protect our clients behind the firewall with only a few simple rules. These rules will use matchers based on connection states, allow connections to be initiated only from the LAN, allow two-way communication through the firewall for every connection opened by LAN clients, and drop all other traffic through the firewall. It will also allow you to add rules to block certain ports and protocols, even if your LAN clients initiate them.

The first rule in our forward chain will allow customers on the LAN to create new connections through the firewall. Since all connection states begin as new connections, by controlling the creation of new connections, we effectively control all access through the firewall. For this purpose, we can use the source address packet matcher in a firewall rule to restrict the first rule to only match packets coming from the LAN. This can be done by simply entering the network address of the LAN in the "Src. Address" field. For example, if your LAN network is 192.168.1.0/24, enter that address in the blank on the General tab. Next, we can use the Connection State matcher to match new connections. Finally, the action of accept will allow "new" connections, sourced from our LAN to be accepted.

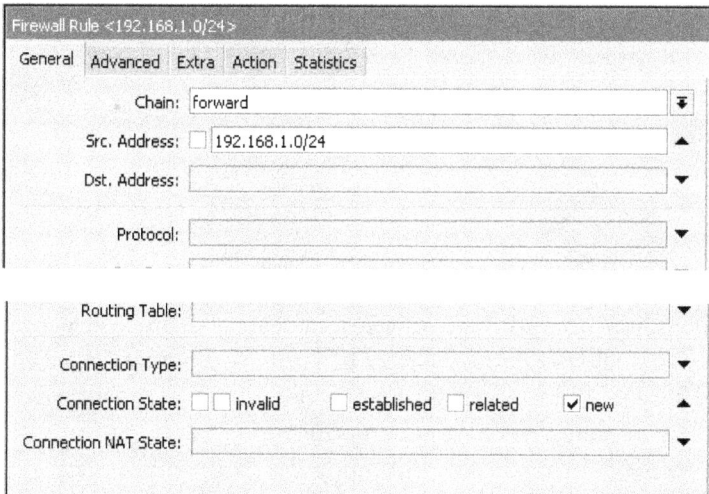

Note that only if the source address is on the LAN will the connection be allowed, so hosts on the WAN side of the router will not be able to open new connections through our firewall.

The next rule will allow related connections. This rule is less restrictive because we have already controlled new connections and secondarily restricted all other connections through this single control. The second rule matches "related" connections in the forward chain with an action of "accept".

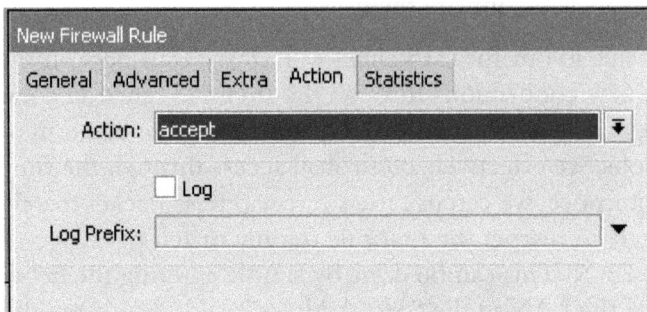

The third rule is similar to the second and allows established connections. Finally, for good measure, we drop invalid connections in the forward chain and drag it up to the top of the rule list, so it gets processed first.

#	Action	Chain	Src. Address	Dst. ...	Prot...	Src...	D. I...	Out...	Connection State	Bytes	Packets
0	✖ drop	forward							invalid	324 B	8
1	✔ accept	forward	192.168.1.0/24						new	0 B	0
2	✔ accept	forward							established	302.7 KiB	1 091
3	✔ accept	forward							related	0 B	0

It is important to note a change made in Version 6. The Connection State matchers are now check boxes, instead of a single selection combo box, allowing you to select multiple connection states in one rule. That can reduce the number of rules, but you must be careful to make sure that if you combine connection states, your rule still makes sense. For instance, combining the Connection State "Invalid" and "New" with the Source Address in a forward chain rule doesn't makes sense because the rule for "Invalid" connections is a drop rule and the rule for "New" connections is an Accept rule. I typically leave the new connection rule by itself to keep my mind straight, and then combine some of the others to make it more logical. Again, there are many ways to accomplish the same goal, but your focus should always be on efficiency and keeping things logical and easy to understand. Also, read the rule out loud to be sure it makes sense.

For instance, this rule:

would read "any packets going through the forward chain, that is, packets with a destination address not bound to this router itself, if they originated from the 192.168.1.0/24 subnet, regardless of destination, port or protocol, if they are a new connection packet, accept them." That is an uncomfortably long sentence, but descriptive of all the packet matchers we have selected in this example, so read it again slowly and ensure it makes sense. If you go through this process with each rule you write, at least at first, things will begin making sense and you will fully grasp the firewall rule-writing process.

Address Lists

The final piece of the basic firewall puzzle is the one that really simplifies our lives in the firewall world: the Address List. Address lists are created to allow a single rule to apply to one or more groups of IP addresses or subnets.

Without an address list, it would be necessary to write a separate rule for each IP address, range, or subnet for which we wanted to match packets. With an address list-based rule, we simply reference an address list name instead of an IP.

To create a new Address List, click on the IP button, select Firewall, and click on the Address List tab. From there, you can click the plus sign to create a new entry and name it as you wish. If this is the second entry for a list, you can use the pull-down list to select the list name. In the address blank, you can type an IP address, a subnet, or a range. Once the address list entry is created, it can be referenced in a firewall rule on the Advanced tab again using the pull-down.

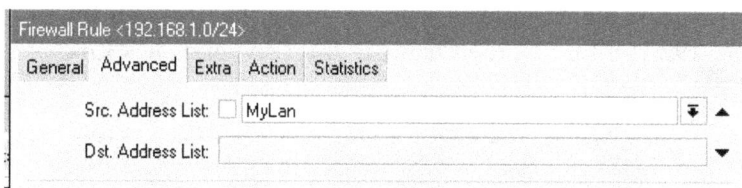

All of this may sound a bit confusing until we tie it all together with some examples. A basic firewall will need two groups of rules on the input chain to protect the router itself and rules on the forward chain to protect the clients on the LAN. Let's dig in now to a comprehensive example.

Example – The Basic Firewall

The default configuration for RouterOS contains a basic firewall. That one is fine for a home router, but quickly becomes too restrictive when you start modifying the default configuration. Always consider removing the default configuration and writing your own firewall. For purposes of this example, we will assume that the LAN is on the 192.168.1.0/24 subnet.

1. In WinBox, click the IP button, select Firewall, and click on the Address List tab.

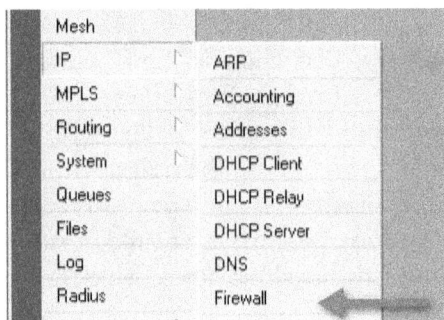

Mesh		
IP	▶	ARP
MPLS	▶	Accounting
Routing	▶	Addresses
System	▶	DHCP Client
Queues		DHCP Relay
Files		DHCP Server
Log		DNS
Radius		Firewall

2. Create a new address list entry using the plus sign for 192.168.1.0/24, then name it "MyLan" and click OK.

(Continued on next page)

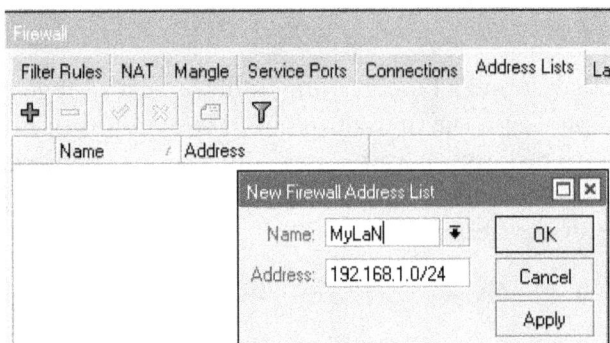

Firewall

| Filter Rules | NAT | Mangle | Service Ports | Connections | Address Lists | La |

| ✚ | ─ | ✓ | ✕ | ▱ | ▼ |

| Name | Address |

New Firewall Address List   ☐ ✕

Name: MyLaN ▼   OK

Address: 192.168.1.0/24   Cancel

Apply

104

3. Click the IP button, select Firewall, and then the Filter tab. Click the plus sign to create a new rule.

   Rule 1: On the chain, select "input". On the connection state, select "invalid" and on the action tab, select "drop".

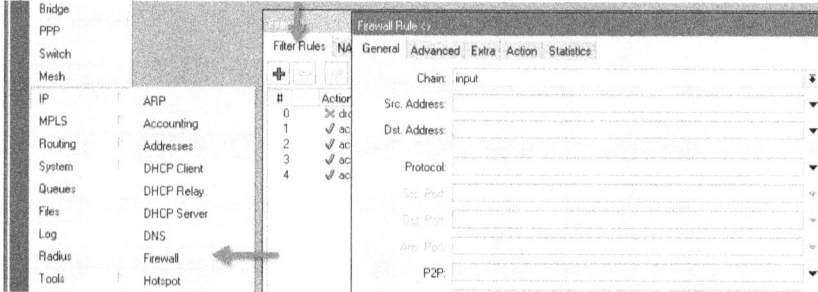

(Continued on next page)

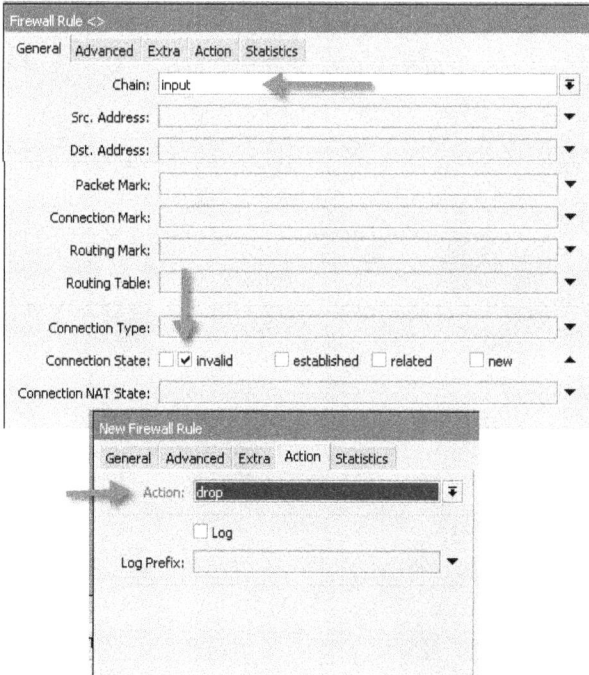

Rule 2: Click the plus sign to create a new rule.

On the chain, select "forward", on the connection state, select "invalid", and on the action tab, select "drop".

(Continued on next page)

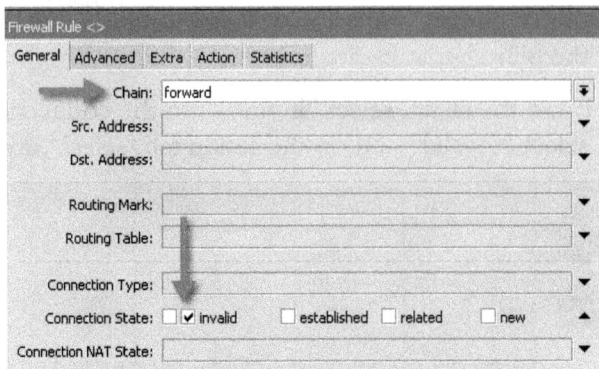

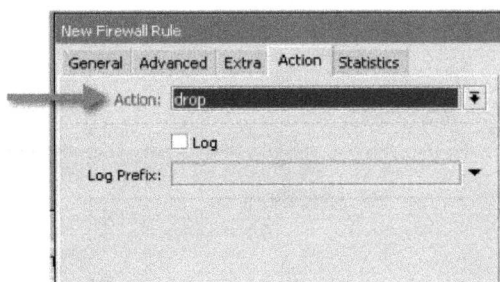

These two rules drop invalid connections to and through the router.

Rule 3: Click the plus sign to create a new rule.

On the chain, select "input", on the advanced tab, select "Src. Address List", on the pull-down, select the new entry you just created for "MyLan", and on the Action tab select "accept". This rule will allow anyone on your LAN to administer the router. Obviously, you can be more restrictive if you wish.

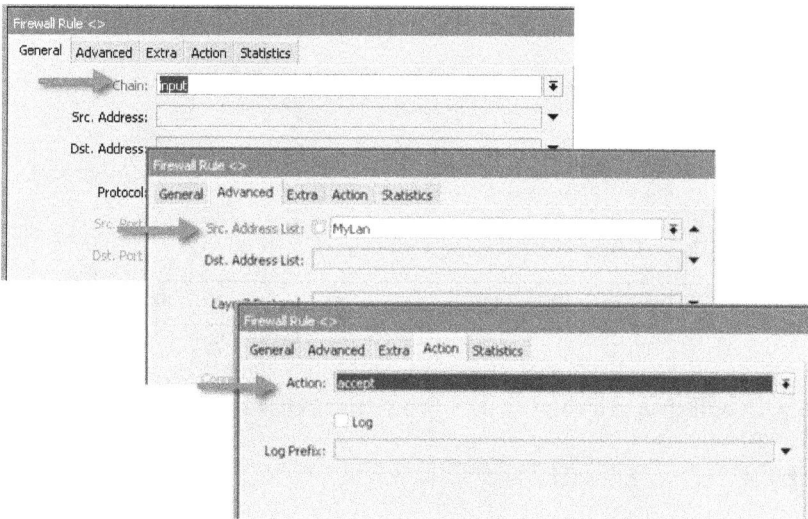

Rule 4: Click the plus sign to create a new rule.

On the chain, select "input". On the "Connection State", select "established" and on the "Action" tab select "accept". This rule will allow our router to communicate with other hosts for services like ping or telnet.

(Continued on next page)

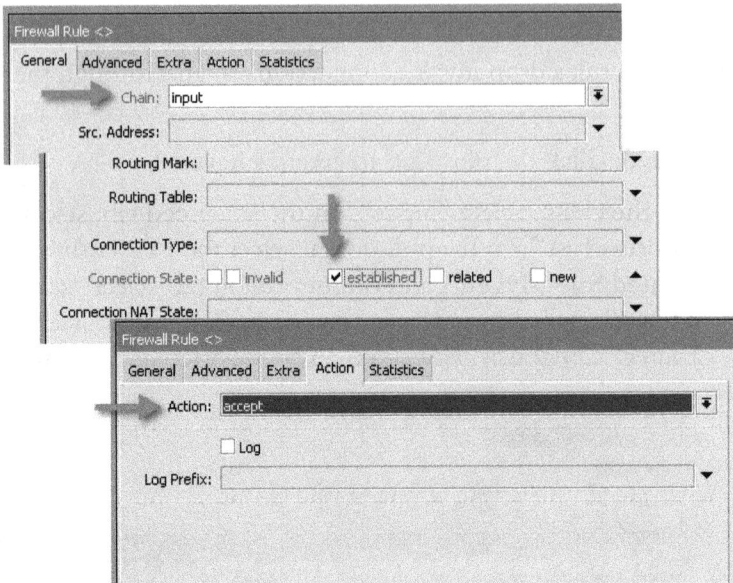

Rule 5: Click the plus sign to create a new rule.

For this rule, make sure you are in Safe Mode, as a mistake here will disconnect you from the router. On the chain, select "input". On the "Action" tab, select "drop". This rule will drop all other hosts trying to access our router.

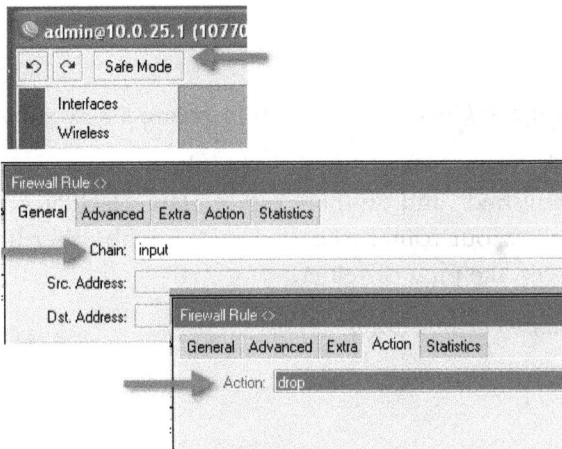

Rule 6: Click the plus sign to create a new rule.

On the chain, select "forward". On the connection state, select "new". On the advanced tab, select the Src. Address

List as "MyLan" previously created, and on the action tab, select "accept". This rule will allow new connections from our LAN to pass through the router.

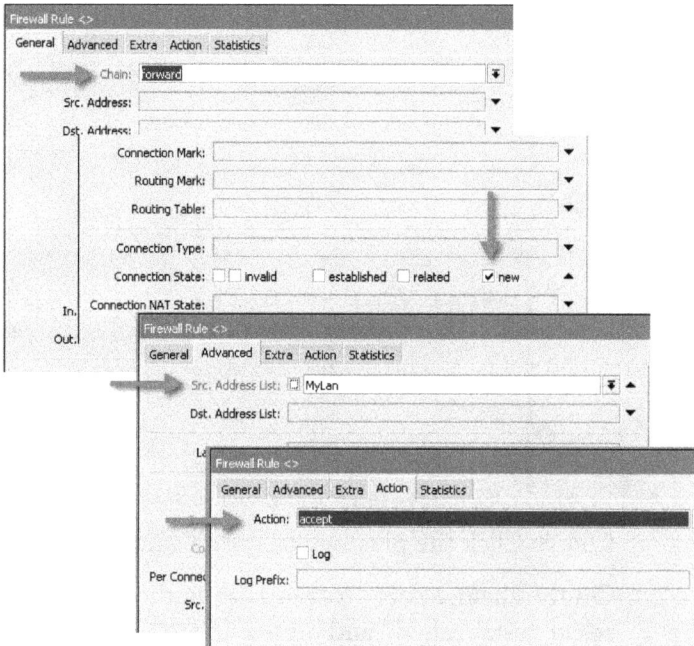

Rule 7: Click the plus sign to create a new rule.

On the chain, select "forward". On the connection state, select "related" and on the action tab, select "accept". This rule will allow related connections through the router.

(Continued on next page)

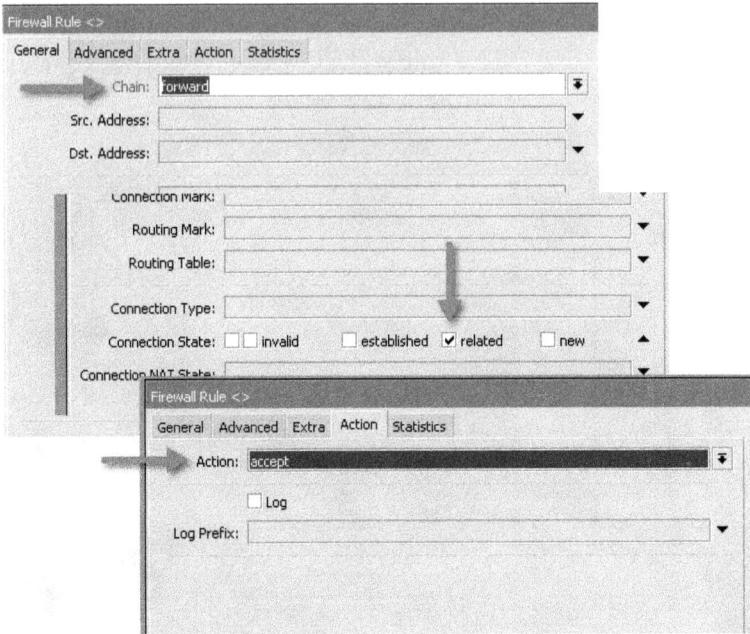

Rule 8: Click the plus sign to create a new rule.

On the chain, select "forward". On the connection state, select "established" and on the action tab, select "accept". This rule will allow established connections through the router.

(Continued on next page)

Firewall Rule <>

General | Advanced | Extra | Action | Statistics

Chain: forward

Src. Address:

Dst. Address:

Protocol:

Src. Port:

Dst. Port:

Routing Table:

Connection Type:

In | Connection State: ☐☐ invalid ☑ established ☐ related ☐ new ▲

Out | Conne

Firewall Rule <>

General | Advanced | Extra | Action | Statistics

Action: accept

☐ Log

Log Prefix:

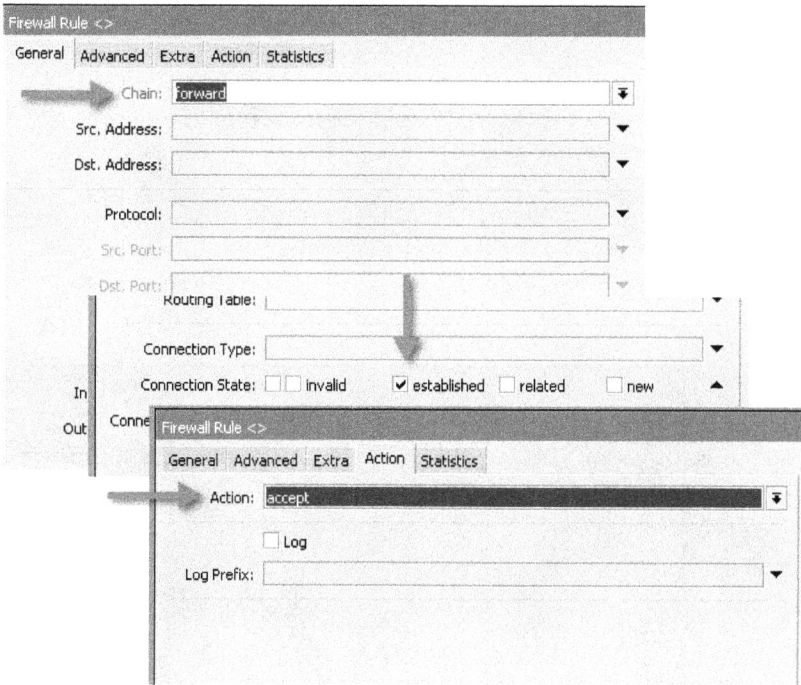

The last rule drops all other connections through the router.

Rule 9: Click the plus sign to create a new rule.

On the chain, select "forward" and on the action tab select "drop".

Firewall Rule <>

General | Advanced | Extra | Action | Statistics

Chain: forward

Src. Address:

Dst. Address:

Protocol:

Src. Port:

Dst. P

Any. P

In. Interfa

Out. Interfa

Firewall Rule <>

General | Advanced | Extra | Action | Statistics

Action: drop

☐ Log

Log Prefix:

Summary of Rules

Rule 1 &2: Drops invalid connections on input and forward chains.

Rule 3: Allows administration of the router (and any other services the router can provide, such as DNS to LAN clients) from the LAN.

Rule 4: Since we aren't restricting the creation of new connections on the input chain, we assume new connections from the router are only created if we are administering the router and trying to initiate a connection from it such as pinging, opening a telnet session from WinBox, etc. If a new connection is created, the response must be acceptable, so we allow established connections. This makes everything work correctly.

Rule 5: This is our drop rule for the input chain. The assumption is that we have already allowed everything that should be allowed, so we drop everything else, which is standard firewall philosophy.

Rule 6: This is where we control the creation of new connections and restrict them only to connections that are sourced from our LAN.

Rule 7: Since we restricted new connections in step 6, we can now allow related connections.

Rule 8: Since we restricted new connections in step 6, we can now allow established connections.

Rule 9: This is our drop rule for the forward chain. The assumption is that we have already allowed everything that should be allowed, so drop everything else, standard firewall philosophy.

This example can be extended and serves only as the foundation of a stateful firewall. If you want to restrict certain protocols, for instance, SSH from the LAN, it is now fairly simple to create a rule to drop that protocol on the forward chain by matching port 22 with an action of drop. Put that rule at or near the top of your list, and LAN clients will not be able to initiate SSH connections outside the firewall.

For Further Study: RouterOS also offers some "smart" rules to detect port scans, match connections, and many other more complex functions that are outside the scope of this book.

Chapter 9 – NAT, Network Address Translation

In the previous chapter, it was made clear the importance of understanding the source IP, destination IP, source port, and destination port of an IP packet with respect to firewalls. Combined with connection states, these four simple pieces of information can be leveraged to assemble powerful firewalls that rival equipment that costs much more than a MikroTik RouterOS device. In addition to the firewall function, these four pieces of information can be tracked and manipulated using a function called NAT (Network Address Translation).

NAT is the process of changing the original source IP, destination IP, source port, or destination port of an IP packet. It allows functions such as masquerading, which is hiding a private network behind a public network address. It also allows the opposite function, destination NAT, which grants public access to a private server.

NAT functions, similar to firewall functions, are organized in chains. The default chains are:

1. Source NAT ("srcnat"), which is changing the source IP address of the packet.

2. Destination NAT ("dstnat"), which is changing the destination IP address of the packet.

Source NAT

With source NAT, the most common function is masquerading, hiding a private network behind a public address. This function allows a router with a single public IP address to function as an Internet gateway for a handful or even thousands of hosts or computers located behind the device on a private network. Like all NAT functions, the process is fairly simple: change the source or destination IP address or port based on a rule. Like all firewall functions, the rule itself is based on a packet matcher. The most simple source NAT rule, the masquerade rule, simply involves configuring the chain as "srcnat", matching packets going to the Internet by matching the "out interface", and setting an action of masquerade.

The first matcher "srcnat" tells the router to strip off the source IP address from the packet. In this case, the source IP address will be the private address of the host or computer on the 192.168.1.0/24 network. For example, if a host at 192.168.1.2 sends a packet to the Internet, it will be sourced as 192.168.1.2 when it enters our firewall. Since the rule is a source NAT rule, the router knows to strip the source IP address. The second packet matcher, "out interface", tells the router to only apply the rule to packets leaving interface ether1, which is the interface connected to the Internet in this example. The action of "masquerade" tells the router to exchange the source IP address (the private IP) for its own IP bound to the interface from which the packet is leaving (the public IP). Once the switch is done, the departing packet is no longer sourced from 192.168.1.2, instead it is sourced from the public IP of the router, 23.14.55.243. Once this is done, the router makes a record of the source and destination IP addresses and ports in its connection tracking table.

SRC-NAT

SRC IP: 192.168.1.2   SRC IP: 23.14.55.243

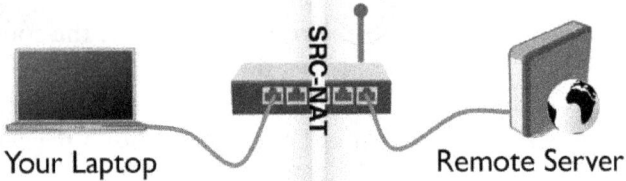

Your Laptop   Remote Server

Figure 9 - Source NAT [1]

This is necessary so that when the packet returns from the host it was sent to, the router will know what to do with it. In this case, a returning packet will enter the router, then the source and destination IP address and ports will be matched against the connection tracking table. If there is a match, the destination IP (now the public IP of the router) will be stripped off and the private IP of the host that sent the original packet will be applied.

Destination NAT

Source NAT is typically used for masquerade, but has other usefulness. First, we must understand the function of destination NAT. With the popularity of enterprises operating their own mail servers, it has become fairly common to host a mail server or web server on the private network. Doing this enables protection of the device with the firewall while still allowing the device to access the Internet via source NAT and masquerade. However, with only a source NAT rule, the device is not accessible from the public Internet. That may be the desired scenario, but in the case of a mail server or web server, the ability to access the device from the public Internet may be desired and that is where destination NAT, or "dstnat" becomes useful.

In source NAT, we described the process of stripping off the private IP address from a packet and replacing it with the public IP address of the router. Destination NAT operates the same way, but instead the rules are located in the "dstnat" chain and the behavior is to strip off the destination IP address from the packet and replace it with a new one. The function can also be performed for destination port as well.

In our example, we have a mail server located on the private network and we want to allow inbound mail to be delivered to the mail server. To accomplish this, we can create a new NAT rule with the chain "dstnat" and match all packets hitting our public IP address ("Dst. Address"). We use our public IP address in the rule because that is the IP address we will publish via DNS (Domain Name System which is handled by Domain Name Servers) as the address of our mail server. Since other mail servers will send packets to that IP, we will then have to take those packets, strip off their destination IP address, and replace it with the private destination IP address in our rule.

The process occurs as follows:

IP Firewall Diagram

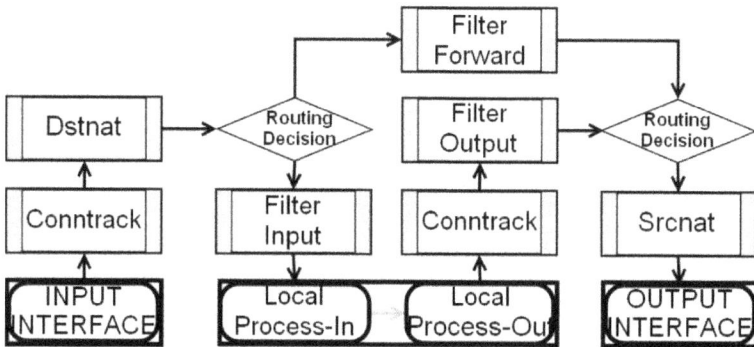

Understand that the preceding figure is what I would term the "simplified" packet flow diagram. The MikroTik Wiki contains a much more complex version that takes into account bridging, IPsec, MPLS, and other advanced protocols that further complicate the packet flow, but this one works for our discussion. Once again, connection tracking tracks the source, destination IP address, and ports, so it knows what to do with the packet when it is returned by the target host.

Destination NAT's do not have to use the same port from the packet matcher on the action tab, instead, we can change the port as well as the IP address if desired. For example, a packet entering the router on port 80 (typical HTTP or web port) can be translated to port 8080 on our internal web server. This allows us to use port 80 on the web server for a different function like a local intranet. The port change is made on the action tab, an example of which follows hereafter. Why would you want to do that? One application is an office that has a single public IP address. Their web server is hosted on the private network and operates on port 80 and they want to give the public access to their web site. The same company operates a second private web server on a separate host server that runs a web server on port 80 for their partners. With only one public IP address and two web server machines that run their web service on port 80, we now have a quandary. The answer lies in using destination NAT to change the destination port.

Host 1 – Public Web Server

Public IP: 12.238.96.5, standard HTTP port 80

Private IP: 192.168.1.10, web service runs on standard HTTP port 80

Host 2 – Partner Web Server

Public IP: 12.238.96.5, non-standard port 8080

Private IP: 192.168.1.11, web service runs on standard HTTP port 80

Now we need two NAT rules:

> The first rule is in the dstnat chain, protocol TCP, destination port 80, action destination NAT, destination IP is 192.168.1.10 and the destination port is 80.

> The second rule is in the dstnat chain, protocol TCP, destination port 8080, action destination NAT, destination IP is 192.168.1.11 and the destination port is 80.

To summarize these processes, NAT is simply the function of changing or manipulating the source or destination IP address and/or ports of packets entering or leaving the router. In simple terms, source NAT refers to packets leaving the router and destination NAT refers to packets entering the router. The most common use of source NAT is for the masquerading action and the most common type of destination NAT is to NAT a public IP to a private IP.

Special Types of NAT Rules

Source NAT With Multiple Public IP addresses

If you have a single public IP address on your Internet facing interface and a default route to your provider on that subnet, it is fairly easy to see that any packets processed by the masquerade rule will result in packets being sourced from your router's public IP address. In many scenarios this is acceptable, but what if you add a secondary IP to the Internet facing interface on a different subnet and use that IP for a mail server located on the private network? With the amount of unsolicited email (SPAM) that is processed every day by mail servers around the globe, careful controls are now in place almost universally to control the origin of emails. One of these controls is reverse DNS, the ability to look up the source address of the mail server trying to deliver mail to our mail server and ensure it is a member of the domain name, which it reports to be. In the preceding example, if the forward DNS entry for our mail server resolves to the secondary IP address on our router, the reverse DNS is set the same. We would need a way to manipulate packets so that the source IP of all packets leaving our mail server is set to the secondary address. This would not be the normal behavior for a single source NAT rule with the action masquerade.

Here is an example:

> Public IP of our router: 23.0.12.2
>
> Default gateway of our router: 23.0.12.1
>
> Mail Server private IP: 192.168.1.2
>
> Secondary public IP used for inbound access to our mail server: 23.0.12.3

For inbound email, if we use a destination NAT rule to receive mail on 23.0.12.3 and destination NAT it to 192.168.1.2, that works well. However, with only a masquerade in place to masquerade everything leaving our public interface, all traffic including mail being sent by our mail server, will be sourced from 23.0.12.2, thereby breaking mail. The solution here is a source NAT rule. The rule would match packets coming from 192.168.1.2 and have an action or source NAT to IP address 23.0.12.3. This rule solves the issue.

Destination NAT with Action Redirect

Each of the actions you set for a NAT rule accomplishes a more complex function in the background. The masquerade action, for instance, strips the source IP and applies the router's public (outgoing) IP, while destination NAT strips the destination IP address or port and applies a different destination IP address or port. There is another useful action called "redirect" that is often used for certain applications.

Consider this example: You operate a network and use your upstream provider's DNS servers for your customers. Many of your customers have static IP's and static DNS entries. For whatever reason, the decision is made to change upstream providers, however, your current provider does not allow DNS resolution from IP's outside its network. Obviously, you could use a NAT rule with masquerade to masquerade the old provider's public IP's and treat them as private IP's while you are transitioning over to the new provider, but what about the static DNS entries? This is where the redirect action can step in.

Think of redirect as a transparent NAT. It transparently applies a NAT action to packets based on matching criteria. The other important thing to remember for a redirect rule is that it captures the traffic and processes it on the router itself. This is a different action than a destination NAT rule with the action destination NAT.

To summarize the difference between these two types of rules, think of it like this: A NAT rule with an action of destination NAT sends the traffic to a host, while a destination NAT rule with an action of redirect "captures" the traffic and processes it on the router.

Getting back to our example, we can remedy the DNS issue by capturing the DNS requests on the router and processing them there using the router's internal caching DNS server. We will discuss caching DNS later in this book, but let it suffice to say for now that we have already configured caching DNS on the router and it is able to resolve DNS requests from the new provider's DNS servers. In this case, simply create a new destination NAT rule with matchers for protocol TCP, port 53, and an action of redirect to port 53. The second rule we need is a duplicate of the first with a protocol of UDP. These two rules will capture all DNS requests trying to go to our old provider's DNS servers and answer them on the router itself. We can then take our time doing the IP transition on the network to the new provider's IP's.

Another example of using redirect is to create a transparent proxy. If we aren't familiar with proxy servers (the most popular one is called Squid), their function is to accept web requests (HTTP traffic) and then proxy those requests to the public network. These pages, after being fetched, may be stored in memory or on disk for later serving to proxy clients. This speeds up network access, enables the use of access rules to restrict use of the Internet, and gives us the ability to redirect web pages (there are many other useful functions described later in this book under the IP Web Proxy function).

If we want this function to be applied without the knowledge of your clients or users and without intervention on their part, a redirect rule is again the answer. In this scenario, create a new destination NAT rule matching protocol TCP, port 80, with an action of redirect to port 8080 (or whatever port we have IP Web Proxy running on at the router). Once configured, all HTTP requests to the Internet will be intercepted at the router and handled by the proxy server.

APPLICATION

Use this example for masquerading a private subnet or subnets behind a single public IP address.

Example – A Simple Masquerade Rule

For purposes of this example, we will assume the Internet is connected to ether1.

1. Create a new Nat rule using the IP button, then Firewall, and then click the NAT tab and the plus sign.

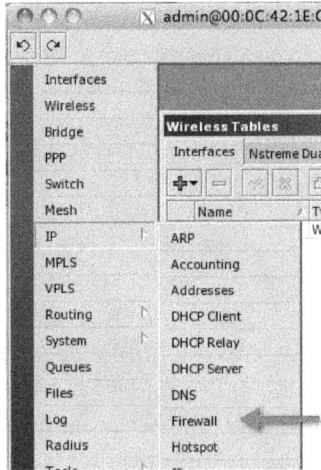

2. Select the chain "srcnat" and set the outgoing interface to ether1.

Interfaces	**NAT Rule <>**
Wireless	General Advanced Extra Action Statistics
Bridge	Chain: srcnat
PPP	
Switch	Src. Address:
Mesh	Dst. Address:
IP	
MPLS	Protocol:
VPLS	Src. Port:
Routing	Dst. Port:
System	Any. Port:
Queues	In. Interface:
Files	Out. Interface: ☐ ether1
Log	
Radius	Packet Mark:
Tools	Connection Mark:
New Terminal	Routing Mark:
Make Supout.rif	Routing Table:
Manual	
Exit	Connection Type:

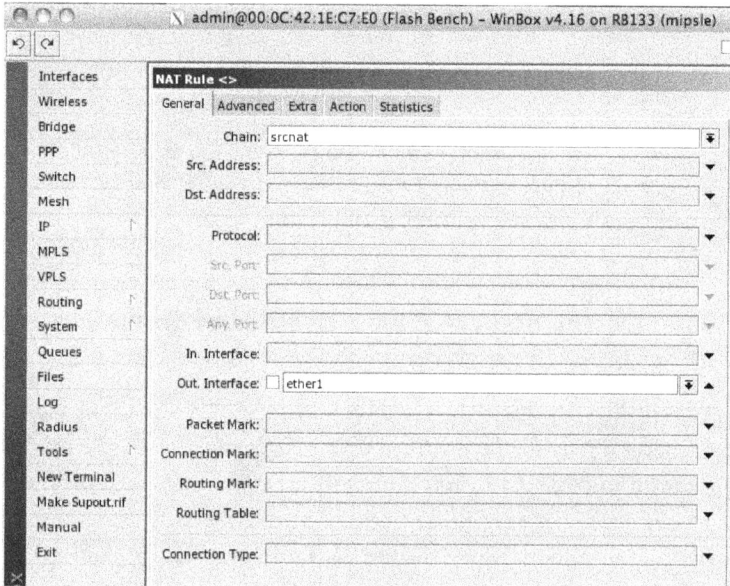

3. Select the Action tab and select "masquerade".

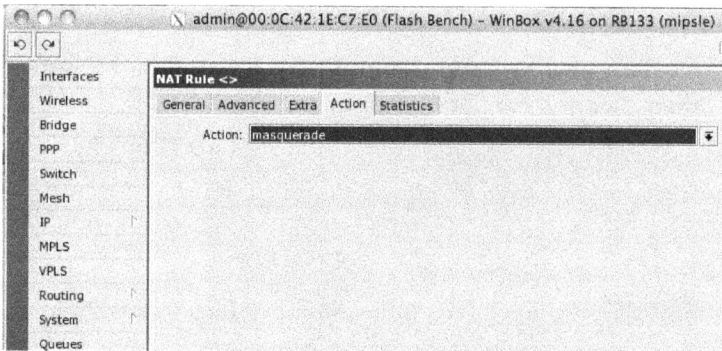

Interfaces	**NAT Rule <>**
Wireless	General Advanced Extra Action Statistics
Bridge	Action: masquerade
PPP	
Switch	
Mesh	
IP	
MPLS	
VPLS	
Routing	
System	
Queues	

This rule matches all traffic going out the Internet interface (not local
traffic) and applies the masquerade action to it. I have seen many
knowledgeable people use more complex packet matchers, but this
rule is all that is required and works well.

Use this example for creating a NAT rule that will allow inbound services for a host on a private IP address behind a router with a public IP address.

Example – Destination NAT for a Web Server on the Private Network with Port Translation

In this example, you want to run a web server on your local area network using a private IP address, but also make a website available to the general public. On your web server, you run your company's Microsoft SharePoint server on port 80 and only want it available to local hosts. Your company's public web site runs on port 8080 on the server, and you want available to the general public outside your firewall on the standard HTTP port 80.

To accomplish this:

1. Create a new Nat rule using the IP button, then Firewall, and then click the NAT tab and the plus sign.

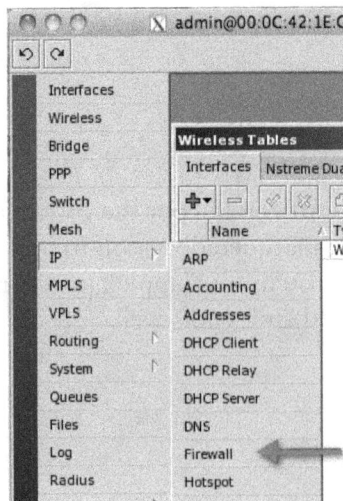

2. Select the chain "dstnat", the Dst. Address as the address of the public IP (in this case 66.76.100.2), the protocol as "TCP", then the destination port as port 80.

NAT Rule <66.76.100.2:80>	
General Advanced Extra Action Statistics	
Chain:	dstnat
Src. Address:	
Dst. Address: ☐	66.76.100.2
Protocol: ☐	6 (tcp)
Src. Port:	
Dst. Port: ☐	80
Any. Port:	
In. Interface:	
Out. Interface:	

3. On the action tab, select the action "dst-nat", the destination address as the private IP of your web server, and the destination port as 8080.

NAT Rule <88>	
General Advanced Extra Action Statistics	
Action:	dst-nat
	☐ Log
Log Prefix:	
To Addresses:	192.168.1.2
To Ports:	8080

The rule matches all TCP packets going to the public IP on port 80, strips the destination address, and replaces it with the private IP address of the web server. It also replaces the destination port with port 8080. To the outside world, there appears to be a web server running on port 80 on 66.76.100.2.

Use this example when your WAN interface has multiple IP addresses and you want some traffic to leave your router sourced from a specific IP address.

Example – Source NAT to Source Traffic From a Certain IP Address

The example above assumes that you only have a single IP address on your public-facing interface. In some setups, you may have multiple public IP addresses on some or all interfaces, including the public-facing interface. In this scenario, traffic being masqueraded by the router with a single masquerade rule and no other NAT rules will generally be sourced from the IP address that is common to the default route. This is certainly true in the example described above.

To be clear, if your public IP is 66.76.100.2 and your default gateway is 66.76.100.1, any traffic that goes out the public interface will be sourced from 66.76.100.2, even if other IP's are bound to that interface. So, what if you get another IP address from your provider for a new web server to operate publically on 66.76.100.3, and you create a destination NAT rule similar to the example above for this new IP to go to 192.168.1.10? This will work fine, except for the fact that traffic leaving the router will still be sourced from 66.76.100.2. This may appear to work, but it may break certain protocols or cause other issues. To solve this problem we can use source NAT.

1. Create a new Nat rule first using the IP button, then Firewall, then the NAT tab, and finally, the plus sign.

(Continued on next page)

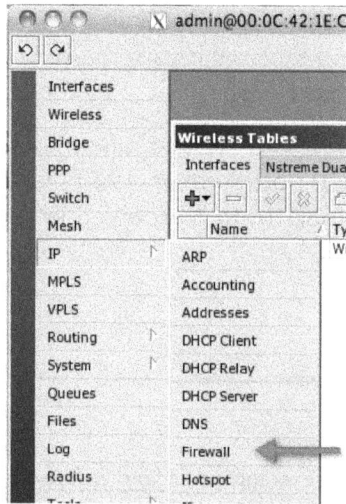

2. Create a new NAT rule in the "srcnat" chain.

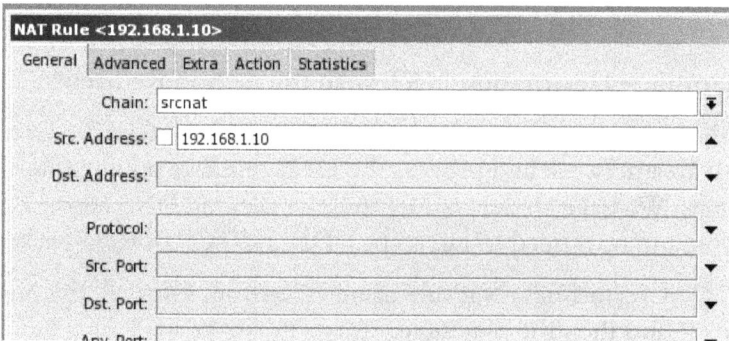

3. On the Action tab, select the action "src-nat" and set the "To Address" value to 66.76.100.3.

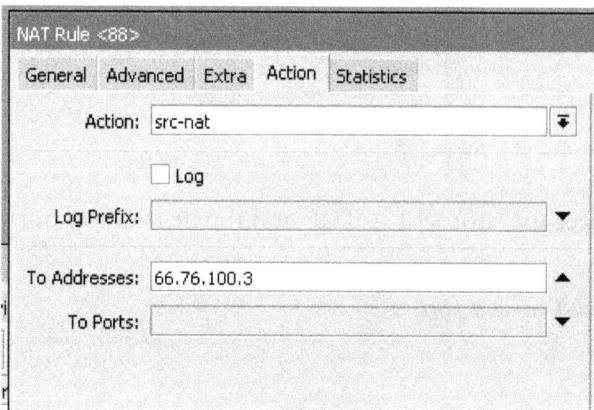

This rule matches all traffic coming from the new web server, strips the source address, and replaces it with the secondary public IP 66.76.100.3 for outbound traffic.

In this scenario, two rules are needed: one to destination NAT inbound traffic on TCP port 80 to go 192.168.1.10 and one to source any traffic from 192.168.1.10 to be sourced from 66.76.100.3 as it leaves the router.

Use this example when you want to capture traffic going through the router and respond to it using processes running on the router. This is typically called "proxying" and it can be used for DNS and web proxy.

APPLICATION

Example – Destination NAT with the Action Redirect

In this example, we want to trap all DNS outbound traffic from the local area network and process the DNS requests on our Internet router. We have already configured the caching DNS server on the router and now need to intercept UDP and TCP port 53 packets.

1. Create a new Nat rule using IP button, Firewall, the NAT tab, and then the plus sign.

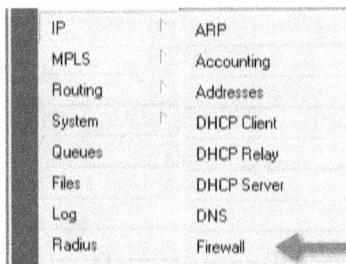

IP	ARP
MPLS	Accounting
Routing	Addresses
System	DHCP Client
Queues	DHCP Relay
Files	DHCP Server
Log	DNS
Radius	Firewall

2. Select the protocol as TCP and the destination port as port 53.

(Continued on next page)

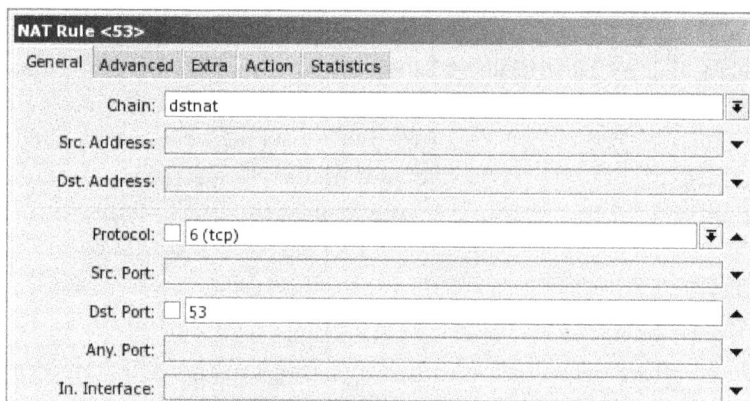

3. On the action tab, select the action "redirect".

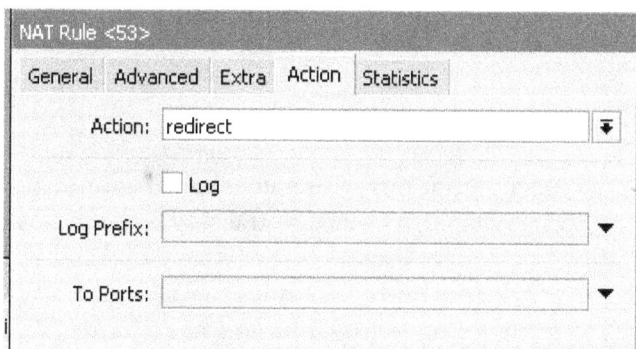

4. Repeat the process for UDP port 53.

These rules will match all DNS packets, (UDP and TCP), intercept them, and process them directly on the router. This example is useful when you want to force the use of your DNS server.

Service Ports - NAT Helpers

You will likely never find yourself looking for the menu to configure NAT helpers, as this feature is seldom changed and usually only discovered by accident. If you happen to click the IP button, then select Firewall, and click on the Service Port tab, there you will see the NAT Helpers that have been included with the NAT facility. These modules, enabled by default, can be disabled or manipulated by changing the port on which they operate. Their function is to help certain protocols by identifying packets that are using that protocol. Connection tracking can be given knowledge of application-layer protocols and thus understand that two or more distinct connections are "related". A great example of this is FTP (File Transfer Protocol). During a FTP session, a control connection is established, but whenever data is transferred, a separate connection is established to transfer it. The function of the NAT helper is to identify the first packet of a new FTP control connection so that the data connection will be marked as related, instead of new, as it is logically part of an existing connection.

Typically, there is no reason to make changes to these Service Ports, unless you are running these protocols on non-standard ports. There is also no reason to disable them. Simply know they are there to make NAT work better and leave them alone.

Connection Tracking (on and off)

By default, connection tracking, sometimes called conntrack, is set to auto. As previously stated, connection tracking is the facility that makes RouterOS a stateful firewall and enables NAT and filter rules. Turning it off will disable both NAT and firewall functions completely, so it is typically a good idea to leave it alone. However, there is always an exception to the rule and in this case, there may be an application where turning it off is desired. For example, if a router is located in the interior of a secure network, that is, it has no access from the outside world and no chance of being attacked, turning connection tracking off will make a slight improvement in the performance of the router. It will be able to route more packets because it isn't using resources for tracking connections. Again, this will disable NAT so it cannot be turned off on an Internet or gateway router or firewall.

One example of where you might want to turn connection tracking off is a device that has a wireless interface bridged to an Ethernet interface. Turning connection tracking off will improve the performance of the wireless link provided, which is the limiting factor, so there isn't an issue with interference, Fresnel zone encroachment, and the like.

Please note that with version 6 came auto mode for connection tracking. If you do not have any NAT or firewall rules, and if Connection Tracking is set to auto, it will turn itself off. Adding one NAT or firewall rule, when in auto mode, will turn it back on.

To further quantify the increase in performance by turning off connection tracking, consider the published performance of the RouterBOARD 750 with connection tracking off.

RB750GL @400MHz (2 port test)			1518 byte frames	
IP Firewall	Conntrack	Mode	Mbps	Fps
off	off	Bridging	949.66	78200
on	off	Routing	631.49	52000
on	off	Bridging	650.92	53600
on	on	Routing	479.69	39500
on	on	Bridging	386.18	31800

Figure 11 - Conn Track On/Off [1]

As you can see, with connection tracking turned off, the router enjoys a 32% increase in throughput. Again, with auto mode now available in Version 6, there is no real reason to make changes to the Connection Tracking settings.

Use this example for routers with versions prior to Version 6 when you do not need connection tracking. This will disable firewall rules and NAT rules, but save a small amount of router resources.

Example – Disable Connection Tracking

1. Select the IP button and then Firewall menu.

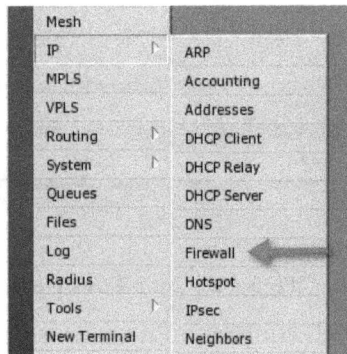

Mesh	
IP	ARP
MPLS	Accounting
VPLS	Addresses
Routing	DHCP Client
System	DHCP Relay
Queues	DHCP Server
Files	DNS
Log	Firewall
Radius	Hotspot
Tools	IPsec
New Terminal	Neighbors

2. Select the Connections tab and click the Tracking button.

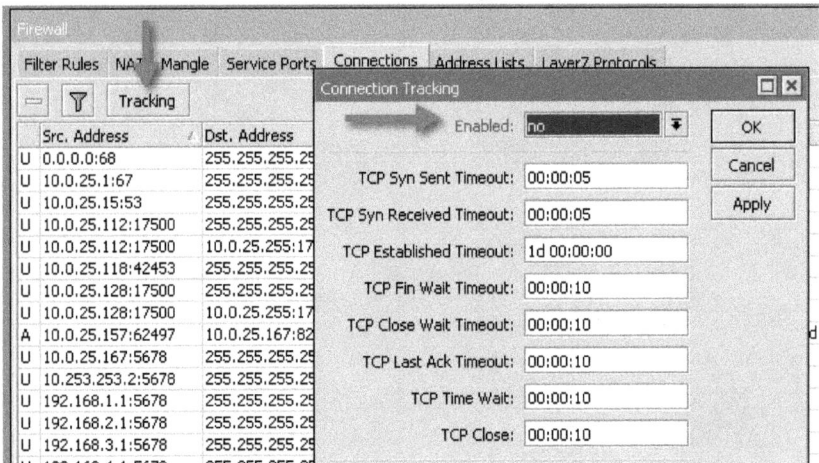

Firewall

Filter Rules   NAT   Mangle   Service Ports   Connections   Address Lists   Layer7 Protocols

Tracking

Connection Tracking

Enabled: no   OK

Src. Address	Dst. Address
U 0.0.0.0:68	255.255.255.25
U 10.0.25.1:67	255.255.255.25
U 10.0.25.15:53	255.255.255.25
U 10.0.25.112:17500	255.255.255.25
U 10.0.25.112:17500	10.0.25.255:17
U 10.0.25.118:42453	255.255.255.25
U 10.0.25.128:17500	255.255.255.25
U 10.0.25.128:17500	10.0.25.255:17
A 10.0.25.157:62497	10.0.25.167:82
U 10.0.25.167:5678	255.255.255.25
U 10.253.253.2:5678	255.255.255.25
U 192.168.1.1:5678	255.255.255.25
U 192.168.2.1:5678	255.255.255.25
U 192.168.3.1:5678	255.255.255.25
U 192.168.4.1:5678	255.255.255.25

Cancel

Apply

TCP Syn Sent Timeout: 00:00:05
TCP Syn Received Timeout: 00:00:05
TCP Established Timeout: 1d 00:00:00
TCP Fin Wait Timeout: 00:00:10
TCP Close Wait Timeout: 00:00:10
TCP Last Ack Timeout: 00:00:10
TCP Time Wait: 00:00:10
TCP Close: 00:00:10

3. Select "no" and click OK.

Connection tracking is now manually disabled.

Note: It is best to leave this setting at the default of "auto" which disables it any time there is no mangle, NAT, or firewall rules.

Tools – Torch

Having used equipment for many years, all from many different manufacturers, I would have to say that one feature that really makes RouterOS stand above the rest is the number of tools that are available to the user inside the user interface. I would venture to say that RouterOS has the most tools, more than any other software, and Torch is one of those very useful tools.

Torch is a real-time tool that will give you an instant picture of all traffic passing through an interface. Better yet, it gives you the ability to sort that traffic, filter it by IP address and port, and to sort the traffic ascending or descending by rate. By using Torch, you instantly know who is using your bandwidth and how they are using it. It is great for determining the effectiveness of queues and firewall rules in real-time. Torch is available in many different places in RouterOS, such as by right clicking queues, interfaces, or the Tools menu by selecting Torch.

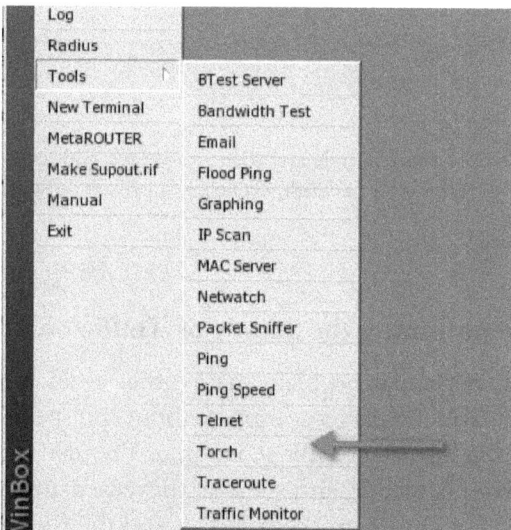

Once Torch loads, you will be presented with a display that allows you to select the interface to be monitored. It also allows the defining of several filters to further restrict the traffic that is observed.

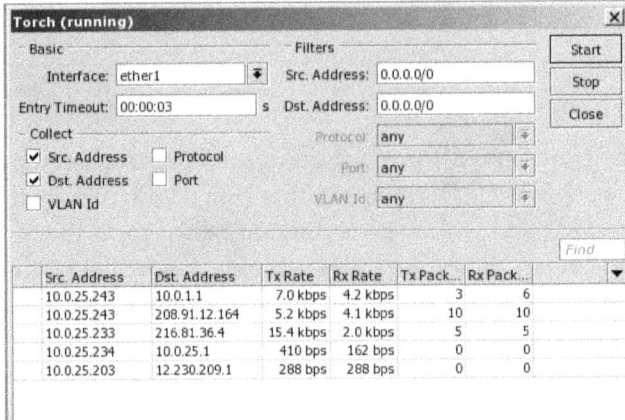

Torch (running)

Basic			Filters		Start
Interface:	ether1		Src. Address:	0.0.0.0/0	Stop
Entry Timeout:	00:00:03	s	Dst. Address:	0.0.0.0/0	Close

Collect
- ☑ Src. Address ☐ Protocol
- ☑ Dst. Address ☐ Port
- ☐ VLAN Id

Protocol: any
Port: any
VLAN Id: any

Find

Src. Address	Dst. Address	Tx Rate	Rx Rate	Tx Pack...	Rx Pack...	▼
10.0.25.243	10.0.1.1	7.0 kbps	4.2 kbps	3	6	
10.0.25.243	208.91.12.164	5.2 kbps	4.1 kbps	10	10	
10.0.25.233	216.81.36.4	15.4 kbps	2.0 kbps	5	5	
10.0.25.234	10.0.25.1	410 bps	162 bps	0	0	
10.0.25.203	12.230.209.1	288 bps	288 bps	0	0	

From Torch, it is possible to collect the source address and port, the destination address and port, and/or the ability to filter by protocol. Combined with the real-time rate of traffic flow, this becomes a very powerful diagnostic tool for IP networks. Torch is available from the tools menu, by right clicking an interface and by right clicking a Queue.

Use this example any time you want a real-time view or traffic on a network, especially a private network.

APPLICATION

Example – Determining the Source of Traffic on a Network

I have seen this particular problem many times as an Internet service provider: A customer calls to complain about the speed of their connection. I log into their CPE (Customer Premise Equipment), in this case a MikroTik router, and see that they are using the full 2 Mb they are paying for. I inform them of this and their response is: "That is impossible. I don't have any programs running and I am the only one using the Internet." By using Torch, I quickly learn that there is a constant 2 Mb stream from a private IP on their LAN subnet. After a few minutes of talking, we discover the IP address streaming the traffic does not belong to their machine, and finally track it down to a child's computer. This machine is currently sharing files with many other peers via bit torrent. So how do we learn the identity of this host on the private network? Here is an example:

1. Click the Tools button and then select Torch.

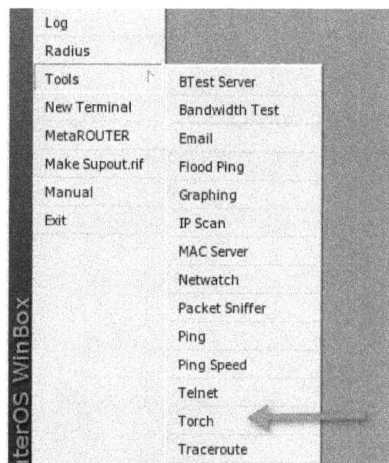

2. From the Torch window, select the interface where you want to discover traffic and then click Start. With Torch running, you can sort by Tx (Transmit Rate) or Rx (Receive Rate), and learn the source of the highest rate traffic on the network.

(Continued on next page)

Torch (running) ☒

Basic — Filters — Start

Interface: ether1 ⬇ Src. Address: 0.0.0.0/0   Stop

Entry Timeout: 00:00:03 s Dst. Address: 0.0.0.0/0   Close

Collect
- ☑ Src. Address ☐ Protocol   Protocol: any ⬇
- ☑ Dst. Address ☐ Port   Port: any ⬇
- ☐ VLAN Id   VLAN Id: any ⬇

Find

Src. Address	Dst. Address	Tx Rate	Rx Rate	Tx Pack...	Rx Pack...	▼
10.0.25.238	65.55.87.95	376.1 kbps	12.3 kbps	35	24	
10.0.25.243	10.0.25.1	6.0 kbps	4.1 kbps	2	5	
10.0.25.2	80.108.117.15	5.0 kbps	58.5 kbps	8	12	
10.0.25.225	208.91.11.14	2.3 kbps	2.0 kbps	0	0	
10.0.25.2	166.205.15.219	0 bps	2.1 kbps	0	0	

Torch is a great customer service tool. It ends customer complaints quickly with proof to support your data.

Chapter 10 - Bandwidth Limits

If I had to name one area where I see the greatest interest in RouterOS, it has to be with bandwidth limitation and Quality of Service (QoS). These two topics really go hand in hand, and incorporating them into your network will almost certainly "tame the savage beast." It will at least fend off the gremlins that are stalking your network, trying to steal your resources. RouterOS offers several schemes to control bandwidth and each has its benefits and costs.

Simple Queues

I always begin my classroom instruction on simple queues by saying, "The best thing about simple queues is that they are simple and the worst thing about simple queues is that they are simple." Simple queues are intelligent facilities that were created to allow you a simple and fast means of limiting bandwidth. They are extremely powerful in what they do behind the scenes and they allow even a RouterOS novice to quickly implement a basic bandwidth limitation and QoS system. In versions prior to version 6, simple queues were very resource-intensive, but all of that has changed in Version 6.

That being said, it is important to use everything wisely. For a more evolved queuing system, rely on more complex queues that are actually more efficient in their operation. For example, PCC, Per Connection Classifiers, enable you to create a handful of queues that can control bandwidth for thousands of clients. These will be discussed later in this chapter.

Simple queues are configured by referencing the target address of the device you are trying to control bandwidth to and then initiating a limit for upload and download. This "device" referenced here is typically a customer or client IP address or an interface name. These are the only pieces of information that need to be configured to have a working queuing system. To further explain, let's look at an example.

Simple queues are configured from the Queues menu on the Simple Queues tab.

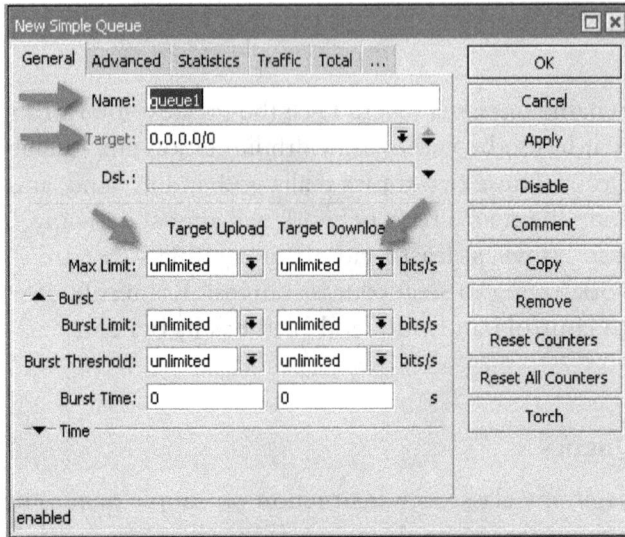

Name the queue anything you like, but I advise that it be descriptive of the function of the queue, such as using a customer name. Next is "Target Address", which is the IP address of the target customer or device, or the interface facing the customer(s). This blank has the availability of a down arrow at the end, such that multiple IP addresses or interfaces can be assigned to the same queue. In addition, a network or subnet can also be assigned to the queue. For example, setting a target address of 192.168.1.0/24 will limit bandwidth to 254 hosts in that network. It is important to note that simple queues, when used with multiple IP addresses or networks, do not create a separate queue. Instead, all hosts defined by the target address will share the queue.

In the example above, a max-limit setting of 1M for the queue will be shared by all 254 hosts in the subnet. It is also important to note that the "sharing" of bandwidth behavior described is in no way allocated evenly. In reference to the "max-limit" setting, these are the limits that are applied to the target address for upload and download. These four settings, Name, Target Address, Max limit upload, and Max limit download, are the only settings required to have a full functioning simple queue.

In this first example, our goal was to influence bandwidth supplied to a customer, but limitations can also be applied to servers or websites. While customers or clients are considered target addresses, servers or host destinations are referred to as destination addresses and can be limited in a similar fashion.

For example, if you wanted to limit bandwidth to a website like mikrotik.com, the process would be to create a new queue exactly as described above, with the exception of one change. Instead of specifying an IP address on the target address line, leave that line blank and click the Advanced tab. On the Advanced tab, specify in the "Dst." blank, the IP address for www.mikrotik.com. You can determine that IP address by pinging www.mikrotik.com and writing down the IP address that is resolved. This function gives you a lot of granularity because you can restrict bandwidth to certain destinations, subnets, address ranges, and the like.

Bursting

The term bursting is used to describe a behavior of the bandwidth limitation system where a destination is allowed to reach a certain level of upload or download bandwidth for some period of time. A lower limitation is then applied for the duration of the upload or download. By allowing these short bursts of bandwidth, the overall customer experience for browsing the web, checking email, etc., is enhanced, while large downloads are throttled back. This controls the average bandwidth usage of the client.

This strategy was once used widely, but with the recent popularity of streaming movies and similar service offerings, bursting now has less appeal for the service provider. The problem created by allowing bursting for clients who are streaming movies is that the movie appears to load at first, but is viewable for only a few seconds because the quality is quickly reduced to an unacceptable level once the maximum limit is applied after the burst. This behavior, although intended by the service provider, will certainly generate technical support phone calls or unhappy customers. Therefore, you should consider your clientele before configuring bursting queues on your network.

With simple queues, bursting can be applied to a queue that references a target IP address or a queue that references a destination IP address, so bursting is applicable to both queue types previously described herein.

Let's take a look at the configuration of a queue with reference to bursting.

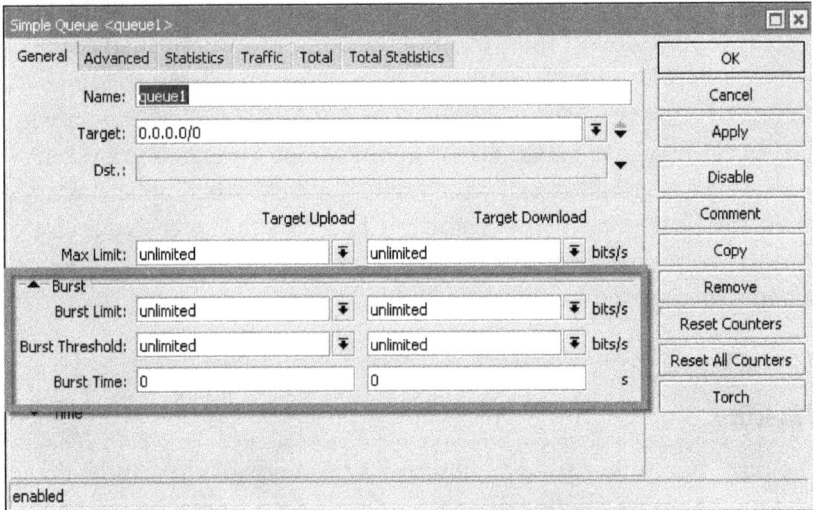

Note: If you don't see the options in the preceding simple queue, you may need to click the triangle next to the word "Burst" to expand the burst section.

The settings that configure burst are Burst Limit, Burst Threshold, and Burst Time.

Quoting from the MikroTik Wiki:

burst-limit (NUMBER): maximal upload/download data rate, which can be reached while the burst is allowed.

burst-time (TIME): period of time, in seconds, over which the average data rate is calculated. (This is NOT the time of actual burst).

burst-threshold (NUMBER): this is the value of the burst on/off switch.

Of these values, the first appears fairly obvious; "**burst-limit**" is the maximum bandwidth you are going to allow during this bursting period. Slightly less obvious is the burst threshold. Think of the burst threshold as an on/off switch. When we hit the value of the burst threshold, the timer starts and we are allowed to burst up to the burst limit for some period of time. I have seen many theories on the proper setting of the burst threshold, but for purposes of our discussion, I rely on the MikroTik RouterOS manual, which states that for the optimal performance, the **burst-threshold** must be less than the **max-limit**, which must be less than the **burst-limit.** To state it another way:

$$burst\text{-}threshold < max\text{-}limit < burst\text{-}limit$$

That having been said, what is the optimal setting for **burst-threshold**? I recommend setting it at half the max-limit because it is an easy calculation and it satisfies the premise that the **burst-threshold** be less than the **max-limit** as prescribed by the manual.

The final setting required is the Burst Time. Again, referring back to the manual "The actual duration of burst does not depend on **burst-time** alone. It also depends on the **burst-threshold/burst-limit** ratio and the actual data rate passing through the bursting class." What does that exactly mean? I can demonstrate through the use of a formula. To calculate the Burst Time, use the following method:

First, calculate the burst ratio as follows:

Burst Ratio = burst-threshold/burst-limit

Then, calculate the burst time:

Burst Time = (Clock Time to Burst) /(Burst Ratio)

To summarize, here is an example.

Given:

We want to create a simple queue with a 256k max-limit and we want to burst to 512k for 5 seconds on the clock.

Therefore:

Max-Limit: 256k (given)

Burst-Limit: 512k (given)

Burst-Threshold: 128k (half the max-limit as recommended above)

Burst-Time: 20s

We calculate the burst time as follows:

Burst Ratio = 128k/512k = .25

Burst Time = 5sec / .25 = 20

Therefore, if we set the burst time to 20, we will get the desired 5-second burst. It would be great if the value of burst time was equal to clock time, but as you can see, it isn't. The calculation described here is required to get proper queue behavior.

Use this example any time you want to allocate a block of bandwidth for a single computer or group of computers, providing a rate limit or shared speed restriction to all of them as a group.

Example – Creating a Simple Queue for Computers in an Office Network

For purposes of this example, we want to limit all computers on our 192.168.1.0/24 network to share a 5 Meg allocation of bandwidth. Remember that simple queues with the target address set to a subnet do not allocate the queue amount to each computer in the subnet; instead, it is shared by all IP addresses in the subnet as it is consumed. We will learn other queue strategies in future examples to create separate allocations of bandwidth.

1. Click the Queues button to open the Simple Queues list.

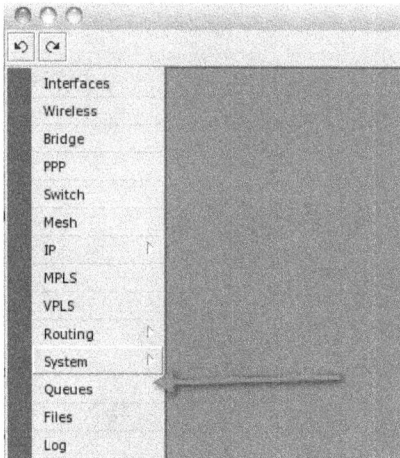

2. In the Simple Queues list, click the plus sign to create a new simple queue.

(Continued on next page)

143

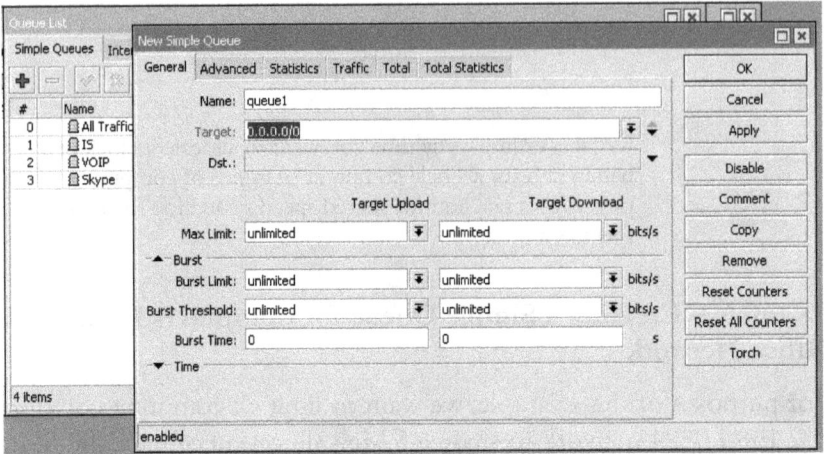

3. Name the queue something descriptive and set the max limit for upload and download. Note here that if the value you want for upload/download is not in the list, you may simply type it in. Acceptable values are expressed in "k" for kilobits or "M" for megabits, but fractional amounts like 1.5M must be expressed in kilobits, such as 1500k.

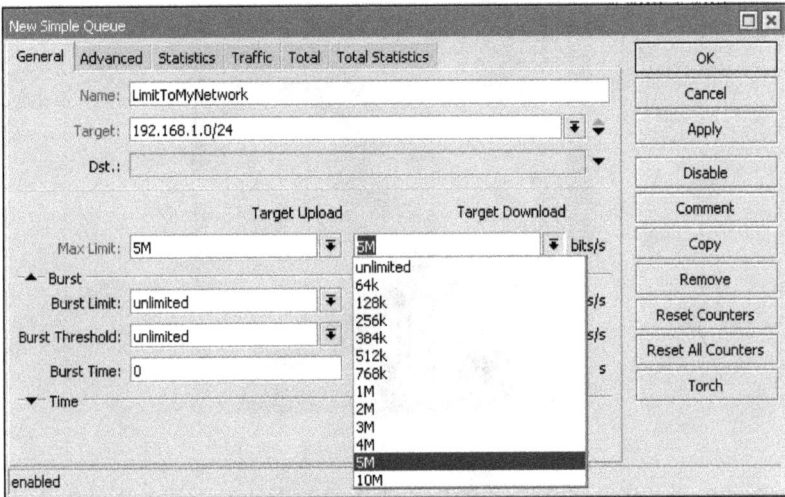

4. Once the settings are entered as above, click the OK button to save and the queue is completed.

Example – Creating a Queue for a Destination Host

In this example, we want to limit bandwidth to a site such as www.mikrotik.com. To create the queue, we must know the IP address of that web host or the range of addresses the host uses. By pinging www.mikrotik.com from a command line, we learn the IP address is 159.148.147.196. Create this queue as follows:

1. Click the Queues button to open the simple queue list.

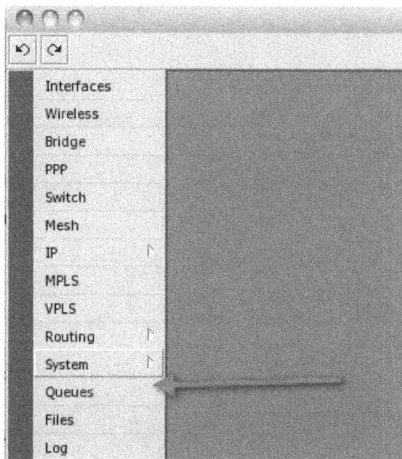

2. In the Simple Queues list, click the plus sign to create a new simple queue.

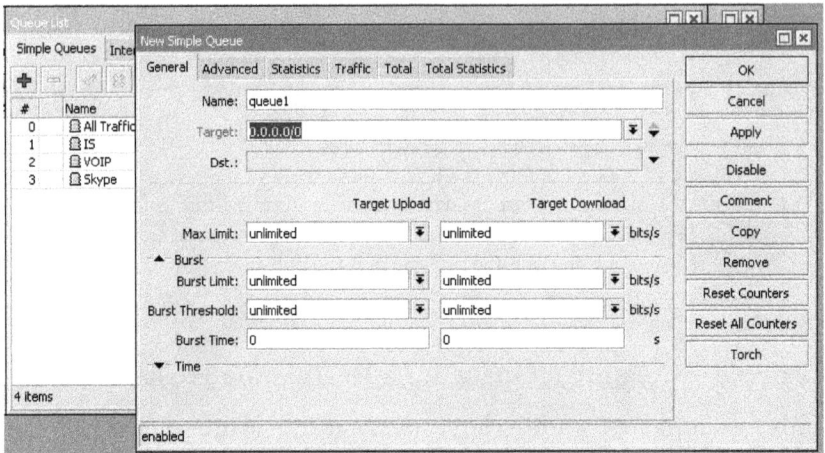

Name the queue as you like, and then click the Advanced tab. On the Advanced tab, insert the value for the destination address, the IP address for www.mikrotik.com, and the bandwidth restrictions you want to impose.

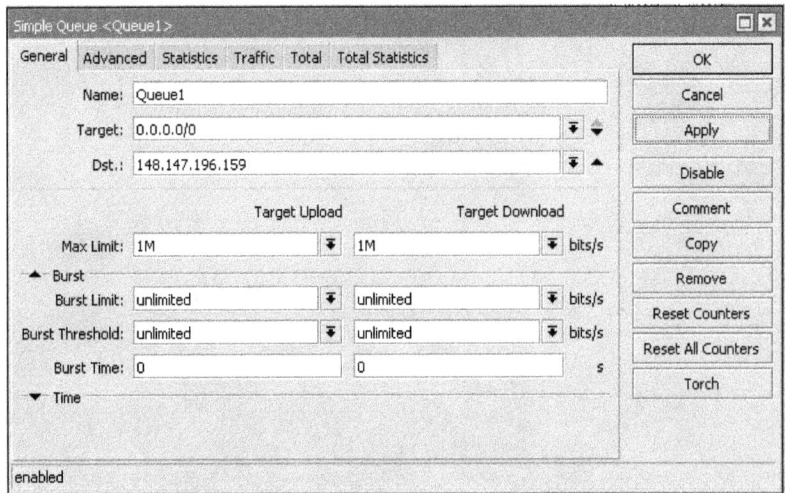

3. Click OK and all traffic to and from MikroTik.com will be restricted to 1M.

Use this example any time you want to impose a rate limit, with the ability to burst to a higher limit for a predetermined period of time.

APPLICATION

Example – Create a Queue for Local Computers with Burst

In this example, we will use the calculated values from the previous section entitled "Bursting".

1. Click the Queues button to open the Simple Queues list.

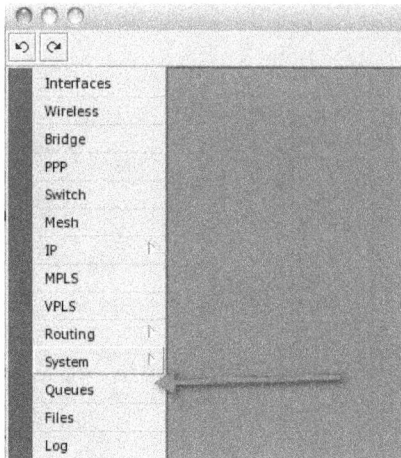

2. In the Simple Queues list, click the plus sign to create a new simple queue.

   (Continued on next page)

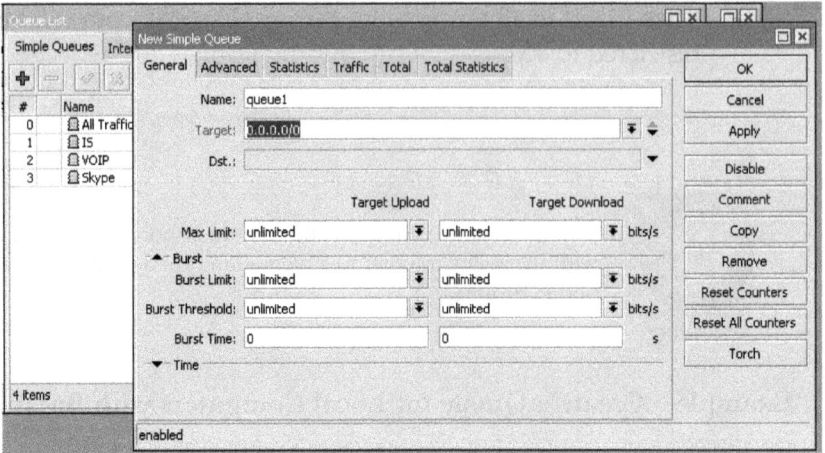

3. Insert the following values in the General tab:

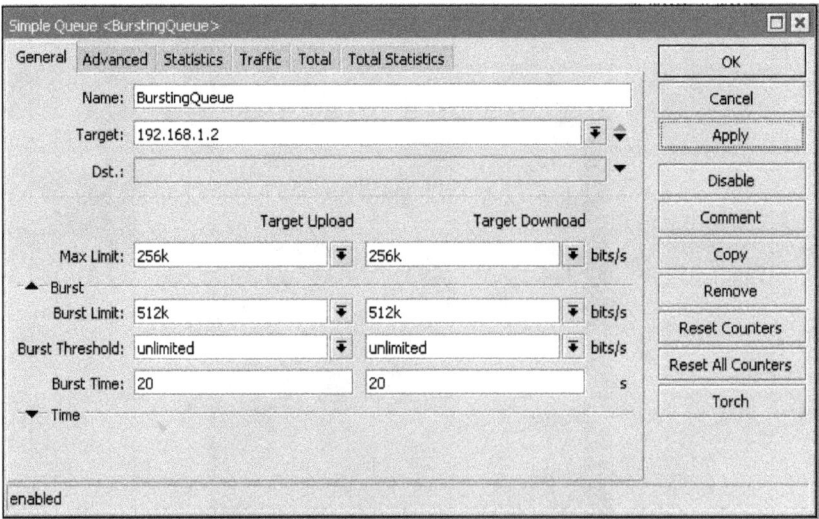

The result will be a 512k burst, up or down for a clock period of 5 seconds.

Packet Mangling

When I introduce this topic in my classes, I typically get a reaction like, "Packet mangling? That sounds painful." But, don't worry; no packets were harmed in the writing of this chapter.

Seriously though, mangling is a facility that allows us to identify packets and mark them for later use. With this mark, we can do wonderful things like force packets with certain marks to take certain routes or go through certain queues. One concern of packet mangling is that it can be very CPU intensive if we have to look at every single packet, make a decision whether or not to mark it, and then perform the marking action. Fortunately, there is a method of marking packets that uses an optimized scheme and is therefore, much less intense. This method is called the optimal mangle, named for the fact that it optimizes the process and accomplishes the task in the most CPU-efficient manner.

There are two steps to the optimal mangle:

1. Identify connections that are flowing the packets we want to mangle.

2. Mark the packets.

To demonstrate why this is the most efficient method, I like to use the analogy of a worker in a factory on the final assembly line whose job it is to place a decal on completed products. If there are a large variety of products passing in front of the inspector and his job is to only mark a single product type, he spends a large portion of his time looking for the actual product to be decaled. It is like looking for a needle in a haystack. However, if we sort the products first and only put on his conveyor belt the actual items he is to mark, his efforts are greatly reduced. He only has to apply the decals and does not waste resources looking for the products. The optimal mangle works the same way.

Use this example to identify and mark traffic in the router for use later by queues or other firewall-type rules.

APPLICATION

Example – Packet Mangling Using Optimal Mangle

1. To perform the mangle, we create two rules in the IP Firewall list under the Mangle tab.

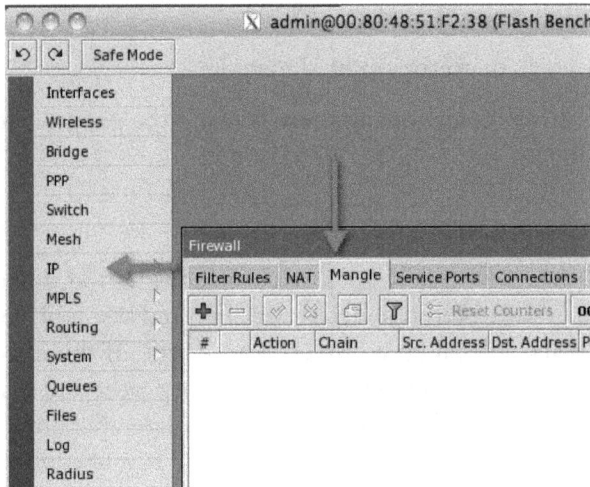

2. Mangles are performed in a certain place within the routing process and the explanation of each of these places or "chains" is outside the scope of this example. However, for most mangling operations, the pre-routing chain is the place to mangle all traffic and the forward chain will mangle traffic going to other hosts. In this example, we want to identify all web-browsing traffic, so we select a minimum of filters on

the packet matcher tab. After creating a new rule with the plus sign, set it as follows:

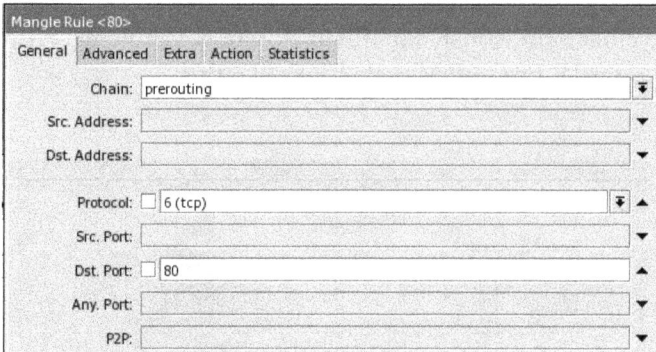

This rule will match all web browsing traffic identified by the fact that it is destined for port 80. The Action tab for this rule is to mark these connections with a mark we have authored ourselves, "WebBrowsingConnections". This mark can be anything, but I like to make it descriptive.

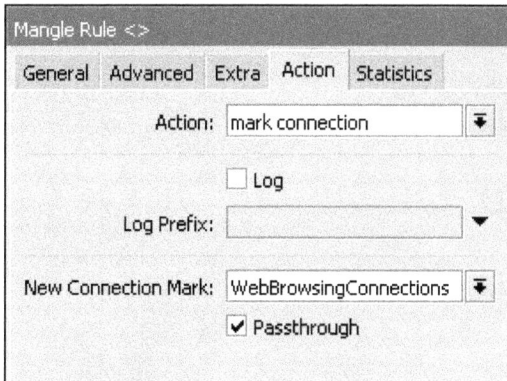

3. Click Ok to save this rule. Now we have narrowed the scope of packets we want to examine greatly by restricting this rule

to port 80 connections and then marking that connection with our mangle rule.

4. Next, we want to mark the actual packets. We don't want to look at every packet, just those that are a part of connections we have previously identified, so the next rule we create under IP Firewall Mangle looks like this:

This packet matcher only matches the previously marked connections. The action tab is where we mark the actual packets with our mark "WebBrowsingPackets".

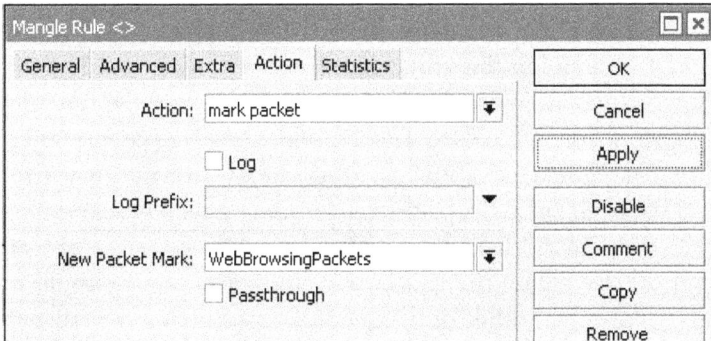

Notice that I have unchecked the box for "Passthrough". This is important because packets can be marked more than once. It is important to understand that multiple marks do not add. For example, if the first rule matches a packet and marks it "AAA" and Passthrough is checked, the packet continues down the mangle chain. If the next rule matches, the packet gets remarked "BBB", not "AAABBB". The marks do not add, they re-mark so the packet will then be marked "BBB". If Passthrough is unchecked, once a rule matches, the packet leaves the mangle chain.

In summary, packets are identified by connections, the connections are marked, and then the packets in those connections are individually marked.

It is important to note that if you have connection tracking off for whatever reason, the optimal mangle will not work. In that case, simply use one rule to identify the packets and mark them all in the same mangle rule. It will be CPU-intensive, but it is your only option.

Traffic Prioritization

Often referred to as QoS (Quality of Service) or traffic prioritization, I would rather call this function Queue Prioritization because it is a more descriptive and accurate means of describing the function. To begin, why is prioritization necessary or desired? Consider two types of traffic: The first is a phone call, and the second is a large file download. Since the phone call is real-time, delays in the delivery of the packets containing the voice data (latency) will cause degradation in quality of the sound received. A similar delay in a file download will go unnoticed. Therefore, for the best network performance, it would be desirable for the voice traffic to have priority over the standard data traffic. This prioritization is achieved by carving out "chunks" of bandwidth and reserving them for each type of traffic. Furthermore, by telling the router that the voice queue should be serviced before the "other data" queue, it is possible to ensure that the phone call always gets handled with the highest priority, as long as there is bandwidth available to serve it. This is QoS or Quality of Service.

To configure prioritization in RouterOS, it is first necessary to identify the traffic to be prioritized. This is best accomplished using a mangle rule and packet matching the traffic by some means. In the previous example, a simple method of identifying Voice Over IP (VoIP) traffic is by destination IP address. If you are the operator of a VoIP gateway or PBX, you can simply packet match traffic to and from the IP address of your VoIP devices and mangle it with some mark. Secondly, a queue is created for the VoIP traffic with a bandwidth allocation and a high priority.

In RouterOS, queues are prioritized based on a numerical value from 1 to 8, where 1 is the highest priority and 8 is the lowest. By default, simple queues are created with a priority of 8. Queues with a higher priority are filled before queues with a lower priority.

Once traffic has been identified with a mangle rule or rules and at least two queues have been created and priorities set, traffic through the router will now be handled based on priority. It is important that traffic prioritization is local to the router and does not carry throughout the network.

For Further Study: QoS

There is a type of traffic prioritization that is carried by the packet throughout the network, but that is a topic for advanced study. If you want to learn more about this type of QoS, I suggest you research setting the DSCP bit (Differentiated Services Code Point bit) of an IP packet. This bit can be set by many VoIP devices or by a mangle rule in RouterOS and is carried throughout the network. Queues can then be created with priority for packets identified by the DSCP bit and thereby provide a much more advanced QoS system.

APPLICATION

Use this example when you want to identify some traffic and ensure there is always sufficient bandwidth for that traffic with VOIP being the main use of this type of QoS.

Example – Queue Priority for VoIP Traffic

In this example, we are a service provider and we desire to prioritize VoIP traffic to and from our imaginary VoIP gateway, which is located at IP address 212.13.14.2. There is one router between our clients and the VoIP gateway and that is where we will create the QoS system.

1. To begin, we want to create a Mangle Rule for traffic destined for the VoIP gateway and traffic from the VoIP gateway. We will use the technique previously discussed for marking connections first and then marking packets. This is done with a mangle rule as follows:

   (Continued on next page)

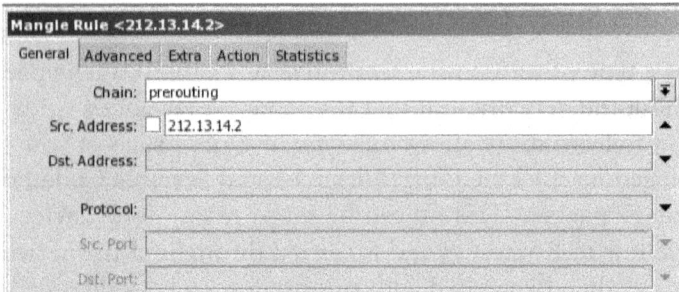

Mangle Rule <212.13.14.2>

General | Advanced | Extra | Action | Statistics

Chain: prerouting
Src. Address: ☐ 212.13.14.2
Dst. Address:

Protocol:
Src. Port:
Dst. Port:

This rule matches packets coming from our VoIP gateway.

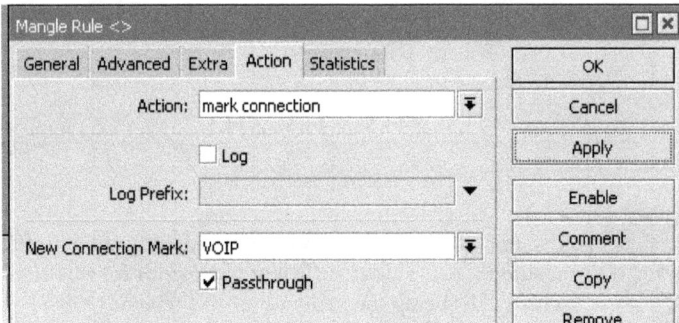

Mangle Rule <>

General | Advanced | Extra | **Action** | Statistics

Action: mark connection

☐ Log

Log Prefix:

New Connection Mark: VOIP

☑ Passthrough

OK | Cancel | Apply | Enable | Comment | Copy | Remove

On the action tab, we are marking these connections with the connection mark "VoIP".

2. Next, we create a rule for traffic in the opposite direction, that is, traffic going to the VoIP gateway.

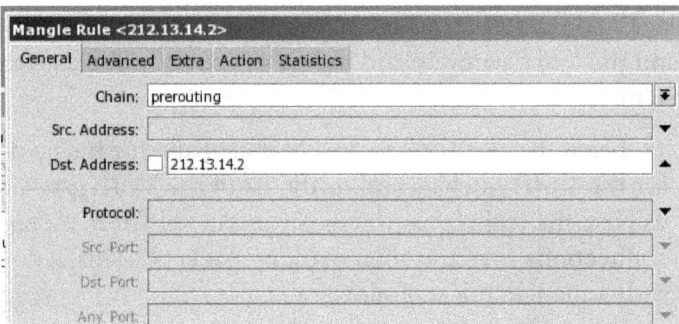

Mangle Rule <212.13.14.2>

General | Advanced | Extra | Action | Statistics

Chain: prerouting
Src. Address:
Dst. Address: ☐ 212.13.14.2

Protocol:
Src. Port:
Dst. Port:
Any. Port:

The Action is to mark the connection as VOIP.

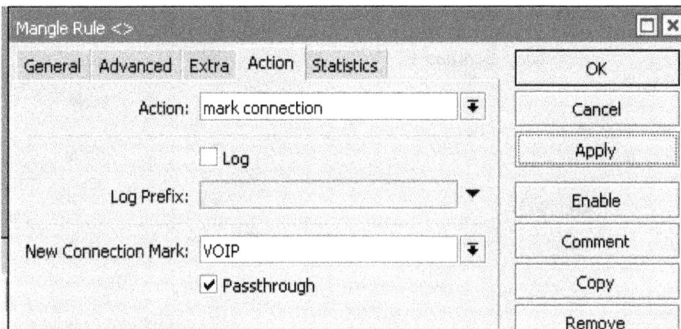

Mangle Rule <>

General	Advanced	Extra	Action	Statistics

Action: mark connection

☐ Log

Log Prefix:

New Connection Mark: VOIP

☑ Passthrough

OK
Cancel
Apply
Enable
Comment
Copy
Remove

3. The last mangle rule will match the connection mark and then mark the actual VoIP packets.

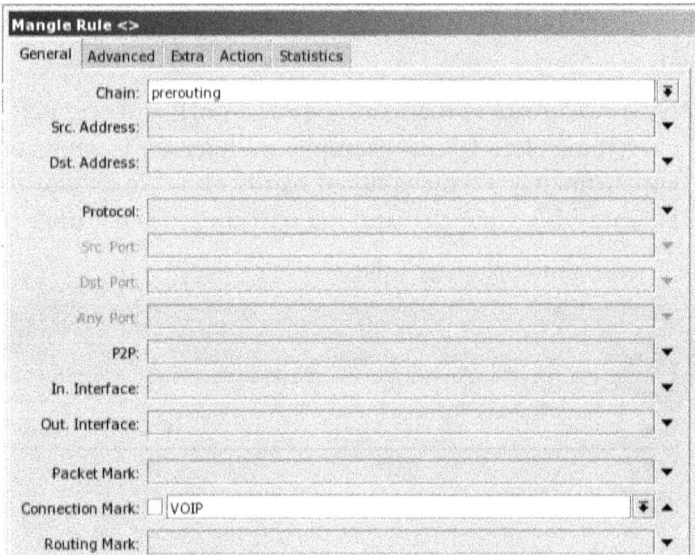

Mangle Rule <>

General	Advanced	Extra	Action	Statistics

Chain: prerouting

Src. Address:

Dst. Address:

Protocol:

Src. Port:

Dst. Port:

Any. Port:

P2P:

In. Interface:

Out. Interface:

Packet Mark:

Connection Mark: ☐ VOIP

Routing Mark:

(Continued on next page)

157

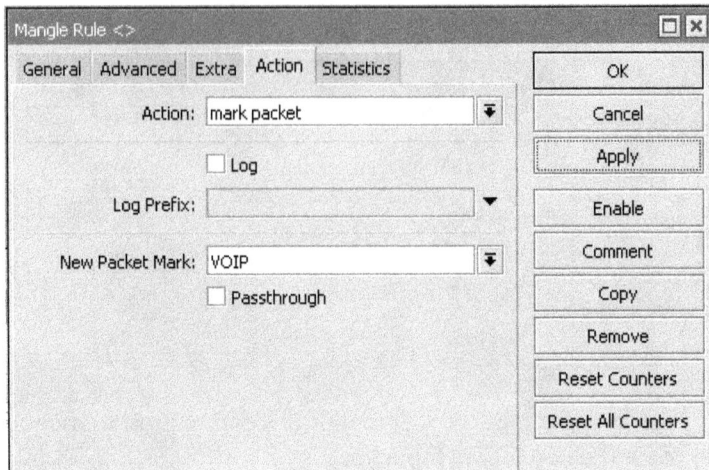

Note that we uncheck "Passthrough" so that the packets will not get remarked.

4. Next, we create two queues, one for VoIP and one for everything else. In this example, we have a T1 connection or approximately 1.5 megabits of bandwidth. We choose to allocate 512k for VoIP and the remainder for all other traffic.

The queues are created as follows:

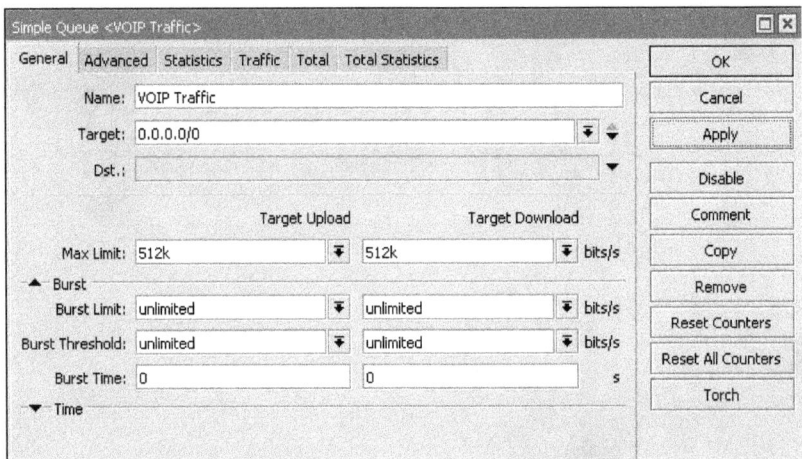

Note that we are identifying traffic with the packet mark "VoIP" and setting this queue priority to 1 for upload and download.

(Continued on next page)

158

```
Simple Queue <VOIP Traffic>                                    [□][×]

General  Advanced  Statistics  Traffic  Total  Total Statistics        |      OK      |

Packet Marks: VOIP                                         [∓][◆]       |    Cancel    |

                    Target Upload        Target Download               |    Apply     |

    Limit At:  unlimited        [∓]  unlimited      [∓] bits/s          |   Disable    |

    Priority:  1                     1                                  |   Comment    |

  Queue Type: default-small    [∓]  default-small  [∓]                  |    Copy      |

    Parent:   none                                [∓]                   |   Remove     |

                                                                       | Reset Counters |

                                                                       | Reset All Counters |

                                                                       |    Torch     |
```

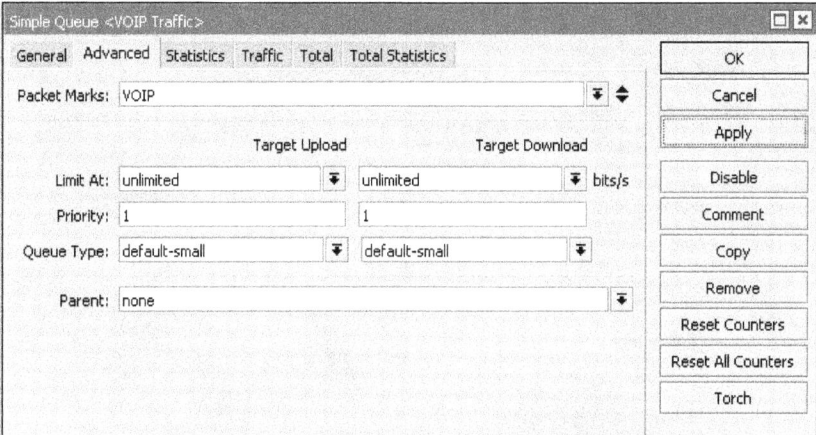

5. Finally, we need a queue for all other traffic and here we can
    make use of a little-known feature, the packet mark "no-
    mark". If a packet is not mangled, it is still actually marked
    with the mark "no-mark". So even without a mangle rule for
    all other traffic, we can queue based on this unmarked status
    of mark "no-mark".

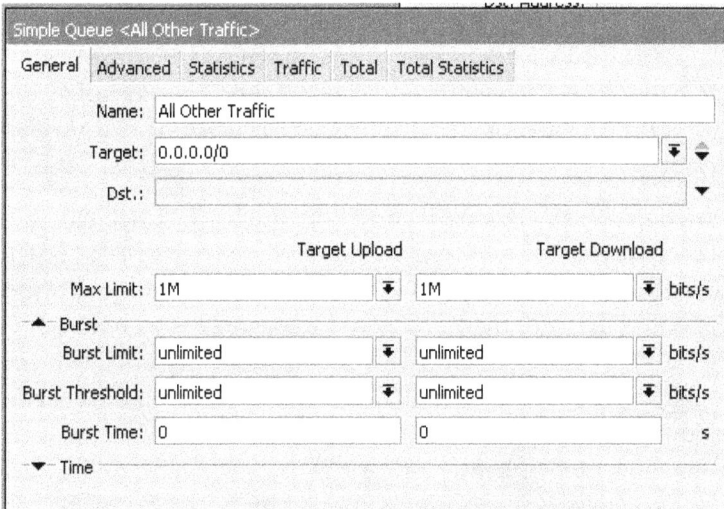

```
Simple Queue <All Other Traffic>

General  Advanced  Statistics  Traffic  Total  Total Statistics

        Name:  All Other Traffic

       Target: 0.0.0.0/0                                  [∓][◆]

        Dst.:                                             [▼]

                    Target Upload            Target Download

   Max Limit:  1M              [∓]   1M              [∓] bits/s
 ▲ Burst
  Burst Limit: unlimited       [∓]   unlimited       [∓] bits/s

Burst Threshold: unlimited     [∓]   unlimited       [∓] bits/s

  Burst Time:  0                     0                    s
 ▼ Time
```

(Continued on next page)

General Advanced Statistics Traffic Total Total Statistics

Packet Marks: | no-mark |

	Target Upload	Target Download
Limit At:	unlimited	unlimited	bits/s
Priority:	8	8
Queue Type:	default-small	default-small
Parent:	none

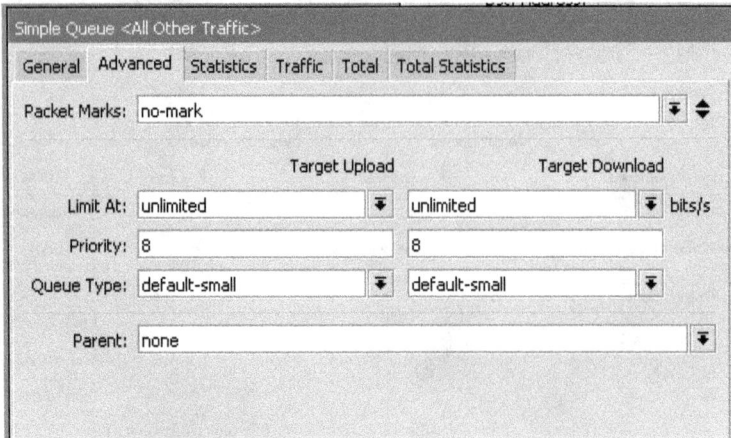

The preceding QoS setup is very effective and easy to configure.

PCQ – Per Connection Queuing

As previously discussed, simple queues are fast and easy, but not very efficient or scalable in their design and operation. For the best balance between resource efficiency, scalability, and ease of configuration, I would like to offer the application of PCQ with a simple queue.

First, what is PCQ? Per Connection Queuing is the queuing discipline that can be used to dynamically divide streams of traffic into upload and download on a per host basis. In addition, once identified and divided, the traffic can be queued. One method allocates a predetermined amount of bandwidth per user with the caveat that once the total available bandwidth is met and exceeded, the bandwidth will then be shared equally. Another method is to create an allocation of bandwidth for all users to be shared equally. These two scenarios are so similar that it may seem confusing, so let's explore some scenarios to explain this concept.

In the first scenario, we have a 512k allocation of bandwidth for our users. We want to divide it amongst them, but limit each user to no more than 128k. Graphically, this scenario is demonstrated using this illustration:

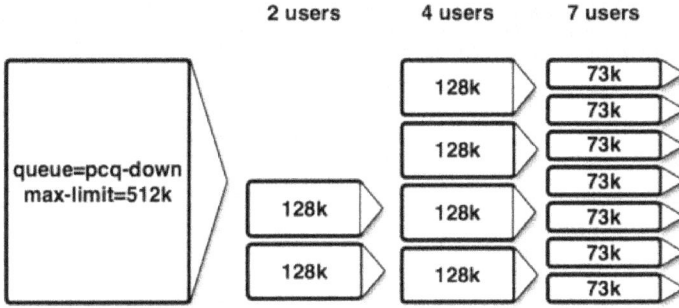

Figure 12 - PCQ Behavior [1]

As you can see, with 4 active users downloading, everyone gets their allocation of 128k. Once we exceed our total allocation of 512k and have 7 active users downloading, the total bandwidth per user drops to 73k.

In the second scenario, we are not imposing any limits until the total allocation of bandwidth is exceeded. We will then share all available bandwidth between all active users. Note that when I say active users, I mean network hosts that are actively downloading or uploading, that is, those hosts for which traffic is currently flowing.

Consider the following diagram:

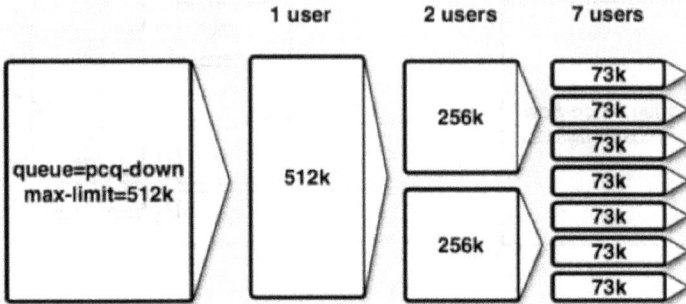

Figure 13 - PCQ Behavior [1]

If only one user is downloading, they get the full 512k allocation, but two users will share it equally.

Which scenario do you choose? The second scenario, in my opinion, will generate the most support calls to the IT department because one user that comes in every morning a half hour before the rest of the office will get an unrealistic expectation about the high speed of the Internet connection. Furthermore, once other users get to work, he or she will call IT and complain that the network slows every day around 8:30 am. This scenario is likely worth some consideration before you choose a method.

Use this example if you want to impose uniform rate limits to all clients on a network.

Example – Using PCQ with a Simple Queue, One Limit to All

The following example demonstrates the easiest way to get started with PCQ's. It is configured by creating a custom queue type that is a PCQ, and applying that to a simple queue. The simple queue controls the bandwidth allocation and identifies the traffic to be queued, while the PCQ type distributes the bandwidth to the targets. With this example, you can experience the scalability of PCQ's using features you have already learned in this book.

1. The first step is to create the custom queue type of upload and download. Remember, PCQ divides traffic using classifiers that determine if it is upload or download, so we need two customer queue types. These are created under the Queues button and then Queue Types.

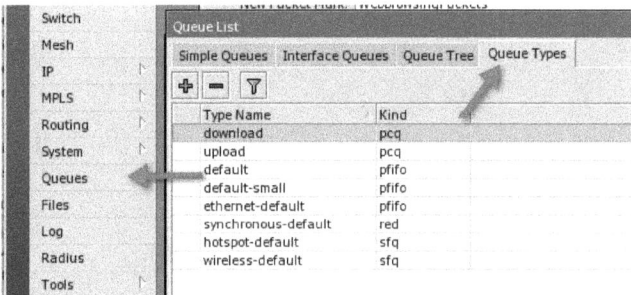

2. Here we create two queues and name them "upload" and "download". For the upload queue, notice we set the Classifier to Src. Address. The rationale is that if traffic is coming from a host, that host is uploading.

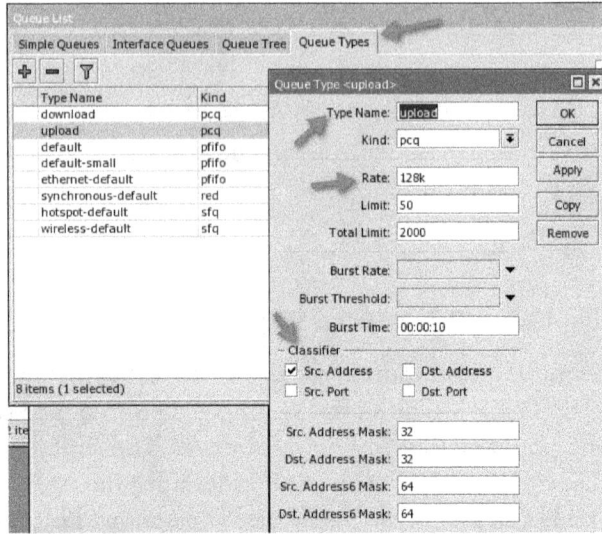

3. For download, pick Dst. Address for the same reason. The Rate setting is the maximum amount of bandwidth each host will receive. If we leave the Rate at 0, there will be no per user rate and everyone will share the available bandwidth equally. This is the only difference between configuring the two PCQ scenarios.

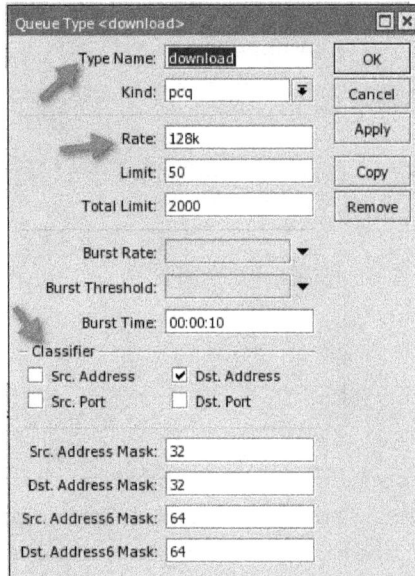

4. Next, we create a simple queue that will identify the hosts to be queued. In this case, we want to identify all traffic to all

hosts on our subnet using the Target address of
192.168.1.0/24 and allocate a maximum of 512k for all traffic.

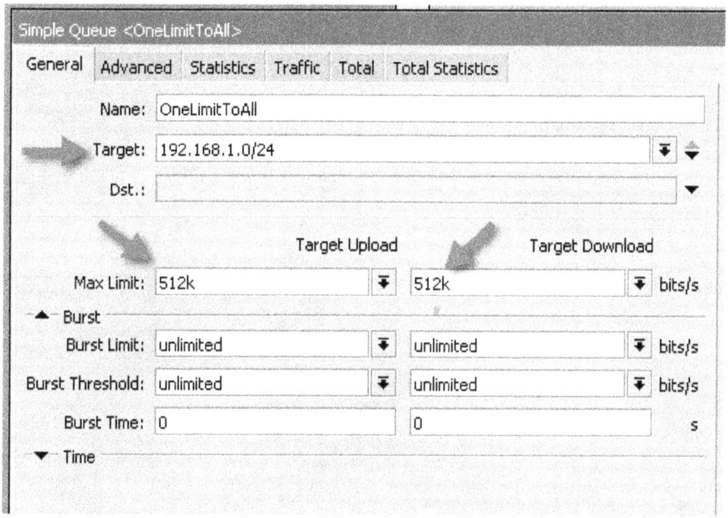

Simple Queue <OneLimitToAll>						

General | Advanced | Statistics | Traffic | Total | Total Statistics

Name: OneLimitToAll

Target: 192.168.1.0/24

Dst.:

	Target Upload		Target Download	
Max Limit:	512k		512k	bits/s
Burst				
Burst Limit:	unlimited		unlimited	bits/s
Burst Threshold:	unlimited		unlimited	bits/s
Burst Time:	0		0	s
Time				

5. On the Advanced tab, we set the queue type to "upload" and
"download", the names of the two custom PCQ queues we
recently created. That is all that is required to create the one
limit to all strategy using PCQ.

(Continued on next page)

Simple Queue <OneLimitToAll>

General | Advanced | Statistics | Traffic | Total | Total Statistics

Packet Marks:

	Target Upload	Target Download	
Limit At:	unlimited	unlimited	bits/s
Priority:	8	8	
Queue Type:	upload	download	
Parent:	none		

enabled

Queue List

Simple Queues | Interface Queues | Queu

Type Name	Kind
multi-queue-ethernet-default	mq pfifo
only-hardware-queue	none
download	pcq
pcq-download-default	pcq
pcq-upload-default	pcq
upload	pcq
default	pfifo
default-small	pfifo
ethernet-default	pfifo
synchronous-default	red

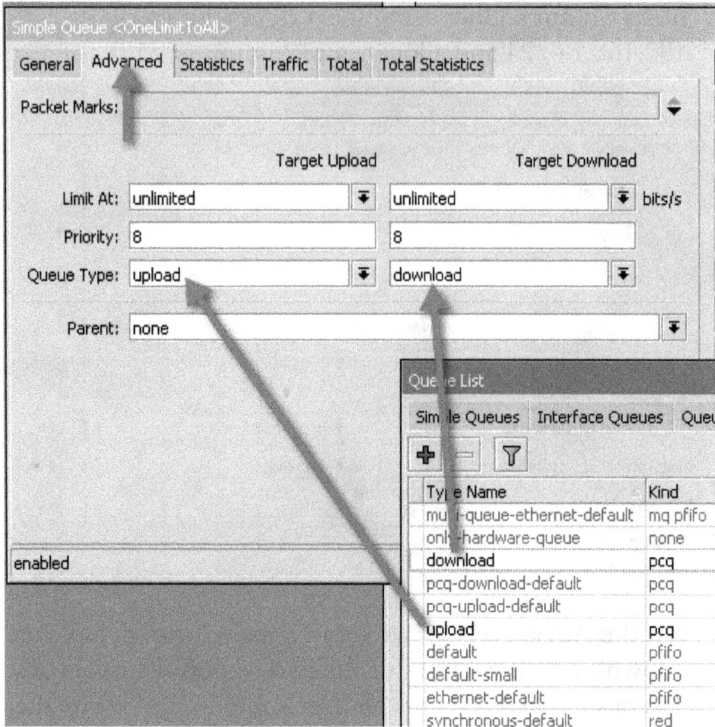

Using mangle, we can further extend this example. First, create PCQ queues and simple queues for each package of bandwidth you want to make available to hosts, just like in this example. Then, create mangles that identify each class of customer by IP address or subnet.

With three packages of bandwidth, you will only need three simple queues, six custom queues, and six mangle rules to queue traffic to thousands of hosts. This is a very manageable, scalable, and efficient way to limit traffic.

PCQ Queue Properties

The default configuration provides two PCQ queue types already
created for you. Feel free to modify and use these, or create your
own as shown in the preceding example. In most setups, the default
values for everything in the PCQ default type work fine and you only
need to modify the Rate settings to match the amount of bandwidth
you want to allocate to your users.

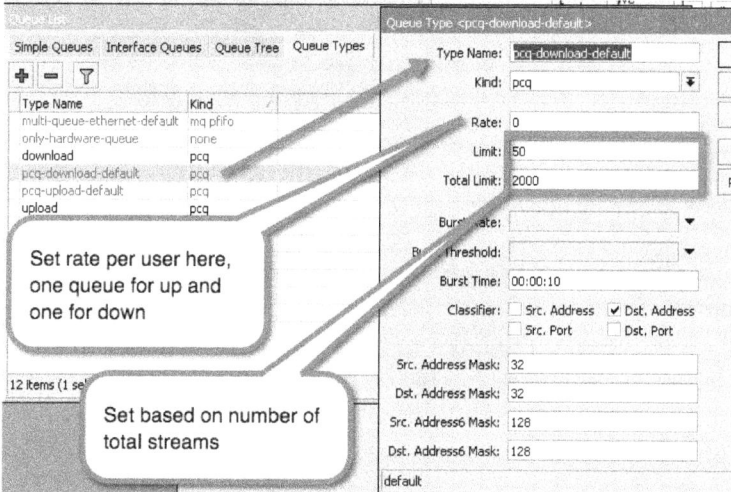

One other setting you may need to modify, depending on the size of
your deployment, is the Total Limit shown in the box above. These
settings allocate sufficient memory for the number of anticipated
queues. I would not change the Limit setting, as the default of 50 is
the optimal setting, but you will need to change Total Limit. To set
this, take the total number of users and multiply it times the Limit of
50 to get the Total Limit.

Example:

> We will have 250 users as a maximum at peak times.
> Therefore, we multiply 250 (number of users) times the
> default Limit of 50 and we get a new Total Limit of 12500.

Chapter 11 – Tools

In my opinion, one of the things that truly separates RouterOS from all the other routing systems I have worked with is the availability of a large selection of very functional tools. I would venture to say that no other dedicated routing system has this large of a selection of network tools contained within the operating system. We will take a look at several of the more commonly used tools and how they can be used to maintain, test, and troubleshoot your network.

Bandwidth Test Utility

The Bandwidth Test utility's function is to test in real time the performance of a link between two devices. The tool is designed as a client server model and the link can be Ethernet or wireless. Best of all, the test can be conducted between two RouterOS devices, between a Windows PC and a RouterOS device, or even between two Windows PC's.

As described previously, the tool is designed as two pieces, a client and a server. The client sends traffic to the server to create an upload test and the server sends traffic back to test the download speed. All results are displayed in real time and there are numerous configurable options. It should be noted that the tool itself requires CPU cycles and resources. To accurately test a link, simply running the tool on the two endpoints of the link will not give accurate results. The most accurate way to test a link is to use two additional routers as the testing endpoints and test through the two link endpoints in a fashion similar to the following illustration created using the MikroTik Dude:

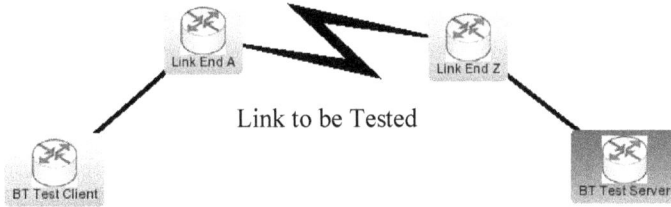

Link to be Tested

Test Client   **Figure 14 - Bandwidth Test Layout**   Test Server

The best way to learn to use the bandwidth test tool is through some examples. In this example, we will do a simple test between two RouterBOARDs. As previously discussed, this is not the most accurate way to conduct a test, but this will simply demonstrate the actual use of the tool.

Use this example for conducting a bandwidth test any time you want to test the bandwidth capability between two hosts.

APPLICATION

Example - Bandwidth Test Utility

1. The server portion requires little configuration and is found in the Tools menu under BTest Server.

(Continued on next page)

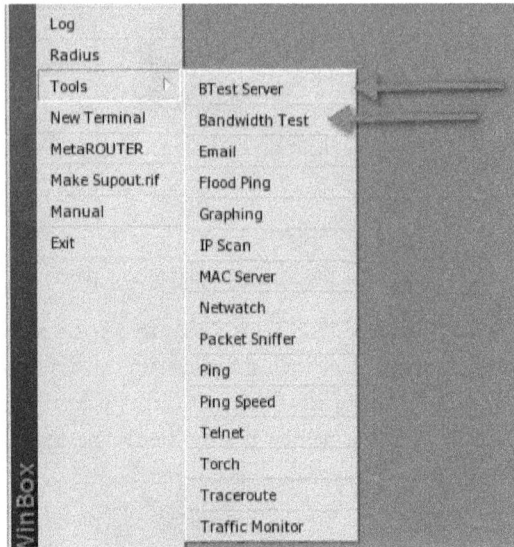

Log	
Radius	
Tools ▷	BTest Server
New Terminal	Bandwidth Test
MetaROUTER	Email
Make Supout.rif	Flood Ping
Manual	Graphing
Exit	IP Scan
	MAC Server
	Netwatch
	Packet Sniffer
	Ping
	Ping Speed
	Telnet
	Torch
	Traceroute
	Traffic Monitor

2. Once the server list is opened, the only configuration is to click "Enabled" and make a decision on "Authenticate". Authenticate simply means the client has to supply a user name and password for a valid router user to run the test. Always check Authenticate or disable the bandwidth test so that someone doesn't use your router as his or her test point.

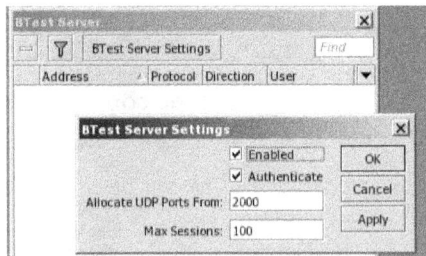

3. When you close the BTest Server Settings window, the BTest Server list shows any clients that may be running a test, so it is empty until a test is started.

4. Once the server end is set up, the client router clicks the Bandwidth Test to open the following dialog box:

```
Bandwidth Test                                    X

              Test To:  10.0.1.1            |     Start

             Protocol:  ⊙ udp      ○ tcp    |     Stop
      Local UDP Tx Size: 1500               |
                                            |     Close
     Remote UDP Tx Size: 1500               |

            Direction:  both            ▼

    TCP Connection Count: 20

        Local Tx Speed:            ▼  bps

       Remote Tx Speed:            ▼  bps

                 User:  admin          ▲

             Password:  +++++          ▲

     Tx/Rx 10s Average:  6.9 Mbps/494.1 kbps

        Tx/Rx Average:  6.9 Mbps/494.1 kbps


    ■ Tx: 7.6 Mbps
    ■ Rx: 71.9 kbps

 running...
```

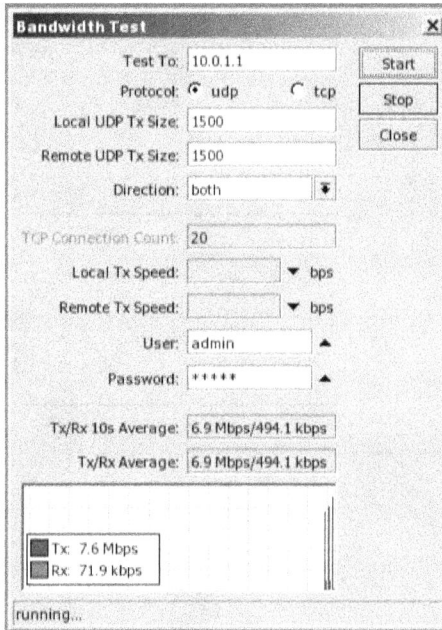

The required items here are a "Test To" IP address of the server, a
user name, and a password for authentication as previously
configured. Everything else is optional, descriptive of its function,
and selectable by the user.

Monitoring Tools

In the beginning of this chapter, I said that in my opinion, one of the
things that really separates RouterOS from all the other operating
systems out there is the availability of a large selection of very
functional tools. The area monitoring is no different. There is no
other routing system that I know of where you can get such advanced
real time traffic monitoring tools as well as such detailed historical
data.

The interface traffic monitor is a real time graph that is available for
every interface in RouterOS. It is accessible within the properties of
an interface on a tab entitled "Traffic".

```
Interface <ether1>                                    [X]

  General  Ethernet  Status  Traffic                    [    OK    ]

        Tx/Rx Rate:  [63.0 kbps    ]  / [27.4 kbps   ]   [  Cancel  ]

  Tx/Rx Packet Rate:  [16 p/s       ]  / [17 p/s      ]   [  Apply   ]

       Tx/Rx Bytes:  [56.6 GiB     ]  / [31.4 GiB    ]   [ Disable  ]

     Tx/Rx Packets:  [90 141 644   ]  / [83 096 569  ]   [ Comment  ]

       Tx/Rx Drops:  [0            ]  / [0           ]
                                                         [  Torch   ]
      Tx/Rx Errors:  [0            ]  / [0           ]

   ┌──────────────────────────────────────────┐
   │  ┌──────────────────┐                     │
   │  │ ■ Tx:  63.0 kbps │                     │
   │  │ ■ Rx:  27.4 kbps │                     │
   │  └──────────────────┘                     │
   └──────────────────────────────────────────┘

   ┌──────────────────────────────────────────┐
   │  ┌─────────────────────┐                  │
   │  │ ■ Tx Packet:  16 p/s│                  │
   │  │ ■ Rx Packet:  17 p/s│                  │
   │  └─────────────────────┘                  │
   └──────────────────────────────────────────┘

  disabled        running       slave      link ok
```

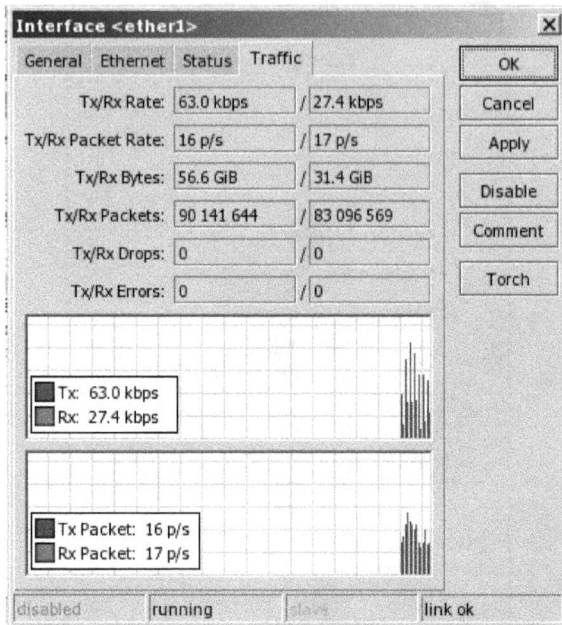

In the interface traffic monitor, traffic passing through the interface is measured and displayed graphically, using directional flow identifiers for Transmit (Tx) and Receive (Rx) rates, as well as a lower-level display of packets per second. In addition, Tx and Rx errors are displayed for the interface, thereby giving the technician a quick and simple view of the traffic passing through the interface. The interface traffic monitor is found on all interfaces by right clicking the interface in the Interfaces list, selecting Properties, and clicking the Traffic tab.

Torch

The operation of the Torch tool was described on page 133.

Use this example any time you want to see, in real time, the traffic passing through an interface, including source/destination IP address, port, and protocol.

Example – Using Torch to Troubleshoot "Slow" Networks

This particular example is more of a story and application rather than a step-by-step guide, as the actual steps are simple. You just click the Tools menu and select Torch. This is a classic example of how Torch and RouterOS can make the operation of a provider network so much simpler and give your technicians fingertip access to diagnostic power that the telecoms only have at their highest level of IP network engineering.

The scenario is simple and common for an Internet service provider. A customer calls in and complains that their Internet connection is slow. "Slow" is a relative term and really makes the possibility of ending this call in a manner that is satisfactory to the customer a real challenge. In addition, it has been my experience that a service provider can give excellent service for years and when there is one "hiccup", regardless of the responsible party, the perception from the consumer is that "the service has always been terrible and has never worked right". Remembering that perception is often reality to our valued customers, we are forced to troubleshoot a problem that is most likely not even a "problem" and thereby defend our honor, or in this case our network. In this scenario, the first tool I launch is Torch on the customer-facing interface.

What I typically find is something that looks like this:

Torch (running)										X

Basic — **Filters** — **Start / Stop / Close**

Interface: ether1   Src. Address: 0.0.0.0/0

Entry Timeout: 00:00:03   s   Dst. Address: 0.0.0.0/0

Collect   Protocol: any

☑ Src. Address   ☑ Protocol   Port: any

☑ Dst. Address   ☑ Port

☐ VLAN Id   VLAN Id: any

Find

Eth. ...	Prot...	Src. Address	Src. Port	Dst. Address	Dst. Port	Tx Rate	Rx Rate	Tx Pack...	Rx Pack...	▼
	6 (t...	10.0.25.243	52445	4.23.45.254	80 (http)	6.3 Mbps	196.4 kbps	580	419	
	6 (t...	10.0.25.243	52227	10.0.1.1	8291 (winbox)	9.7 kbps	4.1 kbps	3	6	
	6 (t...	10.0.25.233	42559	216.81.36.4	2210	7.8 kbps	1426 bps	3	3	
	6 (t...	10.0.25.234	49191	69.171.224.42	80 (http)	6.6 kbps	15.1 kbps	2	2	
	6 (t...	10.0.25.243	52177	208.91.12.164	3389 (ms-wbt...)	4.8 kbps	3.8 kbps	9	9	
	6 (t...	10.0.25.234	49307	208.91.11.5	80 (http)	2.7 kbps	3.9 kbps	2	2	
	6 (t...	10.0.25.243	52168	10.0.1.1	8291 (winbox)	429 bps	421 bps	0	0	

What I have done in this view is to click on the Tx Rate column to sort the traffic based on the highest rate first. As you can see, this customer is maintaining a 6.3 Mbps stream to an IP address of 10.0.25.243. It doesn't take long to explain to a customer that if they are paying for a 6 Meg connection and they are streaming more than 6 Megs, they are getting their money's worth. In addition, you get the opportunity to help them play detective or "informed tech parent", going through the home, checking the IP address of each computer to determine who is streaming a movie (with parental permission or without). Torch gives you a looking glass into the customer's private IP network behind their firewall and empowers you to give quantitate data to the customer that proves the quality and value of the service they are buying.

Traffic Graphing

In a perfect world, all of our customers would be conservative with the network resources to which they have access, decrease their usage during peak times, and schedule their downloads during periods of lowest activity. Obviously, this is not the way it usually works. Many times, as service providers, we are challenged by our clients who believe they are not getting what they have paid for with regard to bandwidth.

It is often a challenge to explain to a customer how we know they are using all the bandwidth they are paying for. Fortunately, a picture paints a thousand words and RouterOS offers such a picture when it comes to bandwidth usage.

Graphing is a method of recording the amount of traffic that passes through an interface over time in an easy-to-read chart, which can be printed or the web link given to a client for his or her own inspection. The graphs can be stored on the device's storage. Although the most common usage is for graphing bandwidth, it can also graph resources such as CPU utilization, memory, and disk usage.

Graphing consists of two parts: the collection of the raw data and the viewing of the compiled data. First, the graph collection is configured in the device, then the graphs become available through WinBox or the web interface.

The configuration of graphs is found under Tools and Graphing.

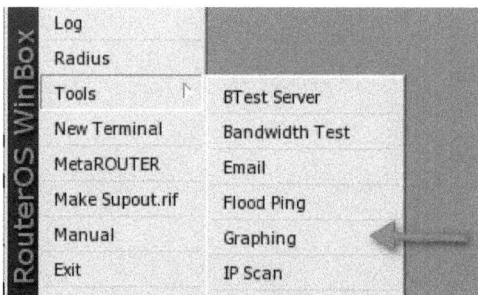

The last three tabs display any graphing rules that have been configured, and by default there, are none.

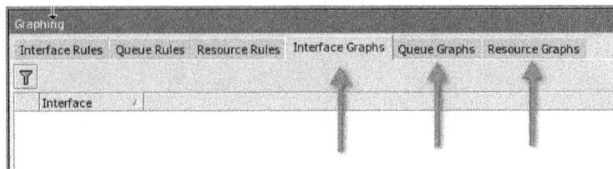

The first three tabs entitled "Rules" are where you configure the items to be graphed. The default when creating a new resource is "all", which is an easy rule to create, but not very selective. There is also the option to limit the hosts that can view the graphs through the web browser interface to a single IP address or a subnet. Limiting to more than one subnet would be better served by using firewall filter rules, as the restriction allowed in graphing is meant to be quick and easy, but is very limited in scope to a single host or a single subnet.

Once you are creating graphs, they can be stored in memory or on disk as configured in your rules you create. They can then be viewed in WinBox or by web browsing to the IP address of your router and clicking the Graphs button.

Graphs are great. They are easy to configure and a quick way to prove to a client, or yourself, that they are using the bandwidth they are buying.

Use this example to automatically create traffic graphs that will document the amount of traffic passing an interface or queue, or the amount of router resource utilization.

Example – Configure a Graph for all Users in a Subnet

This is a quick and easy way to determine whom the "bandwidth hogs" are on your local network. It involves both Queues and Graphs; however, the purposes of the queues here are not to limit bandwidth, but merely to provide a mechanism to measure bandwidth.

The fastest way to create the queues is to use an Excel spreadsheet because of its ability to fill rows of cells with consecutive numbers. With Excel, you can easily create a script, then paste or import the script into RouterOS. If you aren't comfortable with this method, you can create the queues manually.

1. Create a simple queue for each host IP address in your local subnet. In the case of a /24, that is 253 queues, assuming you want to log bandwidth to every single one, excluding the default gateway address.

2. Next, create a queue with a target address for each IP address you want to graph. You must specify a Max Limit for Upload and Download for each queue you create in order for the queue to see bandwidth. This limit can be higher than the network can support. Each queue should look like this:

(Continued on next page)

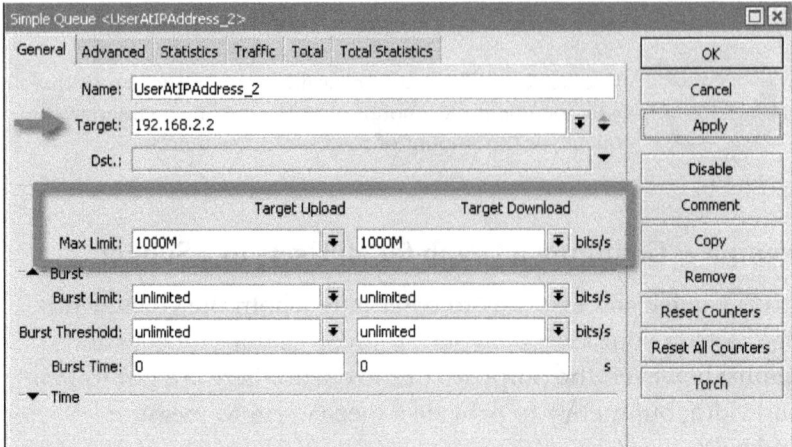

3. In Tools Graphing, create a new rule to graph all queues like this:

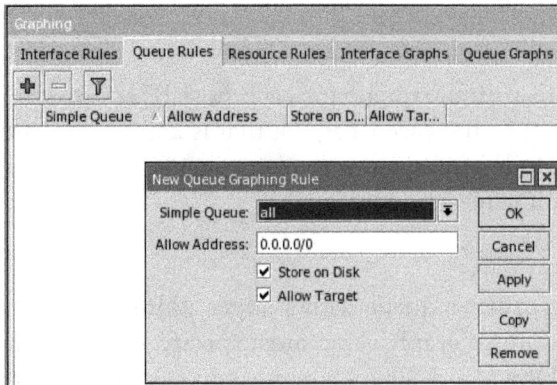

4. Now when I web browse to the router IP address, I can click the Graphs button:

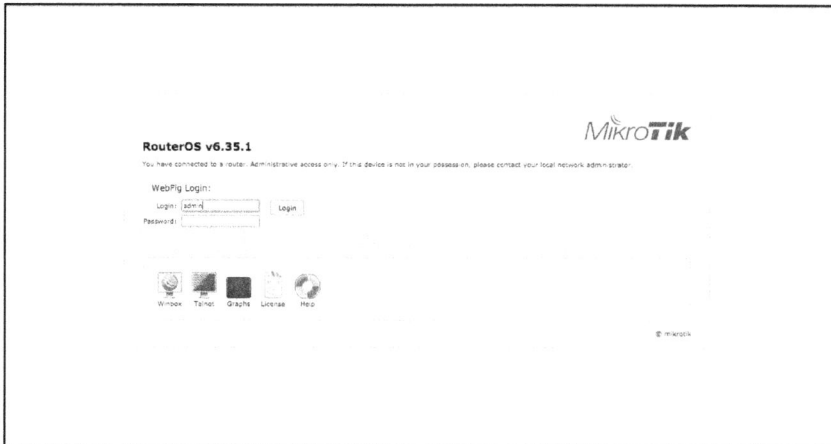

On the graphs page, I will see a list of graphs and a resulting graph for each queue I have created, which will (in this case) equate to one graph per user on the network.   Again, using a script will quickly produce a large number of queues.

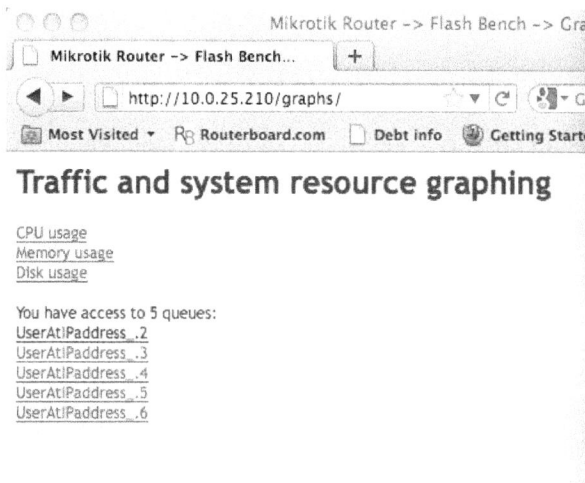

(Continued on next page)

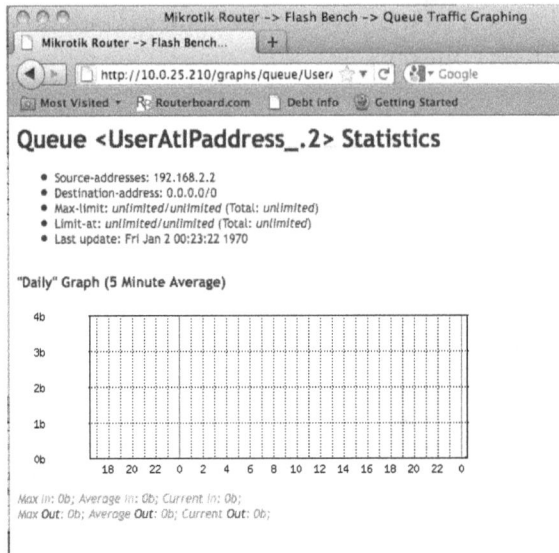

Queue <UserAtIPaddress_.2> Statistics

- Source-addresses: 192.168.2.2
- Destination-address: 0.0.0.0/0
- Max-limit: *unlimited/unlimited* (Total: *unlimited*)
- Limit-at: *unlimited/unlimited* (Total: *unlimited*)
- Last update: Fri Jan 2 00:23:22 1970

"Daily" Graph (5 Minute Average)

Max In: 0b; Average In: 0b; Current In: 0b;
Max Out: 0b; Average Out: 0b; Current Out: 0b;

This method is quick and easy to configure, and it provides a lot of valuable data. For the html-savvy user, it would be quite easy to create a single html web page that included (the <iframe> tag would be a good method to do this) one graph for each user on the network, all on one page for quick and easy analysis.

SNMP – Simple Network Management Protocol

SNMP is a standard Internet protocol to provide management of devices on IP networks. In its simplest terms, SNMP provides a way to get useful information about the performance of a device and then use that in a meaningful way. Some examples of this are producing graphs and charts and recording performance over a historical period.

In RouterOS, it is found through the IP button and then by selecting SNMP. There, by default, you will see an SNMP string that is configured with the name "public". For security, you should remove this entry and configure your own SNMP community string that is a bit tougher for someone to guess and possibly use in some way to exploit your device. Although not common, a good system administrator is always on the watch for ways hackers can exploit his or her network.

By default, SNMP is turned off and can be turned on by clicking the SNMP Settings button and enabling it. Other information can be added as desired and may be used for certain programs that read SNMP information.

If you are using any programs to poll SNMP data from your routers, then by all means, configure it appropriately. Otherwise, there is no need to turn it on or make any changes.

Chapter 12 – Local Area Networks

The LAN (Local Area Network) is a technical term for the network topology that is used in our home, our office, or the campus on which we operate. The attributes that differentiate the LAN from its neighbor, the WAN (Wide Area Network), are typically higher throughput rates, closer proximity of hosts, and the sharing of a common broadcast domain. A broadcast domain is a segment of a computer network where all hosts can communicate directly with each other by broadcast on the data link layer or Layer 2 of the OSI (Open Standards Interconnection) model. Broadcast domains are separated by Layer 3 devices, such as routers or Layer 3 switches. In summary, if two computers are connected to the same Layer 2 switch, they are on the same broadcast domain and they are certainly on the same LAN.

Thus far, we have been working under the assumption that you have at least a basic understanding of the OSI model. To ensure that we are using terms and phrases you are familiar with, I would like to offer some foundation.

Briefly stated, the OSI model defines the framework of our modern IP networks. It is based on a layered topology with seven distinct layers. In this book, we are only concerned with the first three layers.

Layer 1 – The physical layer. This is the cable, the fiber, or the wireless media we use to connect two or more hosts together. It is not intelligent, but it is absolutely necessary.

Layer 2 – The data link layer. In this layer, things become slightly more abstract; however, there is still some firm ground, so let me explain. Every network device comes from its manufacturer with a hard coded "serial number" that identifies it to other devices. This number is called the MAC address or Media Access Control address. The format is something like "00:0C:42:CE:05:1D". Layer 2 network switches understand MAC addresses and not much more. Their job is to pass frames around based on MAC addresses, and because their scope of focus is limited to the MAC address, they can do that very quickly and efficiently.

Layer 3 – The network layer. Now we have reached the heart of an IP network, the network layer. This layer is where routers operate and where IP addresses live. The network layer is even more abstract and dynamic than the data link layer because IP addresses can be assigned to interfaces, changed, or moved to other interfaces. This makes it the most dynamic of the first three layers.

ARP

You can see from this brief description that each of these layers is very unique, distinct, and separate from one another, but to hold them together as a system, we need some "glue". I like to say that ARP or Address Resolution Protocol is the glue that holds together two layers of the OSI model, Layer 2 and Layer 3. The ARP protocol creates a table on the router, which is nothing more than a lookup table, to tie together the MAC address of other hosts on the LAN with their respective IP addresses.

In RouterOS, the ARP table is found by selecting the IP button and the ARP menu.

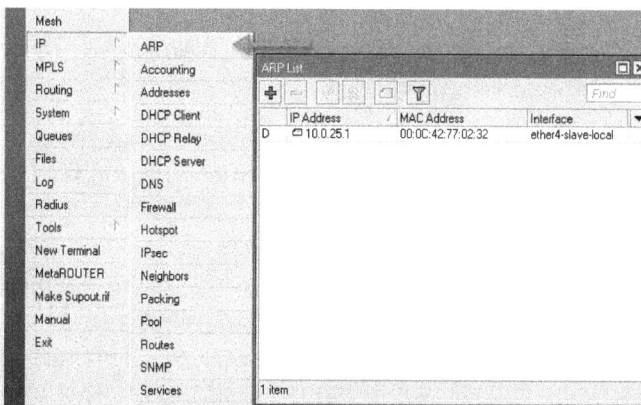

In this ARP table, we currently have one entry for an IP address of 10.0.25.1 with a MAC address of 00:0C:42:77:02:32. The letter "D"

next to the entry designates that the entry was created dynamically. ARP is one of those protocols that just works, so we typically ignore it.

Although ARP entries are normally created automatically (dynamically without our intervention), we can force RouterOS to only use static ARP entries. To make a dynamically created entry in the ARP Table above static, simply double click it and click the button entitled "Make Static". To ensure that no more ARP entries are created, the process is less than intuitive. You actually configure through the interface where the ARP entries are being created and set the interface to "reply-only". No more APR entries will be created.

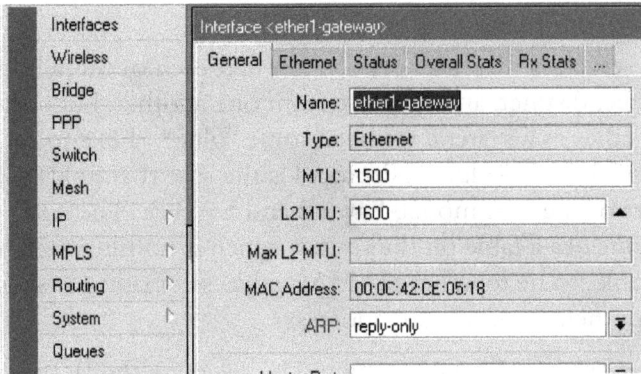

Interfaces	Interface <ether1-gateway>					
Wireless	General	Ethernet	Status	Overall Stats	Rx Stats	...
Bridge						
PPP	Name:	ether1-gateway				
Switch	Type:	Ethernet				
Mesh	MTU:	1500				
IP	L2 MTU:	1600				▲
MPLS	Max L2 MTU:					
Routing	MAC Address:	00:0C:42:CE:05:18				
System	ARP:	reply-only				▼
Queues						

The effect here is that when set to "reply-only", RouterOS no longer creates ARP entries in its table, but instead, only replies to other hosts' ARP requests.

Caution: Do not set the interface to ARP "disabled" or you will lose access through that interface.

Why would you want to set ARP to "reply-only" and create static ARP entries for every host on your network? Did you read the second part of that question "create static ARP entries for every host on your network"? That is important, because if you do not create static ARP entries for every host on your network, this router will not be able to communicate with them. ARP is the glue that binds Layer 2 to Layer 3, so without it, communication stops. The answer to the question is that using static ARP entries is not a common thing; however, if you want to increase the level of security in your LAN, then static ARP will do that. By that I mean, if a new host is brought onto the LAN, the existing hosts will not have static ARP entries for the new host. Furthermore, they will not communicate with it and now the LAN is arguably more secure.

Use this example to understand static ARP. Using static ARP can also be a way to solve an issue created by having duplicate IP addresses on a local area network. Configure static ARP for one host, log into that host, correct his IP address, and then revert to standard, automatic ARP.

APPLICATION

Example – Create a LAN that Requires Static ARP

This example is really meant to be an application that teaches a concept, not a recommended practice.

1. Using the IP Scan tool, scan your LAN subnet. This will cause ARP to create an ARP entry for every host it discovers.

Remember that ARP entries expire and flush after some period of time, so this has to be done quickly.

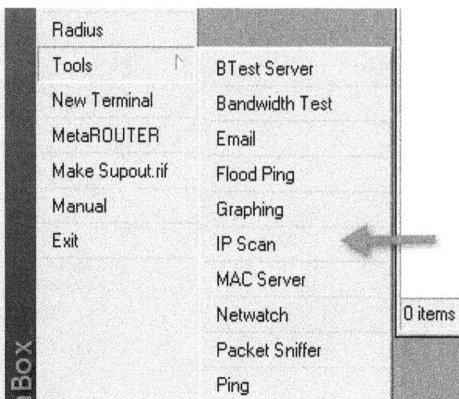

Radius	
Tools ⯈	BTest Server
New Terminal	Bandwidth Test
MetaROUTER	Email
Make Supout.rif	Flood Ping
Manual	Graphing
Exit	IP Scan ⬅
	MAC Server
	Netwatch 0 items
	Packet Sniffer
	Ping

The tool only requires you to enter your subnet in the Address Range blank and click Start.

IP Scan [Running]

Interface:					Start
Address Range:	10.0.25.0/24				Stop
					Close
					New Window

Address	MAC Address	Time (ms)	DNS	SNMP	Netbios
10.0.25.1	00:0C:42:77:02:32	0			
10.0.25.2	00:30:1B:BC:3F:33	1	companyweb		
10.0.25.3		1			

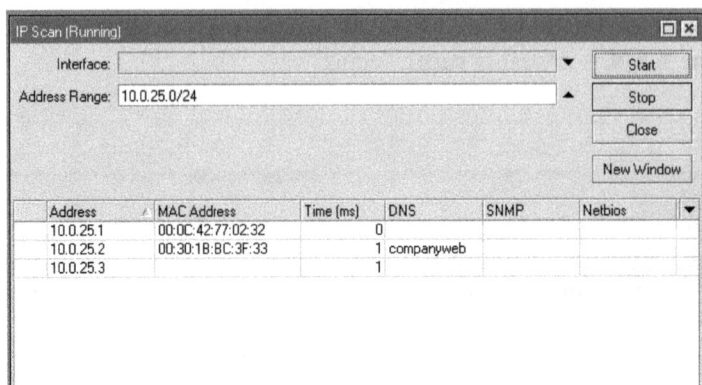

2. ARP entries will be created for each host that replies to the IP Scan probe.

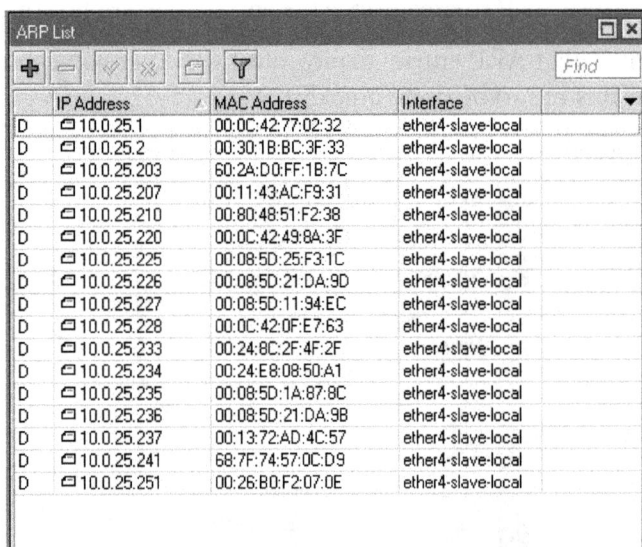

ARP List

Find

	IP Address	MAC Address	Interface	
D	10.0.25.1	00:0C:42:77:02:32	ether4-slave-local	
D	10.0.25.2	00:30:1B:BC:3F:33	ether4-slave-local	
D	10.0.25.203	60:2A:D0:FF:1B:7C	ether4-slave-local	
D	10.0.25.207	00:11:43:AC:F9:31	ether4-slave-local	
D	10.0.25.210	00:80:48:51:F2:38	ether4-slave-local	
D	10.0.25.220	00:0C:42:49:8A:3F	ether4-slave-local	
D	10.0.25.225	00:08:5D:25:F3:1C	ether4-slave-local	
D	10.0.25.226	00:08:5D:21:DA:9D	ether4-slave-local	
D	10.0.25.227	00:08:5D:11:34:EC	ether4-slave-local	
D	10.0.25.228	00:0C:42:0F:E7:63	ether4-slave-local	
D	10.0.25.233	00:24:8C:2F:4F:2F	ether4-slave-local	
D	10.0.25.234	00:24:E8:08:50:A1	ether4-slave-local	
D	10.0.25.235	00:08:5D:1A:87:8C	ether4-slave-local	
D	10.0.25.236	00:08:5D:21:DA:9B	ether4-slave-local	
D	10.0.25.237	00:13:72:AD:4C:57	ether4-slave-local	
D	10.0.25.241	68:7F:74:57:0C:D9	ether4-slave-local	
D	10.0.25.251	00:26:B0:F2:07:0E	ether4-slave-local	

3. Once the scan has completed, click the IP button in WinBox, and select ARP. In the ARP list, click the top entry, hold the shift key, and click the bottom entry in the list to select

everything in the ARP table. Then, right click and select "Make Static".

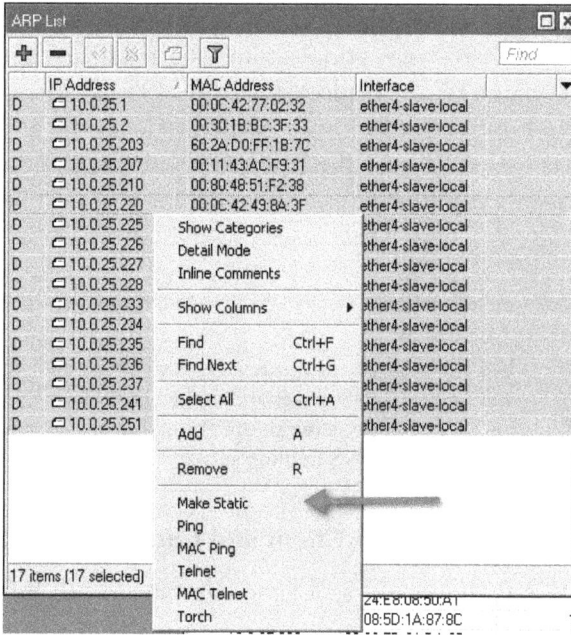

4. Finally, change the interface connected to the LAN to ARP "reply-only".

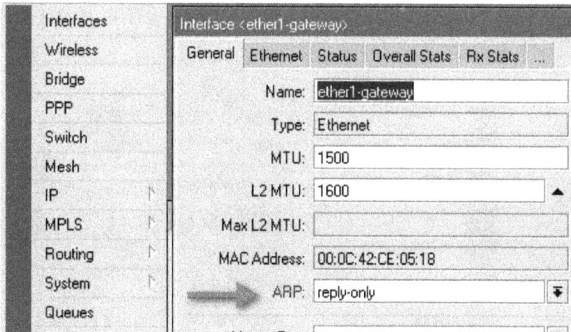

5. That is it. Repeat this process for every device on your LAN so that a new host brought onto the LAN will not be able to communicate with these devices because they lack an ARP entry for the new host. Remember, changing the IP on a host with a static ARP entry will prevent it from working on the network.

DNS

DNS (Domain Name Service) refers to the protocol that binds names to IP addresses. Without DNS, your computer would not be able to web browse to www.google.com, as it must first resolve (convert) that name to an IP address. RouterOS has the ability to store or cache DNS requests locally, which reduces the amount of requests it has to send across the Internet connection and thereby speeds up a user's experience.

Use this example to create a DNS client on your router that will query a DNS server and cache entries locally. This can greatly speed up network operation, but always remember to firewall your DNS caching server.

APPLICATION

Example – Configure DNS Client and Caching DNS Server

This example is fairly simple, so I have combined both functions.

1. Click on IP and select DNS. Click the Settings button and add at least one DNS server. Your Internet service provider typically provides these, but you can also use Google to find a public DNS server. One is fine, but two is better in the case that one fails.

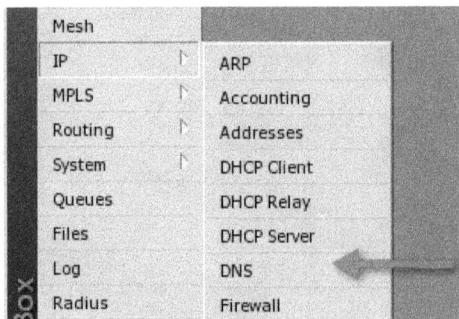

2. If you check "Allow Remote Requests", you can then point hosts on your LAN to the router's IP address and it will answer their DNS requests. It does this by looking in its local cache. If the requested host is not there, it then goes to one

of the servers configured in the DNS client and answers/caches the result. This provides a speed increase on the network. Click Ok to save.

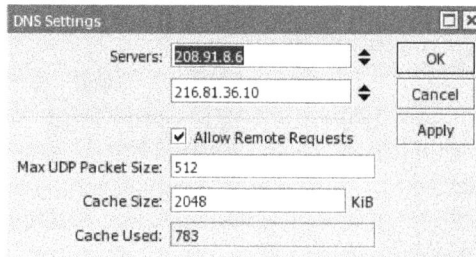

DNS Settings

Servers:	208.91.8.6
	216.81.36.10
	☑ Allow Remote Requests
Max UDP Packet Size:	512
Cache Size:	2048 KiB
Cache Used:	783

OK
Cancel
Apply

3. In the IP DNS window on the Static tab, you may create static DNS entries that will override the DNS server records. This can be used as a simple means to handle local DNS names for devices such as printers or servers.

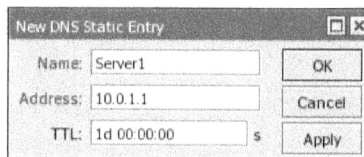

New DNS Static Entry

Name:	Server1
Address:	10.0.1.1
TTL:	1d 00:00:00 s

OK
Cancel
Apply

Note: This is really important, so take a moment to understand it. Enabling "Allow Remote Requests" enables DNS caching on all router interfaces, even the ones facing untrusted networks. This is a problem because left unguarded, your router will quickly become used for launching DNS attacks and you will likely get shut down by your ISP. Therefore, always firewall the WAN port(s) if enabling DNS caching. Firewalling the WAN port is part of the Firewalls Chapter of this book, and if you apply the Basic Firewall provided in the example, your router will be protected.

DHCP – Dynamic Host Configuration Protocol

DHCP is another one of those protocols we often take for granted, that is, unless you remember when everything was statically addressed. DHCP takes the guesswork out of IP address allocation.

The DHCP protocol is comprised of two parts. These two parts are:

1. A <u>server</u> that listens for requests by DHCP clients and responds with an IP address, a DNS server, a default gateway, and possibly some custom DHCP options.

2. A <u>client</u> that makes the DHCP request.

In addition, other information may be sent as options or configurations that can be made on the DHCP server in response to the client request.

DHCP Client

The DHCP client is simple to set up. It merely involves telling the router the interface on which you want to request a DHCP address. You can request a DNS server and default gateway, and in most cases, you will want to receive those configuration pieces, as well as an IP address.

Use this example for adding a DHCP client to an interface. Usually, this is your WAN interface and you are obtaining an address from the ISP.

APPLICATION

Example – Add a DHCP Client

The goal with this exercise is to get an IP address dynamically on the router, assuming there is an active DHCP server on the LAN.

(Continued on next page)

1. From the IP menu, select DHCP Client.

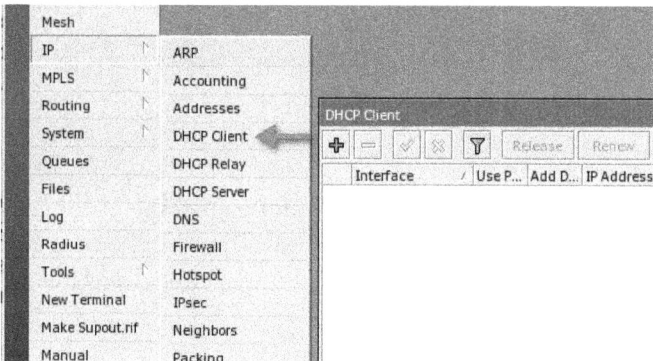

Mesh			
IP		ARP	
MPLS		Accounting	
Routing		Addresses	
System		DHCP Client	
Queues		DHCP Relay	
Files		DHCP Server	
Log		DNS	
Radius		Firewall	
Tools		Hotspot	
New Terminal		IPsec	
Make Supout.rif		Neighbors	
Manual		Packing	

DHCP Client

Interface / Use P... Add D... IP Address

2. Click the plus sign on the new DHCP Client window, and then select the interface on which you want to receive the IP Address, and click OK.

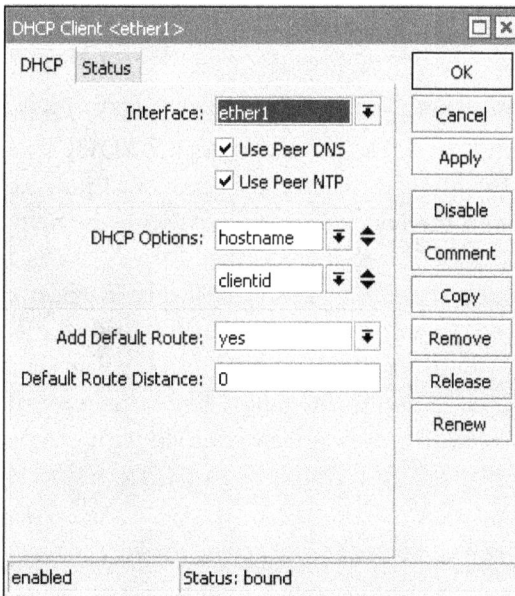

DHCP Client <ether1>

DHCP | Status

Interface: ether1

☑ Use Peer DNS
☑ Use Peer NTP

DHCP Options: hostname

clientid

Add Default Route: yes

Default Route Distance: 0

OK
Cancel
Apply
Disable
Comment
Copy
Remove
Release
Renew

enabled   Status: bound

3. The status of the DHCP client will then be shown in the DHCP Client window, including the IP address that was obtained.

(Continued on next page)

DHCP Client						□ X
✚ ━ ✓ ✕	▼	Release	Renew			▢▢▢▢

Interface	Use P...	Add D...	IP Address	Expires After	Status	▼
▲ bridge1	yes	yes	10.0.25.210/24	2d 23:59:52	bound	

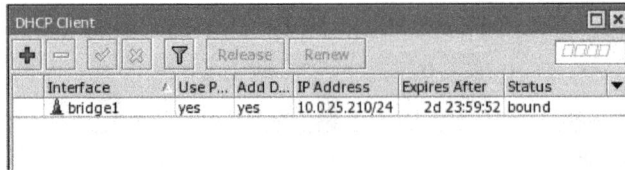

Note: If the interface on which you want to run the client is a port in a bridge, you must put the client on the parent bridge interface, not the Ether(x) interface. (There will be more on bridges later in Chapter 15.)

4. The "Release" and "Renew" buttons perform the functions of releasing or renewing the IP address for the interface selected in the list window.

DHCP Server

Configuring DHCP client was simple, and DHCP server is not much more complicated. The main requirement for DHCP server is a valid IP address on the interface where the server will run. You should then walk through the configuration steps with the help of the included setup script. Note that just like DHCP client, if the interface on which you want to run the server is a port in a bridge, you must put the server on the parent of the bridge interface. Failing to do so will render the server disabled and it will appear in the list window in red, indicating it is invalid. The remainder of the explanation of DHCP server is best handled with examples.

192

Use this example to configure a DHCP server that will automatically allocate IP addresses to clients on the network. Most home or office routers use DHCP server.

Example – Create a DHCP Server

In this example, we have assigned an IP address of 192.168.1.1/24 to interface ether2, where we want our DHCP server to operate. This is an important first step to make the setup very easy.

1. From the IP menu, select DHCP Server.

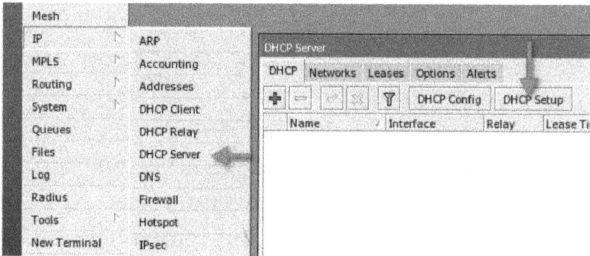

2. Click the DHCP Setup button to begin the configuration script. The first selection is the interface on which you want DHCP to operate.

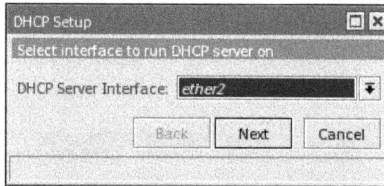

3. From this point forward, you can typically accept the defaults or make adjustments as required. The first window like this is the network address.

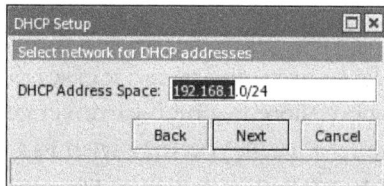

4. Next is the default gateway, typically the IP address you added on the interface previously.

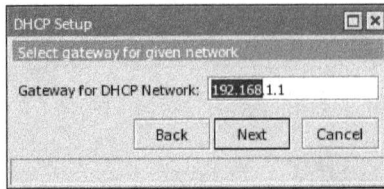

```
DHCP Setup                                    □ ⊠
Select gateway for given network
  Gateway for DHCP Network:  192.168 1.1

                        Back     Next     Cancel
```

5. Next is the pool of addresses that will be created. If you want to exclude certain ranges of addresses from the DHCP pool, now is your opportunity.

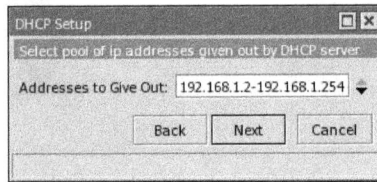

```
DHCP Setup                                    □ ⊠
Select pool of ip addresses given out by DHCP server
  Addresses to Give Out:  192.168.1.2-192.168.1.254 ⬍

                        Back     Next     Cancel
```

6. Next is the IP address of the DNS server(s) you want to give to your clients connecting to this interface. Again, make adjustments here as you wish, but remember you must give clients at least one DNS server, or the setup script will fail. If you want your clients to use your caching DNS server, then use the IP of your local interface. The logic is that we only want our clients to use our router for DNS, since we are caching DNS requests. The router will then either answer from cache or go to its own DNS server to resolve the address.

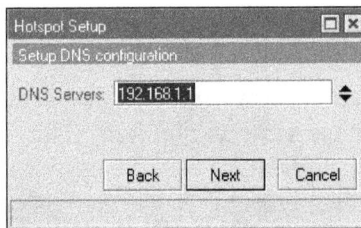

```
Hotspot Setup                                 □ ⊠
Setup DNS configuration
  DNS Servers:  192.168.1.1                      ⬍

                        Back     Next     Cancel
```

7. Next is the lease time, and in most cases, 3 days is fine. In situations where there is a high turnover of clients, such as a public venue or a hotel, you may wish to make this time much lower to prevent exhausting your pool of IP addresses. An IP can not be reused until the lease expires, even if the

client leaves the network, so shorter lease times are better for networks with high turnovers.

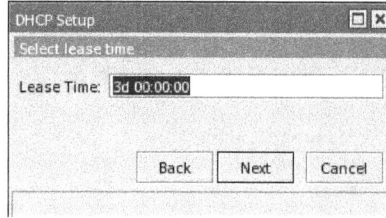

8. DHCP server is now complete.

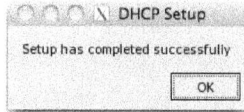

9. Once you have completed the setup script, any changes you would like to make can be done under the DHCP tab or the Networks tab.

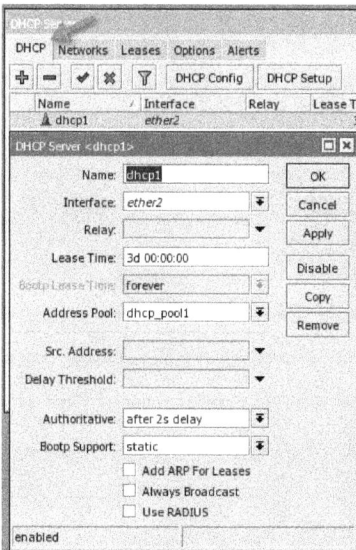

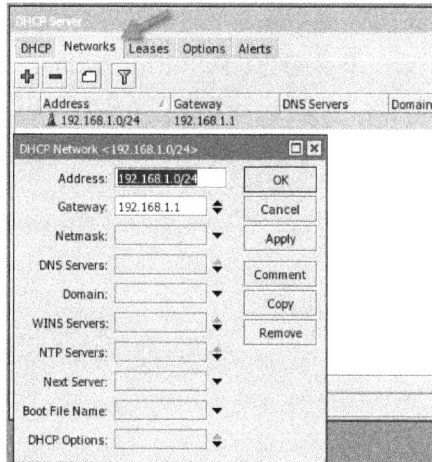

10. Any changes to the IP pool can be done under IP Pool.

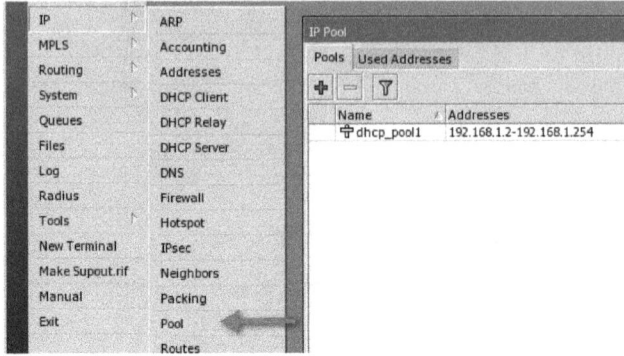

Use this example any time you want a DHCP host on the network to always get the same DHCP lease address. Good examples are printers, servers, and cameras.

Example – DHCP Static Leases

In many cases, it is desired for a host to always receive the same IP address. For instance, you may have a computer on your network that you wish to access via remote desktop. In this case, static leases will ensure a host always receives the same IP address.

(Continued on next page)

In the Leases window, find the lease you want to make static. Double click it to change the properties and click the button "Make Static".

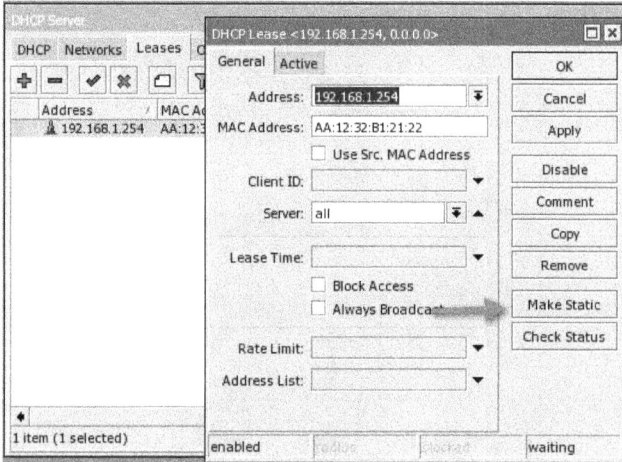

Use this example any time you want to make a DHCP network more secure by only allowing hosts previously seen, for which we have a static lease.

APPLICATION

Example – DHCP Server Without an IP Pool

While DHCP server is typically used with a pool of IP addresses, it can also be run without a pool and only static leases. The application of this is to create a small amount of security for a DHCP network. If a host not previously known is brought onto the network, it will not be able to obtain a DHCP address because there is not static lease. An easy way to implement this policy is to create a standard DHCP server with a pool of addresses. Once all machines on the network have obtained an IP address, convert all of the leases to static as previously described and proceed as follows.

1. On the DHCP Server tab, double click the instance of DHCP server.

2. Change the Address Pool to "static-only". Once this is done, only hosts for which you have a static lease will be able to obtain a DHCP address.

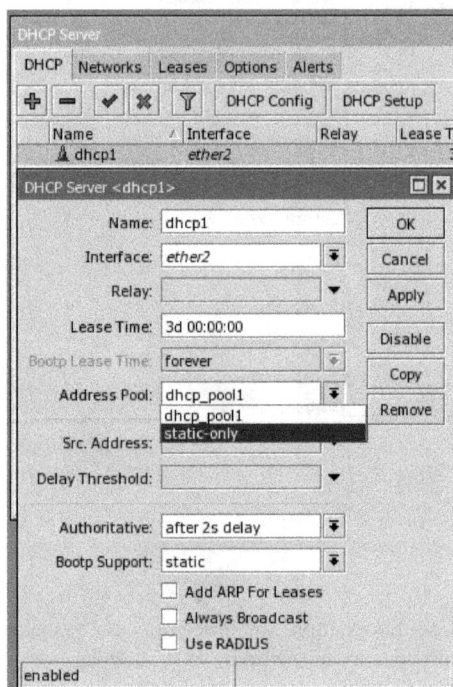

HotSpot – Instant Public Internet

If you have been in the wireless industry long, you likely remember when it was new and trendy to offer free or paid Internet access wirelessly. Hotels were some of the first to jump on the bandwagon, realizing that the RJ-11 modem port on the side of the hotel telephone was no longer going to support the bandwidth-hungry guest. Next, outdoor venues became popular, as well as indoor venues like airports. Now, public WiFi (typically free) is considered a staple like public restrooms in the U.S.A.

What can you do with the HotSpot function? Well, the applications are numerous, but to list a few, you can offer paid Internet access, free Internet access that requires only a user name and password to log in through a web page, restricted Internet access that only allows certain web sites to be accessed after authentication, and access that bombards your clientele with advertisements.

The heart of HotSpot is the redirect page. When a potential user associates with your wireless network or connects through a wired connection, any page they try to visit on their web browser will redirect them to your login page. This redirect page is included with RouterOS, but can easily be customized if you are able to write in html code. Once they authenticate, they can navigate to any page they wish, a page you specify, or a list of pages that you allow. Again, the applications are numerous.

Use this example when you want to create a public network with a splash page or an authentication page.

APPLICATION

Example – Set up HotSpot

In this example, we have a router with at least one wireless interface and existing Internet access. Our goal is to create a default HotSpot on the wireless interface. Setting up HotSpot is very similar to setting up DHCP server. It is easily done through a setup script.

1. In WinBox, click the IP button and select HotSpot. Click the HotSpot Setup button to begin. For your first HotSpot, I recommend accepting the defaults for everything. It is much easier that way.

   (Continued on next page)

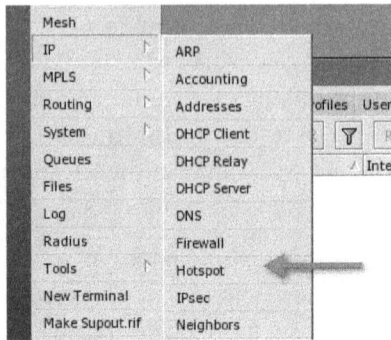

2. Click the HotSpot Setup button.

3. Select the interface where HotSpot will run, in this case, our wireless interface.

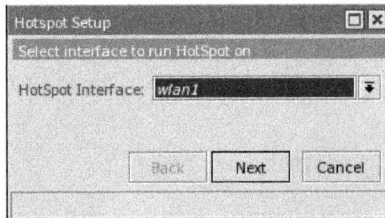

4. Next select the IP address for the interface. We are using the default IP address here.

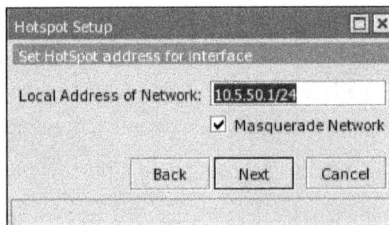

5. Select the pool of addresses to be issued. The defaults are fine.

(Continued on next page)

Hotspot Setup

Set pool for HotSpot addresses

Address Pool of Network: 10.5.50.2-10.5.50.254

Back | Next | Cancel

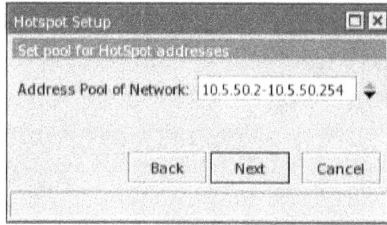

6. This is an advanced option for those wanting SSL encrypted logins. The option "none" is fine for our example.

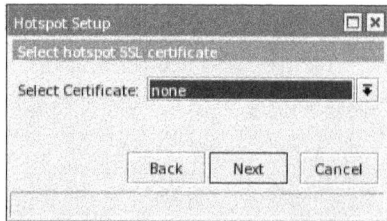

Hotspot Setup

Select hotspot SSL certificate

Select Certificate: none

Back | Next | Cancel

7. This can be dangerous, so I recommend leaving it at the default of all zero's, which means do not configure a default SMTP server. If you configure this option, all emails from your HotSpot network will be redirected to your email server. Unless you want to be a spammer, leave it alone.

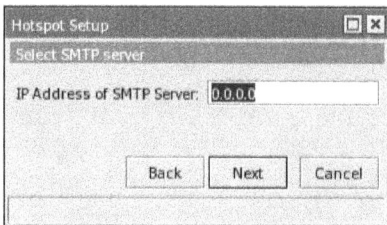

Hotspot Setup

Select SMTP server

IP Address of SMTP Server: 0.0.0.0

Back | Next | Cancel

8. DNS servers are required, so be sure to set them here.

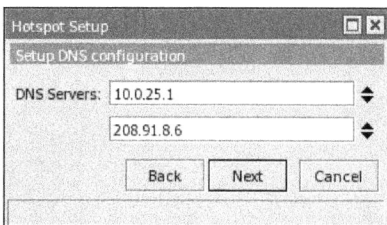

Hotspot Setup

Setup DNS configuration

DNS Servers: 10.0.25.1

208.91.8.6

Back | Next | Cancel

9. This can be anything you want users to see in their web browser on the address line after the redirect. I recommend using a standard URL format. It does not have to be a real domain

because the router will create local DNS for the URL, but some web browsers have trouble if you do not use a format like example.com or myHotSpot.net.

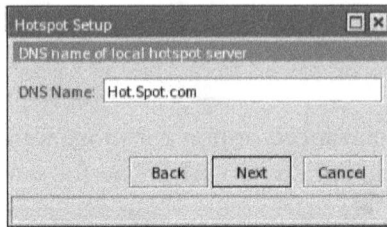

10. This message indicates you are done, and clicking OK will complete the HotSpot.

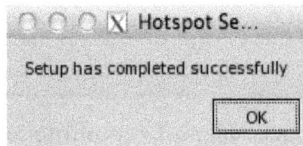

11. Remember that when you complete the last step and click OK, you will immediately be disconnected from the router and will have to log in to regain access. I recommend configuring your first HotSpot on an unused interface, rather than the primary interface you use to access the router. Using that method, you will not lose your ability to access the router.

Use this example with hotspot to keep hosts from having to authenticate with the Hotspot portal. This is useful for cameras, printers, servers, or property owners with whom you might be trading services.

Example – Create IP Bindings

This scenario is very common: You have installed a wireless HotSpot in a venue such as an RV park, and in return for offering a paid service, you have allotted the owner Internet access. Obviously, he or she doesn't want to log into the service each time, so how do you give them open access to the network? The facility is called IP Bindings. To create a binding for a certain host's MAC address, proceed as follows:

1. Click the IP button and select HotSpot.

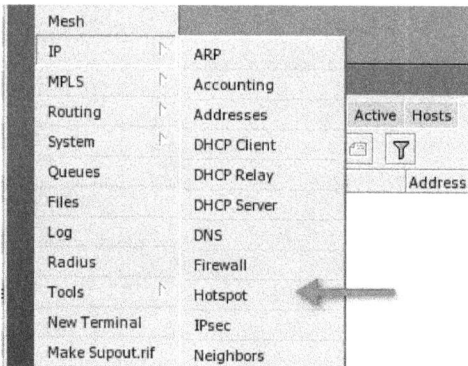

2. On the Bindings tab, click the plus sign to create a new binding.

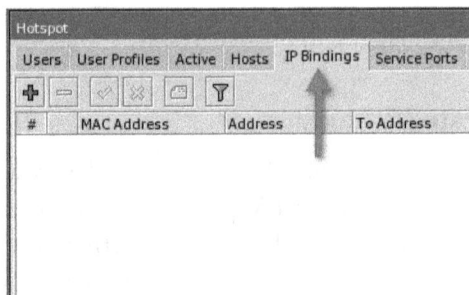

3. Enter the MAC address of the host to be given open access and set the Type to "bypassed".

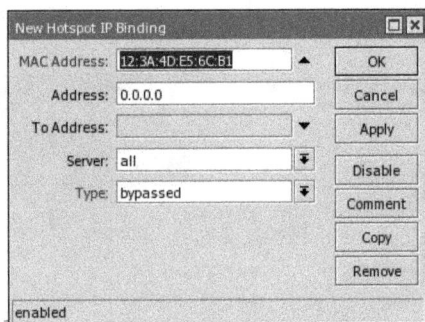

Use this example to add Hostpot users to your local Hotspot database.

Example – Create Additional Users

During the running of the IP HotSpot setup, you were prompted to create a user or set the password for the default user to "admin". It is important to note that the HotSpot user "admin" is not the same admin that can log into the router and configure it. They are two different databases and two different users. If you need to create additional HotSpot users, the process is simple.

1. Click the IP button and select HotSpot.

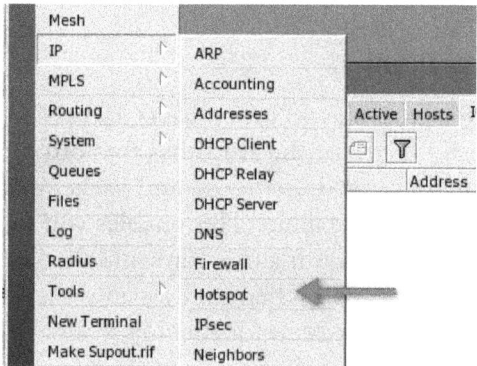

2. On the Users tab, click the plus sign and create a new user, setting the user name and password.

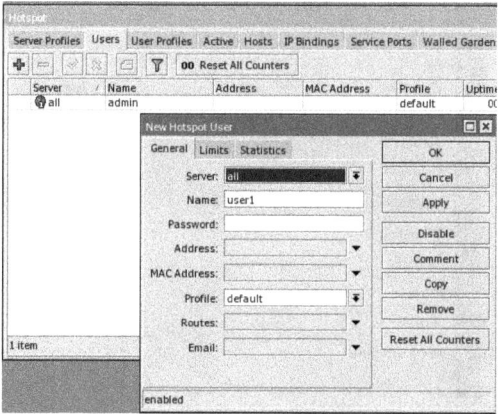

Use this example to create profiles that can be applied to groups of users. This is especially useful for imposing limits like rate limits or maximum number of sessions per user.

Example – User Profiles

User profiles are a great way to group users and assign default attributes to them. A few of the attributes that can be set for these users include rate limits, address pools, and packet marks. The most common application is rate limit. This enables you to create rate packages based on the amount a user pays and then group them manually into these groups. When they log into the HotSpot, they will have a simple queue created for them individually based on their profile.

To create a custom profile:

1. Click the IP button and select HotSpot.

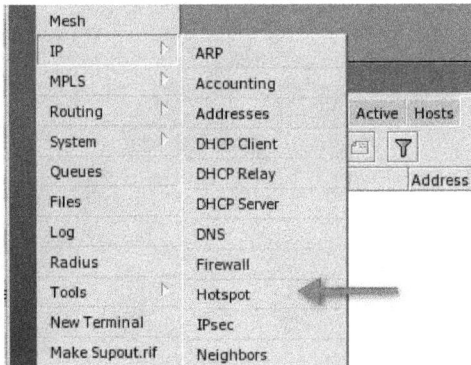

2. Click the User Profiles tab and the plus sign to create a new profile. Name the profile whatever you wish and apply the limits you want. In this case, I have set a rate limit of 1M/1M, that way a simple queue will be created for any user to which this profile is applied.

(Continued on next page)

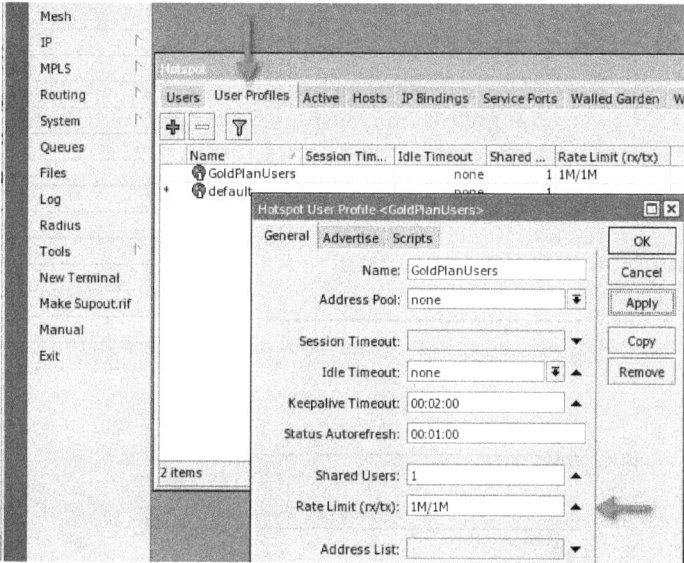

3. Finally, you must apply the profile to the user. In this example, a user, "MrBig", has purchased the Gold plan so that when he logs in, he will get a 1M x 1M rate limit.

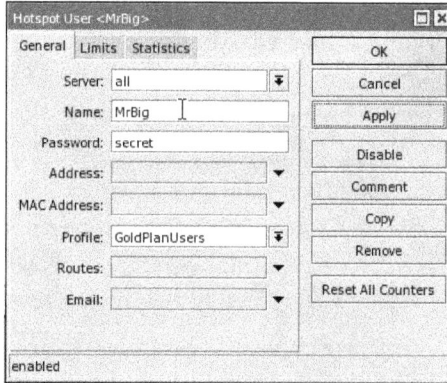

Use this example when you have more than one Hotspot server and you want to apply the same properties to all of the servers.

APPLICATION

Example – Server Profiles

1. Click the IP button and select HotSpot.

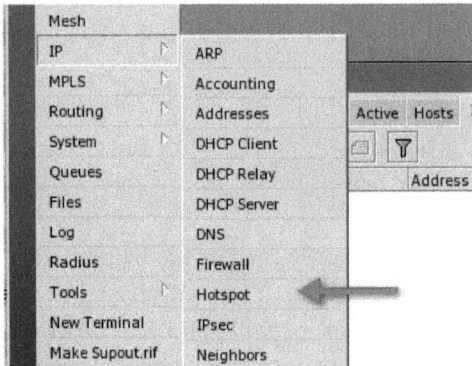

2. On the Server Profiles tab, double click the profile to be modified.

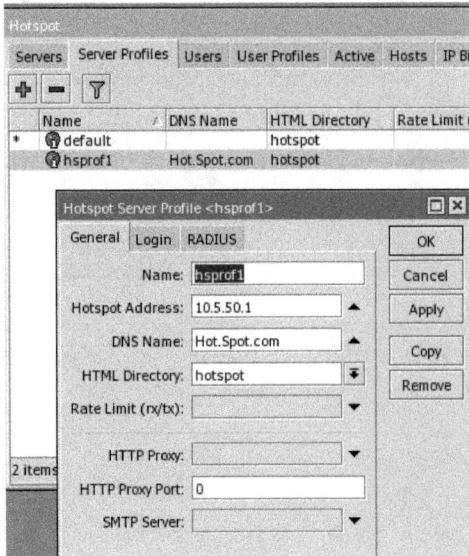

3. Typically, you are going to want the defaults for this profile on the general tab; however, on the Login tab you may wish to make some changes. The most common properties to change here are Cookies and Trial.

Cookies creates a cookie on the router when a user successfully authenticates and allows them to stay logged in for a time period based on the lifetime of the cookie, by default 3 days. This makes troubleshooting the HotSpot difficult so I typically uncheck Cookies.

The other property is Trial. When enabled, Trial will cause a Trial link to appear on the default HotSpot login page and allow unauthenticated access for a time period set below in the uptime limit setting (in this case, 30 minutes of free usage). The host will then have to wait 24 hours before they get another trial. You can also assign a profile to any trial users.

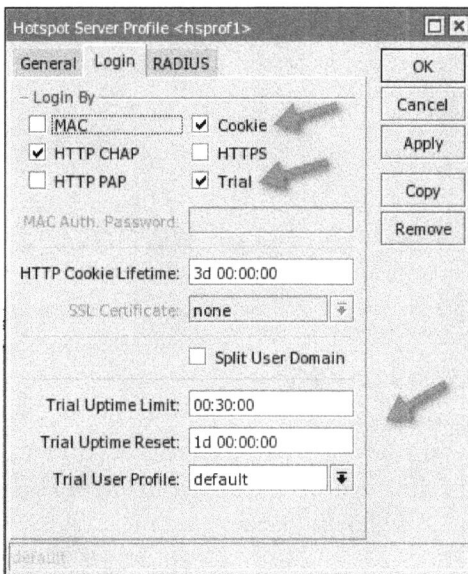

Use this example when you want to give users access to certain sites or IP addresses without authentication. This is useful for advertisements or terms of service.

Example – Walled Garden

Walled garden is a facility that allows unauthenticated access to certain sites based on a list. It can even be restricted to only certain paths on certain sites, so it is very configurable. The typical application is to allow enough access to get users interested in your HotSpot or to allow them to browse your advertisers freely, and then entice them into purchasing an account. To create allowed sites in walled garden:

1. Click the IP button and select HotSpot.

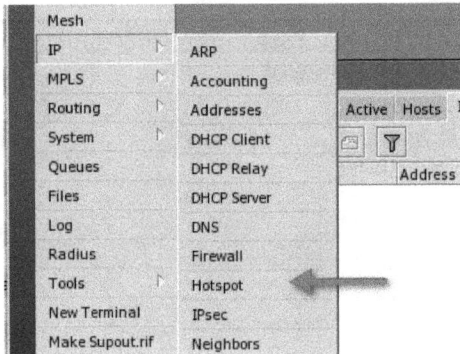

Mesh		
IP	▸	ARP
MPLS	▸	Accounting
Routing	▸	Addresses
System	▸	DHCP Client
Queues		DHCP Relay
Files		DHCP Server
Log		DNS
Radius		Firewall
Tools	▸	Hotspot
New Terminal		IPsec
Make Supout.rif		Neighbors

2. On the Walled Garden tab, create a new entry. In this case, notice I have used the asterisk (*) character so that www.advertisers.com, advertisers.com, and any other URL's that are in the advertisers.com domain will be matched. In this rule, I am allowing access, but access can also be denied.

(Continued on next page)

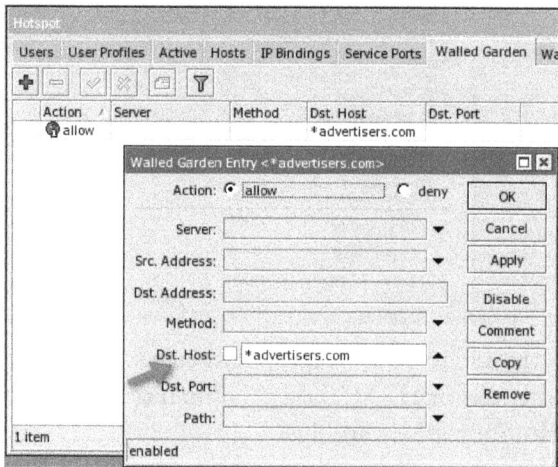

Use this example to create a splash page on which you can publish your logo or terms of service. This can also be used to make the Hotspot login page more aesthetically pleasing.

APPLICATION

Example – Creating a Custom Login Page

How to create a custom login page is probably the number one question I am asked in my classes. Obviously, the default page is basic in design and needs a major facelift for a production site, which can be done quite easily. Coding HTML is beyond the scope of this book, so I will only give you the process here.

1. Click the Files button and find the file login.html in the HotSpot folder.

(Continued on next page)

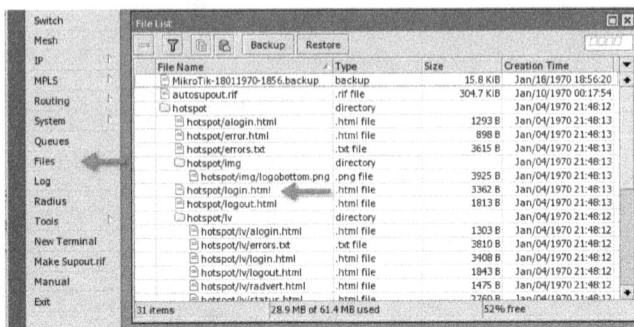

File Name	Type	Size	Creation Time
MikroTik-18011970-1856.backup	backup	15.8 KiB	Jan/18/1970 18:56:20
autosupout.rif	.rif file	304.7 KiB	Jan/10/1970 00:17:54
hotspot	directory		Jan/04/1970 21:48:12
hotspot/alogin.html	.html file	1293 B	Jan/04/1970 21:48:13
hotspot/error.html	.html file	898 B	Jan/04/1970 21:48:13
hotspot/errors.txt	.txt file	3615 B	Jan/04/1970 21:48:13
hotspot/img	directory		Jan/04/1970 21:48:13
hotspot/img/logobottom.png	.png file	3925 B	Jan/04/1970 21:48:13
hotspot/login.html	.html file	3362 B	Jan/04/1970 21:48:13
hotspot/logout.html	.html file	1813 B	Jan/04/1970 21:48:13
hotspot/lv	directory		Jan/04/1970 21:48:12
hotspot/lv/alogin.html	.html file	1303 B	Jan/04/1970 21:48:12
hotspot/lv/errors.txt	.txt file	3810 B	Jan/04/1970 21:48:12
hotspot/lv/login.html	.html file	3408 B	Jan/04/1970 21:48:12
hotspot/lv/logout.html	.html file	1843 B	Jan/04/1970 21:48:12
hotspot/lv/radvert.html	.html file	1475 B	Jan/04/1970 21:48:12
hotspot/lv/status.html	.html file	3760 B	Jan/04/1970 21:48:12

31 items   28.9 MB of 61.4 MB used   52% free

2. Drag the file to your desktop and edit it there using your favorite text or HTML editor. When done, drag it back into the HotSpot folder and test.

For Further Study: For some great login sample pages, check the forums. There is a topic there with many fine examples.

One popular tweak is to change the form field for the user name from type text to hidden, and then set the value of the user name to a shared user you have created. On the login page, users will only see a blank for a password. That way, if you simply want to restrict usage of your wireless network, you can give out the password to anyone that wants to use your wireless and not have the added complication of dealing with user names too. In login.html, look for the login form section:

```
<table width="100" style="background-color: #ffffff">
    <tr><td align="right">login</td>
            <td><input style="width: 80px" name="username" type="text" value="$(username)"/></td>
    </tr>
    <tr><td align="right">password</td>
            <td><input style="width: 80px" name="password" type="password"/></td>
    </tr>
    <tr><td> </td>
            <td><input type="submit" value="OK" /></td>
    </tr>
</table>
```

Change the text identified by the arrows to this:

```
<table width="100" style="background-color: #ffffff">
    <tr><td align="right">login</td>
            <td><input style="width: 80px" name="username" type="hidden" value="sharedguestuser"/></td>
    </tr>
    <tr><td align="right">password</td>
            <td><input style="width: 80px" name="password" type="password"/></td>
    </tr>
    <tr><td> </td>
            <td><input type="submit" value="OK" /></td>
    </tr>
</table>
```

Also note that you will need to create a user profile for the shared user and set the Shared Users setting to a higher number than one. Otherwise, only one person can log into your HotSpot using this method.

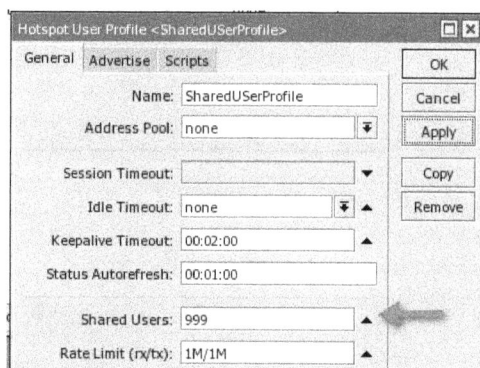

When a user loads the login page, they will only see a password blank to log in. You will obviously want to customize the page further, but that is beyond the scope of this book.

Web Proxy

Web proxy is a utility included with RouterOS that enables your router to act as a web cache and HTTP firewall. Specifically, when a user tries to visit a web page, the proxy receives the request, gets the page from the source, and returns it to the user's browser. If the proxy has previously retrieved the page and stored it to memory or disk, it will deliver it from the cache, rather than retrieve it from the actual web host. This process can significantly speed up a user's web experience and reduce overall utilization of the Internet connection. HTTPS, that is, secure, SSL encrypted web pages cannot be cached. A cached copy of your bank statement would not be helpful.

Note: Some caveats need to be stated here for the safety and proper operation of web proxy on your network. **First, web proxy can be easily misused and exploited by hackers, so it is important to only allow access to certain hosts on your network using firewall rules.** I will demonstrate those rules in the example to follow. Also, simply configuring web proxy is not enough to put it in place in your network. You will need some NAT rules to send HTTP traffic to the proxy.

Use this example to configure a web proxy that will intercept all insecure web traffic and cache it locally.

APPLICATION

Example – Configuring a Transparent Web Proxy

This configuration is referred to as transparent, because it requires no configuration by users on the network. In this scenario, NAT rules intercept all HTTP traffic and send it to the proxy.

1. First, we configure the proxy itself. Click the IP button and select Web Proxy.

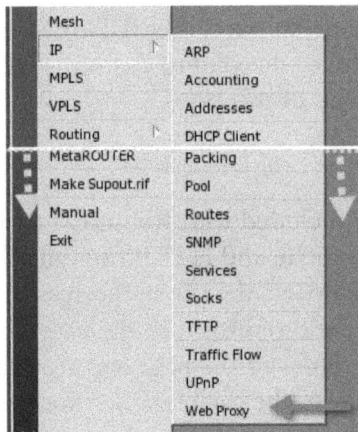

Mesh	
IP	ARP
MPLS	Accounting
VPLS	Addresses
Routing	DHCP Client
MetaROUTER	Packing
Make Supout.rif	Pool
Manual	Routes
Exit	SNMP
	Services
	Socks
	TFTP
	Traffic Flow
	UPnP
	Web Proxy

2. Check the box "Enabled" and the defaults are fine for everything else. You likely do not want to cache on the disk unless your board has an external drive. The RouterBOARD itself has

limited onboard storage and the constant writes to the storage may shorten its life.

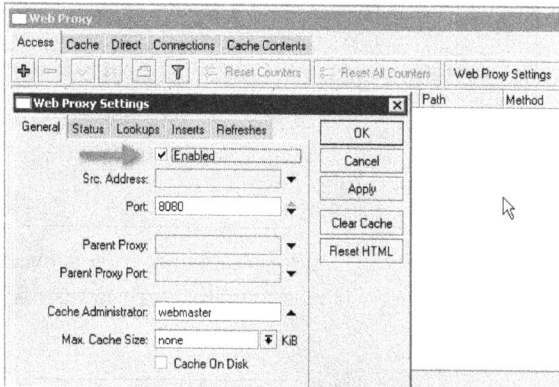

3. Next, we need a NAT rule to send all TCP port 80 (web traffic) to the proxy. This is done under IP Firewall NAT.

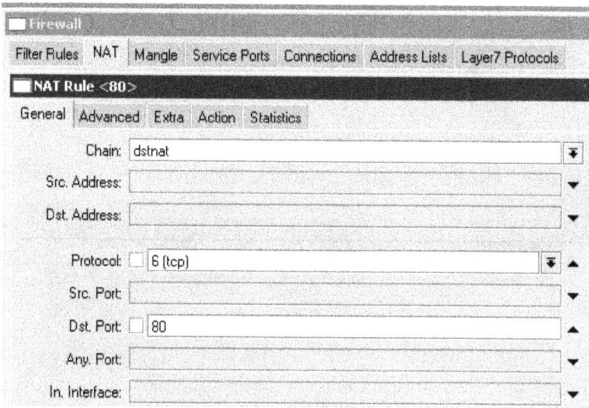

The action for the NAT rule is redirect, which as you may remember, means to intercept the traffic and process it on the router.

(Continued on next page)

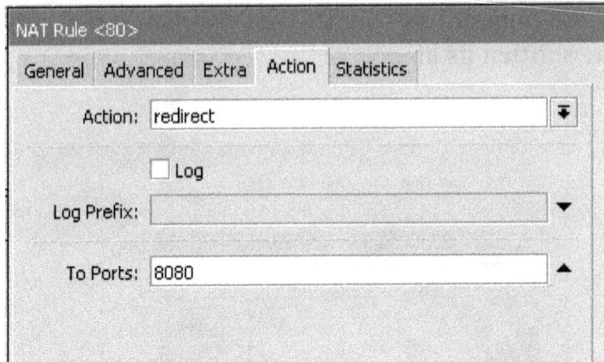

4. Finally, we need a firewall rule (actually two) to prevent unauthorized access to our proxy. This is done under IP Firewall and Filter.

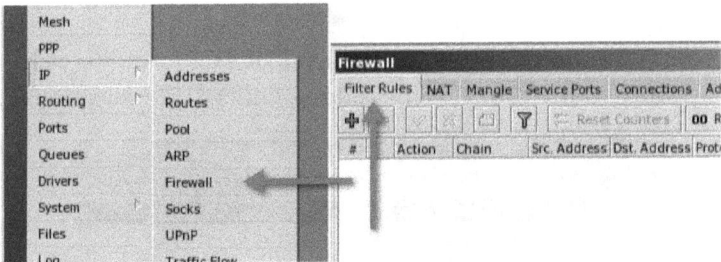

5. Create a new filter rule by clicking the plus sign.

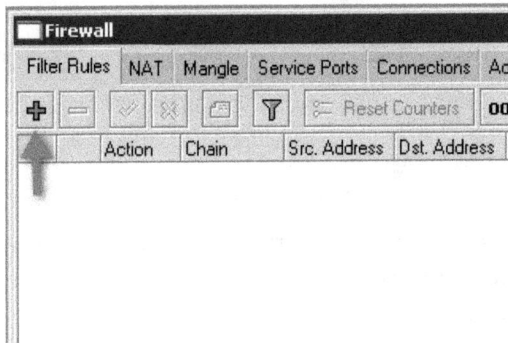

6. The Chain is input, the source address is the address of our LAN, in this case 192.168.1.0/24, the protocol is TCP, and the port is 8080.

(Continued on next page)

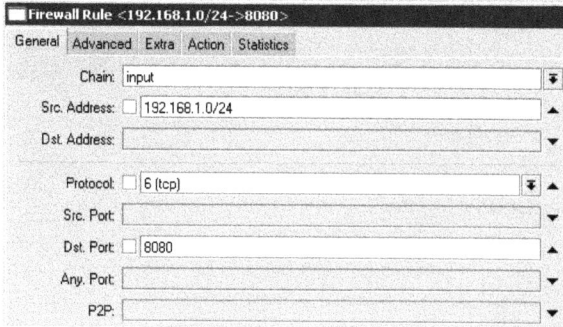

Firewall Rule <192.168.1.0/24->8080>

General | Advanced | Extra | Action | Statistics

Chain: input
Src. Address: 192.168.1.0/24
Dst. Address:

Protocol: 6 (tcp)
Src. Port:
Dst. Port: 8080
Any. Port:
P2P:

7. On the Action tab, select accept.

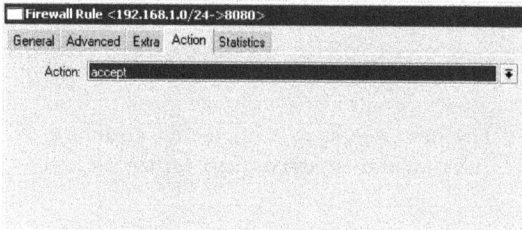

Firewall Rule <192.168.1.0/24->8080>

General | Advanced | Extra | Action | Statistics

Action: accept

8. Next, we need a rule to drop all other traffic to our proxy. Again, the Chain is input, the protocol is TCP, and the port is 8080.

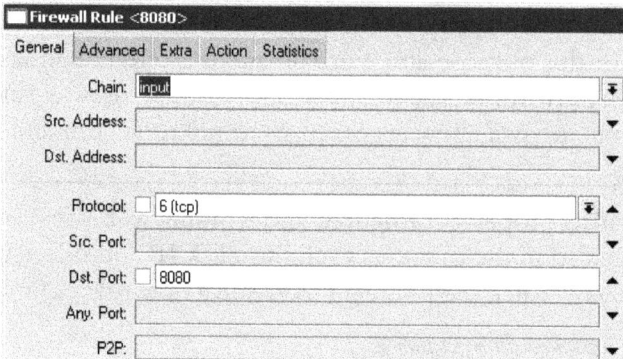

Firewall Rule <8080>

General | Advanced | Extra | Action | Statistics

Chain: input
Src. Address:
Dst. Address:

Protocol: 6 (tcp)
Src. Port:
Dst. Port: 8080
Any. Port:
P2P:

9. On the Action tab, select drop.

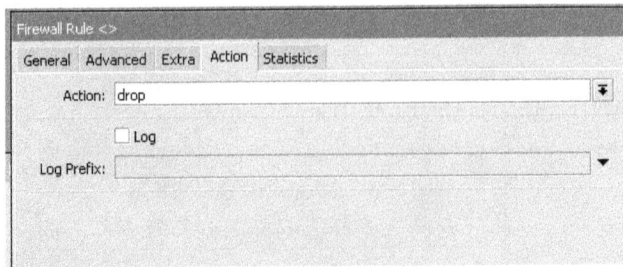

The proxy is now intercepting all port 80 requests and proxying them. In addition, the firewall is allowing access to the proxy from the LAN, but dropping proxy traffic from all other sources.

Use this example to configure the creation of web filtering rules- rules to accept or deny certain sites.

APPLICATION

Example – HTTP Firewall, Allowing or Blocking Certain Sites

With the web proxy in operation, now we can use the full power of this feature to allow, deny, or redirect certain sites. The Access rules are used for this purpose and work on an "if a certain condition exists, then perform this action" concept, just like firewall rules. In this example, we will allow access to www.mikrotik.com and block all other sites.

1. With a properly configured and working web proxy as detailed in the previous example, click IP and select Web Proxy. Click the plus sign to create a new rule.

(Continued on next page)

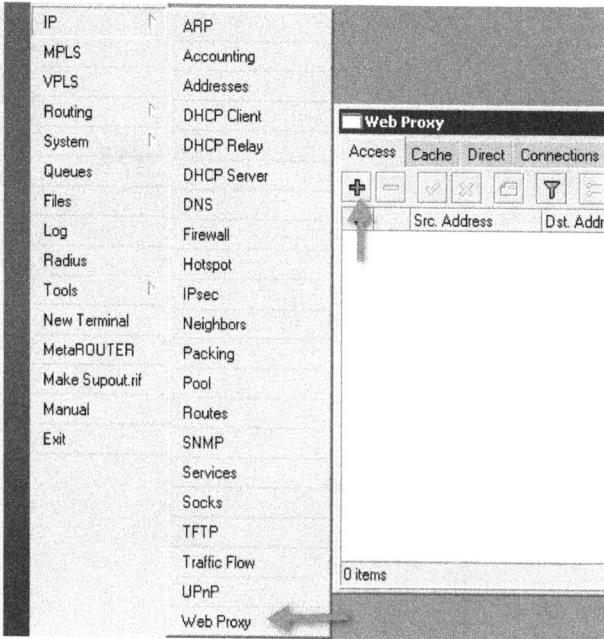

2. The Dst. Host will be the site you want to allow, in this case
   *mikrotik.com. We used the asterisk here so that
   www.mikrotik.com or just mikrotik.com would match the
   rule. Then click Ok.

   (Continued on next page)

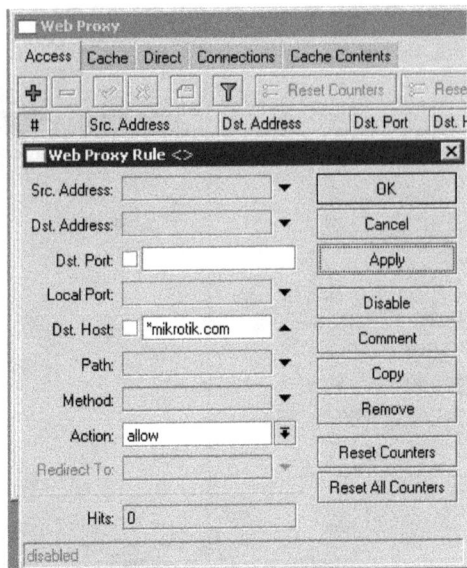

3. Next, we need a rule to block access to all other sites. Remember, rule order is always important. The new rule is created using the plus sign, and the only thing changed is the Action of "deny".

(Continued on next page)

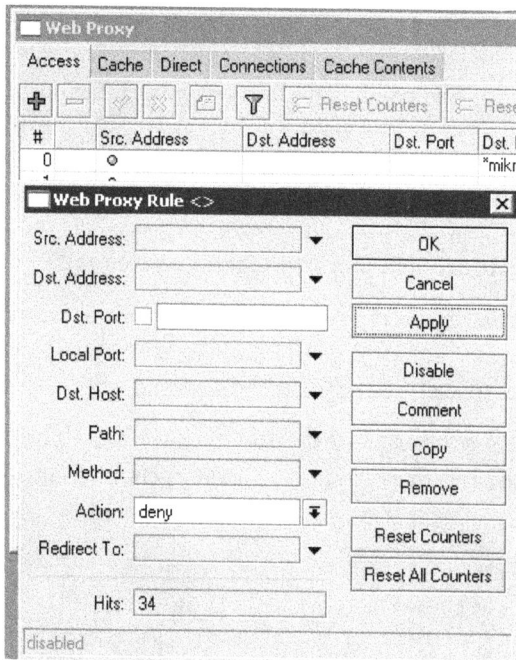

4. Users will now be able to browse mikrotik.com, but not other
   sites. The rule order should be as follows:

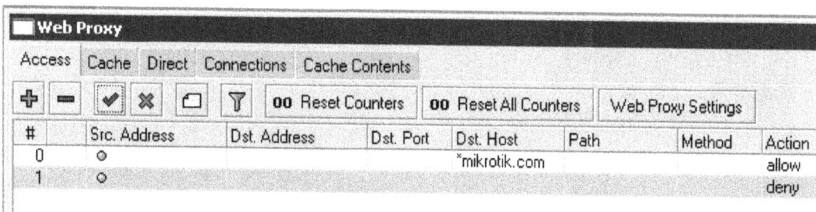

Users will now get this page in their browsers for any site except
mikrotik.com:

ERROR: Forbidden

While trying to retrieve the URL http://www.mozilla.com/en-US/firefox/central/:

- **Access Denied**

Your cache administrator is webmaster.

Generated Fri, 19 Aug 2011 15:04:07 GMT by 199.21.231.193 (Mikrotik HttpProxy)

Use this example to configure web-filtering rules to only allow certain sites.

Example – Redirect Users to Certain Sites

In this example, instead of simply blocking sites, we want to send them elsewhere. For purposes of the example, any users that try to visit yahoo.com will be redirected to google.com.

1. With a properly configured and working web proxy as detailed in the previous example, click IP and select Web Proxy. Click the plus sign to create a new rule.

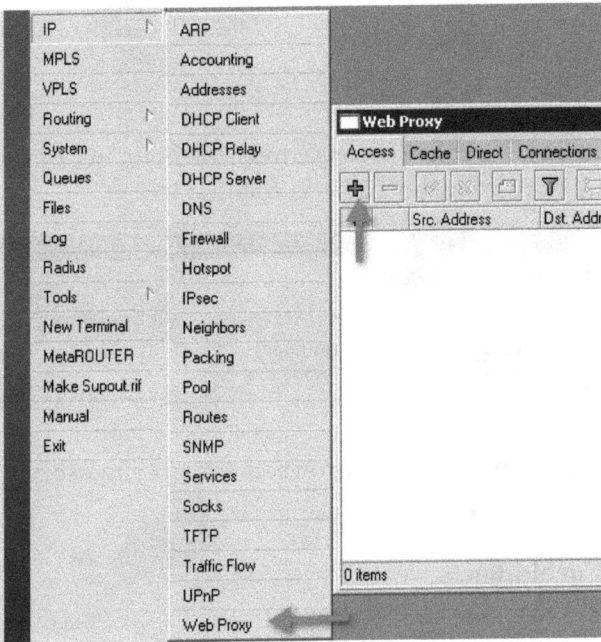

2. The Dst. Host will be the site you want to redirect, in this case *yahoo.com. In the action, select deny as before, but now we add a "redirect to" address of google.com. The net

result is that any users that browse to yahoo.com will instead get google.com.

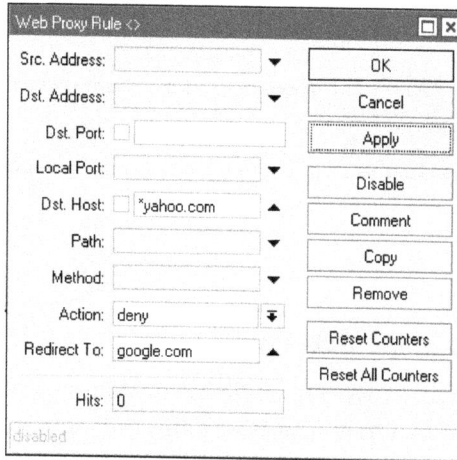

3. Now we need a rule to block access to all other sites. Remember, rule order is always important. The new rule is created using the plus sign, and the only thing changed is the Action "deny".

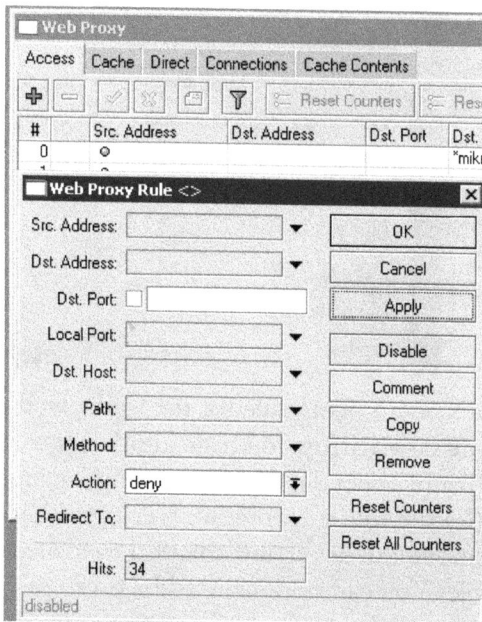

Remember to use your newly acquired knowledge "for good and not for evil". In other words, redirecting your competitor's web site to your web site, although funny, is probably not ethical.

Use this example to log all web traffic with web proxy.

APPLICATION

Example – Logging Web Traffic

The final application we will cover is combining these examples and adding the ability to track our user's Internet activity. This is done simply through the logging facility. With a properly configured web proxy, proceed as follow:

1. Click on System and select Logging.

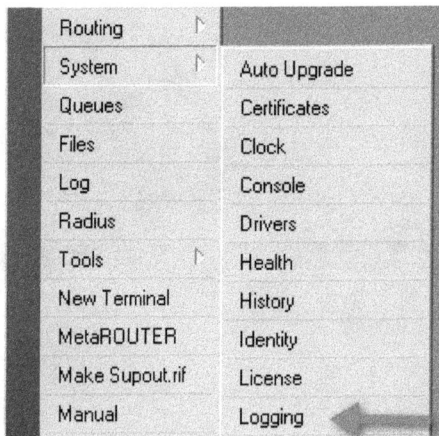

2. Create a new logging rule for the topic- web-proxy. Then click the down arrow to create another row, click the "not" box (!), and select debug. Combining logging rules like this modifies the rule such that we will log web proxy requests, but remove the debug information to make them more readable. You can optionally add a prefix, a text string that will be appended to the beginning of each line in order to

make them easier to identify in the logs. In this case, I have entered "LOGGING->" as the prefix.

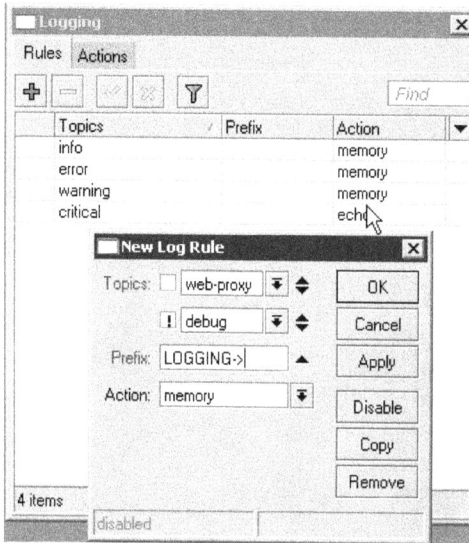

3. Logging to memory is not a good option here, except for purposes of this example. Instead, I suggest logging remotely to a syslog server.

As you can see, web proxy cannot only improve network performance and reduce Internet usage, but can also create an HTTP firewall or a permanent log of sites visited.

Use this example to send your router's logs to a remote syslog server.

APPLICATION

Example – Logging to a Remote Syslog Server

There are many syslog servers available free of charge for a diverse variety of platforms. Syslog is a server daemon (a Linux term for a service or process) that listens for logging streams from remote devices and writes them to a central log. This is a scalable way to design a network because of the ability to centrally monitor the logs of all devices and store many day's of logs with central archiving. The Dude, MikroTik's free monitoring solution, comes complete with a syslog server. To enable remote logging to a syslog server, proceed as follows:

1. Click on the System button and select logging.

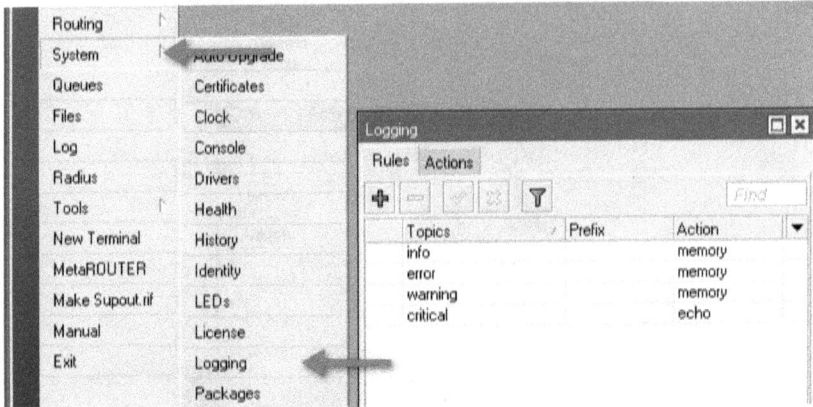

2. On the Action tab, double click the remote list item, and set the Remote Address and Port to match your syslog server.

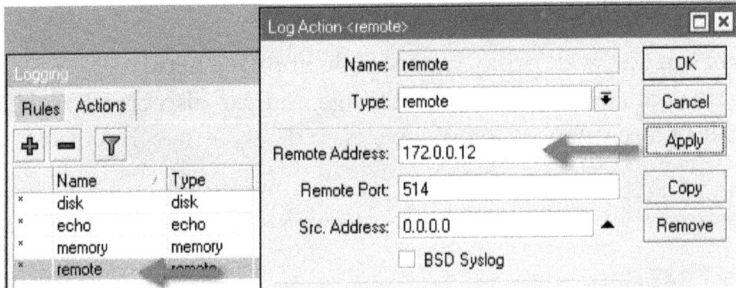

3. On the Rules tab, select the topic you want to send to the syslog server, or create a new topic. On the Action, use the pull-down box to select "remote". All logs for this topic will now be sent to the remote syslog server. Note that topics can be combined in one logging rule.

For example, we might want the web-proxy logs, but not the debug portion of those logs. The "!" symbol tells RouterOS to strip debug info from the web-proxy logs.

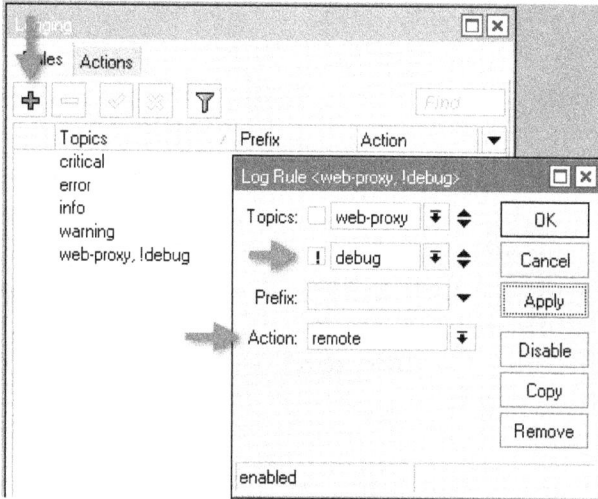

Chapter 13 – Storage

System Storage

While RouterBOARDs have limited onboard storage, RouterOS offers facilities to manage externally attached storage. After Version 6.20, the Stores command has been removed and replaced by the Disk command. Since this transition occurred after Version 6.20, but still within Version 6, the following Stores example is only applicable for versions prior to 6.20. For disk management after Version 6.20, skip to the section entitled "System Disk Management After Version 6.20" on page 231.

Use this example to configure partitions of space on the available disks.

APPLICATION

Example – Explore Stores

1. Storage is manipulated under System Stores.

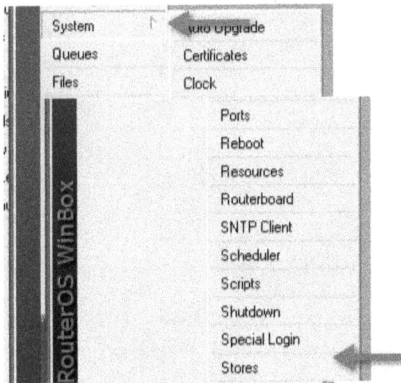

2. Clicking on the Disks tab will display the raw volumes the operating system has access to. On this tab you can check, erase, or format a drive.

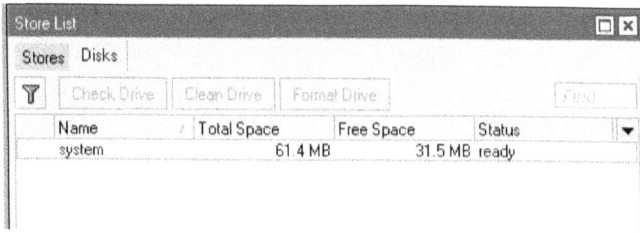

3. The Stores tab allows you to create dedicated partitions on the physical disks.

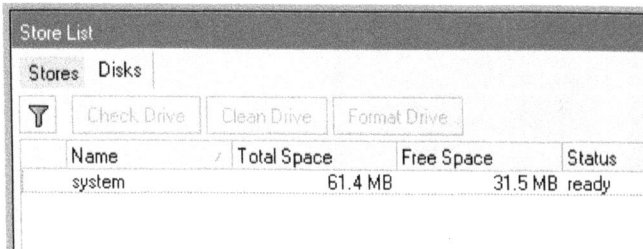

Use this example to configure the allocation of storage on the router where certain partitions are stored and enable external storage for all versions prior to Version 6.20.

Example – Create a Store

1. Click on the System button and select Stores.

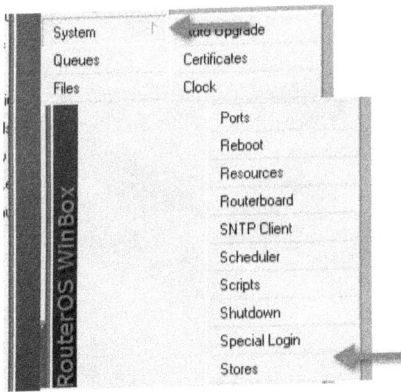

2. On the Stores tab, click the plus sign to create a new store. Name the store anything you wish, and select the type as web-proxy.

3. Select the disk on which to create the store, and check activate.

4. If the Dude is installed on the device, there will be an option in the type pull-down to create a Dude store.

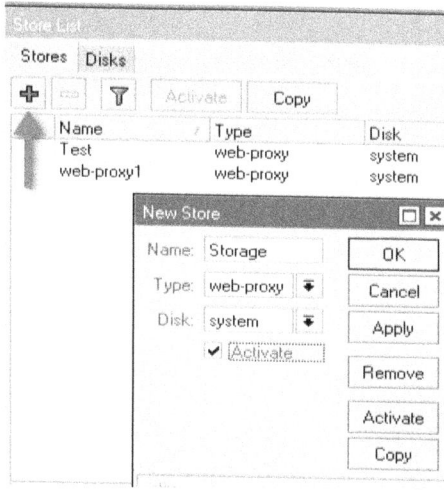

System Disk Management After Version 6.20

Following Version 6.20, information about attached storage is found in the System Disk menu. This is where you will find attached drives. Once an external drive is attached, you will be able to eject and format that drive for use by RouterOS.

The System Disk menu will list all attached storage devices, presuming that they are supported and in working condition.

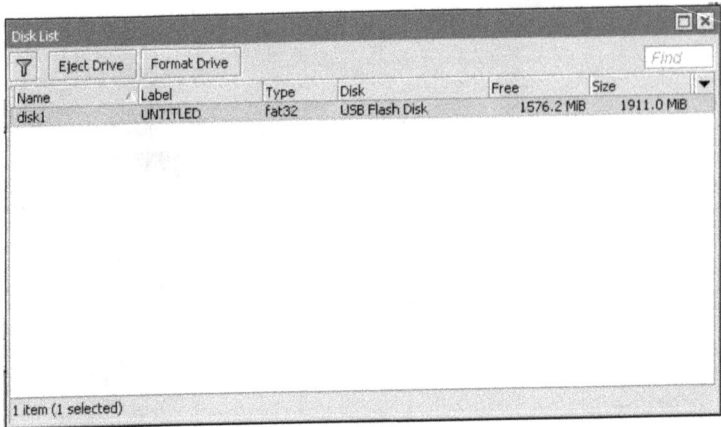

You should note that Web Proxy and User manager storage are now shown as directories in the Files menu once you enable those functions.

In order for you to use the external storage, you will need to format it.

Once it is formatted, it will appear as a folder in your Files list as Type "disk".

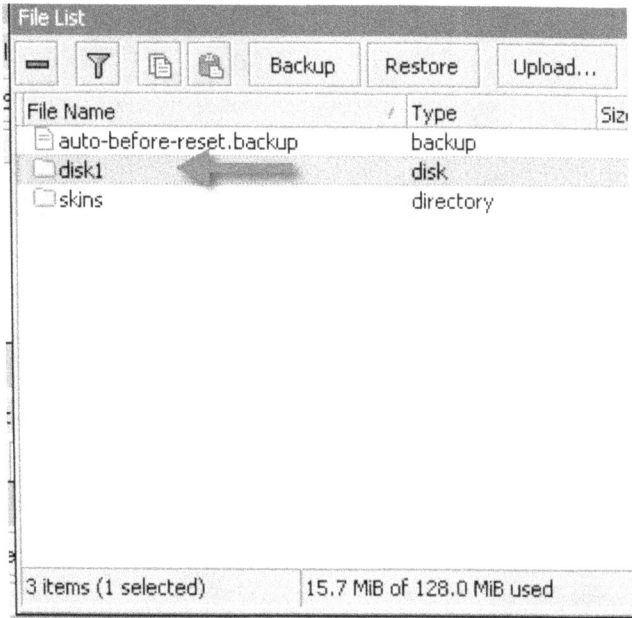

Use this example to configure the allocation of external storage on the router for all versions after 6.20.

APPLICATION

Example – Format and Connect an External Disk

1. First, find a suitable external disk drive. This can be a USB device or any other device supported by your hardware. For this example, I am using a USB thumb drive. Connect the device to the USB connector, and then click System Disk to display it.

   (Continued on next page)

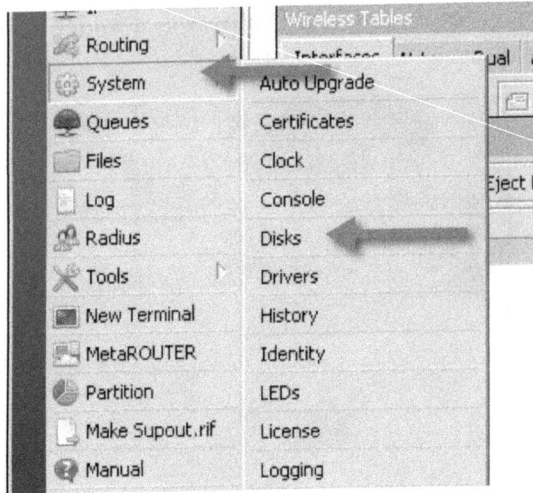

The first and only entry in this list is our external drive.

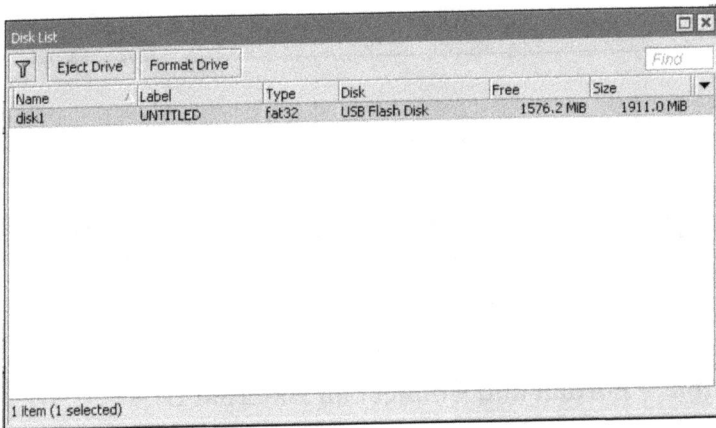

2. Next, eject the drive by clicking the Eject button. Then click the Format button to format it, thereby destroying all data on the disk. Make sure this is a disk that doesn't have important data before formatting.

(Continued on next page)

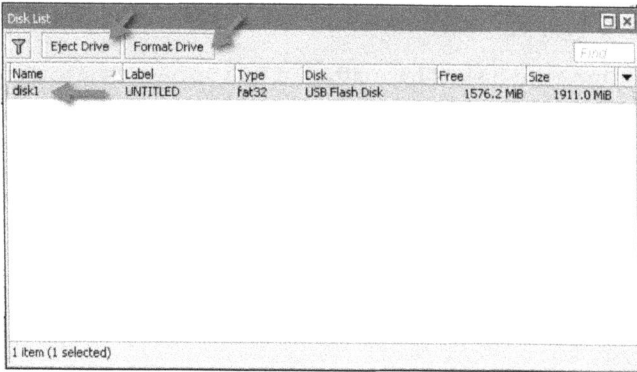

A label can also be added at this point to help identify the disk. Next, click Start to complete the formatting.

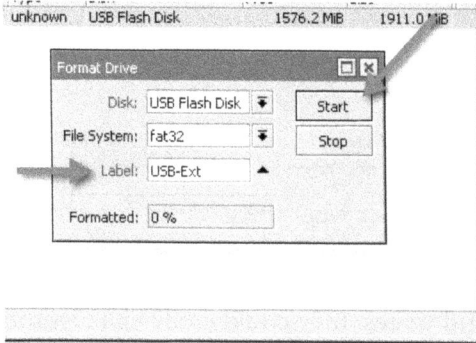

3. Once the disk is formatted, it will appear as a folder in the Files menu.

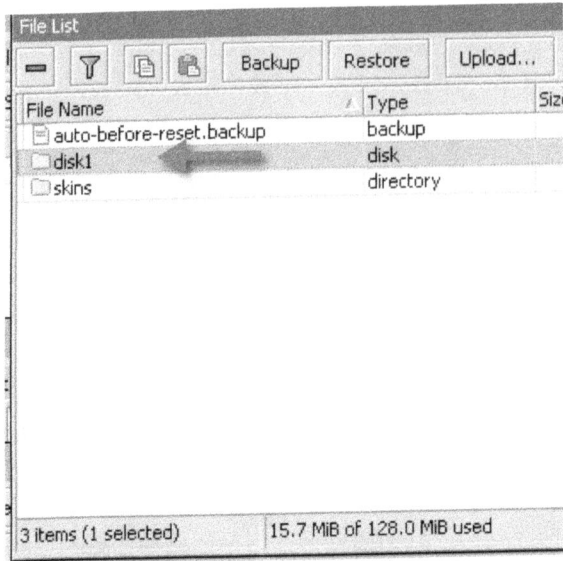

By now, you may wonder what the uses are for external storage. External storage can be used for logging, web proxy, and the Dude and User Manager database storage. Since these services rely on frequent reads and writes, they could easily exhaust the life of the onboard flash disk of a RouterBOARD, so they should only be stored on more appropriate, external storage disks.

Chapter 14 – More RouterOS Tools

When a customer asks me why they should select MikroTik over some other manufacturer, I believe my first response is "because of the tools." Within RouterOS is a vast array of tools to allow you to diagnose network functionality, some of which you have already seen such as torch, as well as tools to extend the functionality of the system. In other words, if you need a function that isn't an included feature, many times you can build that yourself through the integrated tools. The tools we will explore in this chapter are email, netwatch, ping, traceroute, and profile.

Email Tool

The email tool is a configurable function that can be used by other functions within RouterOS. For example, if you want to write a function to create a backup file and then have the router email the backup file to you, the email tool can perform this function. Scripting to conduct backups is fairly straightforward and will be discussed in the following examples; however, a complete discussion of advanced scripting would encompass another book and therefore is not included here. There are many good sources of information on RouterOS scripting on the web, especially on the MikroTik Wiki at http://wiki.mikrotik.com.

The email tool can be configured for your particular email server and then called later through a script, thereby only supplying the details needed for the email such as recipient address, subject line, and email body. If you do not configure the email tool in advance, all of the necessary information can be included when executing the command, but configuring in advance through the following example will certainly improve the usability of the email tool.

Use this example to configure the email tool, which can be used to schedule email backups of the router, email certain events, or complete other tasks that utilize the email abilities in RouterOS.

Example – Configure the Email Tool

1. To configure the email tool, click on the Tools button, and select Email.

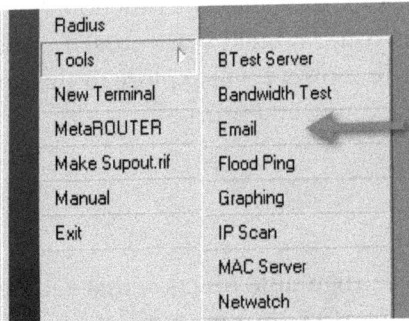

Radius	
Tools ▷	BTest Server
New Terminal	Bandwidth Test
MetaROUTER	Email
Make Supout.rif	Flood Ping
Manual	Graphing
Exit	IP Scan
	MAC Server
	Netwatch

2. In the Email Settings window, configure the settings to match your email server. User and password are only used if your server requires authentication to send email. The "From" blank is the "From" address that will be used in crafting the email.

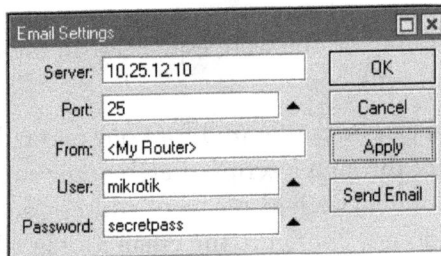

Email Settings	□ ×
Server: 10.25.12.10	OK
Port: 25 ▲	Cancel
From: <My Router>	Apply
User: mikrotik ▲	Send Email
Password: secretpass ▲	

3. The Send Email button will allow you to send a test email to confirm your settings.

(Continued on next page)

Note: The items noted with arrows above may be left at the defaults if the tool has been previously configured as in steps 1 and 2 above. If you have not configured the tool, you may provide those values here.

Use this example to create a script that will automatically create router backups and email them to someone.

APPLICATION

Example – Use a Script With the Email Tool and Scheduler to Create and Send a Backup

This example demonstrates the power of scripting and scheduler to allow unattended backups of your router that can be created and emailed to you. It is a simple process, but nonetheless a powerful and often requested script. This example uses the export function to create an ASCII backup that may be imported as a backup or edited and imported. An image backups backup can be created using a similar scheme with the appropriate commands.

239

1. Click the System button and select Scripts.

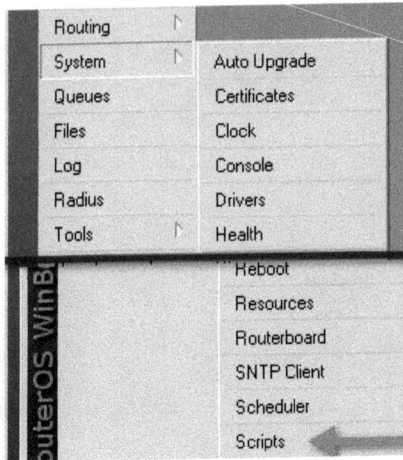

2. Click the plus sign to create a new script. Configure the script as shown.

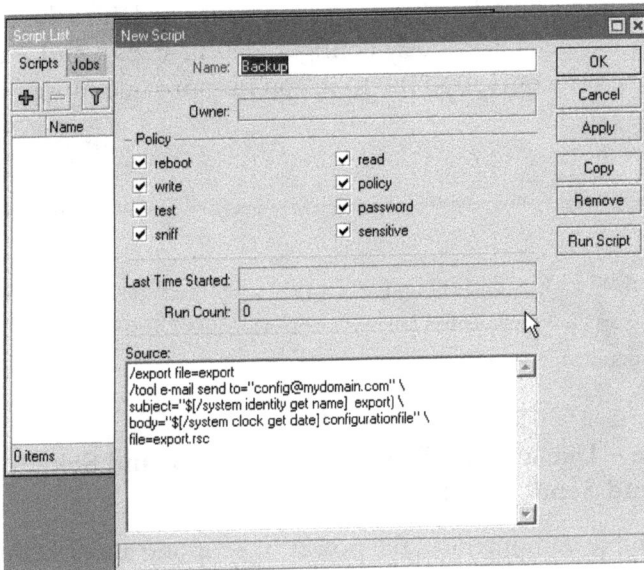

The command to create the script from the command line is:

```
/export file=export
/tool e-mail send to="config@mydomain.com" subject="$[/system identity get name]  export) \
body="$[/system clock get date] configuration file" file=export.rsc
```

3. Now, create a Scheduler job to run the script under System Scheduler.

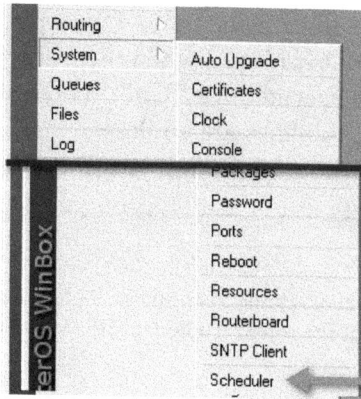

4. Click the plus sign and create a new scheduler job for our Backup script.

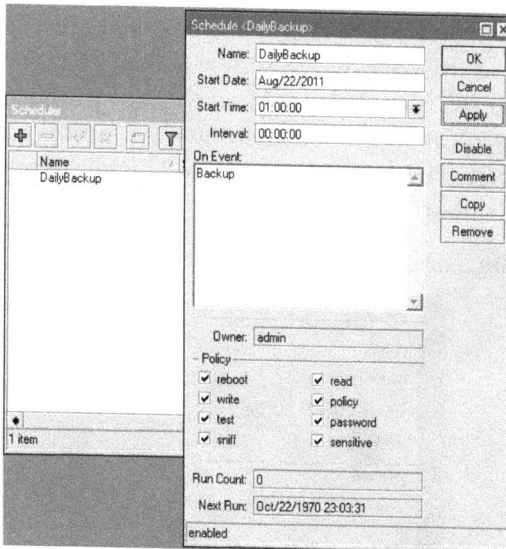

In this scheduler job, our backup script will run every day at 1:00 am and email the export file to us. Scripts are great for extending the features of RouterOS. Almost any command can be scripted to run at a predetermined time and thereby allow unattended functions that make this system really powerful. The "On Event" property can be a series of RouterOS commands like lines from a script or the name of a stored script file.

Netwatch

The purpose of Netwatch is to execute a command if a host IP address is no longer reachable by ping. Upon ping timeout, a script can be executed for "Down" and when the host responds again, another script can be executed for "Up". There are many uses for Netwatch and the possibilities are endless.

Use this example to configure a Netwatch event that can reboot the router if a certain IP address is not pingable.

APPLICATION

Example – Reboot the Router Using Netwatch

RouterOS is extremely stable. I have many times seen router uptimes of over a year, so the chance of a router needing a reboot like a Windows-based PC is really low. However, for purposes of an example, here's a way to reboot the router if it is no longer able to ping the Internet. The command executed by Netwatch is entirely up to you. Again, this is only an example.

1. Click the Tools button and select Netwatch.

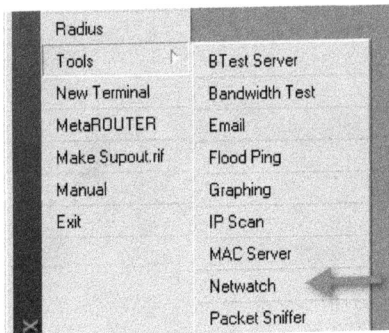

Radius	
Tools	BTest Server
New Terminal	Bandwidth Test
MetaROUTER	Email
Make Supout.rif	Flood Ping
Manual	Graphing
Exit	IP Scan
	MAC Server
	Netwatch
	Packet Sniffer

2. Click the plus sign to create a new Netwatch. Enter the IP address of the host to be pinged.

(Continued on next page)

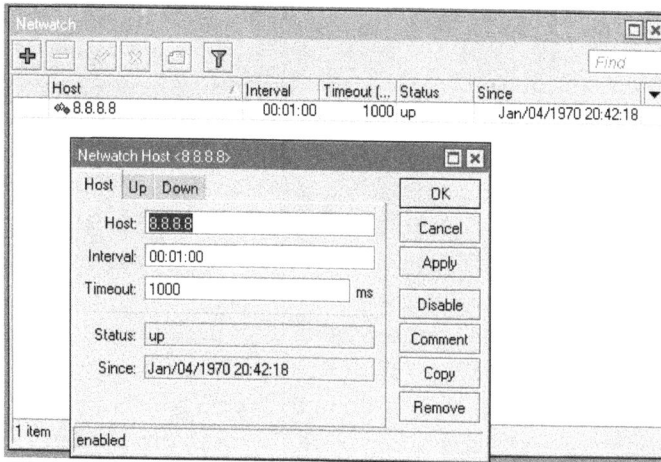

3. On the Down tab, enter the command to be executed.

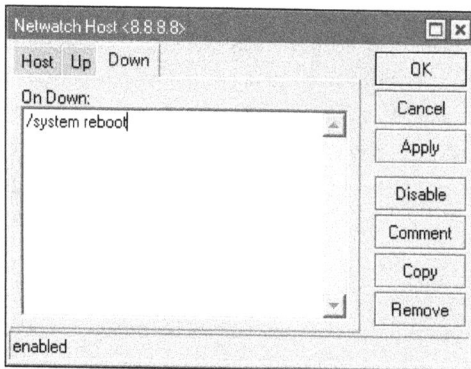

When this host is no longer reachable, the router will be rebooted.

Ping

Ping is a utility to test the reachability of a network host. It is a really basic tool and the most often used tool. I typically invoke ping from the command line out of habit, but it is also available in WinBox under Tools and Ping.

Traceroute

Traceroute is a tool to trace the path an IP packet passes through to get from source to destination. It works by using the TTL (Time To Live) function of a packet. If you aren't already familiar with TTL, whenever a router receives a packet, it looks at the TTL value to determine whether it needs to handle the packet. If the TTL is greater than 1, it routes the packet according to its routing table. If the TTL is equal to one, the router drops the packet. The reason for this is before sending the packet on its way, the router decreases the TTL by one as a way to say, "I am done with this packet." It then sends it down the pipe. This is done to keep a packet from bouncing around the network forever in case of a routing problem in a network. If the packet entering the router has a TTL of one, the router knows it will be reducing it to zero, so it drops the packet.

Traceroute works by increasing the TTL value of each successive set of packets sent. The first set of packets sent has a TTL value of one, and traceroute knows they will not be forwarded by the first router. The next set has a TTL value of two so that the second router they enter will send the error reply. This continues until the destination host receives the packets and returns an ICMP Echo Reply message. Traceroute uses the returned ICMP messages to produce a list of routers that the packets have traversed. The timestamp values returned for each router along the path are the delay (also known as latency) values, typically measured in milliseconds for each packet. [4]

Understanding now how traceroute works, the application for traceroute is to learn the path a packet takes from source to destination. Traceroute can be invoked from the command line or by clicking the Tools button and selecting Traceroute.

Profile

Profile, or Profiler as it is sometimes called, is a tool to display CPU usage and allocation of CPU resources across all processes that are consuming resources.

There are no configurable options in profiler, but it is a great diagnostic tool for determining what is consuming system CPU resources.

Name	Usage
bridging	1.0
ethernet	0.0
idle	92.5
management	0.0
profiling	1.5
queuing	0.5
unclassified	0.5
wireless	4.0

Chapter 15 – Wireless

Wireless is a subject that is really a discipline all of its own, yet combines two very different disciplines into one. Because of that complexity and the lack of control over the environment in which wireless networks are operated, it is probably one of the most challenging fields with which I have ever been involved. Wireless combines standard packet based networking with radio frequency engineering, so to be a wireless master, you really need to be experienced in both areas.

Wireless Theory

This book is about RouterOS, but a certain, basic understanding of wireless theory is necessary to ensure the comprehension of what the different settings and features really mean. Specifically, the IEEE 802.11 is a set of standards for implementing Wireless Local Area Network (WLAN) communication in the 2.4, 3.6, and 5 GHz frequency spectrums. They were created and are maintained by the IEEE LAN/MAN Standards Committee. The base version of this standard has had several amendments as the technology has evolved over the years and provides the basis for wireless networking products using the Wi-Fi band.

The 802.11 standards employ a series of over-the-air modulation techniques using the same basic protocol. The most common standards are referred to as 802.11a, 802.11b, 802.11g, 802.11n, and the newest, 802.11ac. The spectrum available for 802.11 networking varies by country and there are additional restrictions on power output for various configurations. The reader is encouraged to contact their local regulatory authorities to ensure they are operating in accordance with local regulations.

802.11a

The 802.11a standard operates on 5 GHz and supports a maximum data rate of 54 Mbits/s with a real life throughput of around 25 Mbits/s. There is a variation of 802.11a called "turbo mode", which is capable of 108 Mbits/s maximum data rate using 40 MHz channels instead of the standard 20 MHz channels. The 802.11a standard uses a modulation technique referred to as OFDM (Orthogonal Frequency Division Multiplexing).

802.11b

The oldest standard is 802.11b, which operates on 2.4 GHz, has a maximum data rate of 11 Mbits/s, and contains a real life throughput of about 5 Mbits/s. 802.11b suffers from massive interference problems in our "everything is wireless" world. The 802.11b standard uses a modulation technique referred to as DSSS (Direct Sequence Spread Spectrum).

802.11g

IEEE 802.11g extends the operation of 802.11b, which operates on 2.4 GHz by increasing the maximum data rate to 54 Mbits/s and typically achieves a real-life throughput of about 25 Mbits/s. However, 802.11g also suffers from interference. Similar to 802.11a, 802.11g uses a modulation technique referred to as OFDM (Orthogonal Frequency Division Multiplexing).

802.11n

IEEE 802.11n further extends the operation of 802.11g and 802.11a by increasing throughput, reach and reliability through the use of numerous protocol enhancements. At the time of this writing, these have only partially been implemented in commodity devices. Among these enhancements, the most visible improvement comes through multiple streams or chains of data transmitted between devices, which require multiple antennas, or at the least dual polarity antennas on each end, greatly improving throughput. MIMO (Multiple Input Multiple Output) is the technology that makes this possible. 802.11n operates on either 2.4 or 5 GHz and supports data rates up to 600 Mbits/s.

802.11ac

IEEE 802.11ac pushes the improvements of 802.11n even farther by adding new technologies such as extended channels bonding, mandatory 80 MHz channel bandwidth capability for station devices, and more MIMO spatial streams. Like the standards that came before it, the goal is always improved speeds and dependability in noisy environments. The ac protocol delivers that with theoretical data rates up to 867 Mbps.

Channelization – 2.4 GHz 802.11b/g/n

Wireless devices suffer most from interference. Interference is the phenomenon that occurs when two wireless devices in close proximity are able to sufficiently receive or "hear" each other's transmissions due to other transmissions on the same or near frequencies. The best analogy of this is a crowded room. When everyone is talking at the same time, it is difficult to discern whom the speaker is, much less what they are saying. The same happens when many wireless devices are all trying to communicate at the same time on the same, or nearly the same, frequencies.

In the 2.4 GHz spectrum, there are many devices that share a very small section of the unlicensed frequencies. Therefore, noise or interference abounds. The standard channel width for 802.11 is 20 MHz and the U.S.A has 11 channels, but not enough spectrum for those channels to co-exist side by side, so they overlap. With the available spectrum, we can only concurrently use three channels without overlap. By overlap, I mean that the center frequency of the channel and the 11 MHz of spectrum that is used on either side crosses over the adjacent channels. For example, channel 1 on 802.11b, 20 MHz wide, stretches up to overlap with channel 2 and 3. Channel 6 is the next available, non-overlapping channel. Because of this, if you are using 802.11b with multiple devices, the only available channels are 1, 6, and 11. Any other combination of channels would cause your devices to interfere with themselves. Cordless household phones use these same frequencies.

Consider the following diagram:

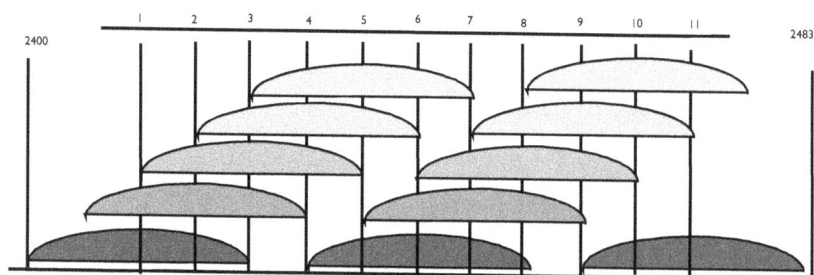

Figure 15 - 802.11 b/g Channels, 2.4 GHz [1]

As you can see, the channels centered on 1, 6, and 11 do not touch or overlap, therefore they do not create interference with each other. On the other hand, channels 1 and 2 clearly overlap, thereby causing interference and poor performance. In some cases, the interference can cause the inability for two devices to communicate with each other at all. The same is true for any 802.11 device operating on the 2.4GHz band using the full channel width (typically 20-22 MHz wide).

Channelization – 5 GHz 802.11a/n/ac

The 5 GHz spectrum offers much more promise, because even if you are operating with standard 20 MHz channels, all channels are usable since they do not overlap like 802.11b.

This book is not meant to be a guide to the legality of operating in any frequency band, but instead, I feel it is important to understand the rules, so I will offer a summary. The FCC recently changed the portion of the Federal Code that governs unlicensed wireless operations, specifically with respect to the 5Ghz devices. In 47 C.F.R. §15.5(b), typically referred to as "Part 15", the most significant changes were as follows:

1. Remove the indoor restriction for 5.15 – 5.25 GHz.

2. Modifications to requirements for devices operating in (U-NII-1) 5.25-5.35 GHz and (U-NII-2) 5.47-5.725 GHz with regard to Dynamic Frequency Selection (DFS).

3. The Commission grandfathered U-NII devices certified under old standards that are already installed for "the life of the equipment".

At the time of the writing of this book, a summary of these new changes was present on the FCC web site at https://apps.fcc.gov/edocs_public/attachmatch/DA-15-575A1_Rcd.pdf .

Portions of the new law were immediately contested by manufacturers, and some phase in periods and delays were imposed.

The 5GHz band is divided up into several segments:

802.11a/n/ac Channels

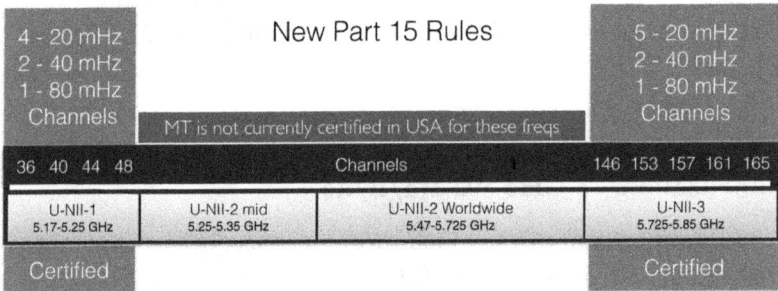

4 - 20 mHz 2 - 40 mHz 1 - 80 mHz Channels	New Part 15 Rules		5 - 20 mHz 2 - 40 mHz 1 - 80 mHz Channels
	MT is not currently certified in USA for these freqs		
36 40 44 48	Channels	146 153 157 161 165	
U-NII-1 5.17-5.25 GHz	U-NII-2 mid 5.25-5.35 GHz	U-NII-2 Worldwide 5.47-5.725 GHz	U-NII-3 5.725-5.85 GHz
Certified			Certified

Figure 16 - 5.8 GHz Channels

These segments are named U-NII 1, 2 ,and 3. The U-NII-3 band is the one with the least amount of restrictions in the USA, and therefore most manufacturers target that band.

All MikroTik wireless devices certified before January 2016 were certified only for U-NII-3, even though the other frequencies appear in the wireless device channels. As they began producing new devices, the new ones are being certified under the new Part 15 rules, thereby opening up the U-NII-1 band. MikroTik at the time of the writing of this books says, "we will continue certifying new products under the new Part 15 rules, and gradually re-certify legacy products under the new rules."

The takeaway point here is to be aware of the regulations in your area, and consult the manufacturer's certification documents before using any frequency.

Small Channels

The Atheros chipset (used in many WiFi radios) brought an enhancement to the 802.11 protocol in the form of small channels or half and one quarter channels. By reducing the size of the channel, the overlap is reduced or eliminated, and many more channels are available.

The disadvantage of small channels is compatibility with products that don't support this feature and the reduced aggregate throughput available to devices using the smaller channels.

As a rule of thumb, if a link is capable of passing 25 Mbits/sec with 20 MHz channels, expect half of that for 10 MHz channels and one-fourth for 5 MHz channels.

Small channels in a service provider scenario, such as a WISP (Wireless Internet Service Provider), offer some additional advantages, including higher power density (goes farther), lower noise floor (better throughput), and better interference avoidance with the only drawback being reduced aggregate throughput. I would certainly make the argument for using small channels, keeping access point user numbers low, and making cells as small as possible. The result will be better quality networks and less interference.

Bridged Versus Routed Access Points and Stations

There are two primary modes of operation for wireless devices: bridged and routed. Although the actual configuration of their wireless components is very similar, there are differences that need to be explained and understood.

Routed

A routed device consists of multiple interfaces, in this case wired and wireless. There is no Layer 2 connection between these interfaces in a routed device, meaning that for traffic to pass between the interfaces, the device must follow routing rules to determine packet flow. All packets must follow the routing rules, firewall rules, and various queue rules. By default, all RouterOS devices operate in routed mode unless you create bridges and bridge ports together.

Bridged

A bridged device consists again of multiple interfaces, but one or all of these physical interfaces are joined together into a logical interface called a bridge. The bridge interface joins the physical devices at Layer 2, such that any packets entering one interface pass freely out the other interface on the bridge (except in the case of a bridge firewall). In the configuration of a wireless interface joined to an Ethernet interface, think of a bridged device as a media adapter, joining two dissimilar media together.

Bridges are a useful configuration, especially with respect to wireless, however they must be used with caution, because it is very easy to create a network with bridges that is not scalable and quickly outgrows itself. As a general rule of thumb, never connect two bridged devices together, either directly or with a switch. Instead, separate bridged links with routers. Routers block broadcast traffic and allow you to use bridged devices while building a scalable network.

The examples that follow later in this chapter can each be configured in succession to build a complete wireless AP solution.

Configure an Access Point (PtMP) With DHCP Server

PtMP (Point to Multi Point) is a phrase that refers to the configuration of a wireless access point that can support multiple wireless stations. One common way to configure such an access point is a routed configuration with DHCP server. This example combines several different concepts and ties them all together. For this reason, it introduces new concepts as well as cross-references to other sections of this book, tying them all together.

Use this example to configure a wireless interface to act as an Access Point for one or more station devices.

APPLICATION

Example - Initial Wireless Interface Configuration

1. Begin by configuring the wireless adapter on the device. This is done by clicking the Wireless button and double

clicking the wireless interface to be configured, typically wlan1.

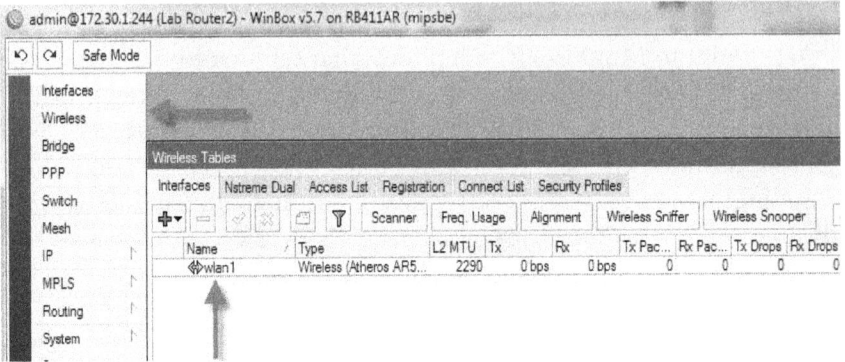

2. On the wireless tab, select the wireless mode as "ap bridge".

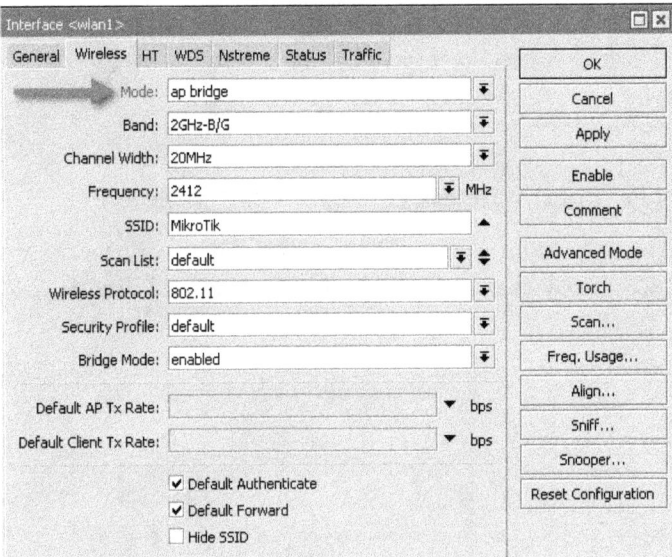

3. Next, select the band on which you are going to operate. For standard wireless clients such as laptops, you can use "2.4GHz-B/G" or "2.4GHz-B/G/N" if your wireless adapters support 802.11n.

(Continued on next page)

Interface <wlan1>

General Wireless HT WDS Nstreme Status Traffic

Mode:	ap bridge	
Band:	2GHz-B/G	
Channel Width:	20MHz	
Frequency:	2412	MHz
SSID:	MikroTik	
Scan List:	default	
Wireless Protocol:	802.11	
Security Profile:	default	
Bridge Mode:	enabled	
Default AP Tx Rate:		bps
Default Client Tx Rate:		bps

☑ Default Authenticate
☑ Default Forward
☐ Hide SSID

OK
Cancel
Apply
Enable
Comment
Advanced Mode
Torch
Scan...
Freq. Usage...
Align...
Sniff...
Snooper...
Reset Configuration

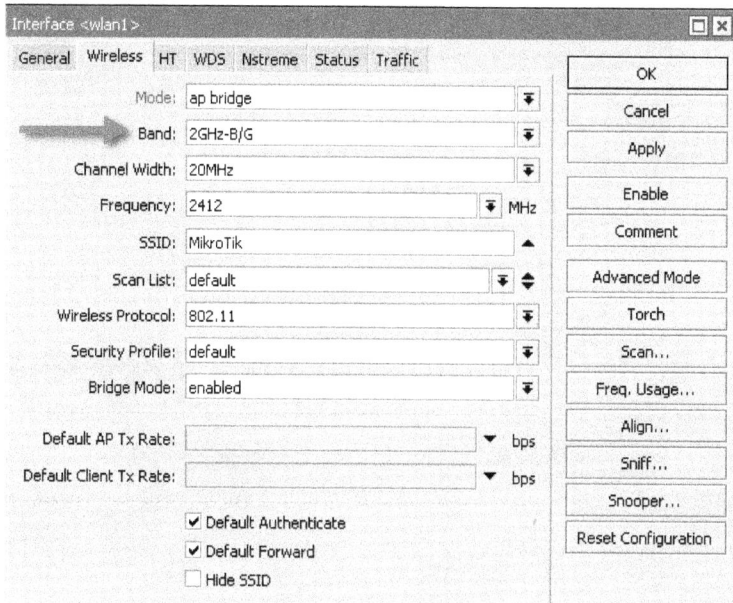

4. The next step is to select the frequency. Taking into account the limitations previously described for 2.4 GHz, you should first find a free frequency by clicking the Freq. Usage button. This will scan for available frequencies.

(Continued on next page)

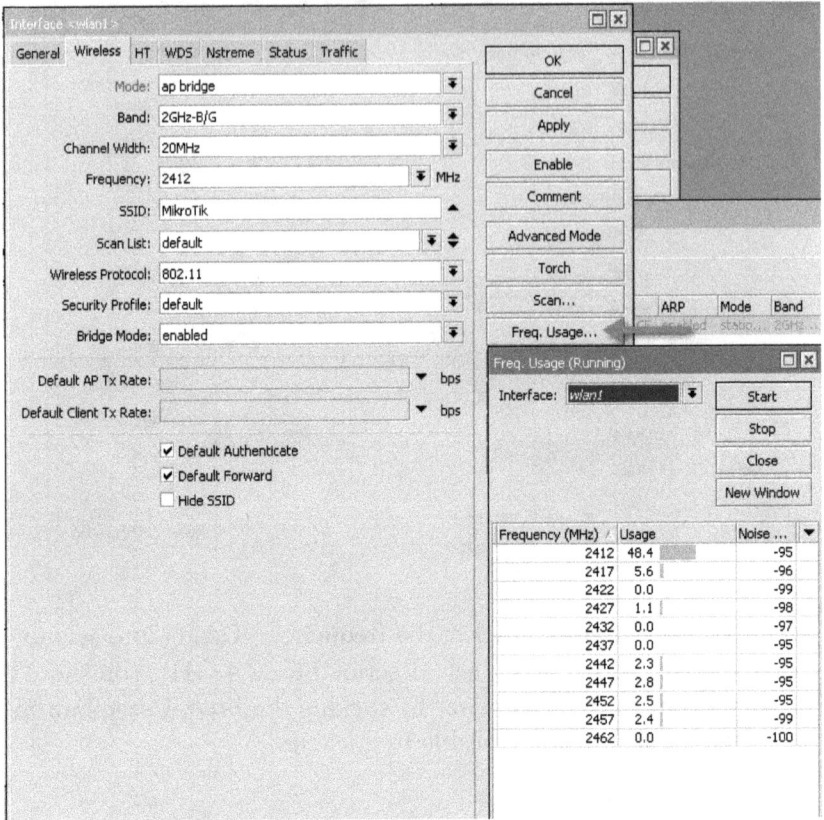

Interface <wlan1>

General Wireless HT WDS Nstreme Status Traffic

Mode:	ap bridge
Band:	2GHz-B/G
Channel Width:	20MHz
Frequency:	2412 MHz
SSID:	MikroTik
Scan List:	default
Wireless Protocol:	802.11
Security Profile:	default
Bridge Mode:	enabled
Default AP Tx Rate:	bps
Default Client Tx Rate:	bps

☑ Default Authenticate
☑ Default Forward
☐ Hide SSID

OK
Cancel
Apply
Enable
Comment
Advanced Mode
Torch
Scan...
Freq. Usage...

ARP Mode Band

Freq. Usage (Running)

Interface: wlan1

Start
Stop
Close
New Window

Frequency (MHz)	Usage	Noise ...
2412	48.4	-95
2417	5.6	-96
2422	0.0	-99
2427	1.1	-98
2432	0.0	-97
2437	0.0	-95
2442	2.3	-95
2447	2.8	-95
2452	2.5	-95
2457	2.4	-99
2462	0.0	-100

5. Once you have decided on an available frequency, select it using the Frequency selector. Note that if there are no other access points in the area, it is best to stick with channels 1, 6, or 11, and pick your channels to not cause interference between your own access points. If there are other AP's in the area outside your control, you will likely need to pick a free channel by using the Frequency Usage tool as described above.

6. Next, decide on the SSID or Service Set Identifier, the text string that will be broadcast to identify your network.

(Continued on next page)

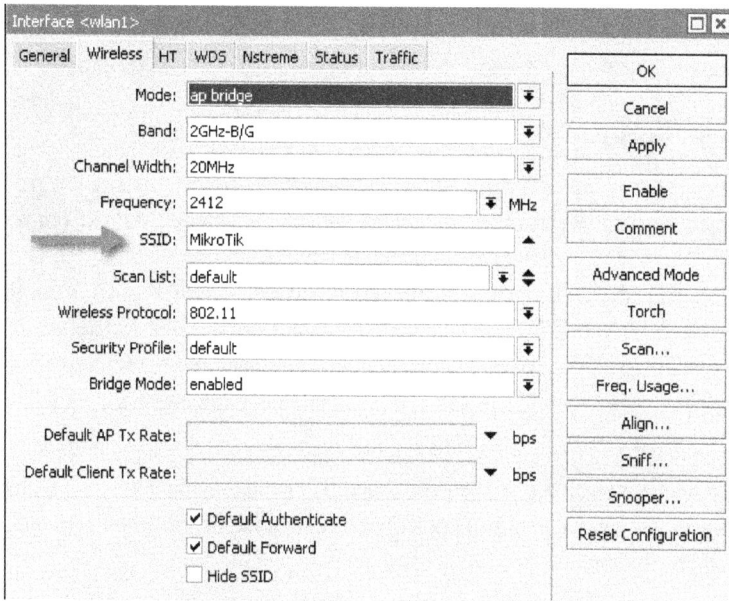

7. Finally, set the Wireless Protocol to 802.11 to support standard, non-RouterOS as well as RouterOS stations.

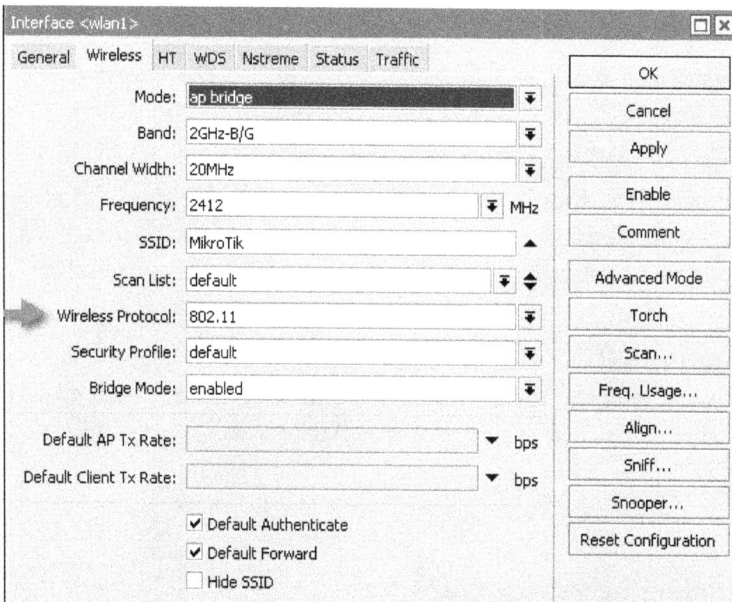

Next comes security. RouterOS supports several wireless security protocols and the most common are WEP (Wired Equivalency Privacy) and WPA2 (Wi-Fi Protected Access). WEP is antiquated and not very secure, yet it is supported for legacy applications. Wireless Security Profiles are explained beginning on page 264.

Wireless Security

I always tell my classes that security is not simply a button we push and then walk away feeling safe and secure. Instead, we go for a layered approach, understanding that the more layers we add, the more secure the network will be. In addition, we stress that each layer of security has a cost and that cost is paid in performance and maintainability. The more complex the security, that is, the more layers, the more work it is for a potential hacker to get in, and the more work it is for us to maintain.

In this book, we discuss several ways to secure your wireless network and again, we opt for a layered approach. The layers that can be applied easily are:

MAC Filtering – Controlling access at the MAC layer. If the station can't associate, it can't gain access. MAC filtering can be circumvented by spoofing the MAC address of an allowed station, so it is not very effective for seasoned hackers.

Encryption – WEP, WPA, and WPA2 are some encryption protocols supported in RouterOS. By encrypting the data transmission, the network is greatly fortified.

Proprietary Protocols – using Nstreme or NV2 is a way to control access to the network. The hacker will have to use RouterOS to gain access, and statistically, this helps improve our odds of resisting attack.

Hiding the SSID – A very basic approach, nevertheless it is effective in keeping the existence of your wireless network away from most unsophisticated users, but true hackers will not even be slowed down.

Controlling Access with MAC Lists

The most basic layer of security we can add is MAC filtering, that is, controlling access based upon the MAC address of the station trying to associate with us or controlling which access points our station can associate with. This can be done on both the access point and the station. MAC filtering on an access point is done with "Access Lists". On a station, it is done with "Connect Lists".

There is a global setting on the wireless interface that can influence the behavior of MAC filtering. It can be found on the wireless tab called "Default Authenticate". This setting is enabled by default and basically tells the wireless interface to associate with any station or access point it can without restriction. If you uncheck "Default Authenticate", stations will only be able to associate with AP's in their connect list and will only allow association from stations in their access lists.

Use this example to create an access list on an AP that will prevent any unknown MAC addresses from associating with the AP.

APPLICATION

Example – Create an Access List on an AP

1. To create an access list on an access point, click on the Wireless button and select the Access List tab.

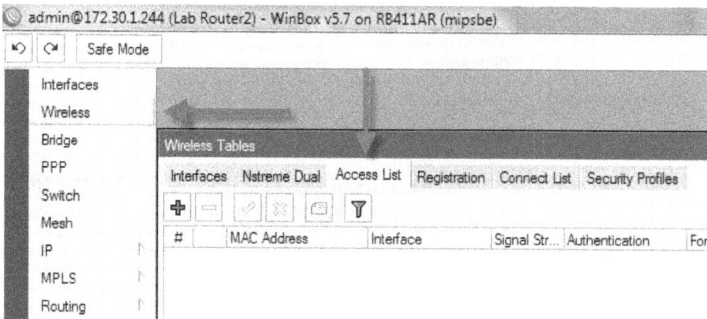

2. Click the plus sign to add an access list entry for a station, and click OK.

The only required information here is the MAC address.

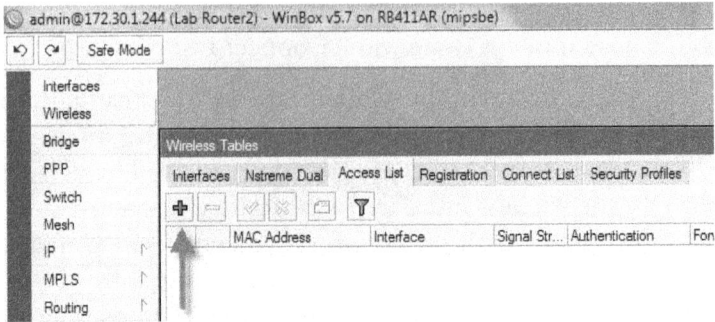

3. An easier method is to click on the Registration tab, right click an already associated station, and pick the menu item "Copy to Access List". This assumes you have the "Default Authenticate" checked on the AP, allowing the station to associate. Once the station is added to the access list, you can uncheck "Default Authenticate".

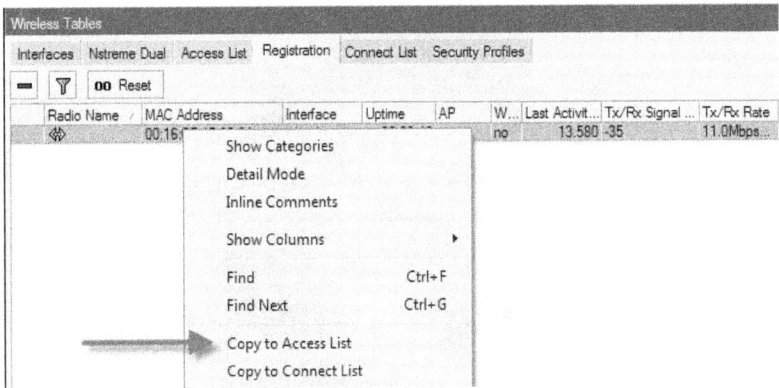

4. An alternative method to using the "Default Authenticate" method is to create a "drop rule" in the access list. Since the rules are processed in order, the last rule can be a new rule that does not specify the MAC address and has Authentication unchecked. By placing this rule at the bottom of your list, only the stations specified in the access list will be allowed to associate. Note that the access list entries take precedence over the global setting of "Default Authenticate" on the interface.

(Continued on next page)

Wireless Tables						
Interfaces	Nstreme Dual	Access List	Registration	Connect List	Security Profiles	
#	MAC Address	Interface		Signal Str...	Authentication	Forwarding
0	00:A0:C9:14:C8:29	all		-120..120	yes	yes
1	00:A0:C9:14:C8:30	all		-120..120	yes	yes
2		all		-120..120	no	yes

Use this example to create a connect list that will only allow a station to associate with known AP's.

APPLICATION

Example – Create a Connect List on a Station

Why would a station need a connect list? Association to an access point is based on the setting of the SSID. If you do not specify an SSID, the station will connect to the strongest AP it sees. Even if you do specify an SSID, and some malicious person wants to create trouble for you, they can configure the same SSID. If their signal is stronger, your station may "jump" to their AP. That is likely a bad thing. To prevent this action or to allow your station to connect to several different SSID's, you can use connect lists. Much like the access list, the connect lists is arranged in a hierarchical manner with the most preferred AP's at the top. If the "Default Authenticate" setting is unchecked, or if you use a drop rule, your device will only associate with the intended AP, the one in the connect list.

1. To create a connect list on a station, click on the Wireless button, and select the Connect List tab.

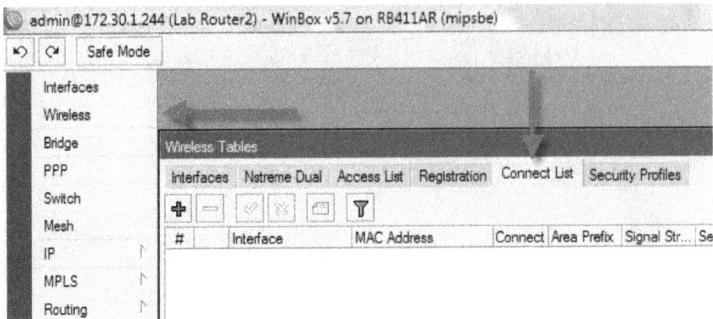

2. Click the plus sign to add a connect list entry, specify the SSID and/or MAC address, and click OK.

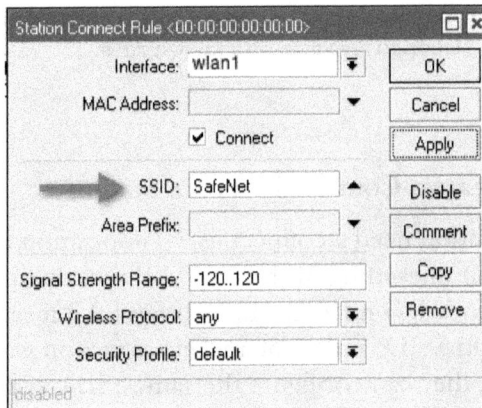

3. An easier method is to click on the Registration tab, right click on an already associated AP, and pick the menu item "Copy to Connect List".

Once the entry is copied to the connect list, you can uncheck "Default Authenticate".

(Continued on next page)

Wireless Tables

Interfaces | Nstreme Dual | Access List | Registration | Connect List | Security Profiles

Radio Name	MAC Address	Interface	Uptime	AP	W...	Last Activit...	Tx/Rx Signal ...	Tx/Rx Rate
	40:1				no	5.060 -36		11.0Mbps...

Show Categories
Detail Mode
Inline Comments

Show Columns ▶

Find   Ctrl+F
Find Next   Ctrl+G

Copy to Access List
➡ Copy to Connect List

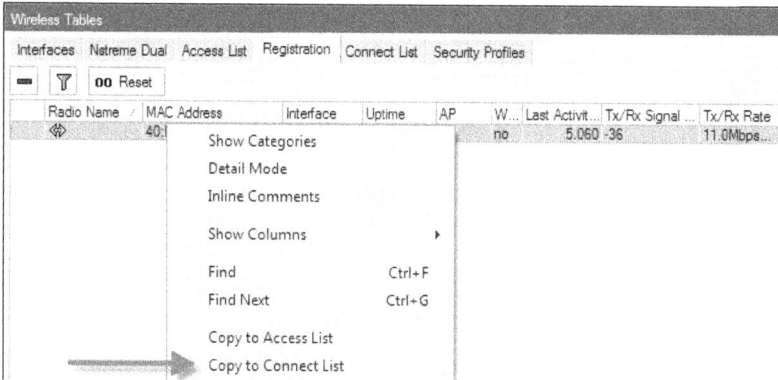

4. An alternative method to using the "Default Authenticate" method is to create a "drop rule" in the connect list. Since the rules are processed in order, the last rule can be a new rule that does not specify the MAC address and has Authentication unchecked. By placing this rule at the bottom of your list, the station will only associate with the AP's specified in the connect list and no others.

   Note that the connect list entries take precedence over the global setting of "Default Authenticate" on the interface.

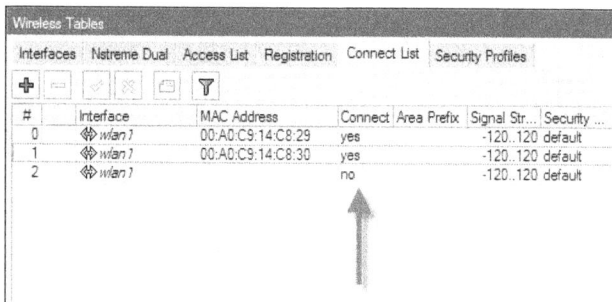

Wireless Tables

Interfaces | Nstreme Dual | Access List | Registration | Connect List | Security Profiles

#	Interface	MAC Address	Connect	Area Prefix	Signal Str...	Security ...
0	wlan1	00:A0:C9:14:C8:29	yes		-120..120	default
1	wlan1	00:A0:C9:14:C8:30	yes		-120..120	default
2	wlan1		no		-120..120	default

5. Also note that in a connect list entry, you can specify as much or as little information as you want in order to be more or less restrictive. For example, if you specify the SSID, then the station will connect to any AP with that SSID; however, adding the MAC address of the AP restricts it to a single AP.

For Further Study: Some other features that can be configured on a connect list are interface (if you have multiple wireless interfaces) and signal strength (to only allow a station to associate if it has a certain signal strength). Other features include the time of day or days of the week.

Example - Encryption Using WEP

Configuring any security protocol in RouterOS involves two steps. First, create a profile that dictates the protocol and keys. Second, apply that profile to the interface.

To create the security profile for WEP:

1. Click the Wireless button and then the Security Profiles tab. Click the plus sign, create a new profile, and name the profile whatever you wish. Change the mode to "Static Keys Required".

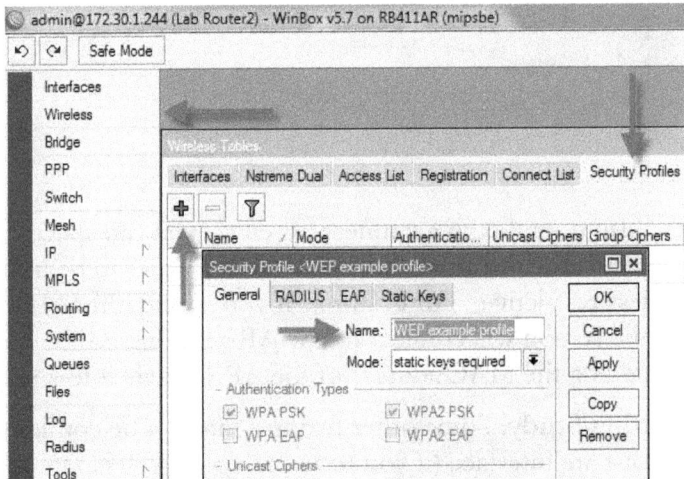

2. On the Static Keys tab, select Key 0 using the key type you require, typically 40 bit or 104 bit. A 40 bit key is 10 digits

and a 104 bit key is 26 digits. In the blank, type the key you want to use, and then click Ok.

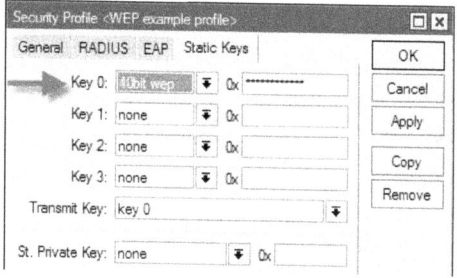

3. Back on the Wireless tab, double click the wireless interface to be configured with security.

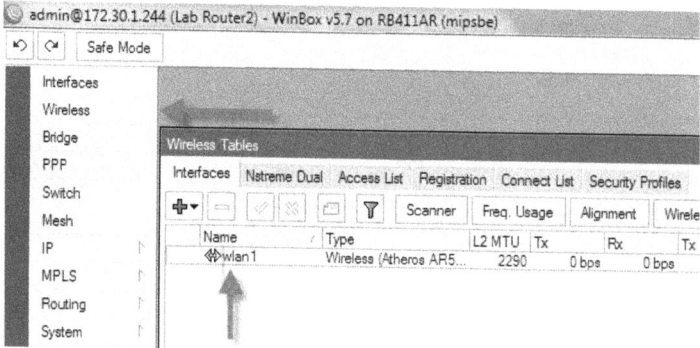

4. On the Wireless tab, select the interface and use the pull-down to select the security profile you just created.

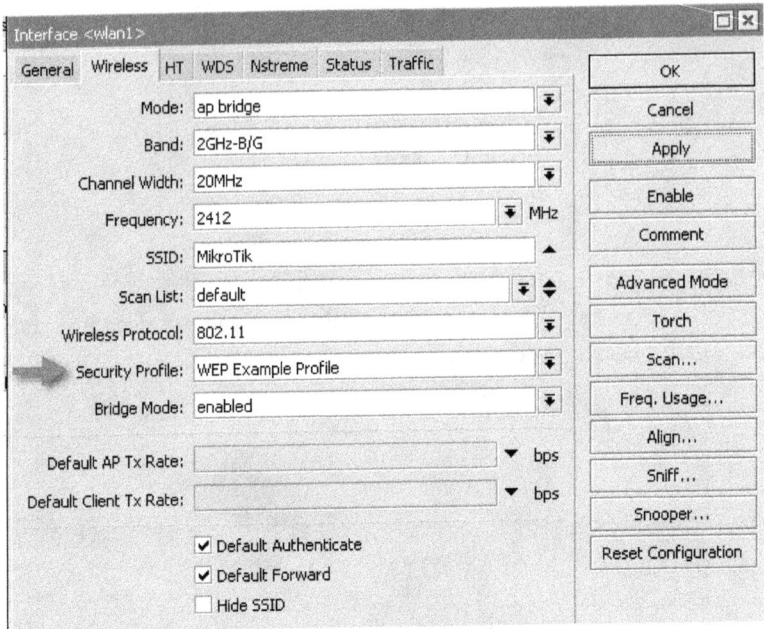

Use this example to create a wireless encryption security profile that will support WPA. Use wireless security any time you want to protect a wireless network, which is typically always!

APPLICATION

Example – Encryption Using WPA(2)

To create the security profile for WPA or WPA2:

1. Click the Wireless button and then the security tab. Click the plus sign, create a new profile, and name the profile whatever you wish. Change the mode to "Dynamic Keys". For the Authentication Types, select WPA PSK and/or WPA2 PSK, depending on the type of security you want to support.

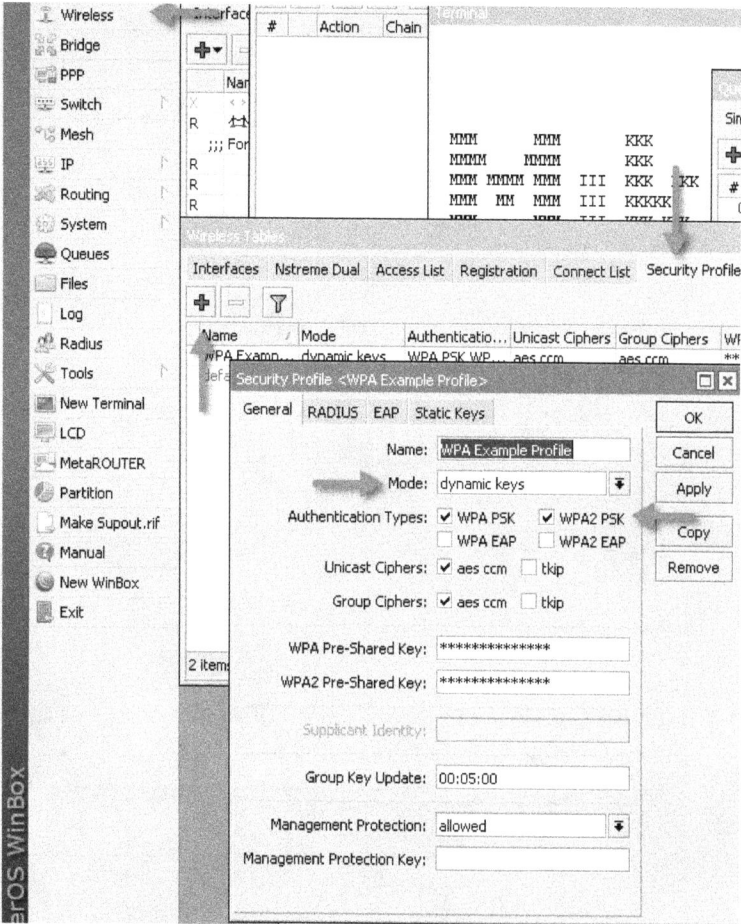

Unicast and Group Ciphers are also dependent on the type of station security you want to support. Checking more will result in supporting more types of stations. See the note below.

2. On the Security Profiles Tab in the WPA Pre-Shared Key and/or the WPA2 Pre-Shared Key blank, type the passphrase you want to share between the AP and station.

NOTE: I recommend using AES for the Unicast and Group ciphers. It is supported in hardware for the fastest modulation rates, while TKIP is done in software, so it is more resource-intensive and. Additionally, there are often compatibility problems with TKIP.

NOTE: In the upper right corner of WinBox is a check box labeled "Hide Passwords". Uncheck that box at any time to ensure what you have typed is what you intended. Click OK to save the profile.

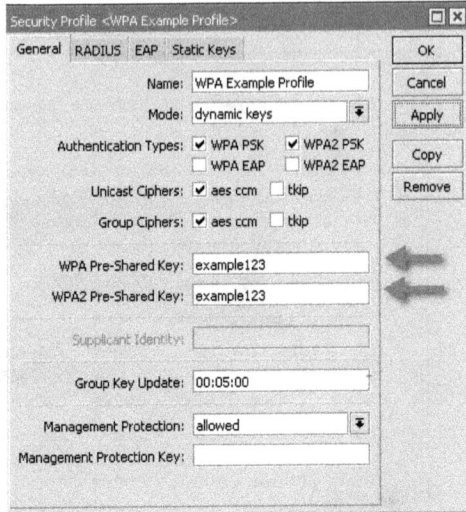

3. Back on the Wireless tab, use the pull-down to select the security profile you just created, and click OK.

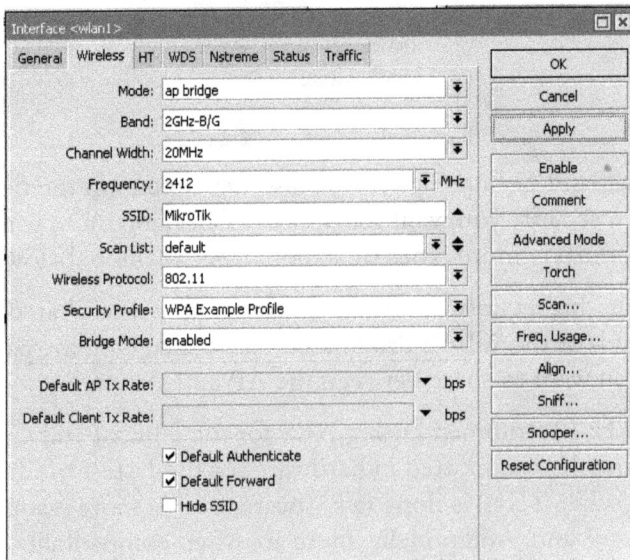

Use this example as a final checklist to configure a router for IP connectivity. Each of these concepts has been previously described in this book.

Example - IP Addressing, DNS, Masquerade

1. With the wireless interface configured and security established, next we need to handle IP addressing. Typically, the device will receive an IP address from the network it is connected to in order to receive Internet access. Assuming you receive your address using DHCP, add a DHCP client to the Ethernet interface that will connect to the Internet, typically ether1. The process of adding a DHCP client is outlined on page 190.

2. Next, we need to add an IP address on the wireless interface as demonstrated on page 37.

3. We likely want our router to be a caching DNS server, thereby reducing our Internet usage and speeding up the DNS process. Enable caching DNS as demonstrated on page 188.

4. With an IP address in place, we likely want to add DHCP Server to automatically give out IP addresses to our wireless clients. This is demonstrated on page 193.

5. Finally, we will need a NAT masquerade rule to hide our LAN behind a public IP address as shown on page 122.

At this point you should have a fully functioning wireless access point.

Use this example to create a wireless station device. This device will be able to connect to a wireless AP and route packets between the wireless and Ethernet interfaces.

Example – Configure a Wireless Interface to be a Routed Station (client)

As previously explained, when a router is outfitted with multiple interfaces, not tied together by a bridge, it is operating in routing mode. In this example, we will configure a routed station that can associate with an access point. The Ethernet port will be connected to our laptop or a switch, and the wireless interface will connect to a wireless access point that provides DHCP and Internet access.

1. Click the Wireless button and double click the wireless interface to be configured.

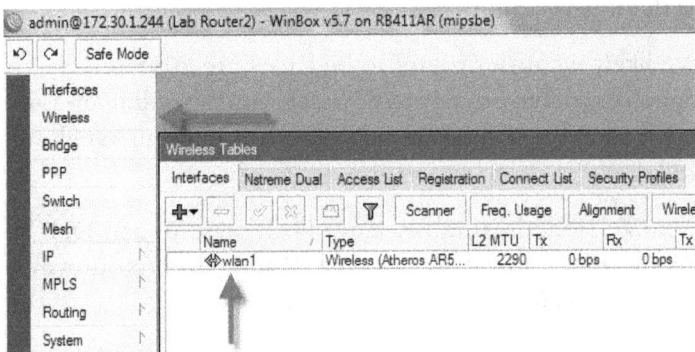

2. The minimum information to be configured is the Mode, the band, the SSID, and the Wireless Protocol. Set the Mode to station, the Band to the frequency of your access point

(typically 2.4 GHz, 802.11 b/g/n), and the Wireless Protocol to 802.11. Then click Apply.

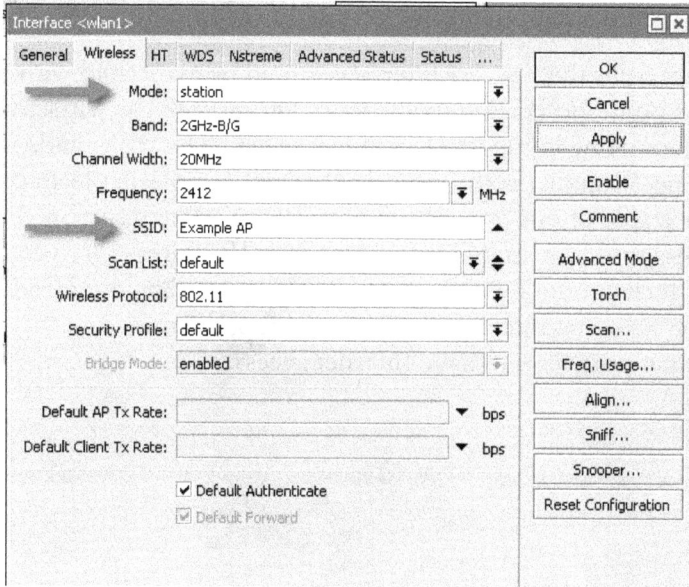

If you are unsure of the SSID, you can scan for it by using the Scan button and then clicking Start. This will scan for wireless networks in the band you previously specified.

To select an SSID, click the Connect button and that SSID will be loaded into the SSID blank. Stop and close the Scan tool. The router should then be connected to the AP. If the AP requires security, it can be configured exactly the same way as security for an access point as described on page 264.

3. At this point, the wireless station should be associated with the access point.

4. Add DHCP client to the wireless interface as shown on page 190.

5. Add an IP address to the Ethernet interface as shown on page 37.

6. Configure DNS as instructed on page 188.

7. Add DHCP server to the Ethernet interface as demonstrated on page 193.

8. Add a masquerade NAT rule as shown on page 122.

At this point the wireless interface should be associated with the access point, designated by the letter "R" next to the wireless interface name in the wireless interface list. The "R" stands for running. Running is the same as "linked" in Ethernet terms, meaning there is at least one association between an AP and station. The wireless interface should have a dynamic IP address received from DHCP client, the DHCP server should be handing out IP addresses on the Ethernet interface, and your laptop, connected to the Ethernet port, should have Internet access.

APPLICATION

Use this example to create secondary wireless SSID's. These virtual interfaces can supply connectivity to stations as if they were a physical interface. One application for this is to add a guest network to an existing wireless infrastructure.

Example – Create a Virtual AP

Virtual AP's are a great way to provide diverse functions with a single wireless interface. To the router, they behave like a physical interface, but only require a single adapter. The only real difference between a virtual wireless interface and a physical one is that they share the same physical card so they can only operate on one channel, the same channel as the physical interface. Virtual AP's can hand out DHCP addresses, be bridged, addressed, run HotSpot, etc.,with few limitations.

To create a virtual AP:

1. Click the Wireless button. Then in the Wireless Tables window, click the plus sign.

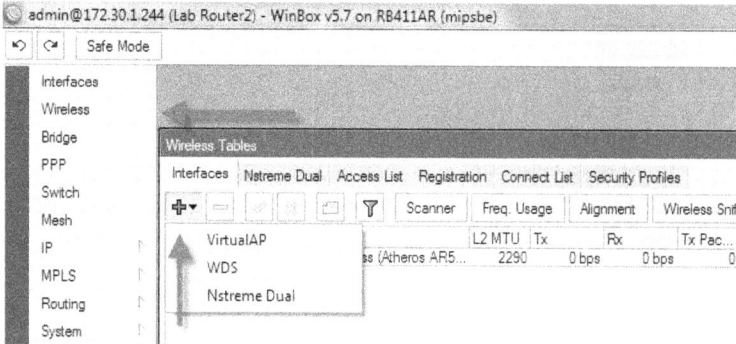

2. Select Virtual AP. On the Wireless tab, enter the SSID you want it to broadcast. Once configured, you can apply a separate security profile as previously described, or configure the Virtual AP as any other physical interface.

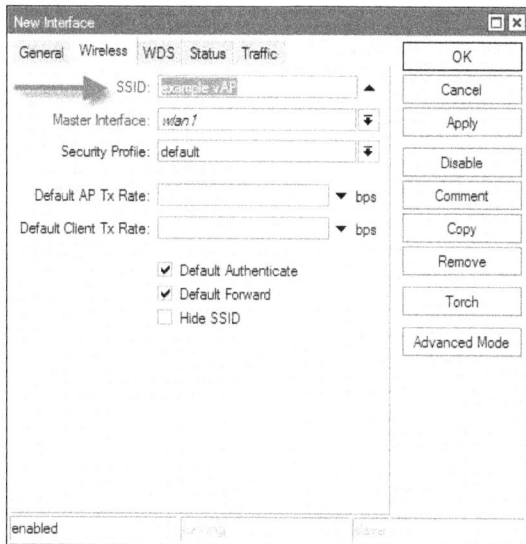

Bridging – Point to Point or Point to Multi-Point

There are several ways to bridge a RouterOS device, but the goal is always the same: to join dissimilar physical interfaces into one logical interface. RouterOS supports several methods of bridging, but I advocate only one, station-bridge mode. This method can be used in a mixed wireless network, an access point that will support routed stations as well as bridged stations.

Bridging an access point is straightforward and completely accepted in the IEEE 802.11 standard. Bridging a device while configured in station mode is, however, not acceptable in the IEE standard. For that reason, we need a workaround to perform bridging.

Bridging MikroTik Station to a Non-MikroTik AP that Supports WDS

The wireless mode that will enable bridging a station to a WDS compliant AP is named "station-wds" mode and is simple to set up on the station, but requires support on the access point. Both configurations will be described here. "Station-wds" is no longer my first choice when I am in an all-MikroTik environment. In that scenario I prefer "station-bridge" mode, which is described later in another example.

Use this example to create a bridged link when the non-MikroTik AP device supports WDS and the station device is a MikroTik. If both devices are MikroTik, mode "bridge-station" is a better choice.

APPLICATION

Example – Transparently Bridging a Link With WDS

Station End

1. To bridge the station device, click the Wireless button and then double click the wireless interface.

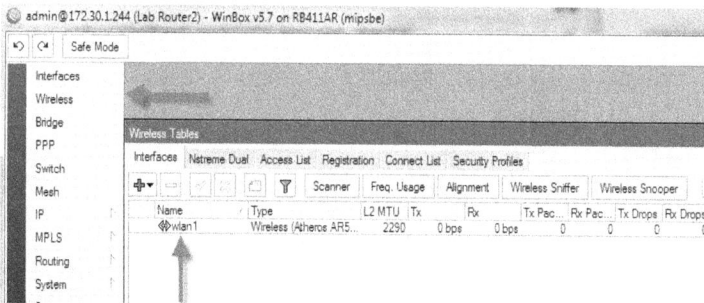

2. Set the Mode to station-wds and set the SSID to the one to be used on the AP. In this example, we are using "MikroTik" as the SSID. Set the Band to the frequency you are using, such as 2.4 GHz or 5 GHz, and set it to the desired Wireless Protocol. In this example, we are using 802.11. Then click Ok.

(Continued on next page)

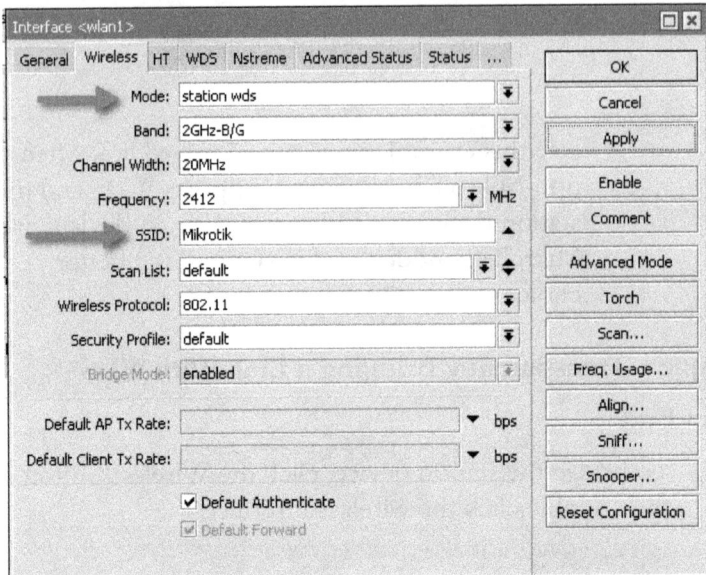

3. Click the Bridge button and the plus sign to add a new bridge interface and click Ok.

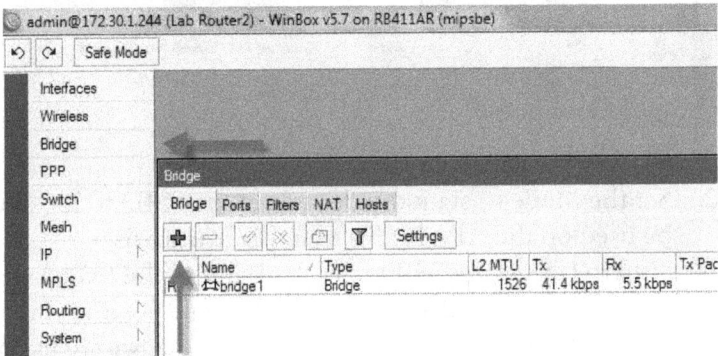

4. On the Bridge Ports tab, click the plus sign, add the Ethernet port to be bridged (typically ether1) to the new bridge you just created, and click Ok. Repeat for the wireless interface.

(Continued on next page)

| Interfaces |
| Wireless |
| Bridge |
| PPP |
| Switch |
| Mesh |
| IP |
| MPLS |
| Routing |
| System |

Bridge

| Bridge | Ports | Filters | NAT | Hosts |

Interface	/	Bridge	Priority (h...	Path Cost	Horizon
ether1		bridge1	80	10	
wlan1		bridge1	80	10	

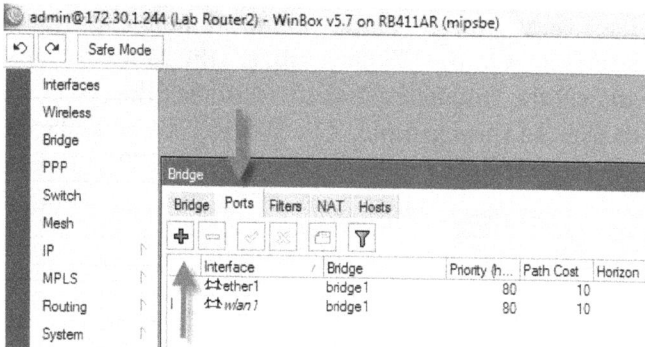

The station is now bridged, but now we must adjust the access point.

Access Point End

1. On the access point, create a new bridge interface, and click Ok.

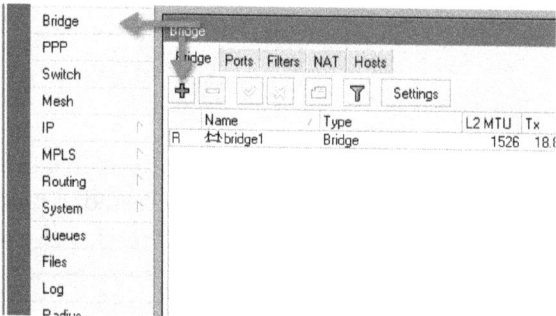

| Bridge |
| PPP |
| Switch |
| Mesh |
| IP |
| MPLS |
| Routing |
| System |
| Queues |
| Files |
| Log |

Bridge

| Bridge | Ports | Filters | NAT | Hosts | | Settings |

	Name	/	Type	L2 MTU	Tx
R	bridge1		Bridge	1526	18.6

2. On the Bridge Ports tab, add the wireless interface to the bridge, and click Ok.

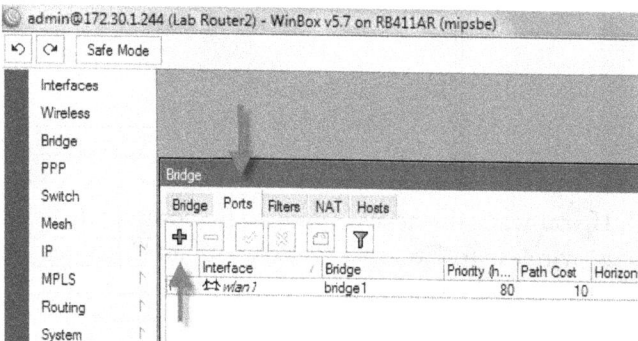

| Interfaces |
| Wireless |
| Bridge |
| PPP |
| Switch |
| Mesh |
| IP |
| MPLS |
| Routing |
| System |

Bridge

| Bridge | Ports | Filters | NAT | Hosts |

Interface	/	Bridge	Priority (h...	Path Cost	Horizon
wlan1		bridge1	80	10	

3. Back on the wireless interface list, double click the wireless interface. On the Wireless tab, set the Mode to "ap-bridge", and set the frequency desired. Also, set the SSID you want to use. In this example, it is "MikroTik". Finally, set the desired Wireless Protocol. We are using 802.11 here.

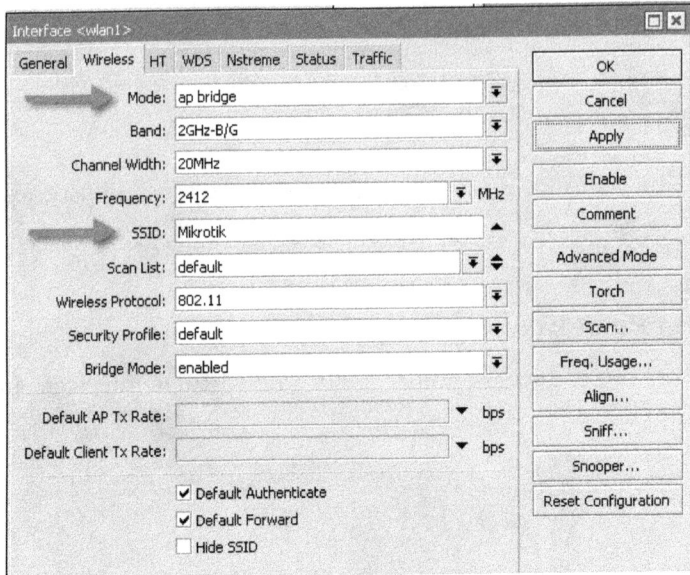

4. On the WDS tab, select WDS Mode as dynamic and WDS Default Bridge as the bridge you created, typically bridge1. It may be necessary to disable and re-enable the wireless interface on the station to cause it to re-associate with the access point now that it supports WDS.

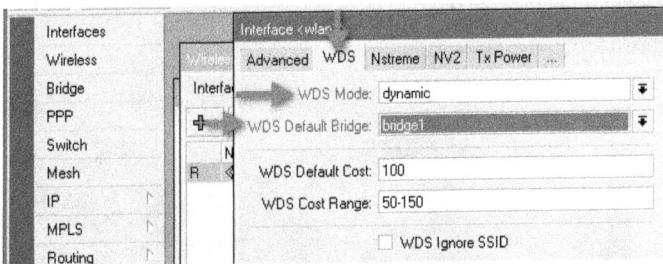

5. If you want the access point to be completely bridged, that is, wireless to Ethernet, simply add its Ethernet interface as another port on the AP's bridge.

Use this example to create a bridged link when both AP and station are MikroTik devices. It is the simplest, fastest method, and is very stable.

Bridging a Station Using Station-Bridge Mode

This is my preferred way to bridge a station device when both devices in the link are MikroTik devices. The setup is exactly as described above with two changes:

Station End

1. On the wireless interface, select station-bridge as the mode, instead of station-wds.

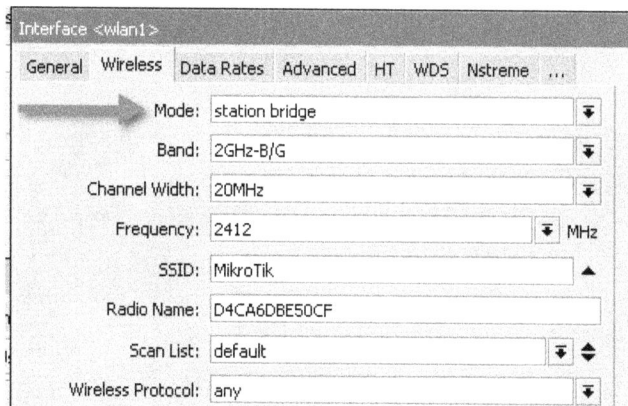

2. Bridge the wlan1 to the ether, just as you did in the previous example.

Here is the detailed procedure:

3. To bridge the station device, click the Wireless button, and then double click the wireless interface.

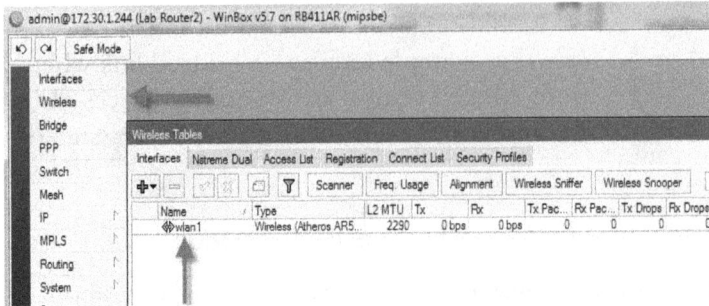

4. Set the Mode to station-bridge and set the SSID to the one to be used on the AP. In this example, we are using "MikroTik" as the SSID. Set the Band to the frequency you are using, such as 2.4 GHz or 5 GHz, and set it to the desired Wireless Protocol. In this example, we are using 802.11. Then click Ok.

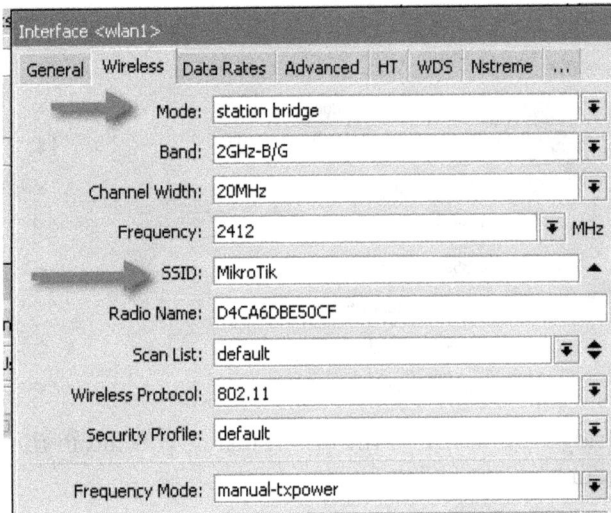

5. Click the Bridge button and the plus sign to add a new bridge interface, and click Ok.

(Continued on next page)

Safe Mode

Interfaces
Wireless
Bridge
PPP
Switch
Mesh
IP
MPLS
Routing
System

Bridge

| | Bridge | Ports | Filters | NAT | Hosts | |
| | | | | | Settings | |

Name	Type	L2 MTU	Tx	Rx	Tx Pac
bridge1	Bridge	1526	41.4 kbps	5.5 kbps	

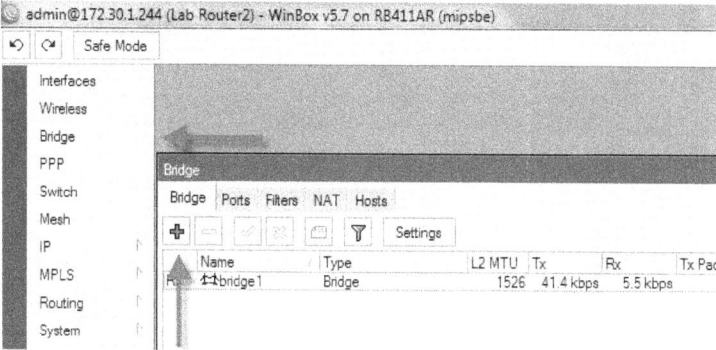

6. On the Bridge Ports tab, click the plus sign, and add the Ethernet port to be bridged (typically ether1) to the new bridge you just created, and click Ok. Repeat for the wireless interface. The station is now bridged, but now we must adjust the access point.

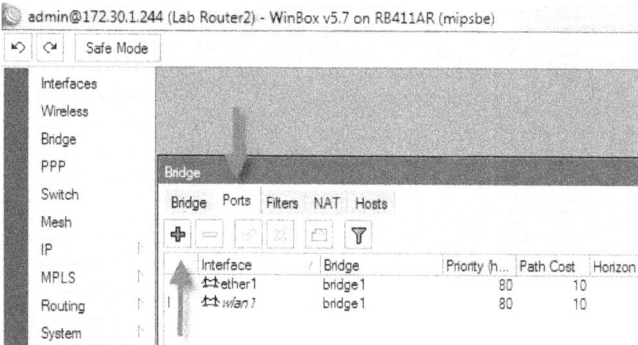

admin@172.30.1.244 (Lab Router2) - WinBox v5.7 on RB411AR (mipsbe)

Safe Mode

Interfaces
Wireless
Bridge
PPP
Switch
Mesh
IP
MPLS
Routing
System

Bridge

| | Bridge | Ports | Filters | NAT | Hosts | |

Interface	Bridge	Priority (h...	Path Cost	Horizon
ether1	bridge1	80	10	
wlan1	bridge1	80	10	

Access Point End

1. The configuration is exactly the same as the previous AP

with WDS support example, but the WDS tab settings are not required.

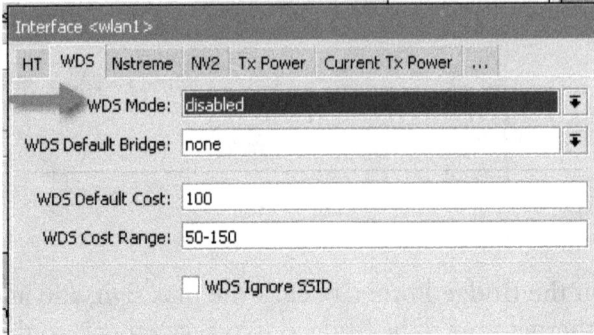

Here is the detailed procedure:

1. On the access point, create a new bridge interface, and click Ok.

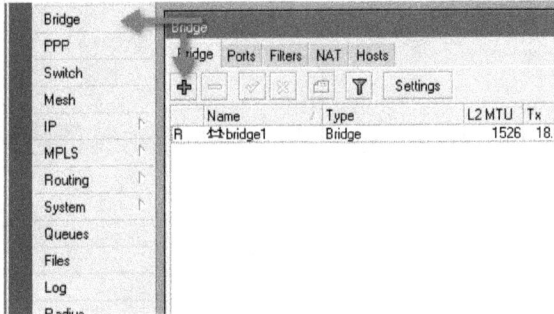

2. On the Bridge Ports tab, add the wireless interface to the bridge, and click Ok.

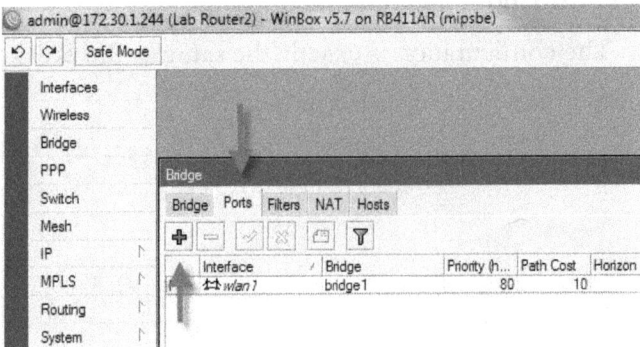

3. Back on the wireless interface list, double click the wireless interface. On the Wireless tab, set the Mode to "ap-bridge", and set the frequency desired. Also, set the SSID you want to use, in this example it is "MikroTik". Finally, set the desired Wireless Protocol. We are using 802.11.

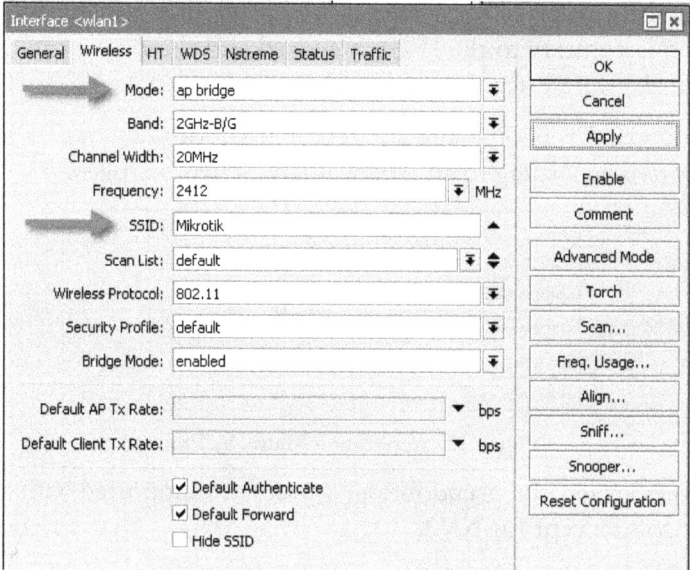

4. If you want the access point to be completely bridged, that is, wireless to Ethernet, simply add its Ethernet interface as another port on the AP's bridge.

Point to Point Links

If your access point is being used with a single station as in a backhaul or point-to-point link, you can set the wireless mode to "bridge". This mode is available in the Level 3 license, while ap-bridge mode is not available in the Level 3 license. In bridge mode, the device is still an access point, but will only support one station, ideal for low cost point-to-point links.

Pseudobridge Modes

In some scenarios, it is not possible to use an access point that supports WDS or a MikroTik AP. If the station must still be bridged, you may use one of the two pseudobridge modes as a last resort. I state that with reluctance because any mode that defies the standard is fraught with possible problems. As previously stated, bridging a station is contrary to the IEEE standard and should only be used where absolutely necessary.

In RouterOS version 5 and above, the pseudobridge modes are supported according to an Applicability Matrix as follows:

	802.11	ROS 802.11	nstreme	nv2
station	v	v	v	v
station-wds		v	v	v
station-pseudobridge	v	v	v	
station-pseudobridge-clone	v	v	v	
station-bridge		v	v	v

Figure 17 - Application Matrix by Protocol [1]

As you can see, the pseudobridge modes are supported with most protocols, except for NV2.

If you need to use pseudobridge mode, there are two options: station-pseudobridge and station-pseudobridge-clone.

Wireless Mode Station-Pseudobridge

In this mode, the wireless station works very much like source NAT in the firewall facility. Specifically, the devices source NATs frames sent to the access point using the MAC address of its wireless card. A MAC translation table is maintained on the wireless station, and any frames entering the device from a client are stripped of their MAC address. The MAC of the station is then inserted in their place. Returning packets are treated in the opposite manner, returning the originating host's MAC address. This masquerading process will not work with many non-IP-based protocols, so as stated before, pseudobridge modes should always be avoided when possible.

Wireless Mode Station-Pseudobridge-Clone

This mode works in a similar fashion to the station-pseudobridge mode, with the exception that the station's wireless card connects to the access point using the MAC address of the first frame that passes through the device. In the case of a laptop being connected to the bridged station, this means the access point would see the MAC address of the laptop rather than the actual station's wireless card, hence the name "clone".

APPLICATION

Use this example to create a bridged link when the AP is not a MikroTik AP and does not support WDS. You will be able to use only one device behind the bridged station, as only a single MAC address is supported.

Example – Bridge a Station Using Pseudobridge

This example will work for either station-pseudobridge or station-pseudobridge-clone.

1. To bridge the station device, click the Wireless button, and then double click the wireless interface.

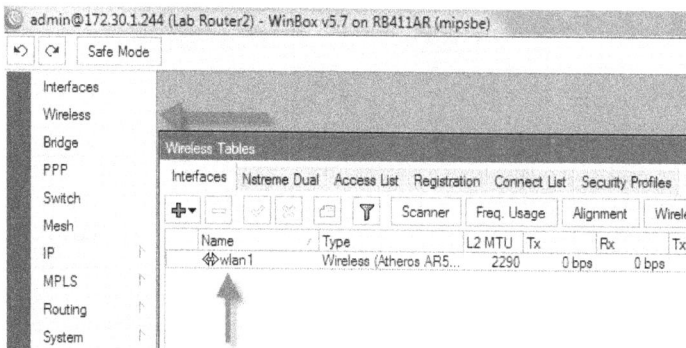

2. Set the mode to station-pseudobridge or station-pseudobridge-clone mode, and click Ok.

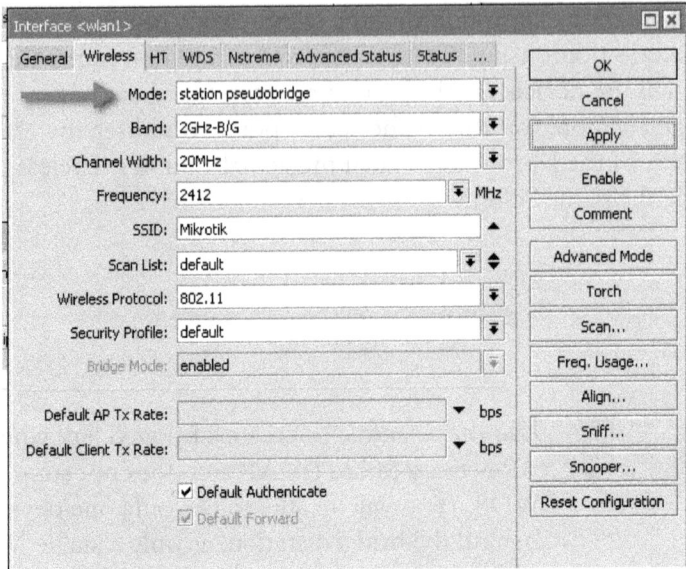

3. Click the bridge button and the plus sign to add a new bridge interface, and click Ok.

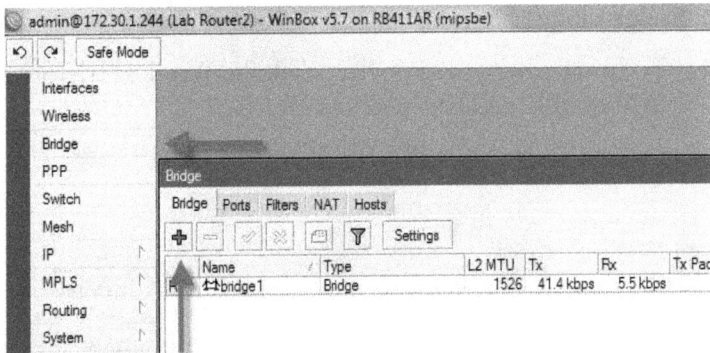

4. On the Ports tab, click the plus sign and add the Ethernet port to be bridged (typically ether1) to the new bridge you just created. Then click Ok and repeat for the wireless interface.

(Continued on next page)

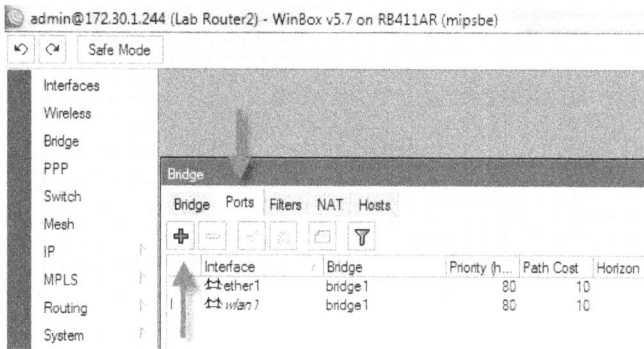

admin@172.30.1.244 (Lab Router2) - WinBox v5.7 on RB411AR (mipsbe)

Interface	Bridge	Priority (h...	Path Cost	Horizon
ether1	bridge1	80	10	
wlan1	bridge1	80	10	

The station is now bridged.

For Further Study: It is also possible to bridge two devices using a PPP tunnel, EoIP tunnel, or VPLS.

Supporting Mixed Clients, Routed Stations, and Bridged Stations

Once WDS bridging is set up on an access point as demonstrated on page 275, it is possible to support both routed stations and bridged stations that have been configured using the transparent bridging method. This is a good scenario for Internet service providers, as it gives them several different customer configurations they can offer.

For example, if a customer wants a standard managed connection using a routed station, firewalling, private addressing on the LAN, public addressing on the WAN, and the ability to support destination NAT for inbound services to servers on the LAN, this is all possible using a standard routed station. If the access point is configured with support for WDS clients as outlined on page 275, that makes it possible to offer an alternate configuration on the same access point for non-managed clients. For example, if a client wants to run their own router and firewall and have it receive a public IP address via your PPPoE server, that can be done by configuring that station in station-wds mode. Since the AP supports both WDS and non-WDS clients, one access point can support either configuration and neither of these scenarios require station-pseudobridge mode, although that is still supported.

WDS, Wireless Distribution System

In some scenarios, it is desired to provide wireless access, yet it is not possible to get network cabling in place to the access point. This scenario lends itself well to a protocol called WDS. We have previously used a function of this protocol to create a transparent wireless bridge, yet the true power of WDS is the application just described. In a WDS system, each access point serves double duty, in that it acts as both an access point and a station at the same time. This is both helpful and hurtful, so let me explain.

By design, 802.11 devices are half-duplex, meaning they cannot transmit and receive at the same time. By contrast, modern Ethernet devices are typically full duplex, meaning they can transmit and receive at the same time, which explains why a 100 Mb Ethernet device can transfer data at line speed, both directions, simultaneously. Wireless devices with a single transmitter must either be in transmit mode or receive mode, but not both simultaneously, which explains why a device connected at 54 Mbps will only maintain about half that in one direction and one fourth if passing data both directions simultaneously.

In a WDS system, if a device is both a station and an AP at the same time, the total throughput of the system will be reduced by a factor of about one half when a second device is added to the system. That trend continues as more devices are added, until the system grinds to a screeching halt. That being said, a few devices in WDS will perform quite well for client Internet access where you are typically trying to deliver a few megs to each client, and in that situation, a two or three node WDS system running 802.11g is quite adequate. The same system running 802.11n with dual chains becomes substantially more robust and expandable before this throughput "wall" is reached.

Use this example to create a bridged mesh network without wired uplinks. In this example, each AP is also an uplink for the other AP's so that the mesh is self-building and self-healing. As explained, this is not without a performance cost.

Example – Build a WDS System

To build any WDS system requires a bridge interface. It is not mandatory that the Ethernet interface be added to this bridge, so the AP can still be a routed device. However, a bridge interface is a requirement for the wireless portion of the configuration. In this example, we want to build a WDS system that will both extend our network to a second AP and allow non-WDS clients to connect to an access point in the WDS system and receive network access.

1. In WinBox, click on the Wireless button, and then double click the wireless interface to view its properties.

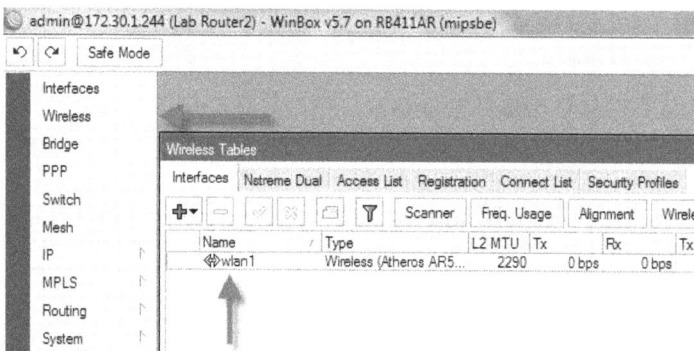

2. On the wireless tab, set the mode to ap-bridge, the Frequency to a free frequency, and the SSID to something of your choice. In this case, we will use "MikroTik" as the SSID.

(Continued on next page)

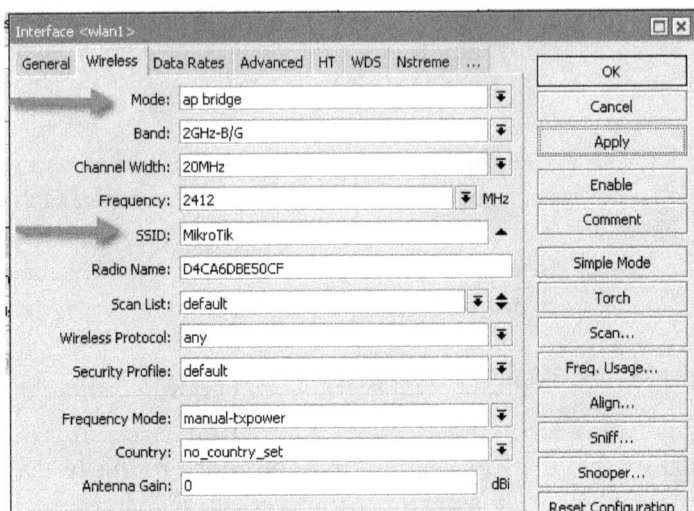

Interface <wlan1>

| General | Wireless | Data Rates | Advanced | HT | WDS | Nstreme | ... |

Mode: ap bridge
Band: 2GHz-B/G
Channel Width: 20MHz
Frequency: 2412 MHz
SSID: MikroTik
Radio Name: D4CA6DBE50CF
Scan List: default
Wireless Protocol: any
Security Profile: default
Frequency Mode: manual-txpower
Country: no_country_set
Antenna Gain: 0 dBi

OK | Cancel | Apply | Enable | Comment | Simple Mode | Torch | Scan... | Freq. Usage... | Align... | Sniff... | Snooper... | Reset Configuration

3. Create a new bridge interface, and click Ok.

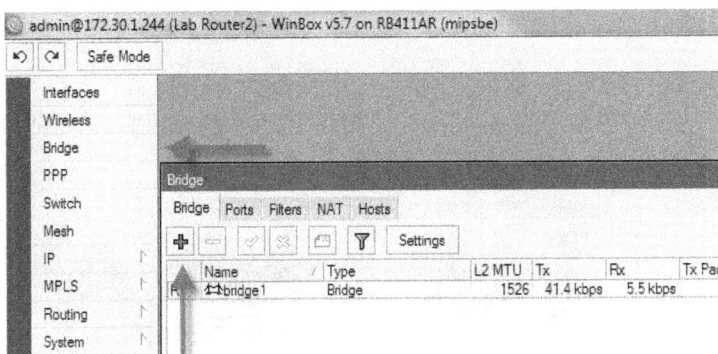

4. On the ports tab, add the wireless interface to the bridge, and click Ok.

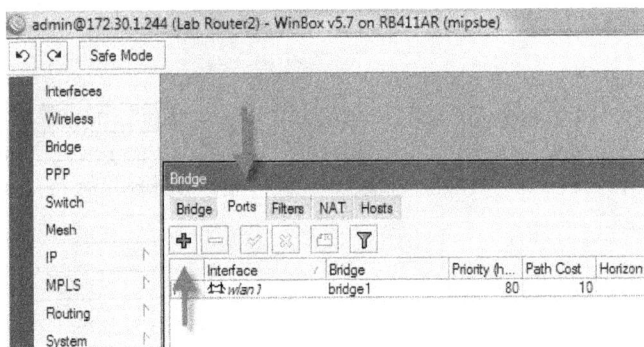

290

5. Back on the wireless interface list, double click the wireless interface. On the WDS tab, select WDS Mode as dynamic and WDS Default Bridge as the bridge you created, typically bridge1.

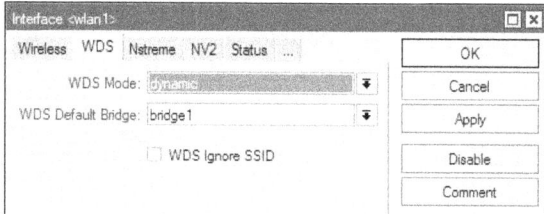

6. Repeat steps 1 through 5 for the second device in the WDS system. Note that it is essential for you to set the SSID and the frequency to the same settings for all devices to participate in the WDS system, or they will not associate.

7. Once the wireless interfaces are associated, and the WDS interfaces are dynamically created, you can either configure the device as a routed access point (as shown on page 253), or add the AP's Ethernet interface to the bridge you just created, and push the Layer 3 services to another router in the network.

NV2- Nstreme Version Two

Nstreme Version Two is one of the most exciting features to be added to RouterOS. Nstreme Version Two (NV2) is a TDMA (Time Domain Multiple Access) protocol, meaning wireless stations are allowed to transmit only during a specific time slice. This negates the need for a station to "listen" before it transmits, as is the case with conventional 802.11, which uses CDMA (Carrier Sense Multiple Access) and greatly improves the speed and scalability of the network. TDMA has only been available in very expensive devices in the past, so this was a welcomed addition to RouterOS.

"TDMA media access technology solves hidden node problems and improves media usage, thus improving throughput and latency, especially in PtMP networks." [1] So the question is, "Why would you want to use the NV2 protocol in your network?" I would pose the question, "Why would you _not_ want to use NV2?" The benefits are higher throughput, longer links, improved stability in noisy environments, lower latency, no hidden node effect, and reduced frame overhead. The only reason for not using NV2 is the incompatibility with standard 802.11 devices in a mixed network of RouterOS and non-RouterOS devices.

Use this example for all outdoor wireless deployments using MikroTik devices for the highest capacity outdoor network.

Example – Converting an 802.11n PtMP System to NV2

In this example, we will take an imaginary service provider or WISP network tower running 802.11n protocol with all RouterOS stations and convert it to NV2. The goal is to improve performance of the network without substantial customer downtime.

Note: Although the method described herein is accurate, there is always the chance a station will not re-associate with the access point or that an upgrade could fail. Therefore, understand this risk before you begin, and perform the operation inside your standard maintenance window.

1. Step one is to ensure every station is running the latest version of RouterOS, so we will upgrade each station on the access point using the technique previously described on page 44.

2. Once all stations have been upgraded and rebooted, they should still be associated with the access point.

3. Upgrade the access point to the latest version, as previously described.

4. Log in with WinBox to each station, click the Wireless button, and double click the wireless interface.

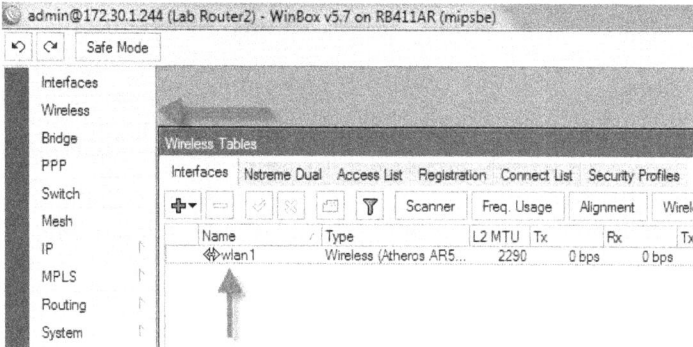

5. On the wireless tab, change the protocol to "nv2 nstreme 802.11", and click OK. This ensures that the station will re-associate now and after you have converted the access point to NV2.

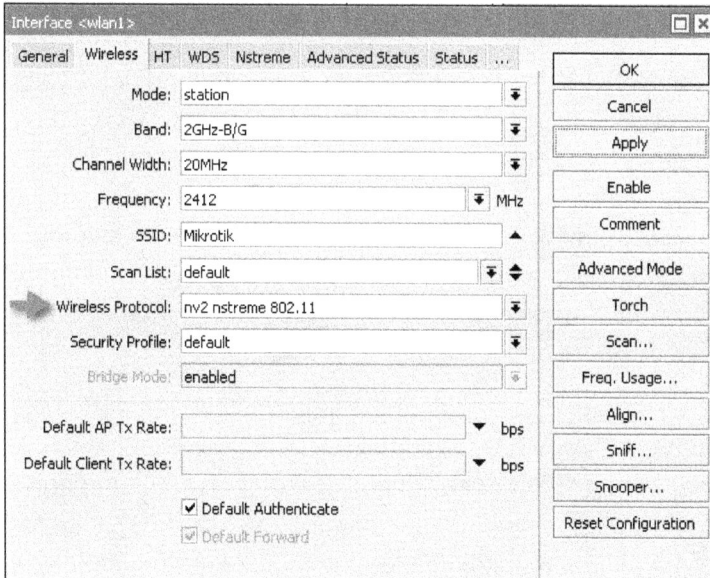

6. Once all stations have been set this way, WinBox to the access point. On the wireless tab, set the protocol to NV2.

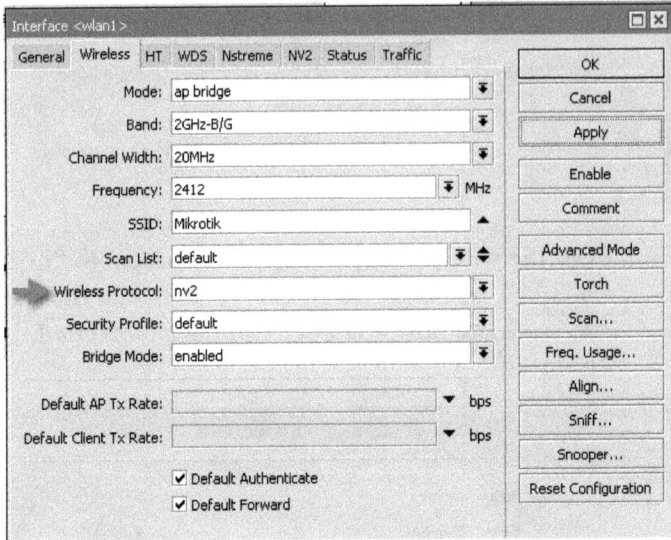

7. On the NV2 tab, set the cell radius to a value equal to the distance to the farthest client on this AP in kilometers.

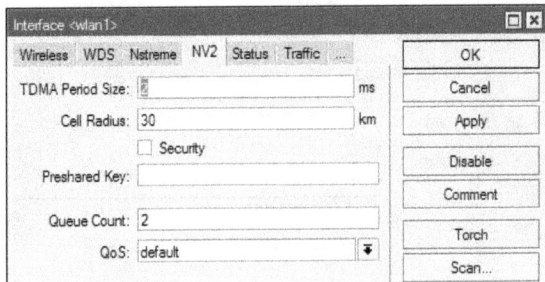

8. Once you click OK, all clients should re-associate in NV2 mode and you should have a stable TDMA network.

For Further Study: NV2 supports its own security, which can be set by checking the Security box on the NV2 tab and setting a "Preshared Key" on both the access point and all stations. This will further enhance the security of your wireless network.

Use this example any time you want your SSID to be hidden from standard Wi-Fi clients.

Example – Hiding the SSID

To hide the SSID from prying eyes:

1. In WinBox, click the Wireless button, and double click the wireless interface.

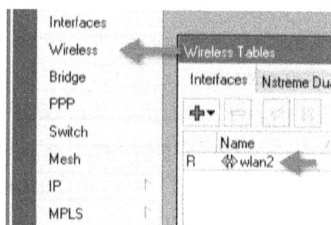

2. On the wireless tab, check the box "hide SSID".

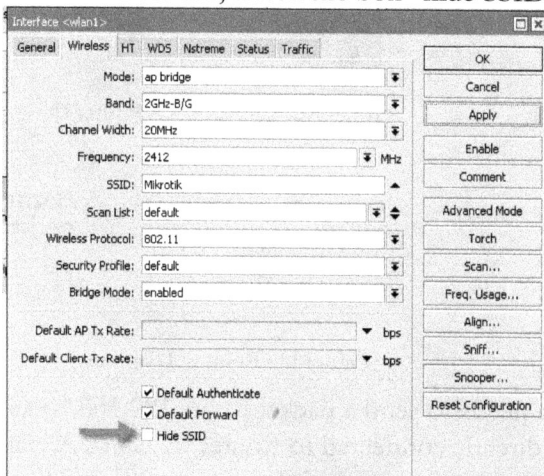

Chapter 16 – Routing

In simplest terms, routing is the process that determines the interface through which a packet leaves a router. Routing takes place at Layer 3, and the process is governed by a list of rules called routes. When a packet enters the routing process, the router looks at the destination IP address of the packet and then compares that address to the route rules to determine where to send the packet.

There are some basic rules that govern simple routing. First, routers can only send packets to routers they are directly connected to. By directly connected, I am describing two routers with a Layer 1 connection, such as an Ethernet cable or wireless link connecting them, both of whose interfaces are configured with IP addresses on the same subnet. Understanding this term "directly connected" is essential in understanding IP routing. Secondly, routers have to "trust" that the router to which they send a packet can ultimately get the packet to its final destination. To explain this "trust" relationship, consider the following example:

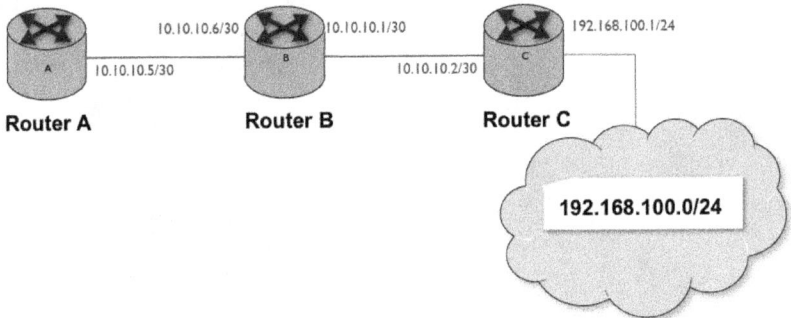

Figure 18 - Routing Diagram

Router A needs to send a packet to the 192.168.100.0/24 subnet, which is directly connected to Router C. Since A is not directly connected to C, it must send the packet to B and "trust" that B can get the packet to its final destination. Why does it send the packet to B? Because Router A's routing table or routing "rules" tell it that Router B is the gateway for the 192.168.100.0/24 subnet. With routing, there is no "leap frogging", meaning that A must send the packet to B, who sends the packet to C. A can not jump over B and send packets directly to C.

This concept of sending packets to an adjacent or directly connected router is referred to as the "next hop", which is descriptive of a packet hopping from Router A to Router B to Router C, and finally to the destination subnet. In this scenario, the next hop for router A is Router B.

Simple Static Routes

With a basic understanding of how routing works, let's explore the rules that routers use, specifically the routing table. In RouterOS, the routing table is found in WinBox by clicking IP and Routes.

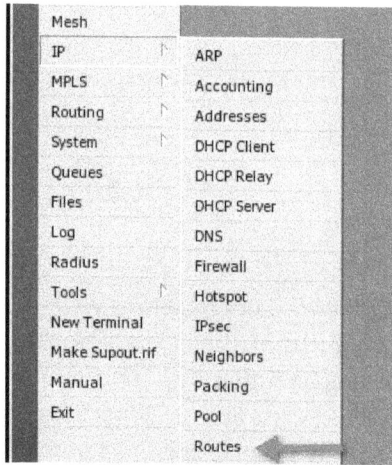

The routing table looks like this:

	Dst. Address	Gateway	Distance	Routing Mark	Pref. Source
AS	▶ 0.0.0.0/0	66.76.13.1 reachable ether1	1		
DA	▶ 66.76.13.0/24	ether1 reachable	0		66.76.13.10
DA	▶ 192.168.101.0/24	bridge1 reachable	0		192.168.101.1

In every route, there are two key pieces of information: the destination address and the gateway. The destination address is the network that contains the host we are trying to send a packet to, and the gateway is the router that knows how to route the packet to its destination. It is feasible that the destination address could be a single host address. In this scenario, we would need one route for every single host we ever wanted to reach. In the case of an IPV4 Internet connected router, that would be nearly a billion host routes, one for every host on the Internet. Obviously, this is unreasonable, so we always use network routes as our destination address.

Most Specific Route

It is important to interject here that there is an additional rule for routes we must consider. When a router has multiple routes to get to the same destination, the router will use the most specific route. By most specific, I am referring to the size of the range of the IP addresses in the destination network.

Consider the following routes:

#	Destination Address	Gateway
0	192.168.1.0/24	10.0.0.1
1	192.168.1.0/30	10.0.0.2

In this example, the router wants to send a packet to 192.168.1.1. That host address is defined by the IP address range of route 0 and the range of route 1, meaning that 192.168.1.0/30 includes the host addresses .1 and .2, while 192.168.1.0/24 includes the host addresses .1 through .254. Since the smaller range is that defined in route 1, route 1 is the most specific and therefore the packet will be sent to 10.0.0.2. The concept of "most specific route" is very important for understanding the routing decision.

Default Routes

A default route is best described by borrowing the phrase "gateway of last resort" from a competitive router operating system. I like this phrase because it tells me that if the router doesn't have a route for a packet that fits into one of the destination network routes in our table, we send that packet to the gateway of last resort, the default route.

Examining the default route, the destination address is always 0.0.0.0/0, which matches everything. Therefore, if this is the only route in the routing table, then all packets will be sent to the default route. If there are other, more specific routes to the desired destination, those will take precedence over the default route.

Use this example to work through a real life routing example to better understand static routing.

Example - Tying it All Together With Static Routes

By now you should understand the basic rules of static routing:

1. Routers must route packets using gateways that are directly connected.

2. Routers must "trust" adjacent or directly connected routers, that is, they are able to get the packet to its final destination.

3. With simple static routes we cannot "leap frog" to our destination.

With these three pieces of information, we can now apply this knowledge to a real life scenario.

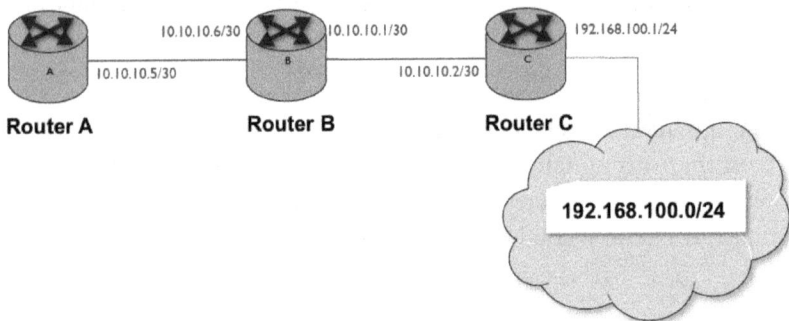

Figure 19 - Routing Diagram

In the above diagram, we have a system of three routers with no routes. The goal is to add enough static routes to each router in order for the hosts in the subnet at the far right to reach every router in the network and so that every router can reach the other routers as well as the hosts in the 192 subnet. The only default route we will use is configured on the hosts in the subnet at the far right; so all other devices must have a complete routing table.

All routes will be written in the format Destination Network and Gateway.

Solving first for router A:

#	Destination Network	Gateway
0	10.10.10.0/30	10.10.10.6
1	192.168.100.0/24	10.10.10.6

Looking at these routes, what you see is the embodiment of our three routing rules. In route 0, Router A only references a gateway to which it is directly connected. Router B's 10.10.10.6 address is directly connected to Router A and on the same subnet as Router A's 10.10.10.5 address, so the first rule is satisfied. Secondly, Router A trusts that Router B can get the packet to the destination network. It has no way to ensure that, it only trusts it is so. Thirdly, we aren't leapfrogging, because B is only one hop away from A. The second route, route 1, satisfies the same rules and enables Router A to send packets to the192 subnet. This completes Router A's routing table.

Router B will also need a static route:

#	Destination Network	Gateway
1	192.168.100.0/24	10.10.10.6

You may also be asking why does Router B only need one route? That is a good question, however, it is easily answered because Router B is in a unique position in that it is directly connected to both Routers A and C, therefore no static routes are needed. Router B can ping both Router A and Router C, because they are one hop away, so it only needs a route to the 192 subnet.

Router C is in a situation similar to Router B. It is directly connected to the 192 subnet, so no static routes need to be added. It is also directly connected to Router B so no static routes are needed there either. It only needs one static route to Router A as follows:

#	Destination Network	Gateway
1	10.10.10.4/30	10.10.10.1

The only other question that might remain in your mind is, "Why are we using the network addresses like 10.10.10.4/30, instead of the host IP addresses like 10.10.10.5 or 10.10.10.6?" If you remember back at the beginning of this chapter, we discussed that although you could add a route for every single host IP on the network, to do so would be a waste of time because network references include many hosts, rather than a single host. In this example, 10.10.10.4/30 includes 10.10.10.5 and 10.10.10.6, so packets to either IP address would be included in that single route.

Route Distance

There is an additional piece of information in a route that we can use to influence how the device treats the routes. This attribute is called distance or cost. Distance is an arbitrary value assigned to the route so that if there are multiple routes to the same destination, they can be ordered (prioritized) by their distance, meaning a route with a lower distance takes priority over a route with a higher distance. By default, certain distances are applied to routes by the router. These distances can be changed to alter how a route is treated. Consider the following routing table:

#	Destination Address	Gateway	Distance
0	192.168.1.0/24	10.0.0.1	10
1	192.168.1.0/24	10.0.1.1	20

There are two routes here to the same destination with different gateways. In this scenario, since route 0 has a lower distance (sometimes called cost), it will be the active route and route 1 will be inactive. In the routing table, this will be evidenced by the active route being displayed in black and the inactive route(s) displayed in blue as shown below.

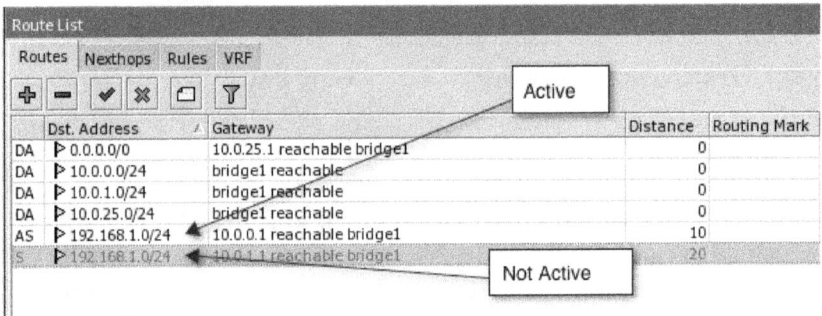

Also note that the routing flags will designate the active route(s) as "A" for active. If the interface for the active route is disabled or loses its link, that route will become inactive, and the route via gateway 10.0.1.1 will become the active route. This is a simple way to provide some basic redundancy, but it relies on the interface to actually go down for the active route to become inactive.

For Further Study: An additional feature called "check gateway" can be enabled on the active route to constantly check not only that the interface is active, but also that the gateway on the other end is reachable. This further enhances this type of failover configuration.

Dynamic Routes

Routes can be added to the routing table manually (static routes) or dynamically. Dynamic routes can either be added by a dynamic routing protocol or by the operating system as a part of the normal configuration of an IP address. More specifically, when you add an IP address to the router, it dynamically creates a companion route to tell the router on which interface to look for other hosts on that subnet.

In the above illustration, there are two dynamic routes designated by the routing flag "D", both of which are active, designated by the letter "A". Notice that the gateway for both routes is an interface rather than a host address. The reason is that these routes were dynamically added by the system in response to the configuration of an IP address. Now the router knows that other hosts on the 192.168.101.0/24 subnet will be found on interface bridge1, and similarly, hosts on the 66.76.13.0/24 subnet are found on interface ether1.

Routing Flags

In the previous illustration, to the left of each route in the route list, there is a flag or group of letters that describes the state or origin of the route. In this example, the flags "A", "S", and "D" stand for Active, Static, and Dynamic, respectfully. There are several other routing flags in RouterOS. Those that appear below in bold are the most common.

X – Disabled, not active

A – Active, in use

D – Dynamic, received from a dynamic routing protocol or added by the operating system

C – Connected, a directly connected host route

S – Static, added manually

R - RIP route, received from the routing information protocol

B – BGP, received from the border gateway protocol

O – Received from the open shortest path first protocol

M – Received from the mesh made easy protocol

B – Blackhole route, packets are silently discarded

U – Unreachable, discards the packets and sends an ICMP unreachable messages

P – Prohibit, discards packet and sends an ICMP communication administratively prohibited message

OSPF – A Dynamic Routing Protocol

Open Shortest Path First (OSPF) is the name of a simple to configure, yet robust routing protocol that anyone can implement and should implement in their networks as they grow past a single router. OSPF routers dynamically trade routing information as well as the state of the links that join routers together in order to determine the best path between routers. If a path becomes unreachable, they adjust their routes accordingly to maintain the reachability of all hosts in the OSPF cloud.

OSPF provides two main benefits. The first is the automatic propagation of routes in a network, and the second is failover to ensure the reliability of an IP network.

In this book, we will explore the basics of the OSPF protocol and learn how to create basic, single area OSPF networks that will provide all the routes necessary for the networks to operate without using static routes.

Link State Protocol

The basic communication of an OSPF network is done using the link state protocol. This protocol begins working when two routers in a network are similarly configured with OSPF, and the first OSPF packet is sent. This packet is called a hello packet. The hello packet is the first phase of the OSPF neighbor negotiation.

The second phase is called the link state advertisement or LSA. This communication involves sending a list of all the OSPF neighbors the router has learned. This link state information is sent by "flooding" LSA's (Link State Announcements) or sending the LSA's to every OSPF interface on the router. If a router receives a packet already seen, it is discarded so the router only processes new LSA's.

Once a router has learned all of its neighbors and all the neighbors they know, it builds a Link State Database. Once the link state database is fully populated, the routers begin the final and most complex portion of the process: calculating the routes. A Dutch computer scientist, Edsger Dijkstra2, originally proposed this particular algorithm. A famous quote by Edsger Dijkstra that I really like says, *"Program testing can be used to show the presence of bugs, but never to show their absence!"*

Dijkstra's Algorithm works by constructing a tree of the network. The tree's root is the system performing the calculations, and its branches are linked to other systems. The result is the shortest path to each router in the system. If a link fails, all routers in the system must perform a new set of calculations, and this results in utilizing router resources[3]. Networks with unstable links are not good candidates for OSPF, as the constant recalculation of these routes can utilize a large amount of resources. The network should be stabilized before configuring OSPF.

Areas

The concept of OSPF areas is included in the advanced RouterOS certification course I teach, the MikroTik Certified Routing Engineer (MTCRE), but a basic discussion is necessary for purposes of the configurations discussed in this book. The purpose of OSPF areas is to organize or group OSPF routers in logical divisions in the network. These divisions are typically made with some basis of geography, proximity, or function. OSPF routers are typically all contained within one AS (Autonomous System). In simple terms, an AS is a group of routers controlled or owned by a single entity. When the number of routers within that AS becomes too large or unwieldy, it can be broken up into smaller groups or OSPF areas.

By default, there is an OSPF area named backbone. For purposes of a small OSPF network, all routers can be made members of the backbone area. As the network groups, additional areas will become desirable, but these areas will continue to have some attachment to this backbone area. Single area OSPF networks are the simplest and can work well for most applications. They can also be easily scaled as the network grows.

When a new area is created and routers are assigned to this area, they operate as standard OSPF routers flooding their LSA's, building their databases, and performing their route calculations. This information is only shared with other routers in their particular area (if there are multiple areas). If one router in the area is also connected to the special area called backbone, it becomes a special type of router called an ABR (Area Border Router). The ABR is special in that it participates in normal OSPF functions inside its area, but on the backbone interface, it only sends a special type of LSA called a summary LSA. The summary LSA summarizes the routes to the routers in its area. The primary purpose of areas is to partition the network so that the size of the database is kept to a manageable size, and router resources are conserved, because the number of LSA's is reduced.

Configuring OSPF

In RouterOS, the first step to configuring OSPF is the addition of a network statement. Although the process sounds confusing, the goal is to determine which interface or interfaces OSPF should use to find other OSPF routers. OSPF determines the interface or interfaces through the network statement, using it to find an IP address that falls within that network subnet. It then determines on which interface that IP address is bound. In summary, OSPF is looking for other OSPF routers. It will only find them on the interfaces where you want it to look, and it will determine which interfaces those are based upon the network address, and then find on which interface that IP address is bound.

Once a network statement is entered, the router dynamically creates an OSPF interface. This is the interface where it looks for other OSPF speaking routers. OSPF starts working immediately when the network statement is added, but no routes are exchanged until we tell OSPF what to share or redistribute.

Redistribution is configured in the Instance tab by telling OSPF to redistribute connected routes, static routes, default routes, or routes learned through other processes like RIP or BGP.

Generally, you will want to redistribute connected and static routes. By redistributing connected routes, any time you configure a new IP address on your router, that network route will be sent to the remainder of the area, thereby telling them, "I am the way to get to this subnet". Do you need to add a new /24 to your router to serve new clients? Instead of adding tons of static routes to every router in your network, simply add the IP address, and the route is built and redistributed automatically by OSPF.

The final piece of information involves redistribution of the default route. If you check the box to redistribute default route, the router will send the default to other routers in the area. Typically, there are only one or two routes in the area that are actually connected to the default gateway, so those will be the only two routers to redistribute default. With two routers connected to the Internet, both redistributing default, you can create a fault-tolerant network with automatic failover if one default gateway fails.

APPLICATION

Use this example any time your router needs to be able to route packets to subnets to which it is not directly connected. An example of this could be two offices on different routers. Router A clients need to get to Router B clients. Static routes on both routers will solve this problem.

Example – Add a Static Route

Adding a static route is very simple. The goal of a static route is to tell this router how to get to other networks. In this example, we want to add a route to get packets to the 192.168.1.0/24 network. This router is directly connected to another router that is directly connected to this target subnet. The route is added as follows:

1. In WinBox, click IP and Routes.

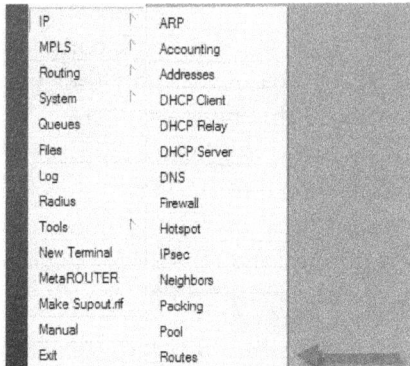

2. Click the plus sign, and enter the destination address of 192.168.1.0/24.

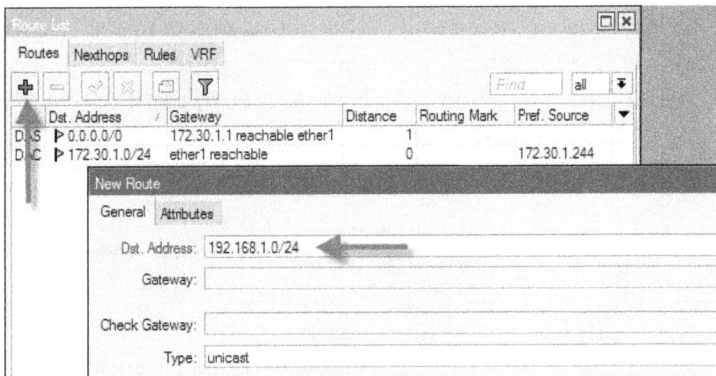

3. On the gateway blank, type 10.0.0.2, which is the IP address of the directly connected router that is attached to our router as well as the destination subnet.

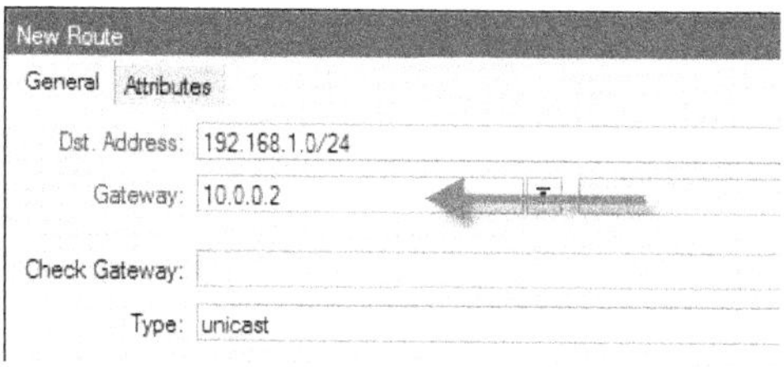

New Route

General | Attributes

Dst. Address: 192.168.1.0/24

Gateway: 10.0.0.2

Check Gateway:

Type: unicast

4. Click Ok.

Use this example any time your router needs to be able to route packets to subnets to which it is not directly connected, but wants to send them all to one upstream router. The most typical scenario is a default route pointing to the ISP.

Example – Add a Default Route

Adding a default route is exactly like a static route. The goal of a default route is to give the router a place to send all packets for which it does not have a specific route. This router is directly connected to another router that is connected to the Internet. The route is added as follows:

1. In WinBox, click IP and Routes.

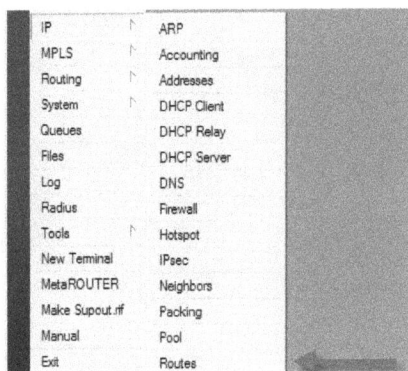

IP		ARP
MPLS		Accounting
Routing		Addresses
System		DHCP Client
Queues		DHCP Relay
Files		DHCP Server
Log		DNS
Radius		Firewall
Tools		Hotspot
New Terminal		IPsec
MetaROUTER		Neighbors
Make Supout.rif		Packing
Manual		Pool
Exit		Routes

2. Click the plus sign, and do not enter a destination address, as the default of 0.0.0.0/0 matches all packets and is used for the default route.

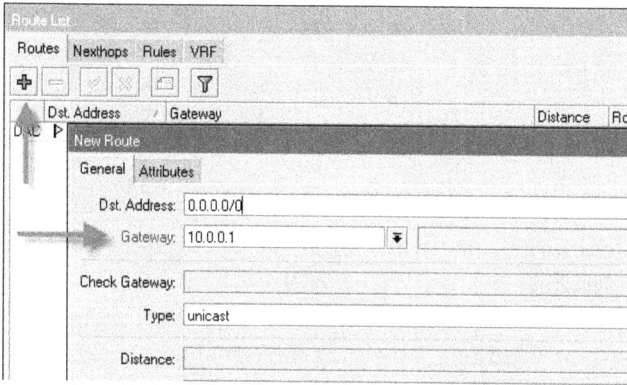

3. On the gateway blank, type 10.0.0.1, which is the IP address of the Internet router.

4. Click OK.

Use this example when your router needs to be able to route packets to subnets to which it is not directly connected, but you do not want the administrative burden of maintaining these routes. OSPF will add the routes for you dynamically.

Example – Set up OSPF, the Basics

While static routes are just as effective as dynamic routes, the use of a dynamic routing protocol like OSPF is the basis of a scalable and mature network that can easily grow without an excessive administrative burden. To set up a basic single area OSPF network, proceed as follows:

1. In WinBox, click Routing and then OSPF.

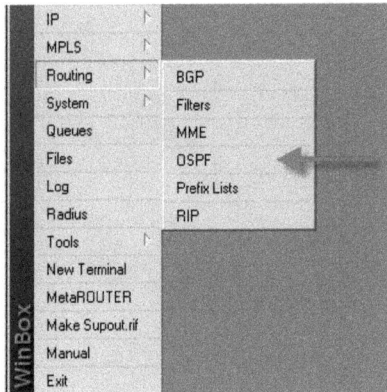

2. Assume we are building a network according to the following diagram. Even though our router has several interfaces and numerous IP addresses, we have selected a management network on which we will run OSPF. These networks all fall within 10.10.10.X/X.

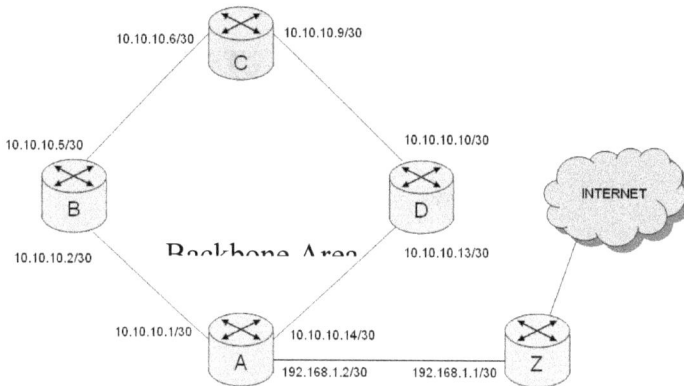

Figure 20 - OSPF Network

3. Now consider router A. It has multiple interfaces with multiple subnets, but we only want to run OSPF with neighbors B, C, and D, but not Z. To do this, click on the Networks tab and then the plus sign. Enter the network address of the network on which you will run OSPF. Notice we do not add the 192.168.1.0/30 network, as we do not want OSPF configured on that interface.

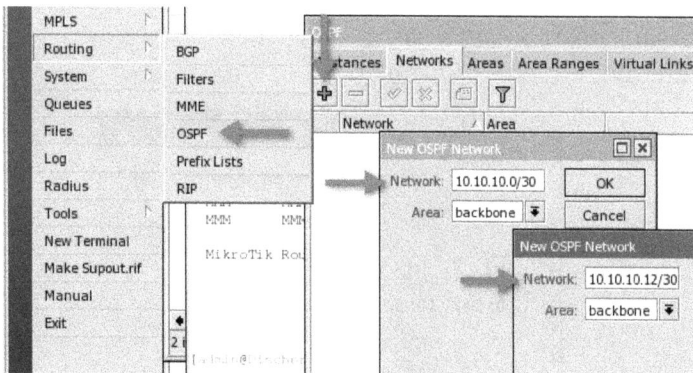

Repeat the process of adding the network statements for routers B, C, and D as you did router A. Each should be configured as follows when you are done:

313

Router B

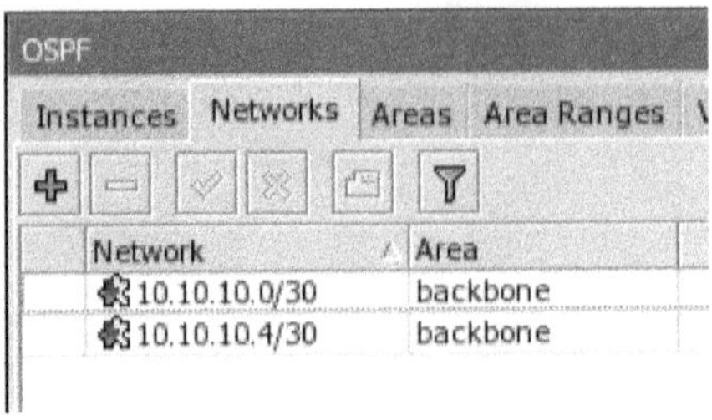

Router C

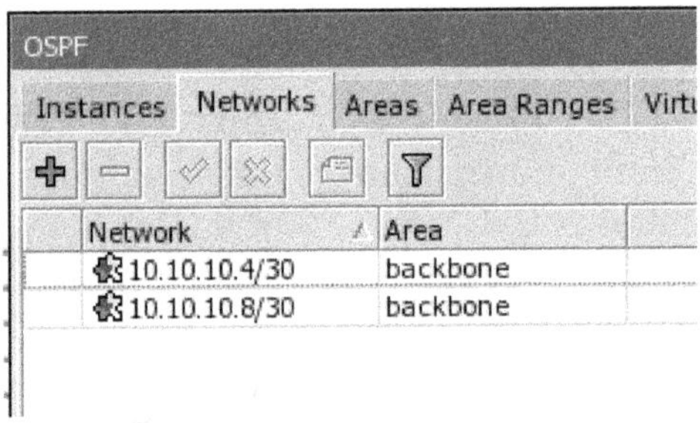

Router D

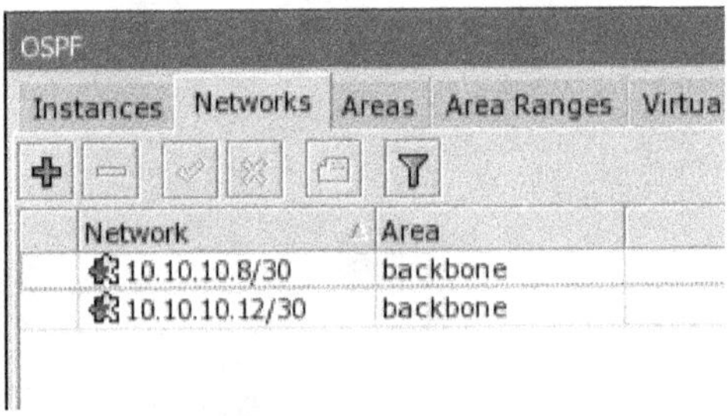

4. Once the network statements are added, OSPF starts working. Now we need to tell it what to redistribute, and this is done on the Instances tab by changing the default instance. For Router A, we want to redistribute static routes, connected routes, and default routes, because router A is the only gateway for our network to get to the

Internet. For routers B, C, and D, we only redistribute static and connected routes. For this small network with a single area, we can use Type I or Type II redistribution.

Configure the instances on all four routers as follows:

Router A

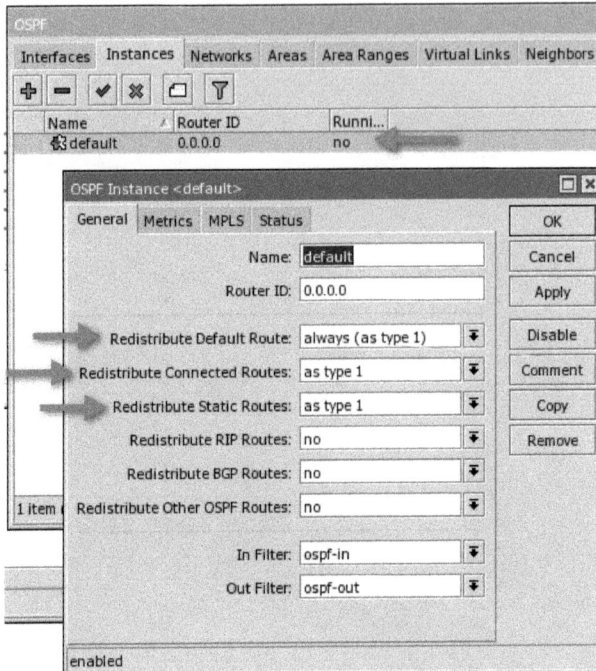

Router B

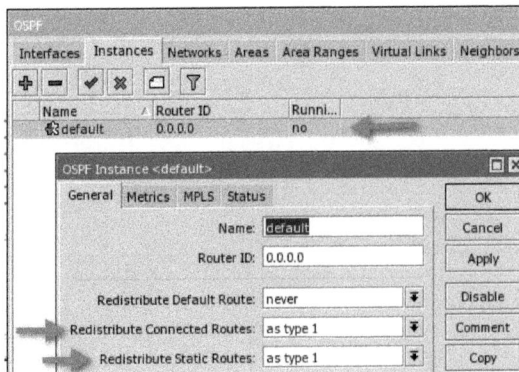

Router C

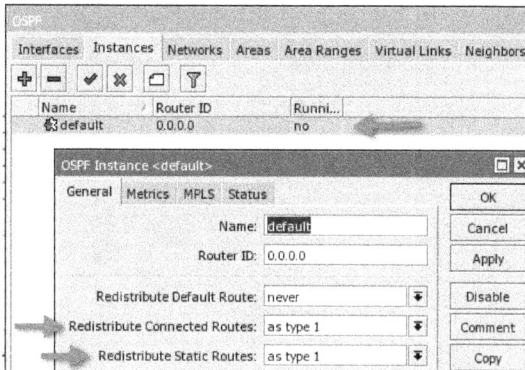

Router D

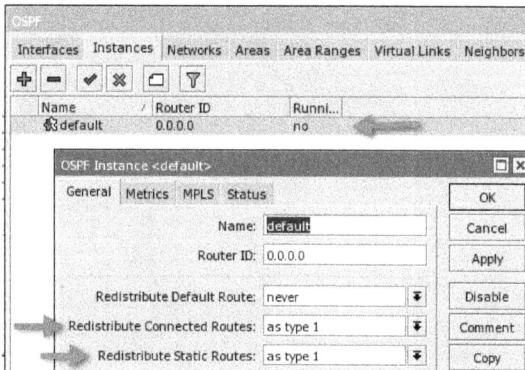

Check the routing table now, and you should see routes to all of the networks configured on all four routers as well as a default route.

For Further Study:

1. As networks grow, multiple areas can enhance network performance by reducing the size of the database and making the network more scalable. Consider dividing the network into multiple areas once you understand the OSPF basics.

2. Using Type I or Type II redistribution is appropriate for multiple areas. With more experience in using OSPF, consider

changing redistribution types as appropriate to engineer traffic flow.

3. You should also consider using authentication between your OSPF routers to enhance security, as well as using passive interfaces and setting a designated router through the priority setting.

Chapter 17 – VPN Tunnels

General

VPN tunnels (Virtual Private Network) tunnels are a method of spanning diverse networks in a manner to allow two network devices to communicate with one another as if they were on the same local area network. Imagine a crowded room full of noisy people with two people on opposite ends of the room that need to communicate with each other. By stretching a pipe across the room and each person speaking into or listening to the end of the pipe, the two would be able to communicate with each other in the noisy, crowded room as if they were the only ones in the room. This analogy roughly describes a VPN tunnel, where the two people wanting to communicate are the tunnel end point hosts and the crowded, noisy room is the public Internet. In an actual VPN tunnel, the traffic would follow the same path as other traffic through the Internet, but would be encapsulated or possibly encrypted. When the packet reaches its destination at the remote end of the tunnel, it is unencrypted and sent to its destination.

The most common use of VPN's is for remote hosts to "dial in" to an office network, thereby allowing the remote device to reach office resources such as printers or file servers, as if it was located on the same private local area network. The transport network becomes invisible to the remote host, and it operates as if it were only one hop away from the office, even though there may be many router hops in between.

Tunnels are either Layer 2 or Layer 3 in design, that is, packets are either carried through the tunnel by routing or by switching. PPtP (Point to Point Tunneling Protocol) is one example of a Layer 3 tunnel, while EoIP is an example of a Layer 2 tunnel. With a Layer 3 tunnel, routers on the end points make the decision about which packets to send across the tunnel, but with Layer 2 tunnels, all packets are sent through the tunnel like a switch (unless there are Layer 2 filters in place to prevent certain types of traffic).

Another application of VPN tunnels is to connect two networks together through the public Internet. A company may have two or more locations across the world and by using VPN tunnels, they can tie all these locations together as if they were on the same LAN. This allows hosts in all remote locations to use services behind the company firewall in an unimpeded manner.

In this book, we will explore five different types of tunnels:

1. **PPTP** – The Point to Point Tunneling Protocol is supported in RouterOS as both client and server. The server will be suitable for a central location and will support a mixture of Windows clients, Mac OSX clients, MikroTik routers, or any other standards-based PPTP client. This is also an easy tunnel to set up between two routers and is a Layer 3 tunnel.

2. **L2TP** – The Layer 2 Tunneling Protocol is also supported, and the setup is exactly the same as PPTP.

3. **EoIP** – Ethernet over Internet Protocol is a Layer 2 tunnel and can be bridged to provide a quick and easy method of bridging two networks together over the Internet at Layer 2; however, it provides no encryption.

4. **MPLS/VPLS** – Multiprotocol Label Switching and Virtual Private LAN Service are powerful protocols that help you create complex and scalable provider networks. By using some basic features of each, we can create simple network tunnels.

5. **PPPoE** – Point to Point Tunneling Protocol over Ethernet is a Layer 3 protocol used by many service providers because of it's ability to restrict network access, use central authentication, and provide automatic provisioning of customers. It is by design a tunnel, but not in the sense of a typical VPN tunnel like PPTP or L2TP, in that it is not used to "tunnel through" public networks. PPPoE supports a special type of IP addressing called point-to-point addressing. To fully understand how point-to-point addressing is used in PPPoE, lets explore it first.

Point to Point Addressing

When the Internet was first born, there were few hosts and many addresses available. Networks were designed based upon classes. These classes were based upon letter designations such as Class B or Class C networks, and the classes were descriptive of the subnet mask that formed the boundaries of the classes. LANS were typically given Class C blocks of addresses, and not much thought was given to subnetting or classless networks.

All of this changed as the Internet exploded, and we suddenly saw the necessity to become more conservative with our IP space. When we began seeing the future depletion of our IPV4 address space, we progressively transitioned from classfull to classless networks. Soon thereafter, customers were allocated small /30 subnets or something slightly larger, instead of entire /24's, and networks were masqueraded or source natted behind firewalls. Now that there are few IPV4 blocks available at the time of this writing, providers have become very conservative with their IP allocations, and the entire Internet has transitioned to classless provisioning.

As we make the observation of the relationship between subnet prefix and subnet size, we see the following mathematical progression:

/24 subnet = 256 addresses, including one network address, one broadcast address, and 254 host addresses

/25 subnet = 128 addresses, including one network address, one broadcast address, and 126 host addresses

and so on through:

/30 subnet = 4 addresses, including one network address, one broadcast address, and 2 host addresses

and finally:

/32 subnet = 2 addresses, including one network address and 1 host addresses

Note that as we begin splitting subnets, we always halve the number of total addresses available. Next, we designate one address for the network address and one for the broadcast; the remainder are host addresses. The pattern seems to change when we get to the /32 subnet or point-to-point addressing. Now, there is only one host address, one network address, and no broadcast address. That is both the complexity and the simplicity of point-to-point addressing.

Point-to-point addressing is used most commonly in PPPoE (Point-to-Point Protocol over Ethernet) configurations, so we will use the PPPoE protocol as the basis for our explanation of point-to-point addressing. When using point-to-point addressing, you find that the network resembles a star topology with respect to multiple hosts connecting to the center of the star, the PPPoE server, and through the server, knowing how to get to every other host. Every address has two pieces of information, the actual host address and the network.

Since there is no available address for broadcast, there is no broadcast address. I like to think of point-to-point addressing as an imaginary piece of wire with two ends. Each end has an address (the end point) and a sort of reminder of the address of the other end of the wire (the network address). Take a look at this concept graphically in the figure below.

A IP: 10.0.0.1/32 ———————————————— IP: 10.0.0.2/32 B
   Network: 10.0.0.2   Network: 10.0.0.1

Figure 21 - Point to Point Addressing

The end of our imaginary wire marked "A" has an IP address of 10.0.0.1/32 and a network address of 10.0.0.2, therefore it knows that the host at the other end of the imaginary wire has an IP address of 10.0.0.2. The end of the wire marked "B" has an IP address of 10.0.0.2/32 and a network address of 10.0.0.1, therefore it knows the host at the other end of the imaginary wire has an IP address of 10.0.0.1. As you can see, there is no availability of an extra address to use as a broadcast address, nor is it needed since each end host already has the information needed to find the other end of the point-to-point connection.

PPPoE – Point to Point Protocol over Ethernet, Applying PTP Addressing

You may be wondering, "How is this useful in a network of more than two hosts?" This concept is useful because it can support a large number of hosts in a very scalable star topology as follows:

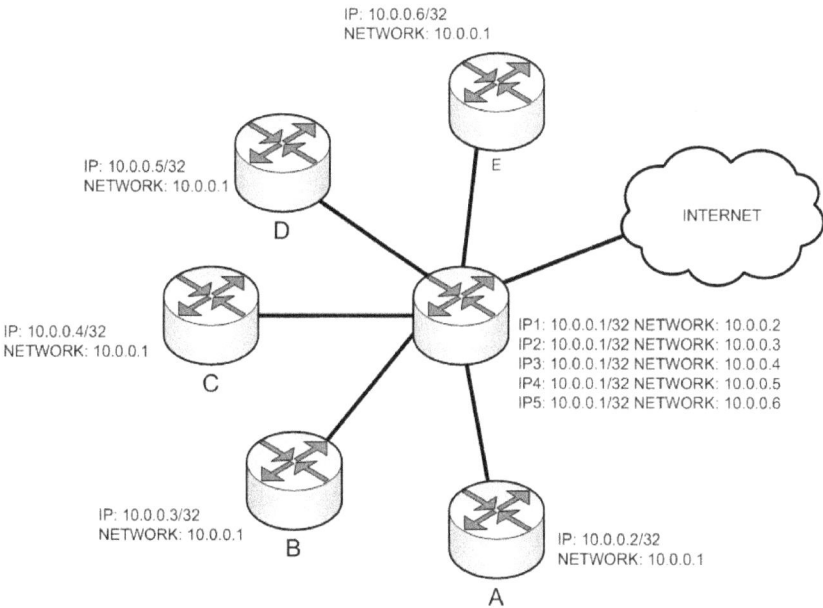

IP: 10.0.0.6/32
NETWORK: 10.0.0.1

IP: 10.0.0.5/32
NETWORK: 10.0.0.1

D

E

INTERNET

IP: 10.0.0.4/32
NETWORK: 10.0.0.1

C

IP1: 10.0.0.1/32 NETWORK: 10.0.0.2
IP2: 10.0.0.1/32 NETWORK: 10.0.0.3
IP3: 10.0.0.1/32 NETWORK: 10.0.0.4
IP4: 10.0.0.1/32 NETWORK: 10.0.0.5
IP5: 10.0.0.1/32 NETWORK: 10.0.0.6

IP: 10.0.0.3/32
NETWORK: 10.0.0.1

B

IP: 10.0.0.2/32
NETWORK: 10.0.0.1

A

Figure 22 - PPPoE Network

As you can see, the configuration is similar to the previous illustration of the wire, with the exception that there are now 5 wires, with router Z at the center of the star. The PPPoE concentrator or "server" has multiple addresses, each with a network address that matches the host IP address of the other end. It appears that the server has duplicate IP's, but understand that they are really not duplicates since they have different network addresses.

This illustrates one of the attributes of point-to-point addressing, which is the conservation of address space, as we are no longer wasting addresses on network and broadcast pairs.

PPPoE uses point to point addressing exclusively, so now that you understand the concept and have been briefly introduced to PPPoE, let's dig in deeper. PPPoE is widely used by large DSL and cable modem providers for some important reasons:

1. It provides a scalable way to control network access. Since it is a Layer 2 protocol, it handles IP addresses and default routes in a fashion similar to DHCP, so it secures the network.

2. It interfaces easily with Radius, a server application widely used since the dialup days that centralizes user access control.

3. It allows the return of numerous attributes by the Radius server such as the creation of rate queues, the assignment of IP addresses, and other functions.

4. With Radius controlling the network, it is simple to provision new customers and turn off access for those that don't pay their bills.

5. And finally, since it uses point-to-point addressing, it conserves IP space.

In this book, we will be using PPPoE server with a local user database and local user profiles. Following this, I will give some topics for further study on extending PPPoE with Radius.

Example - IP Pools

IP pools are ranges of addresses that can be allocated automatically.
These pools were created automatically for us using the DHCP
Server setup script on page 193, but they can easily be created
manually and used by server processes such as PPPoE server.

1. In WinBox, click the IP button, and then select Pools.

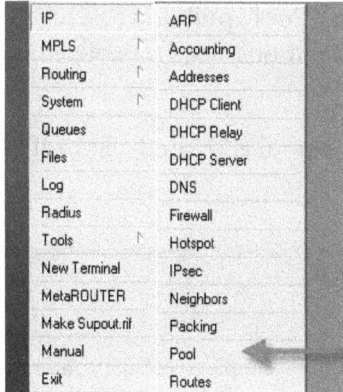

IP		ARP
MPLS		Accounting
Routing		Addresses
System		DHCP Client
Queues		DHCP Relay
Files		DHCP Server
Log		DNS
Radius		Firewall
Tools		Hotspot
New Terminal		IPsec
MetaROUTER		Neighbors
Make Supout.rif		Packing
Manual		Pool
Exit		Routes

2. Click the plus sign to create a new pool.

   (Continued on next page)

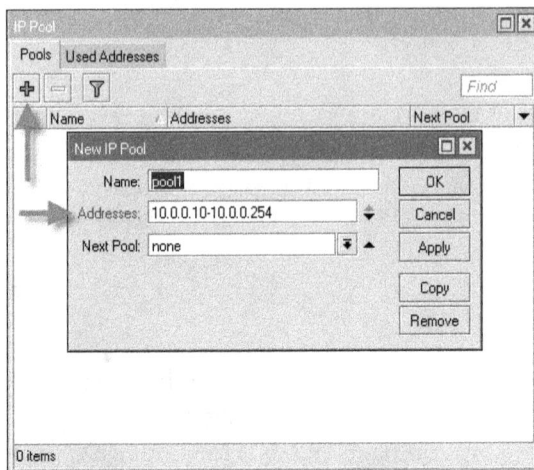

The IP range can be any valid range of IP addresses.

Notice the "Next Pool" pull-down, which can be used to chain pools together, so if one pool is depleted, the next pool can be used.

1. Once the pool is created, click OK.

APPLICATION

Use this example to create profiles that can be shared by VPN servers. Information that is the same for all VPN clients can be put in a profile such as local IP address and the name of the pool of addresses used by the clients.

Example - PPP Profiles

PPP profiles are used by all the PPP-based protocols, including PPPoE, PPTP, and L2TP. The profile is used by the server to cause it to behave based on a policy. It can also be applied to an individual user. We will need a profile to configure PPPoE server, so create one now.

In WinBox, click the PPP button, and select the Profiles tab.
(Continued on next page)

	PPP	
	Switch	
	Mesh	PPP
	IP	Interface PPPoE Servers Secrets Profiles Active Connections
	MPLS	✚ ⊟ ▢ ▽
	Routing	Name Local Address Remote Address Bridge Rate Limit...
	System	default
	Queues	default-encryption
	Files	
	Log	
	Radius	
	Tools	

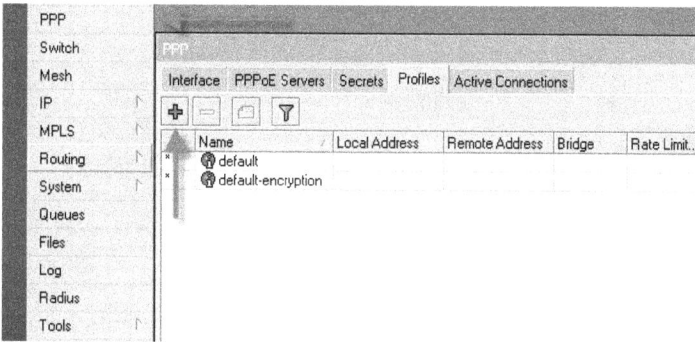

1. Click the plus sign to create a new profile. I suggest you name the profile based on some meaningful criteria, in this case we will call it AP1, meaning it will be used by our access point number 1. The Local Address is the IP used by the point-to-point protocol assigned to this end of the wire. The remote address is the address to be given to the clients, so we want to use the pool we created in the IP Pools example on page 325. The only other setting really required is to set "Change TCP MSS" to "yes". This is necessary to make many secure sites work properly in the client's web browser.

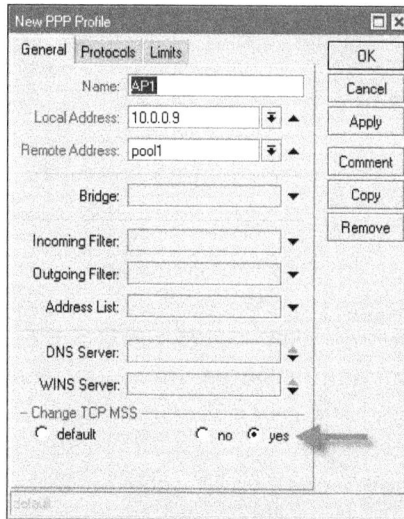

New PPP Profile

General Protocols Limits

Name:	AP1	
Local Address:	10.0.0.9	
Remote Address:	pool1	
Bridge:		
Incoming Filter:		
Outgoing Filter:		
Address List:		
DNS Server:		
WINS Server:		

Change TCP MSS
○ default   ○ no ● yes

OK Cancel Apply Comment Copy Remove

2. Everything else is optional or geared toward a more complex setup, so now click OK, and the profile is completed.

Use this example to configure a PPPoE server that will serve PPPoE clients. Typically, PPPoE is only used in a service provider scenario and is not commonly used in a LAN environment.

Example – Create a PPPoE Server

PPPoE server is the service that handles the incoming clients. It is important to know it is a Layer 2 protocol. This means that it will not work across routers, and the interface on which the server is running must be directly connected to the clients. One way to accommodate this across routed networks is to use a Layer 2 tunnel like EoIP (Ethernet over IP).

1. To create the PPPoE Server, in WinBox, click the PPP button, and select the PPPoE Servers tab.

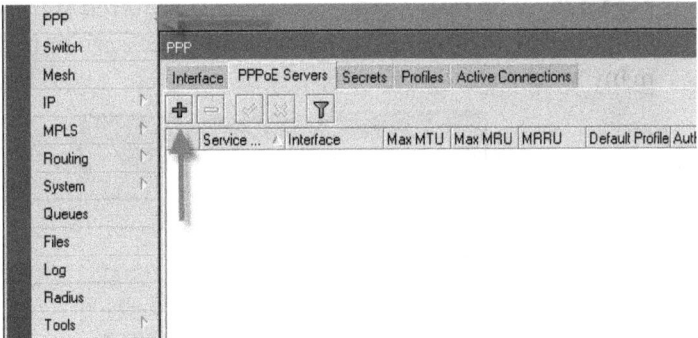

2. Click the plus sign to create a new instance. The Service name is important because of the ability to run multiple servers on the same interface. When this is the case, the client can be configured to request a specific service name, and then that server will answer that client. If no name is specified on the client and if there are multiple servers, there is no control over which one will answer, so keep that in mind. Next, set the interface where it will run. Remember that if you have bridged the physical interface, then the service must run on the bridge, so select the bridge instead of the actual interface.

```
New PPPoE Service                        □ ☒
    Service Name: service1              OK
       Interface: wlan1          ⬇      Cancel
        Max MTU: 1480                   Apply
        Max MRU: 1480
           MRRU:                  ▼     Disable
Keepalive Timeout:               ▼      Copy
                                        Remove
  Default Profile: AP1           ⬇
                 □ One Session Per Host
    Max Sessions:                ▼
─ Authentication ─────────────────────
  ✔ pap            ✔ chap
  ✔ mschap1        ✔ mschap2
enabled
```

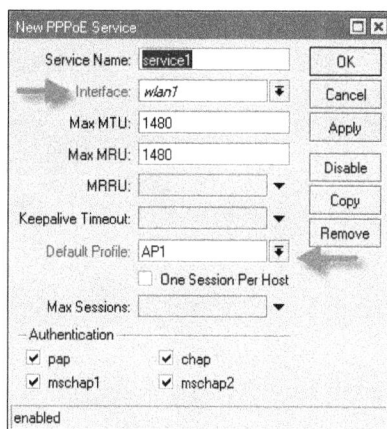

3. Finally, select the profile created in the previous example on page 326, and then click OK.

APPLICATION

Use this example to create a user/password database to be used by any of the VPN servers. For example, a PPTP VPN server will use the secrets to authenticate clients.

Example – Create a User (Secret)

The final step in the server configuration is the creation of a client user name and password, which can be done on the Secrets tab.

1. On the Secrets tab, click the plus sign. Fill in the name as the user name and assign a password. I always set the service type because this narrows the scope of the services that can use this secret for authentication.

    (Continued on next page)

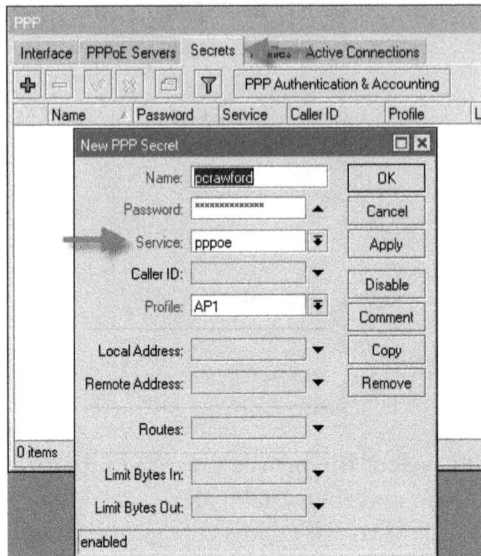

2. All of the other settings are optional, so now click OK.

Use this example any time a group of clients can share similar characteristics when they connect to a VPN server. For example, to limit all PPPoE clients to a certain bandwidth limitation, assign their secret to a profile with a rate limit.

Example – Create a Client Profile

In the same way that profiles can be applied to servers, they can also be applied to PPPoE clients. Typically, this concept is used to assign a static IP to a PPPoE client or to set a rate limit. Creating a rate limit will cause a simple queue to be created for the client when they authenticate.

1. In WinBox, click the PPP button, and select the Profiles tab.

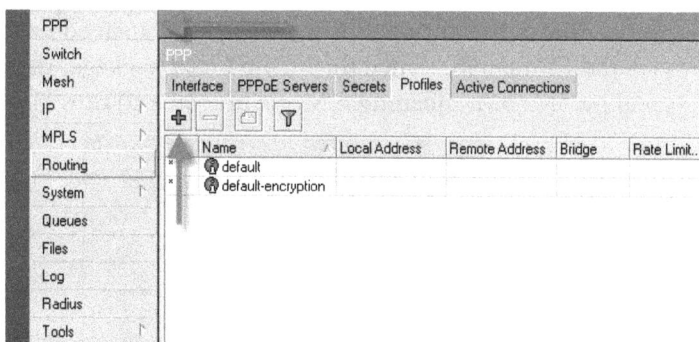

2. Click the plus sign to create a new profile. I like to name the profile based on some meaningful criteria. In this case, we will call it Gold because we have a Gold package with the highest speeds and a public IP address as the options. The Local Address is the IP used by the point-to-point protocol to assign to this end of the wire. The remote address is the address to be given to the clients, so we want to use the pool we created in the IP Pools example on page 325, but in this case we might create a pool of public IP's. The only other setting really required is to set the "Change TCP MSS" to "yes".

This is necessary to make many secure sites work properly in the client's web browser.

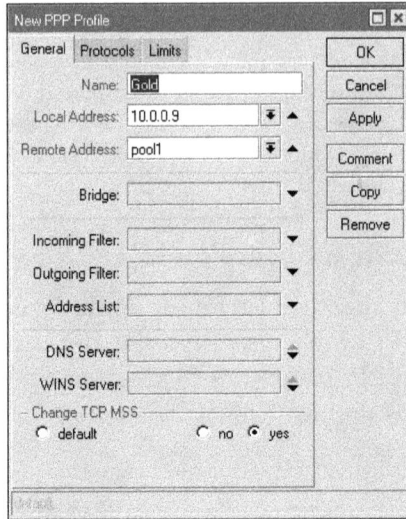

```
New PPP Profile                                    □ ×
General  Protocols  Limits                      ┌──────────┐
                                                │    OK    │
         Name: Gold                             ├──────────┤
                                                │  Cancel  │
  Local Address: 10.0.0.9          ⬇ ▲          ├──────────┤
                                                │  Apply   │
 Remote Address: pool1             ⬇ ▲          ├──────────┤
                                                │ Comment  │
                                                ├──────────┤
        Bridge:                        ▼        │   Copy   │
                                                ├──────────┤
                                                │  Remove  │
 Incoming Filter:                      ▼        └──────────┘

 Outgoing Filter:                      ▼

   Address List:                       ▼

    DNS Server:                        ⬍

   WINS Server:                        ⬍
  ─ Change TCP MSS ──────────────────────
    ○ default          ○ no  ⦿ yes
```

3. Since this is a client profile, we will create a speed limitation on the Limits tab. Since this is the Gold package, the limit will be 5M/5M, meaning 5 Mbps upload and download.

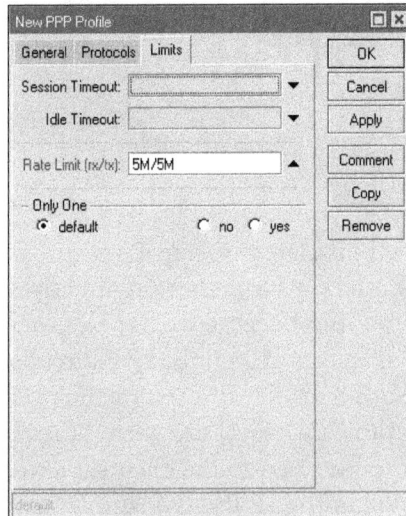

```
New PPP Profile                                    □ ×
General  Protocols  Limits                      ┌──────────┐
                                                │    OK    │
 Session Timeout:                      ▼        ├──────────┤
                                                │  Cancel  │
    Idle Timeout:                      ▼        ├──────────┤
                                                │  Apply   │
                                                ├──────────┤
 Rate Limit (rx/tx): 5M/5M             ▲        │ Comment  │
                                                ├──────────┤
  ─ Only One ──────────────────────────         │   Copy   │
    ⦿ default          ○ no  ○ yes              ├──────────┤
                                                │  Remove  │
                                                └──────────┘
```

4. Everything else is optional or geared toward a more complex setup, so now click OK, and the profile is completed. Back on the secrets tab, assign the profile to any client that buys the Gold package.

5. The profile is now completed and may be assigned to one or multiple clients in the secrets tab.

Use this example any time your router needs to be able to connect to a PPPoE server. Many ISP's require PPPoE such as DSL, WISP, and Cable modem technologies.

Example – Create a PPPoE Client

With the server configured, we need a client, and RouterOS provides that as well. Remember that since RouterOS is standards-based, any PPPoE client should work with a RouterOS PPPoE server. To create a PPPoE client:

1. In WinBox, click the PPP button and in the list, select PPPoE Client.

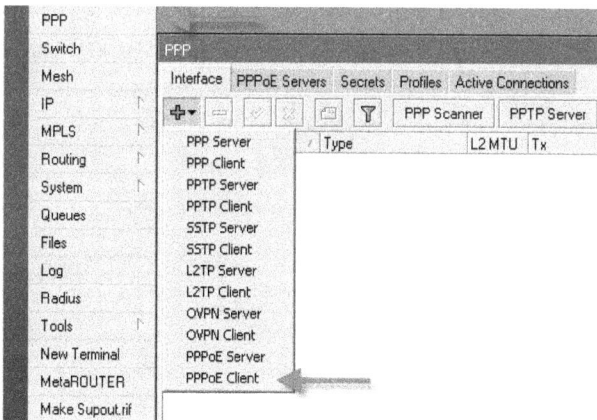

2. The Name is optional, but you will need to select the Interface on the General tab. Remember, this is a Layer 2 protocol, so it needs to know where to look for the server.

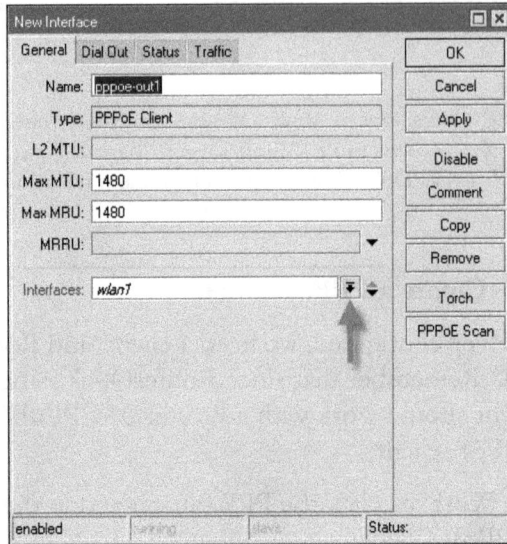

3. On the Dial Out tab, you can select a service name to match the server's service name or leave blank for any service. Next, add the User and Password, and you will likely want to Use Peer DNS, so check that box as well.

(Continued on next page)

New Interface

General | Dial Out | Status | Traffic

Service: ▼
AC Name: ▼
User: pcrawford
Password: ****************
Profile: default

☐ Dial On Demand
☑ Add Default Route
☑ Use Peer DNS

Allow
☑ pap ☑ chap
☑ mschap1 ☑ mschap2

OK
Cancel
Apply
Disable
Comment
Copy
Remove
Torch
PPPoE Scan

enabled | Running | Slave | Status:

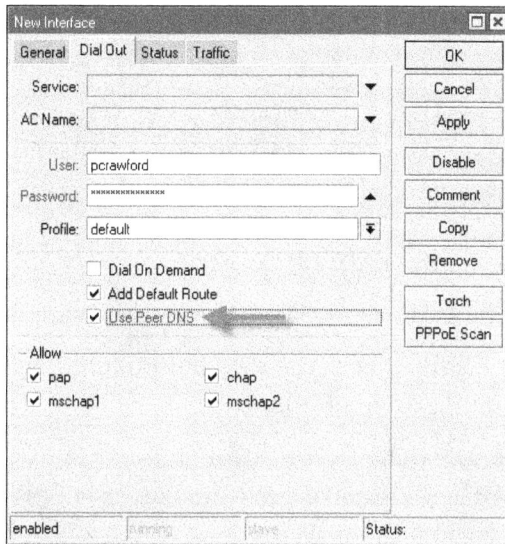

4. Click ok, and the client should immediately negotiate a
    connection to the server.

PPTP and L2TP Tunnels

PPTP tunnels are likely the type of tunnel you want to configure if
you want to "dial in" to your office network or home network. By
configuring your MikroTik router as a PPTP server and connecting it
directly to the Internet, you can create a PPTP client on a Windows,
Mac OSX, or RouterOS device. You can then dial the connection
and once connected, your computer will have access to your home or
office's resources as if it were behind your home or office firewall.

The same configuration can be done between two MikroTik routers,
with one configured as the PPTP server and one as a PPTP client.
RouterOS supports several other tunnel types including L2TP.
These tunnels are Layer 3 tunnels, meaning they need to have IP
connectivity in place prior to initiating the tunnel, unlike PPPoE,
which works at Layer 2 and then creates the Layer 3 connection.

Use this example to create a PPTP server. A PPTP server is one solution for "road warriors", those that work at home and need to access a remote network. Site to site VPN's are another application of PPTP tunnels.

Example – Create a PPTP Server

Setting up the PPTP (or L2TP server) is very simple.

1. In WinBox, click the PPP button. On the interface tab, click the PPTP Server button.

2. Check the box to enable the server, and select a profile. The profile is created exactly the same for PPPoE as is shown on page 326.

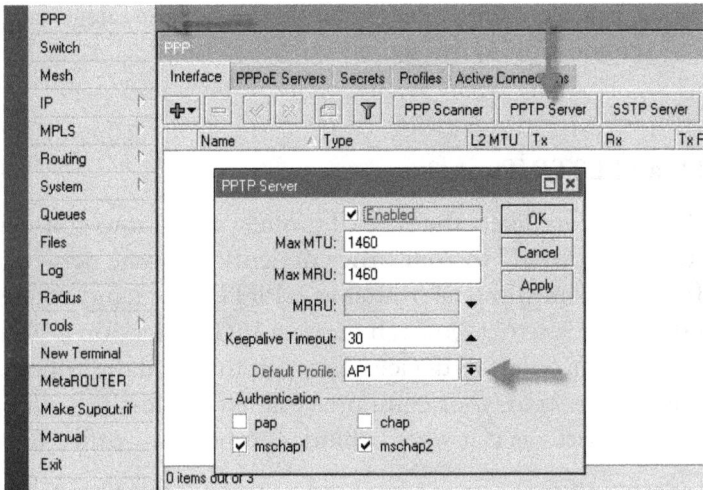

3. PPTP will now accept incoming connections and issue the client an IP address according to the profile. Note that the same secrets database is used as PPPoE and is shown on page 32.

An L2TP server is created exactly like a PPTP server and is more widely supported now due to security concerns with PPTP. An example of L2TP Server follows in this chapter.

Adding Routes for Tunnels

If you are using a PPTP tunnel to join two networks on different subnets, you will need to add routes to each router pointing to the other router's subnet. For example, for a PPTP client, the destination network will be the subnet at the far end of the tunnel, and the gateway will be the IP address of the PPTP server contained in the server's PPTP profile as the Local IP. For the server end of the tunnel, the destination network will be the remote client's subnet, and the gateway IP address will be the PPTP client's tunnel IP.

Tunnels With IP Addresses on Same Subnet as LAN Hosts

This is the remote end tunnel, and the remote LAN is 192.168.1.0/24:

```
Address <10.10.10.2>                    □ ▣ ☒

    Address:  10.10.10.2          ┌─────────┐
                                  │   OK    │
    Network:  10.10.10.1          └─────────┘
                                   ┌────────┐
   Interface: pptp-out2            │  Copy  │
                                   └────────┘
                                   ┌────────┐
                                   │ Remove │
                                   └────────┘




 dynamic
```

This is the server end tunnel, and the server LAN is 192.168.0.0/24:

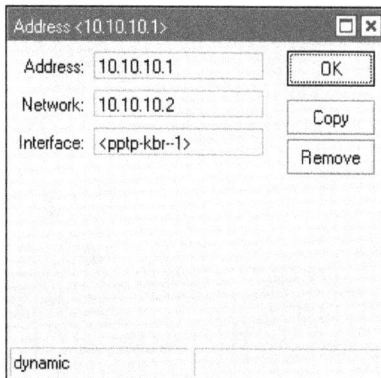

```
Address <10.10.10.1>                    □ ☒

    Address:  10.10.10.1          ┌─────────┐
                                  │   OK    │
    Network:  10.10.10.2          └─────────┘
                                   ┌────────┐
   Interface: <pptp-kbr--1>        │  Copy  │
                                   └────────┘
                                   ┌────────┐
                                   │ Remove │
                                   └────────┘




 dynamic
```

On the remote end, add this route:

Destination: 192.168.0.0/24 and Gateway: 10.10.10.1

On the Server end, add this route:

Destination: 192.168.1.0/24 and Gateway: 10.10.10.2

This will allow the two LAN subnets to be able to reach one another through the tunnel.

Note that if you assign your PPTP clients IP addresses from the same subnet as your PPTP server's local area network, you will need to enable proxy-arp on the interface facing your local area network clients. Proxy-arp transmits the MAC of all connected hosts so that the PPTP server will ARP for the remote client, thereby enabling LAN hosts to communicate with it.

APPLICATION

Use this example to create a L2TP server. This is what you would use for "road warriors" or home workers that want to access a remote network. Site to site VPN's are another application. You can run PPTP and L2TP on the same server.

Example - Configuring L2TP Server

To configure L2TP, follow the exact same steps as for the PPTP server previously described in this chapter, except perform the configuration using the L2TP button on the PPP Interface tab.

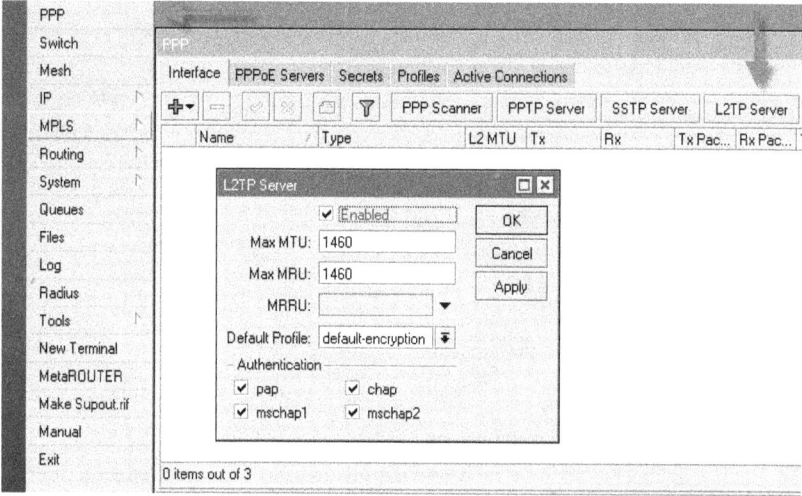

PPP Status Tab

The PPP Status tab shows the status of any clients that may be connected to the router's PPP services. The IP address, user name, and connection time is displayed for each client.

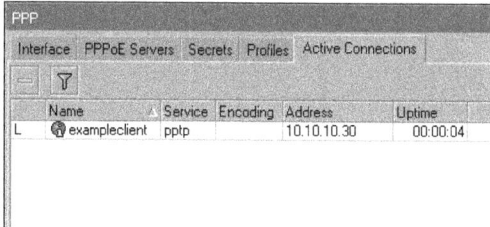

Bridging Tunnels

Thus far, we have explored three tunnel types, PPPoE, PPTP, and L2TP. All three are Layer 3 routed tunnels, but it is also possible to create tunnels that can be bridged. Bridged tunnels work just like any bridge, that is, packets that enter a bridge port are transmitted out the other bridge ports. Bridges join dissimilar interfaces into a single logical interface.

Two types of tunnels that can bridge networks are EoIP (Ethernet Over IP) and VPLS (Virtual Private LAN Service). EoIP is simpler to create, but has increased overhead over VPLS.

Use this example to create an EoIP tunnel between two MikroTik routers. This is a good choice for a site-to-site VPN where you want to extend Layer 2 connectivity between two routers. An example is a tunnel across the internet with each end bridged to an Ethernet interface, thereby resulting in extending a Layer 2 LN between 2 Ethernet ports across the world.

APPLICATION

Example – Create a Bridged EoIP Tunnel

1. In WinBox, click the Interfaces button, and select a new EoIP tunnel interface. The only information that is mandatory is the Remote IP address of the other end of the tunnel. If tunneling across the Internet, this will be the public IP address of the remote host. The tunnel ID must be unique for every tunnel on the router, so use the default or change if adding multiples.

2. Click OK.

3. Repeat the process on the remote end of the tunnel, swapping the Remote IP address for the other end of the tunnel.

Once the tunnel is running, evidenced by the letter "R" next to the interface, you can bridge it to other physical interfaces. For example, if your LAN is on ether1 on both ends of the tunnel, create a new bridge interface by clicking the Bridge button and the plus sign.

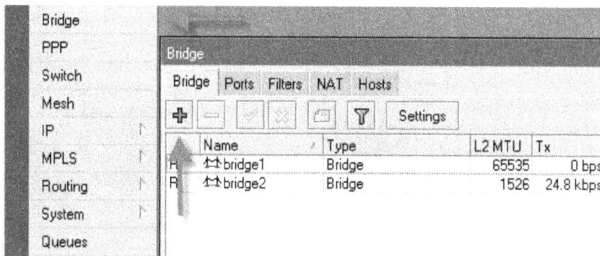

Bridge					
PPP	Bridge				
Switch	Bridge Ports Filters NAT Hosts				
Mesh	➕ ➖ ✓ ✗ 🗀 ▼ Settings				
IP					
MPLS	Name	⁄	Type	L2 MTU	Tx
	R 🔀 bridge1		Bridge	65535	0 bps
Routing	R 🔀 bridge2		Bridge	1526	24.8 kbps
System					
Queues					

On the ports tab, add ether1 and the EoIP tunnel you just created. Repeat on the remote end of the link, and your two networks will be joined at Layer 2.

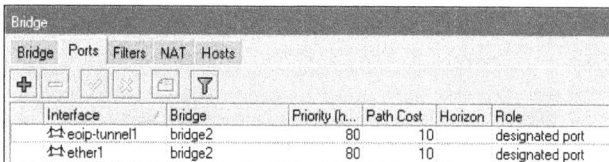

Bridge					
Bridge Ports Filters NAT Hosts					
➕ ➖ ✏ ✗ 🗀 ▼					
Interface	⁄ Bridge	Priority (h...	Path Cost	Horizon	Role
🔀 eoip-tunnel1	bridge2	80	10		designated port
🔀 ether1	bridge2	80	10		designated port

Note: All versions after Version 6.30 support IPsec encryption over EoIP by simply supplying the same IPsec password on both tunnels interfaces.

This can be added during setup or afterward like this:

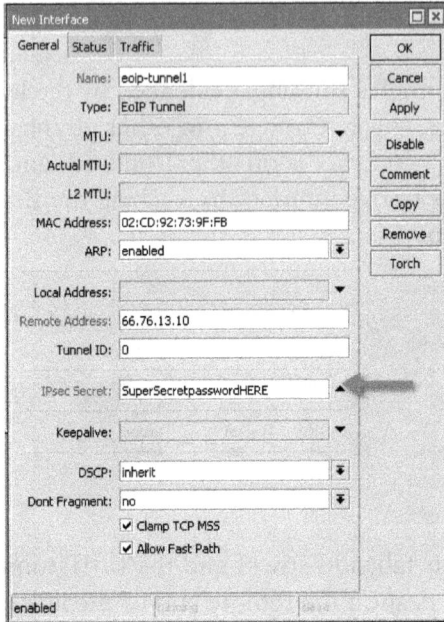

Use this example to create a transparent, Layer 2, bridgeable tunnel between two routers. This does the same thing as the previous EoIP tunnel with less overhead and better performance.

APPLICATION

Example – Create a Transparent VPLS Tunnel

The routing and MPLS packages are required to create a transparent VPLS tunnel. This example assumes you are connecting two hosts with a VPLS tunnel in order to bridge two wireless devices together without using EoIP or station-wds mode.

It is also assumed that you have an existing wireless connection between the two devices (one device in ap-bridge or bridge mode and the other device in station mode), which is associated with the access point. This can be done as demonstrated on page 270.

MPLS also requires Layer 3 connectivity between the two devices, so you will need an IP address on the wireless interface on the AP device and an IP address on the same subnet on the wireless interface on the station device. Adding IP addresses is covered on page 37. The two hosts should be able to ping each other.

In this example, we are assuming that the AP has an IP address of 10.0.0.1/24 on the wlan1 interface and that the station is associated wirelessly with the AP and has an IP address of 10.0.0.2/24 on its wlan1 interface.

Near End of Tunnel (AP)

1. In WinBox, begin by clicking the MPLS button. First, you must turn LDP on by clicking the LDP Settings button and enabling LDP.

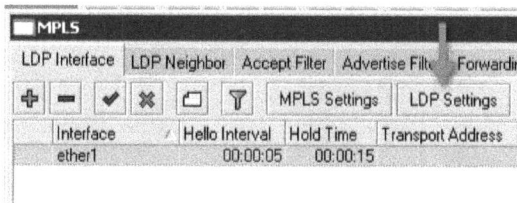

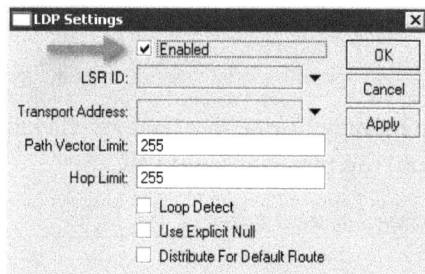

2. On the LDP tab, click the plus sign. Select the interface on which we will create the tunnel, in this case wlan1, and the transport IP address, which is the wlan1 IP of this router, 10.0.0.1, and click OK.

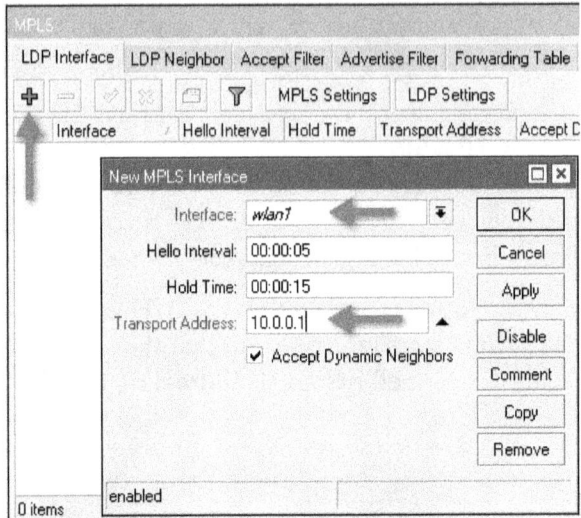

3. In WinBox, click the MPLS button, and select the VPLS submenu button. On the VPLS tab, click the plus sign. Set the Remote Peer to the IP address of the remote end's wlan1 interface, in this example, 10.0.0.2. Set the VPLS ID to the default of 0:0, and click OK.

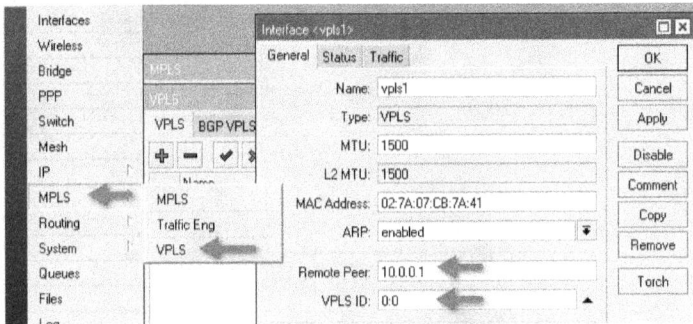

4. Create a new bridge interface by clicking the Bridge button, the plus sign, and OK.

   (Continued on next page)

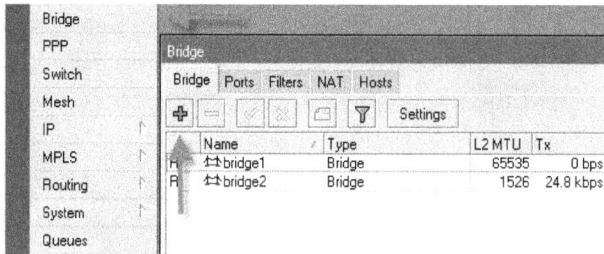

	Name		Type	L2 MTU	Tx
R	bridge1		Bridge	65535	0 bps
R	bridge2		Bridge	1526	24.8 kbps

5. On the bridge ports tab, click the plus sign, and add the LAN interface, in this case, ether1. Click the plus sign again, add the vpls1 interface you just created, and click OK.

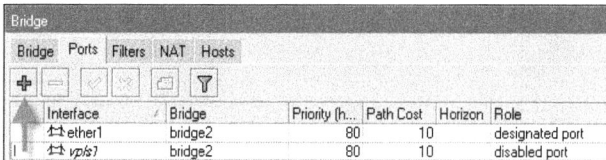

	Interface	Bridge	Priority (h...	Path Cost	Horizon	Role
	ether1	bridge2	80	10		designated port
	vpls1	bridge2	80	10		disabled port

Far End of Tunnel (station)

1. In WinBox, begin by clicking the MPLS button. First, you must turn LDP on by clicking the LDP Settings button and enabling LDP.

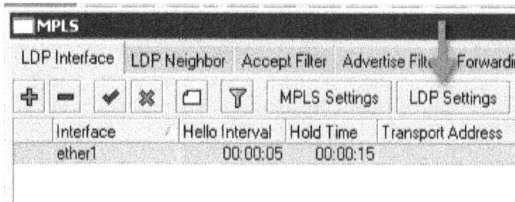

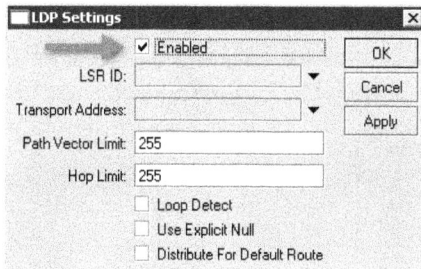

2. On the LDP tab, click the plus sign. Select the interface on which we will create the tunnel, in this case ether1, and the transport IP address, which is the public IP of this router, 10.0.0.2, and click OK.

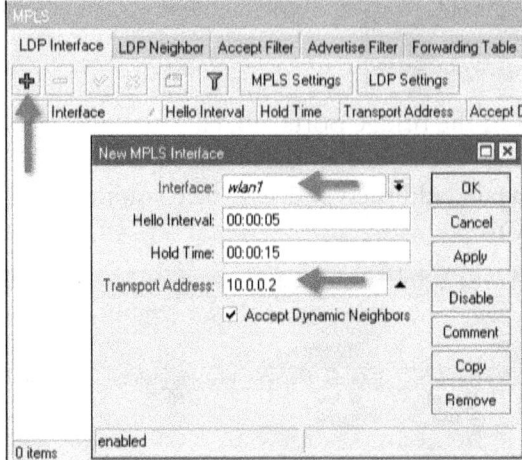

3. In WinBox, click the VPLS button, and on the VPLS tab, click the plus sign. Set the Remote Peer to the IP address of the remote end's public interface, in this example 10.0.0.1. Set the VPLS ID to the default of 0:0, and click OK.

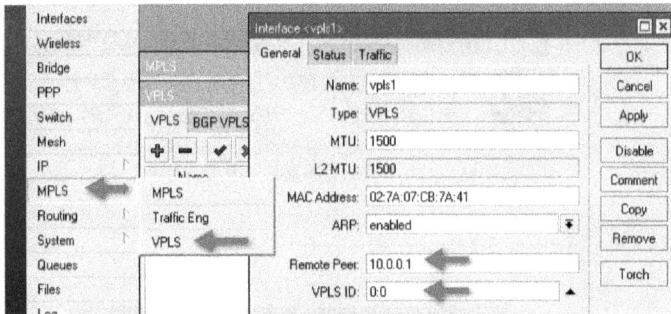

4. Create a new bridge interface by clicking the Bridge button, then the plus sign, and then OK.

(Continued on next page)

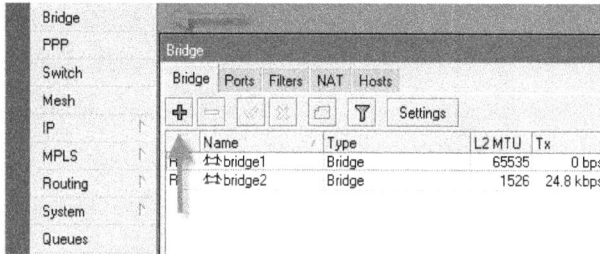

		Name	/ Type	L2 MTU	Tx
H		‡‡bridge1	Bridge	65535	0 bps
R		‡‡bridge2	Bridge	1526	24.8 kbps

5. On the bridge ports tab, click the plus sign, and add the LAN interface, in this case, ether1. Click the plus sign again, add the vpls1 interface you just created, and click OK.

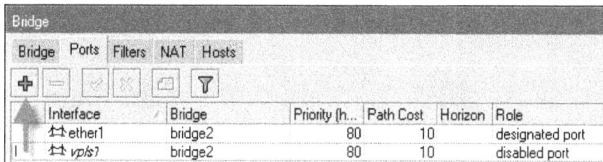

	Interface	/ Bridge	Priority (h...	Path Cost	Horizon	Role
	‡‡ether1	bridge2	80	10		designated port
I	‡‡ vpls1	bridge2	80	10		disabled port

The two LANS are now bridged using VPLS. To confirm that LDP is running, click the MPLS button and then the LDP Neighbor tab. You should see the other end of the tunnel displayed. To confirm that the VPLS tunnel is running, click the Interfaces button, double click the new VPLS interface, and check the status tab. You should see a display of the tunnel details.

For Further Study: MPLS and VPLS are powerful protocols that can do far more than bridge a wireless link. They are a main topic in the MTCINE (MikroTik Certified Internetworking Engineer) certification course and can greatly expand your networks' capabilities.

Chapter 18 – Switching

Introduction

This chapter is fairly long and contains significantly more general information about switching theory and the switch function of the CRS (Cloud Router Switches) as well as topics specific to RouterOS. My reasoning for this is that in my experience using these switches, I have found that little detailed documentation exists. I wanted to create a reference that would stand on its own.

Background of Switch Design

Years ago, routers were routers and switches were switches, but that has really changed. Nowadays, Layer 2 and Layer 3 functions are typically available within the same chassis, and in the case of RouterBOARDS, on the same motherboard. This is done by utilizing a processor or CPU(s) for routing functions and a dedicated switch chip for switching functions. This has many benefits to the end user, including reducing rack space and power consumption. But it does often blur the line between these two functions, thereby adding complexity, at least in the mind of a user who has not taken time to understand the capabilities. The good news is that it is actually quite easy to utilize these functions with some time spent learning.

Switched networks have become more important when deploying wired LANs as common home and office devices are becoming more "network aware". Even homes and small businesses need devices to be able to share information and access the public Internet. That requires connectivity.

It was also not that long ago that most switches used in most deployments were unmanaged switches. As network services evolved, managed switches became necessary to provide the level of service and monitoring capability required for quality of service, support for technologies such as security, and voice over IP (VOIP) on shared data networks.[5]

MikroTik switch/router devices support both Layer 2 and Layer 3 functions in one box. These functions can be used separately or together to reduce deployment cost and conserve space and power.

Switch Operation

Regardless of the manufacturer, Ethernet switches function in basically the same manner. Managed switches specifically have the ability to perform advanced functions and to manipulate the way the switch performs its basic role, which is to move frames from one port to another. The most basic concept of switching is to make a decision based on two traffic flows:

Ingress – Traffic entering a port.

Egress – Traffic leaving a port.

Since switches function at Layer 2, their forwarding decisions are made based upon the destination MAC addresses of the frames they process. Once a switch learns which port a MAC address is located on, that information is saved in the switch's memory, thereby creating a strict association between MAC address and port. The MAC address table is typically populated dynamically, but we can also manipulate it manually.

The Switching Process

Understanding these basic terms, *ingress, egress,* and *forwarding,* is important as you navigate through the functions of a switch. Begin by understanding that a switch learns the location of a MAC address based on the frame's source MAC address and then forwards that frame based on the frame's destination MAC address. This means that source MAC addresses are learned on egress and added to the MAC address table. Through this process, the source MAC is associated with a port of ingress. If an entry already exists, the age timer for that entry is updated or refreshed. If an entry does not exist, the source MAC address is not associated with the ingress port in the MAC address table. Next, the switch examines the destination MAC address. If it is not in the MAC address table, the switch floods that frame to all the ports, except the port that the frame entered (ingress). Once a reply is received from the destination MAC address host, it is added to the table, the frame is forwarded, and the process is complete. Here is the process again, step by step in an example:

1. Frame enters Port 1. Is source MAC in MAC address table? If yes, continue to 2. If not, associate source MAC with ingress port.
2. Switch examines destination MAC address. If it is in the MAC address table, it is forwarded. If it is not, the frame is flooded to all ports and awaits a reply.
3. Source port of reply is recorded and the packet is forwarded.

Collision Domains

Two terms often heard in wired and wireless networking, which are often misused, are collision domain and broadcast domain. We will start by discussing collision domains.

In the long-gone days of Ethernet hubs, all the ports of the hub shared the same collision domain, meaning they all competed for access to the hub to send their frames. Collisions occurred regularly and retransmits were required. The same phenomenon occurs in Wi-Fi networks where all Wi-Fi devices contend for wireless access. This is obviously inefficient and necessitates protocols and workarounds to minimize the effects. Switches, on the other hand, are able to create something called microsegmentation[5], meaning each port of the switch is a separate collision domain. Therefore, collisions cannot occur within switches, allowing them to operate at wire speed.

Broadcast Domains

As discussed previously, switches filter most of the frames based on MAC address, only transmitting frames to the port where the host is located and flooding frames only when they need to learn the port on which a host is connected. Switches, however, do not filter broadcasts because other switches need to be able to receive them so that they too can learn the topology of the network. Therefore, broadcast frames are sent to all the switch ports, except for the port of ingress.

Broadcast frames are generated when certain network services need to make announcements to other hosts on the network and are constantly being generated. In Ethernet networks, a frame that has a MAC address of FF-FF-FF-FF-FF-FF, that is, 48 binary ones, simply means this frame is intended to be received by all hosts on the network and is termed a broadcast frame. Too many broadcast frames can slow down a large network. Therefore, in this example, a broadcast domain comprises all hosts that can receive the broadcast frame. When two switches are connected together, the size of the broadcast domain is increased proportionately to the number of hosts added with the next switch.

Reducing Network Congestion

Managed switches help alleviate (but not eliminate) network congestion. As described previously, each port is a separate collision domain, so there is no contention for the media. Next, they operate in full-duplex mode, meaning a host can transmit and receive at the same time. Finally, they have the ability to reduce the size of the broadcast domain by using a concept called VLANS (virtual LANs).

Integrated Managed Switch Features in RouterBOARD Hardware

The benefits to speed and functionality are immense, so to fully utilize the power of RouterOS and RouterBOARDs with switching functions, especially the CRS (Cloud Router Switch series), it is essential to have at least a basic understanding of how to use these switch chips.

RouterBOARDs, especially the CRS, have a lot of advanced Layer 2 switching capabilities, but in my experience, most of the complex functions are seldom used. Therefore, by getting a basic understanding of the most commonly used functions and applications here in this book, you will have a level of understanding most MikroTik users utilize in their daily work.

Even some of the least expensive RouterBOARDs have switch chips with limited functionality. For example, the RB951 series will allow you to join ports together in a switch group, thereby negating the need for bridging, which requires CPE resources. The RB951 utilizes the Atheros 8327 chip and the capabilities of this chip, as well as other switch chips. It can be found on the MikroTik Wiki by searching for Switch Chip Features. The 8327 for example, supports switching, mirroring, and VLANs.

What are VLANS

A VLAN (Virtual LAN) is any broadcast domain that is partitioned and isolated on a computer network at the data link layer (Layer 2). VLANs can be configured on a router as virtual interfaces that are subordinate to a physical interface or in a switch through a table that controls which VLANs can pass out of a port.

When an Ethernet frame exits a port and an 802.1q tag or VLAN tag is added to the frame, that is called tagging. When we remove the tag, that is called untagging. This is an important step because most of the devices on our networks, like PC's, don't support tagging. Untagging the frames before exposing them to the non-VLAN aware devices allows the traffic to be received by your PC just like any other non-VLAN traffic. By using an access port, your PC doesn't even know VLANs are in use on the switch. They become invisible to the edge device.

When a port accepts tagged traffic from multiple VLANs, that is considered a trunk port. When a switch removes VLAN tags (untagging) and then sends that traffic to a port, that is called an access port or customer/client port because that port is allowed to access a VLAN, typically for one customer or device.

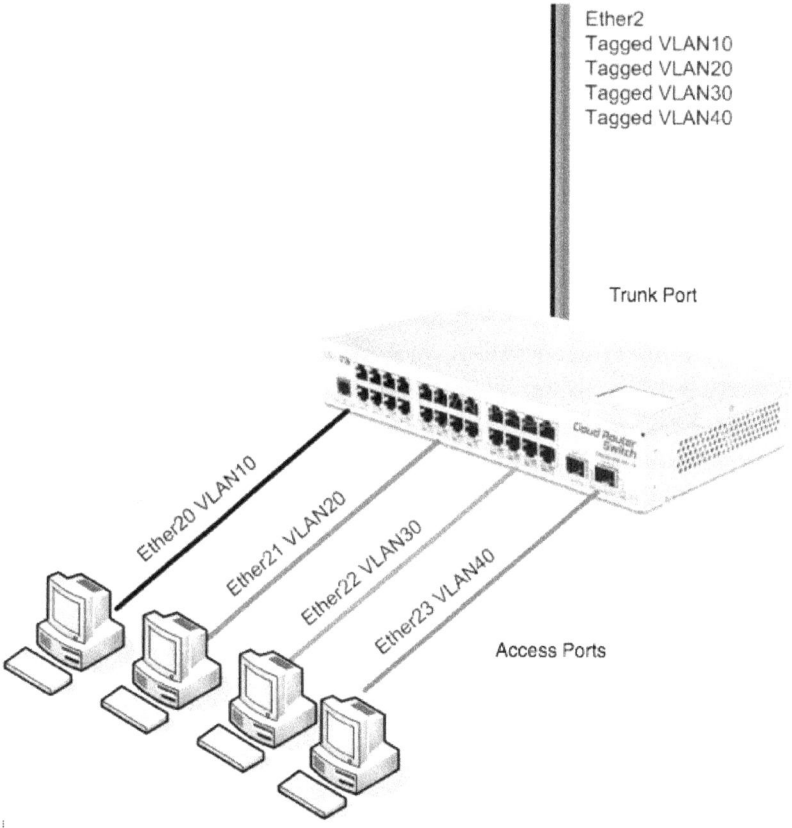

Ether2
Tagged VLAN10
Tagged VLAN20
Tagged VLAN30
Tagged VLAN40

Trunk Port

Ether20 VLAN10
Ether21 VLAN20
Ether22 VLAN30
Ether23 VLAN40

Access Ports

Figure 23 – VLANs in Action

The most common application of VLANs is one or two trunk ports and multiple access ports. These access ports can be individual or multiple ports that access the same VLAN.

The power of VLANs, switching, trunking, and access ports can be combined with Layer 3 routing functions to create slightly more complex, but extremely powerful, scenarios. This is how most carriers design their networks.

Later in this chapter, when we begin discussing the CRS (Cloud Series Routers) with their advanced switching functions, we will cover some common examples of using routers and switches together. But first, we will begin with the simple, non-CRS devices, which have limited switching functionality, entirely adequate for many applications.

Configuring Switching Functions on Non-CRS Devices

Port Switching

Switching means the device allows wire speed traffic to pass among a group of ports as if they were a regular Ethernet switch.

Note: Beginning in version 6.41 of RouterOS is a new bridge implementation that supports hardware offloading (hw-offload). This book has been revised in January of 2018 to incorporate the changes necessitated by this major release. Upgrading to this version or greater will convert all interface "master-port" configurations into a new bridge configuration and eliminate the "master-port" option. The bridge will now handle all Layer2 forwarding, and the use of switch-chip (hw-offload) will be automatically turned on based on appropriate conditions. The rest of the RouterOS Switch-specific configuration remains untouched in the usual menus for now. The goal of this change is to simplify switching by utilizing bridges instead and have the device offload the bridging function to the hardware chip if available.

You configure this feature by creating a bridge interface and adding ports to that bridge. Any of these ports that can be controlled by the hardware switch chip will offload traffic to that chip automatically.

The most common assignment of ports (and also the default assignment) on the low-cost MikroTik routers is to make Ether1 a stand-alone port (typically the WAN), and then switch together Ether2-5 using a bridge (with hardware offload to a switch chip if present).

On some models, such as the RB450G/RB435G/RB850Gx2, port Ether1 is not part of the switching function by default. The default setting is to allow Ether1 to be an independent internal interface from Ether1 to the CPU and from the CPU to the switch chip, thereby allowing the router to achieve more than 1Gbit and up to 2Gbit aggregated routing speed if CPU resources can support it.

This block diagram of the RB850Gx2 helps illustrate this function:

RB850Gx2

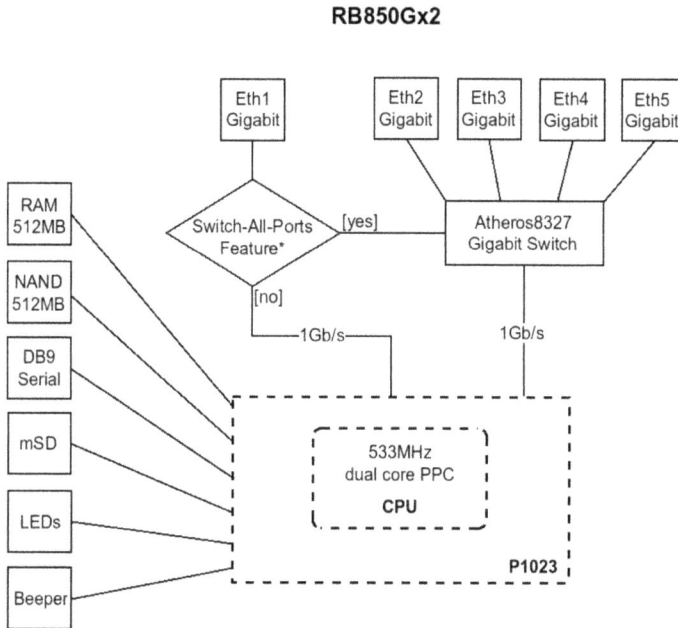

Figure 24 – RB805Gx2 Switching Block Diagram[1]

If you want Ether1 to be a part of the switch chip, there is a setting for that on certain models. Click the Switch button, and double click the switch list item to open the properties:

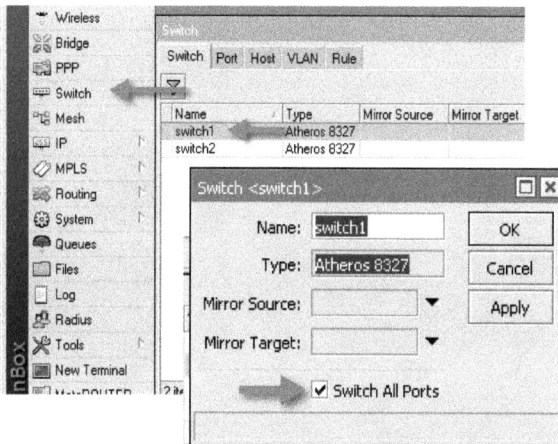

Although this setting option exists in Winbox for all boards besides the RB450G/RB435G/RB850Gx2, it has no effect whether on or off.

Remember that on the RB450G/RB435G/RB850Gx2, if you select "Switch All Ports", you will accomplish putting ether1 on the switch chip, but all ports on the switch chip will now share a single pipe to the CPU which could cut your throughput in half, compared to allowing ether1 to be an independent port and have its own pipe to the CPU. Always keep the block diagram and your settings' effects on overall capacity in mind when making changes.

Port Mirroring

Port mirroring lets a switch copy all traffic that is going in and out of one port (the mirror-source) and send a clone of those frames out of some other port (the mirror-target). This feature is typically used to set up a "tap" device that receives all traffic that goes in/out of some specific port for applications like Wire Shark or a Net Flows collector. One caveat is that the mirror-source and mirror-target ports must belong to the same physical switch. (You can see which port belongs to which switch in the /interface Ethernet switch port menu).

Host Table

The Host Table lists all the switch chip's internal MAC addresses to port mappings. It can contain two kinds of entries: dynamic and static. Dynamic entries get added automatically, which is called learning. When a switch receives a frame from a certain port, it adds both the frame's source MAC address and the port it was received on to the host table. When a frame comes in with a certain destination MAC address, it knows to which port it should forward the frame. If the destination MAC address is not present in host table, then it forwards the frame to all ports in the group and tries to learn from this process. Dynamic entries take about 5 minutes to time out. Learning is enabled only on ports that are configured as a part of a switch group by adding them to a bridge on a device that supports hardware offload. Also note that you can add static entries that override dynamic ones, but that is not a common occurrence.

VLAN Table

The VLAN Table specifies forwarding rules for frames that have an 802.1q tag. Frames with VLAN tags leave the switch chip through one or more ports that are set in the corresponding table entry. The exact logic that controls how frames with VLAN tags are treated is controlled by the VLAN-mode parameter that is changeable per switch port in the Interface Ethernet switch port menu. The VLAN-mode can take the following values:

- **disabled** - Ignore the VLAN table; treat frames with VLAN tags as if they did not contain a VLAN tag.

- **fallback** - The default mode - handle frames with VLAN tags that are not present in the VLAN table just like frames without a VLAN tag. Frames with VLAN tags that are present in VLAN table and where incoming port does not match any port in the VLAN table, do not get dropped.

- **check** - Drop frames with a VLAN tag that is not present in the VLAN table. Frames with VLAN tags that are present in the VLAN table, where the incoming port does not match any port in the VLAN table entry, do not get dropped.

- **secure** - Drop frames with a VLAN tag that is not present in VLAN table. Frames with a VLAN tag that is present in the VLAN table and where the incoming port does not match any port in VLAN table entry, get dropped.

VLAN-header option (configured in Interface Ethernet Switch Port) sets the VLAN tag mode on the egress port (the port where the frame leaves the switch). Starting from RouterOS version 6, this option works with the QCA8337, AR8316, AR8327, AR8227, and AR7240 switch chips and takes the following values:

- **leave-as-is** – The frame remains unchanged on the egress port.

- **always-strip** - If a VLAN header is present, it is removed from the frame.

- **add-if-missing** - If a VLAN header is not present, it is added to the frame.

All of this is probably way more than you care about for most typical uses of the switch chip. Most people only want to join ports together into a switch group, so I believe an example is in order.

Note: For all switch examples in this book, you must reset the router with no default configuration as shown on page 34 or you will encounter problems completing the configurations as written. This is because default-configuration changes often add new features that may conflict with these examples, causing them to not work.

Use this example to create a LAN switch where certain ports on the LAN interface of the router are switched together. A common application of this example is to use several ports as a switch for a home or small office with ether1 being the WAN port and ether2-5 switched together for the LAN.

APPLICATION

Example – Bridge ports Ether2 through Ether5 with Hardware Offload to the Switch Chip

1. In this example, we will be configuring a CRS125-24G-1S. I am assuming you are beginning with no default configuration. First, click the Bridge button and the Plus sign to create a bridge and name the bridge switch-bridge1 or whatever you like. Click OK.

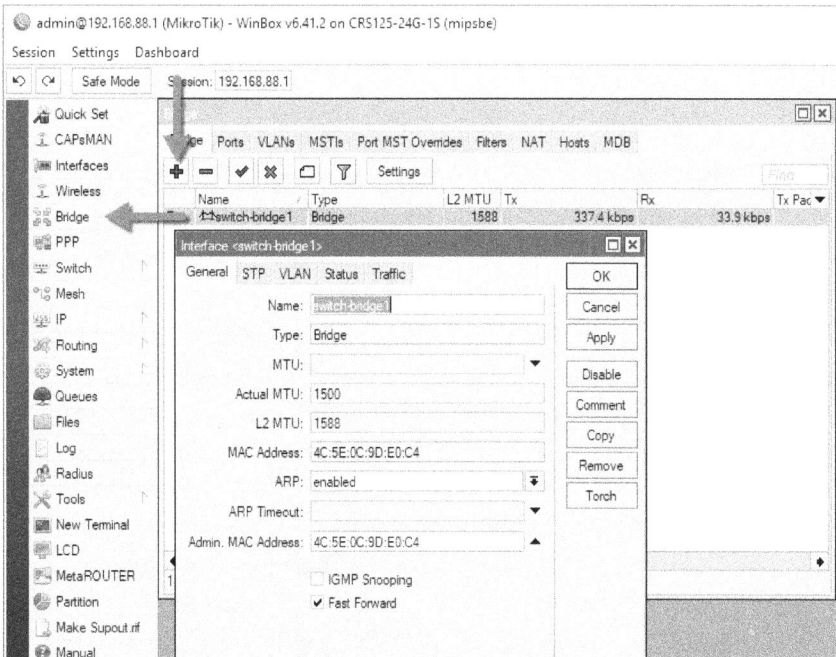

2. Click the Ports tab and add ports ether2-ether5 to that bridge. The router will now bridge ether2-3-4-5 together and offload traffic to the hardware switch chip.

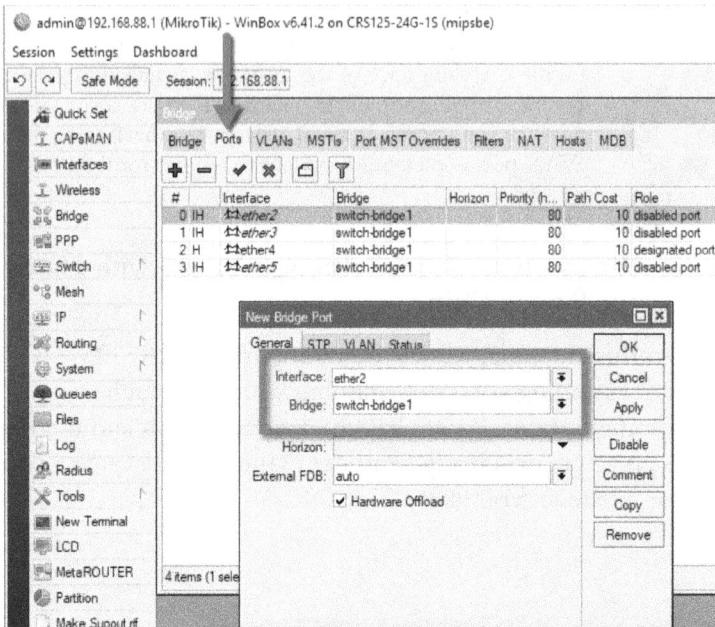

If the router on which you use this bridging method has a hardware switch chip, it will be utilized. If not, the bridging will all be done in software and will use the router's CPE resources.

Configuring Switching Functions on the Cloud Router Switch

The Cloud Router Switches are highly integrated and powerful switches with a high-performance MIPS CPU and a feature-rich packet processor. The CRS switches can be designed into various Ethernet applications, including unmanaged switch, Layer 2 managed switch, carrier switch, and wireless/wired unified packet processing. Many of their advanced switching functions go well beyond the scope of this book and even the needs of the average user. Therefore, I will show you what matters to most people and avoid the complexity of functions the majority of users almost never need. The MikroTik Wiki does a reasonable job of showing some CRS examples, but each is done using the CLI. I prefer Winbox, so I believe this series of examples to follow will have more value to the reader.

CRS Switching Features

The CRS switches support the same functions as the non-CRS switches, including Port Switching, Port Mirroring, VLANs, and the Host Table as described beginning on page 359. In addition, the CRS supports Port Isolation and Leakage, Trunking, Quality of Service, Shaping and Scheduling, and an Access Control List. We will cover most of these through the use of application examples.

Within the CRS model series, slight difference in functionality exists. The following illustration demonstrates those differences:

Model	CPU	Wireless	SFP+ port	Access Control List	Jumbo Frame (Bytes)
CRS112-8G-4S	400MHz	-	-	+	9204
CRS210-8G-2S+	400MHz	-	+	+	9204
CRS212-1G-10S-1S+	400MHz	-	+	+	9204
CRS226-24G-2S+	400MHz	-	+	+	9204
CRS125-24G-1S	600MHz	-	-	-	4064
CRS125-24G-1S-2HnD	600MHz	+	-	-	4064
CRS109-8G-1S-2HnD	600MHz	+	-	-	4064

Figure 25 - PPPoE Cloud Router Switch Models [1]

I want to begin by explaining each of the switch menu buttons and the associated tabs.

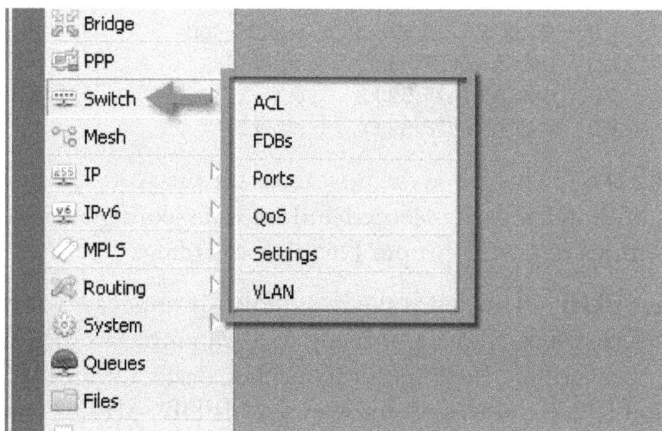

Clicking the Switch button reveals six other buttons. Their functions are as follows:

ACL Button

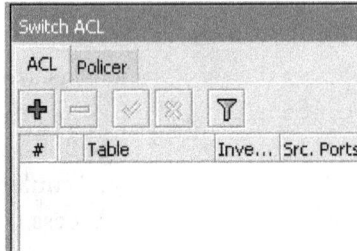

ACL Tab – An ACL (Access Control List) allows you to create policies that match frame ingress or egress ports, VLANS, or even IP addresses, and allows you to apply an action to them. Think of the Switch ACL as a firewall for switches that blurs the line between Layer 2 and Layer 3.

Policer Tab – Allows you to create rate-limiting options, similar to queues, which can then be used in Access Control List entries.

Switch FDBs Button

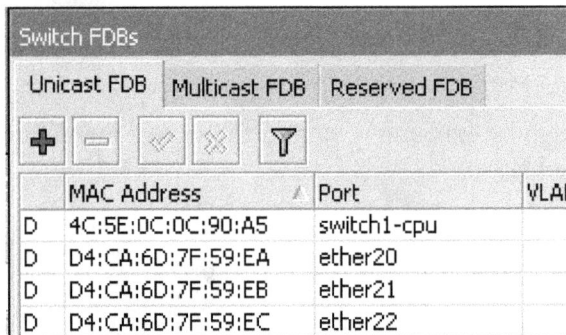

Unicast FDB – This tab is the host table for the switch, which contains both dynamically-learned and statically-configured MAC address entries to ensure proper Layer2 forwarding.

Multicast FDB – This tab is the host table for multicast forwarding. The CRS125 switch-chip supports up to 1024 entries in MFDB for multicast forwarding. Each multicast packet, destination MAC, or destination IP lookup is performed in the MFDB. MFDB entries are not automatically learned and can only be configured statically.

Reserved FDB – This tab contains a list of manually-configured entries that allow you to statically influence how the switch handles frames and will store up to 256 RFDB entries. Each RFDB entry can store either a Layer2 unicast or multicast MAC address with specific commands such as forward, drop, or assign to a QoS group.

Ports Button

Switch Ports			
Ports	Trunk	Port Isolation	Port Leakage

Name	∕	VLAN Type	Isolation Profile	MAC Bas
ether1		network port		29 no
ether2		network port		30 no
ether3		network port		30 no
ether4		network port		30 no

Ports Tab - This tab contains port-specific switch settings for each physical port in the switch. Here you can configure features such as Port-Based Mirroring, Port-Based QoS, MAC-based VLAN translation, and most of the functions that are specific to frames entering or exiting a port.

Trunk Tab – This tab provides the ability to configure static LAG (Link Aggregation Groups) with hardware automatic failover and load balancing. IEEE802.3ad and IEEE802.1ax compatible Link Aggregation Control Protocol is not supported yet, but it is planned. Up to 8 Trunk groups are supported with up to 8 Trunk member ports per Trunk group.

Port Isolation and Port Leakage Tabs[1] – This tab allows you to configure flexible, multi-level isolation features, which can be used for user access control, traffic engineering, and advanced security and network management. The isolation features provide an organized fabric structure, allowing user to easily program and control the access by port, MAC address, VLAN, protocol, flow, and frame type. The following isolation and leakage features are supported:

- Port-level isolation
- MAC-level isolation

- VLAN-level isolation

- Protocol-level isolation

- Flow-level isolation

- Free combinations of the above referenced features

Port-level isolation supports different control schemes on "source port" and "destination port". Each entry can be programmed with access control for either source port or destination port. When the entry is programmed with source port access control, the entry is applied to the ingress packets. When the entry is programmed with destination port access control, the entry is applied to the egress packets.

Port leakage allows bypassing egress VLAN filtering on the port. The "leaky port" is then allowed to access other ports for various applications such as security, network control, and management.

Note: When both isolation and leakage is applied to the same port, the port is isolated.

QoS Button

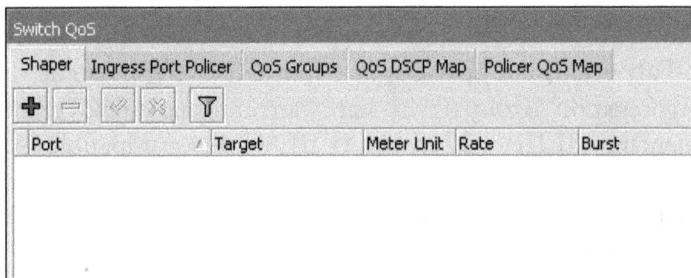

Shaper Tab – This tab allows you to create traffic-shaping policies on a per port basis for egress. Up to eight different queues can be targeted.

Ingress Port Policer – In this tab, ingress rate limiting can be configured for each port and various types of packets. Also, QoS attributes can be applied for limited traffic, which is not dropped.

QoS Groups - The global QoS group table is used for VLAN-based, Protocol-based, and MAC-based QoS group assignment.

QoS DSCP Map - The global DSCP to QoS mapping table is used for mapping from DSCP of the packet to new QoS attributes configured in the table or to change the DSCP bit.

Policer QoS Map - This table contains QoS attribute mapping for Access Control List policers.

Switch Settings Button

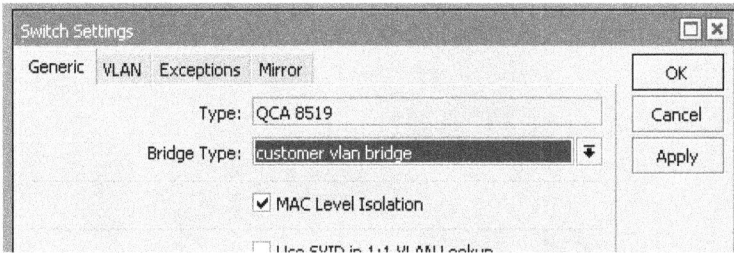

Generic Tab – This tab stores the settings that are global for the switch where generic switch settings are stored. It also allows you to configure the switch VLAN learning in accordance with an 802.1q or 802.1ad tag and adjust MAC address learning timeout setting.

Applications For VLANs

In this first example, we want to segregate every computer on our switch by putting each one in its own VLAN. This is done by creating one trunk port and four access ports. The computers cannot see each other at Layer 2, but they would be able to communicate with a device connected to the trunk such as a router.

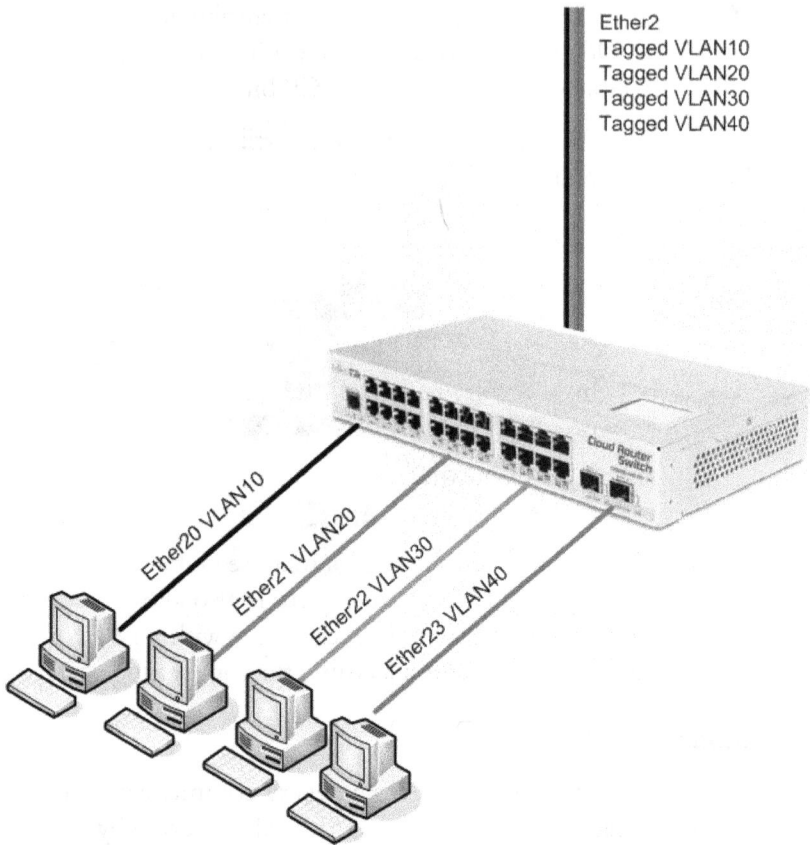

Figure 26 – Multiple VLAN Access Ports

Router on a Stick, also Known as Inter-VLAN Routing

By adding a router to this scenario connected to the trunk port and configuring VLAN virtual interfaces on the physical trunk port, we could add a separate IP range including private DHCP servers, one for each computer. The VLANS would provide Layer 2 isolation and by using firewall rules on the router, we could even prevent these computers from communication with one another at Layer 3. This illustration demonstrates this concept:

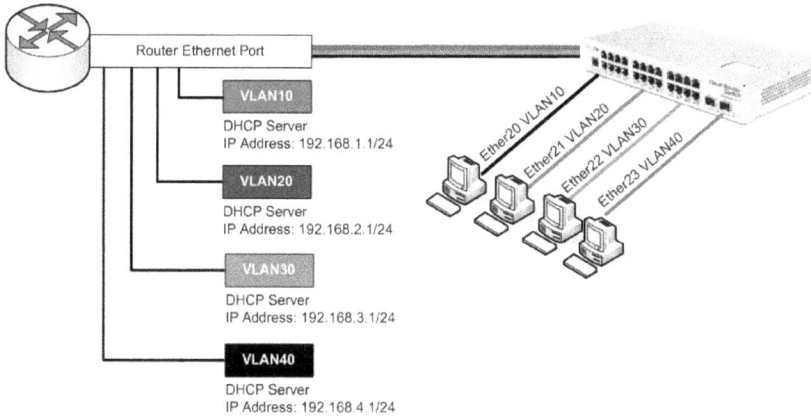

Figure 27 – Inter-VLAN Routing

This configuration is often referred to as a router on a stick, a reference to the fact that the router has a single interface connected to a trunk port (the stick) and many separate routable interfaces on the switch it sees as virtual interfaces on the router itself.

In the early days (when routers were just routers), they had few, and sometimes only one physical interface. Building a "router on a stick" was a great way to have the benefit of many interfaces on that router. One of the benefits of this configuration today with switches/routers is Layer 2 isolation for clients and the ability to restrict or enable inter-VLAN routing on the router.

Multiple Access Ports, Same VLAN

In many scenarios, you aren't trying to restrict each client to a single device broadcast domain, but rather segment groups of machines into their own VLAN groups. A common application would be an office environment where we have departments. Each department needs to be able to communicate with other machines in that department, but we want the ability to restrict inter-VLAN routing through firewall rules. This application would look like this:

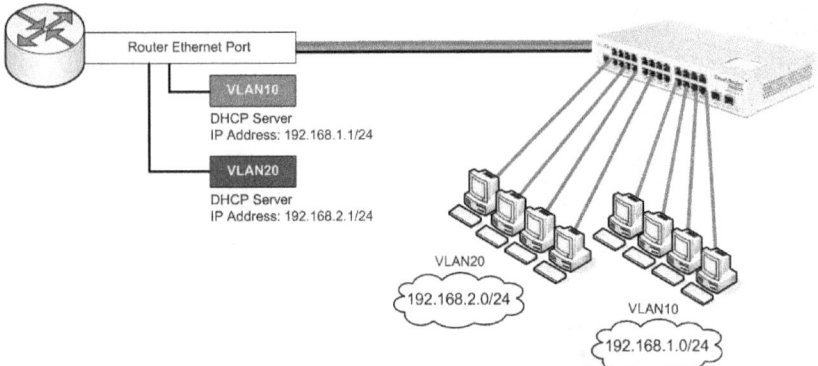

Router Ethernet Port

VLAN10
DHCP Server
IP Address: 192.168.1.1/24

VLAN20
DHCP Server
IP Address: 192.168.2.1/24

VLAN20
192.168.2.0/24

VLAN10
192.168.1.0/24

Figure 28 – Multiple Access Ports on the Same VLAN

Tagged VLANs and Untagged Traffic, Same Port Group

This is another common scenario. A typical application is an office LAN with VOIP phones and computers plugged into the same switch or even the same port. The computers are handling untagged traffic and getting their address via DHCP. The phones are VLAN-aware and handling tagged traffic. The phone VLAN has possibly no Internet access because it is not needed to get to the PBX. In addition, the phone VLAN can be given priority over and isolated from the untagged VLAN subnet using QoS and firewall rules.

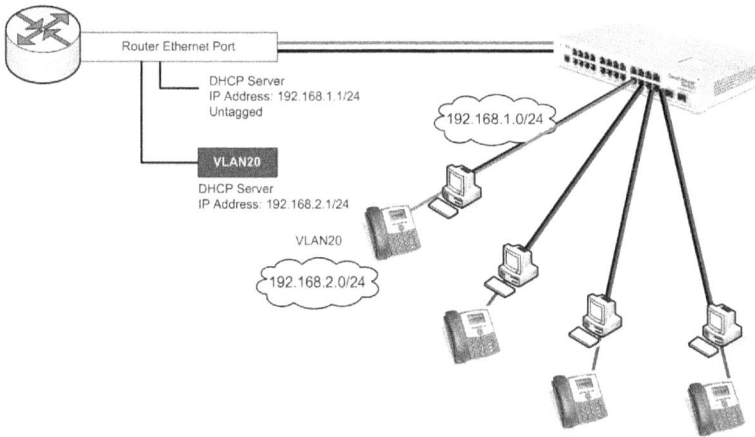

Figure 29 – Tagged VLANs and Untagged Traffic on the Same Port Groups

Hybrid Topology, Trunk and Access Ports on the Same Physical Port

In RouterOS, a port can be a trunk port (passing many VLANs), an Access Port (passing only one VLAN), or a Hybrid port, that is, a trunk and access port at the same time (although this is a much less common scenario, it is still possible). One reason for doing this is if you are extending VLANs to other switches for distribution to access ports on those switches and you want your management traffic for each of those switches on a different VLAN. I usually take the lazy approach here and mark my management IP's as untagged traffic and only tag the customer data traffic. This illustration shows what the hybrid port would look like:

369

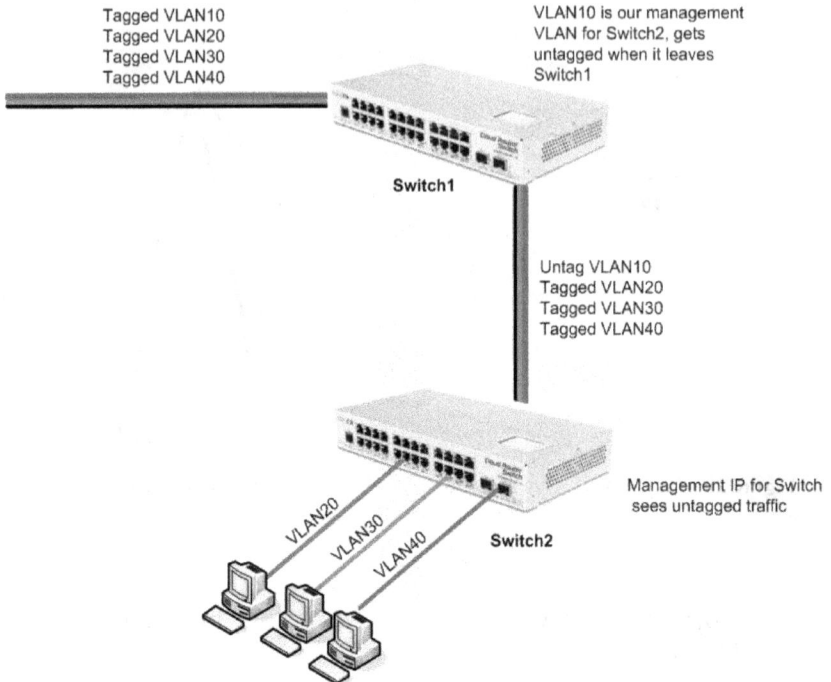

Tagged VLAN10
Tagged VLAN20
Tagged VLAN30
Tagged VLAN40

VLAN10 is our management
VLAN for Switch2, gets
untagged when it leaves
Switch1

Switch1

Untag VLAN10
Tagged VLAN20
Tagged VLAN30
Tagged VLAN40

Management IP for Switch
sees untagged traffic

VLAN20
VLAN30
VLAN40

Switch2

Figure 30 – Hybrid topology, Trunk and Access Ports on the Same Physical Port

Multiple Trunk Ports

While multiple access ports for the same or different VLANs seem
quite useful, sometimes we want to extend out VLANs to other
switches and locations before we untag them and this too is possible,
simple, and useful. In this example, each switch is in a different
physical building, interconnected by a single piece of media, possibly
a pair of fibers. We trunk the VLANs to every switch and break
them out when needed, using VLAN access ports.

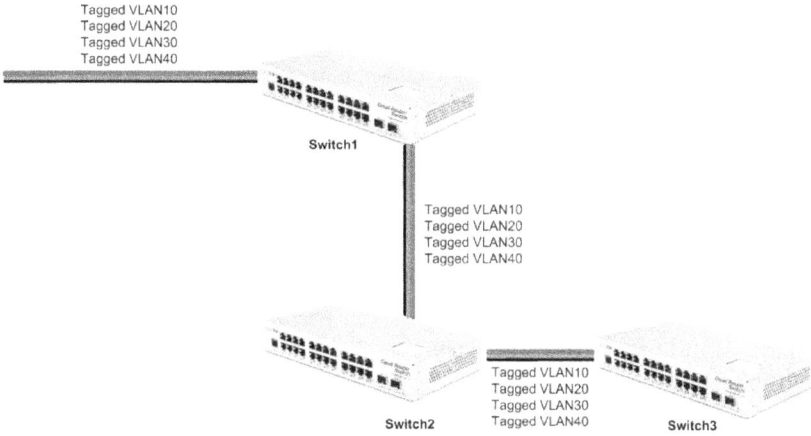

Tagged VLAN10
Tagged VLAN20
Tagged VLAN30
Tagged VLAN40

Switch1

Tagged VLAN10
Tagged VLAN20
Tagged VLAN30
Tagged VLAN40

Switch2

Tagged VLAN10
Tagged VLAN20
Tagged VLAN30
Tagged VLAN40

Switch3

Figure 31 – Multiple Trunk Ports

There are many more combinations possible, but the preceding ones are really the most common. There are also many features in the switching facility that allow you to influence how this works and to create exceptions to the default behavior, but the defaults are typically perfect for most scenarios. Further study of the Wiki pages will help you learn these advanced, but less commonly needed techniques.

Now that we have visited these different configurations, let's go through some examples of how to create them.

Use this example any time you need to add many ports to a bridge. This can be done manually as previously described or by using this automated method with a script.

Example – A Script to Assign Ports to a Bridge

In this example, we will use a script to quickly assign ports to a bridge. Scripts can greatly speed up the way we provision devices by automating repetitive tasks. There are a few variables we will need to change each time, but the script looks like this:

1. Type these commands into a new script named Set Ports and click Ok. The command syntax is at the end of this example.

(Continued on next page)

2. Edit the variables as explained in the comments of the script, and then click Run Script to perform the changes.

This script is featured on my wiki, http://wiki.stevedischer.com, and you can copy and paste them from the provided text. Simply search for "scripts" on my wiki site.

Here is the script in export format:

```
/system script
add name="Set Ports" owner=admin policy=\
    ftp,reboot,read,write,policy,test,password,sniff,sensitive source="#\r\
    \n#\r\
    \n# \r\
    \n# First, set port type i.e.: ether or sfp \r\
    \n# This is for interfaces not named \93ether\94 like SFP\r\
    \n# Second, set the bridge name\r\
    \n# Then set ports in range form using SlavePortStart and SlavePortStop.\r\
    \n:global PortType \"ether\"\r\
    \n:global BridgeName \"bridge1\"\r\
    \n:global SlavePortsStart \"1\"\r\
    \n:global SlavePortsStop \"9\"\r\
    \n:for i from=\$SlavePortsStart to=\$SlavePortsStop do={\r\
    \n/interface bridge port add interface=(\$PortType . \$i) bridge=\$BridgeNam\
    e\r\
    \n}"|
```

Here is the script itself:

```
#
#
#
# First, set port type i.e.: ether or sfp
# This is for interfaces not named "ether" like SFP
# Second, set the bridge name
# Then set ports in range form using SlavePortStart and SlavePortStop.
:global PortType "ether"
:global BridgeName "bridge1"
:global SlavePortsStart "1"
:global SlavePortsStop "9"
:for i from=$SlavePortsStart to=$SlavePortsStop do={
/interface bridge port add interface=($PortType . $i) bridge=$BridgeName
}
```

373

Note: For all of the VLAN examples in this book, it is assumed you will be doing the configuration from the port that is designated in the example as the trunk port or a spare port that does not have VLANs configured on it. This ensures you will not get disconnected from the device in the middle of the configuration process.

APPLICATION

Use this example any time you need a router to have many LAN interfaces located on a switch or to physically place those interfaces at some distance away from the router. These can be stand-alone interfaces or grouped together.

Example – Router on a Stick

In this example, we will configure a router on a stick, that is, inter-VLAN routing, using ether1 as our trunk port (connected to the router) and ether20-23 as our access ports. The final configuration will look like this:

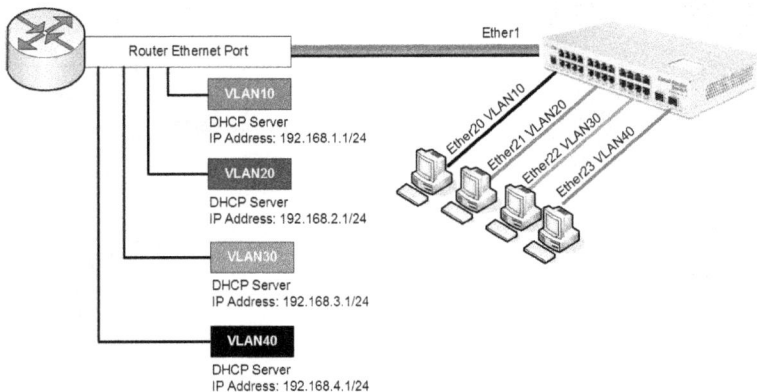

Figure 32 – Router on a Stick

1. Click the Bridge button and the Plus sign to create a bridge and name the bridge switch-bridge1 or whatever you like. Click OK.

(Continued on next page)

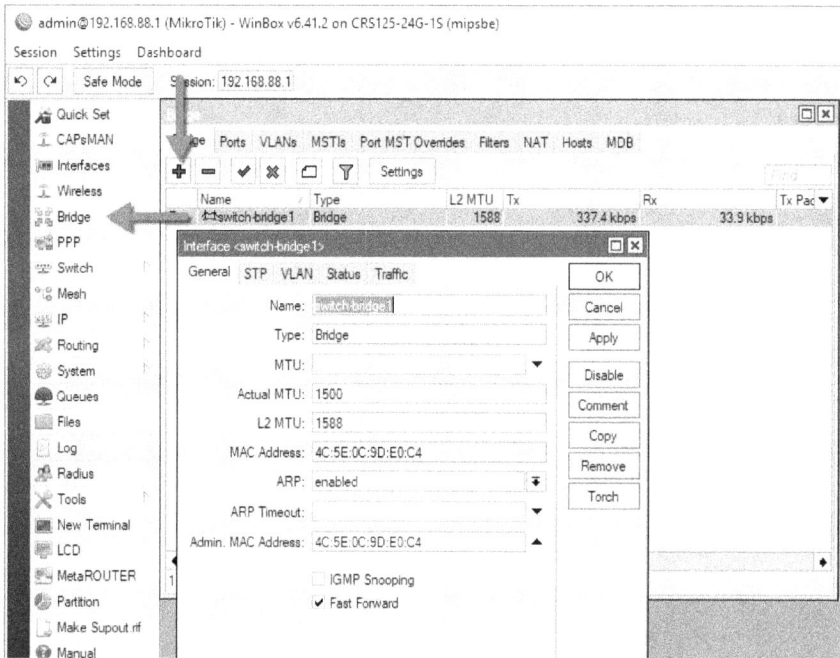

2. Click the Ports tab and add ports ether1 and ether20-ether23 to that bridge. The router will now bridge ether1 and 20-23 together like a switch and offload traffic to the hardware switch chip.

(Continued on next page)

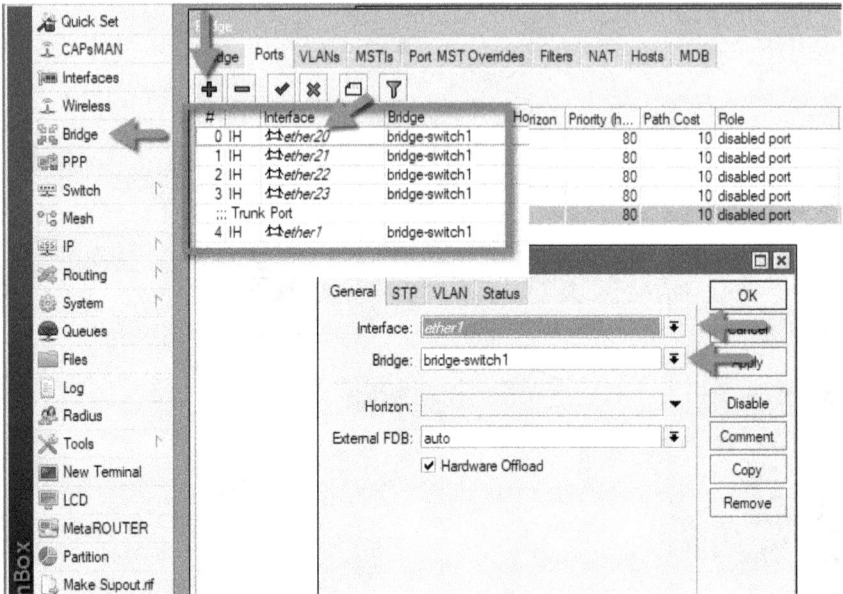

Note: I like to add a comment to certain interfaces based on their function. In this example, the switch is a CRS.

3. When you are done, the access ports should have an "H" next to them, indicating they are being offloaded to the hardware switch chip.

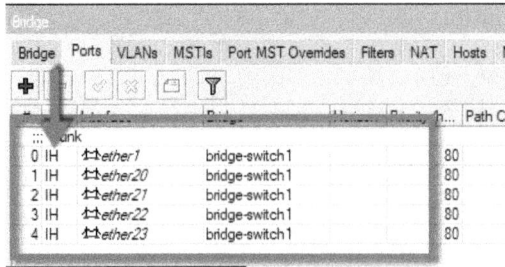

4. The next steps will be to configure the VLANs. Click the Switch button and select VLAN.

(Continued on next page)

On the VLAN tab, click the plus sign, configure the VLAN number to 10, select the VLAN 10 access port, ether20, and select the trunk port, ether1. Repeat for VLAN20 with ether1 and ether21, then VLAN30 with ether1and ether22, etc. Basically, this tells the switch on which ports to expect these tags.

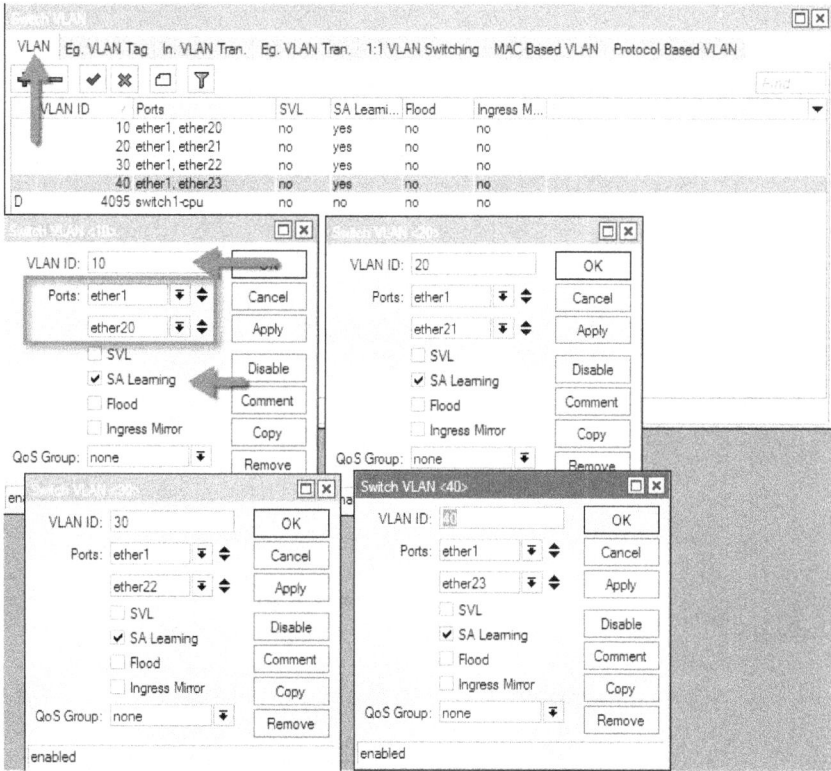

Note: If you want to be able to manage the switch from one of the access ports on an untagged interface (an IP address on the bridge for example), you must add the switch1-cpu virtual port to each VLAN statement above. If not, only the trunk port will be able to manage the switch. In the example below, I want to be able to manage the switch on an untagged interface (bridge) via ports ether1 (trunk) and access ports ether20, ether21, and ether23, but not ether22.

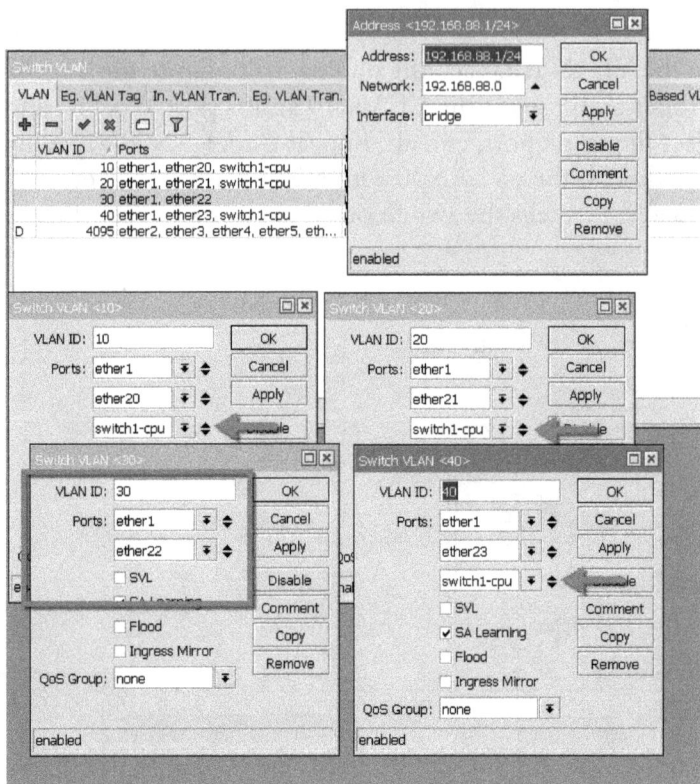

Adding the interface "switch1-cpu" to each applicable entry
accomplishes this. If you think about it, this is logical because once
you add the "Ingress VLAN Translation" statements to the access
ports (ether20-ether23), any traffic entering those ports (ingress) will
get tagged with a VLAN tag, and unless the CPU of the switch
(through which you manage the switch) is VLAN aware, it will not
see that traffic.

5. Click OK on each of these windows, then click the Eg.
   VLAN Tag (Egress VLAN Tagging) tab. On this tab, we will
   establish the trunk port for each VLAN. (At the time of the
   original writing of the Second Edition, I had requested that
   MikroTik change the name of the "VLAN Tagging" tab to
   "Eg. VLAN Tag." to make it coincide with the CLI. That
   change was made and subsequent copies of this book have
   been edited to reflect the change). Click the plus sign and
   create an entry for each VLAN that will exist on ether1 (the

trunk port), including VLAN10, 20, 30, and 40, making one entry for each as follows:

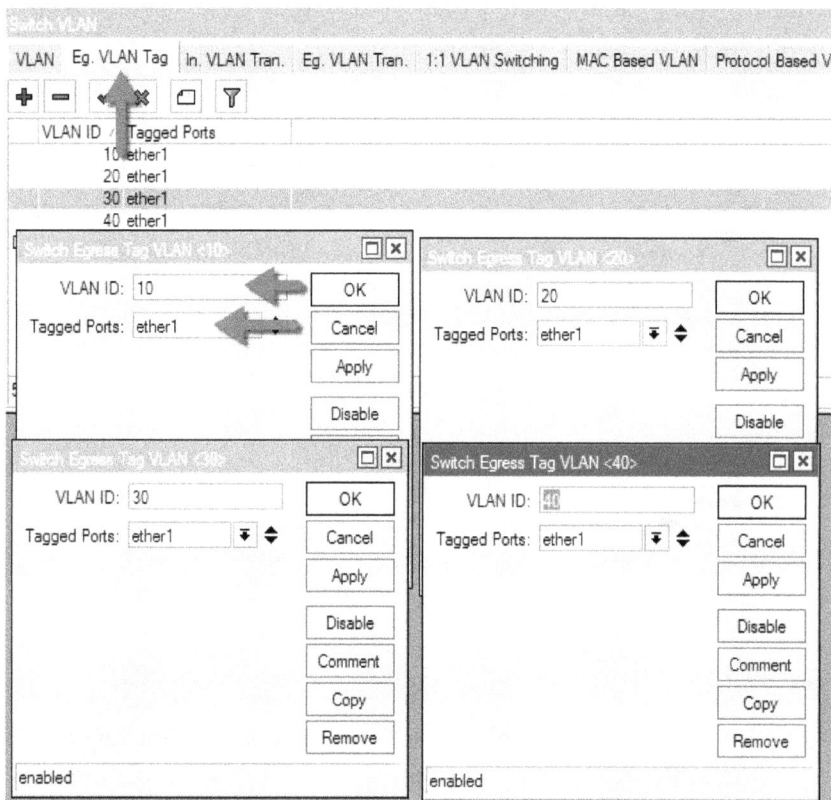

Click OK on all the open windows.

6. Click the In. VLAN Tran. (Ingress VLAN Translation) tab. The purpose of these entries is to tell the switch that frames coming in the access port (not tagged yet) need to be tagged with the proper VLAN before they are sent on their way. For each port, you will need one entry that identifies the port. Then set the New Customer VID.

(Continued on next page)

Switch/VLAN

VLAN | Eg. VLAN Tag | In. VLAN Tran. | Eg. VLAN Tran. | 1:1 VLAN Switching | MAC Based VLAN | Protocol Based VLAN

Find

	Ports	/	Protoc	Service VLAN...	Service VID	Customer VLA...	Customer VID	New Service ...	New Custome...
D				any		any			4095
	ether20			any		any			10
	ether21			any		any			20
	ether22			any		any			30
	ether22			any		any			40

Ingress VLAN Translation <ether20>

Ports: ether20 — OK
Protocol: — Cancel
Service VLAN Lookup For: any — Apply
Service VID: — Disable

Ingress VLAN Translation <ether21>

Ports: ether21 — OK
Protocol: — Cancel
Service VLAN Lookup For: any — Apply
Service VID: — Disable

Ingress VLAN Translation <ether22>

Ports: ether22 — OK
Protocol: — Cancel
Service VLAN Lookup For: any — Apply
Service VID: — Disable
Service PCP: — Comment
Service DEI: — Copy
Customer VLAN Lookup For: any — Remove
Customer VID:
Customer PCP:
Customer DEI:
New Service VID:
New Customer VID: 30
☐ PCP Propagation
☑ SA Learning
enabled

Ingress VLAN Translation <ether22>

Ports: ether23
Protocol: — Cancel
Service VLAN Lookup For: any — Apply
Service VID: — Disable
Service PCP: — Comment
Service DEI: — Copy
Customer VLAN Lookup For: any — Remove
Customer VID:
Customer PCP:
Customer DEI:
New Service VID:
New Customer VID: 40
☐ PCP Propagation
☑ SA Learning
enabled

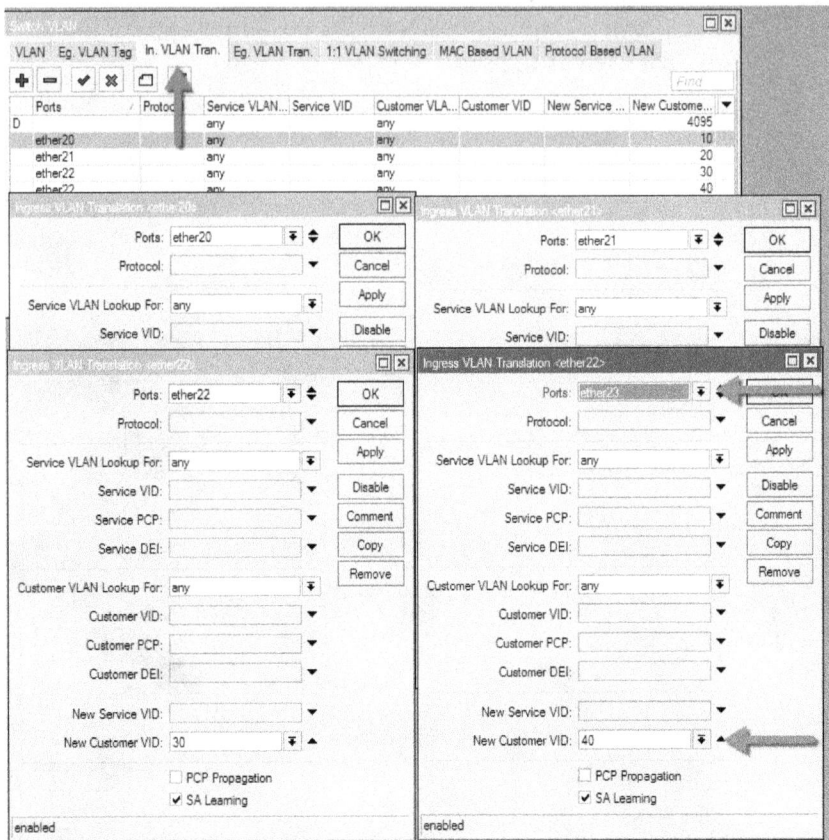

Note: If you read the example on the wiki, they suggest locking the configuration down a bit by dropping invalid VLANs on all ports. This is done by clicking the Switch Settings VLAN tab and enabling "Drop if Invalid VLAN" on all the ports we will be using as access ports. In the wiki, they also show the trunk port on that list. However, if you are managing the switch using an untagged IP address on that port, this will cause you to lose access to the switch. Simply leave the management trunk port out of that list.

7. Click the Switch Settings VLAN tab and enable all the ports we will be using as access ports.

(Continued on next page)

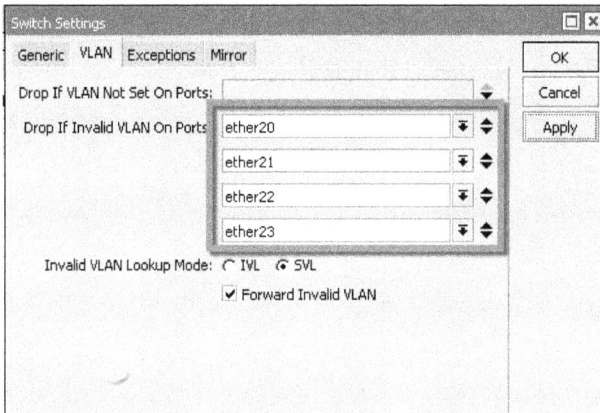

The switch is now configured. To complete the Router on a Stick, we need a router connected to ether1. That router's interface will need VLAN interfaces and IP schemes that complement our switch configuration. Here are some screen shots without explanations, since you are nearing the end of this book and these concepts are already covered!

IP Addresses:

Interfaces:

Our switch is connected to physical interface ether5 of this router:

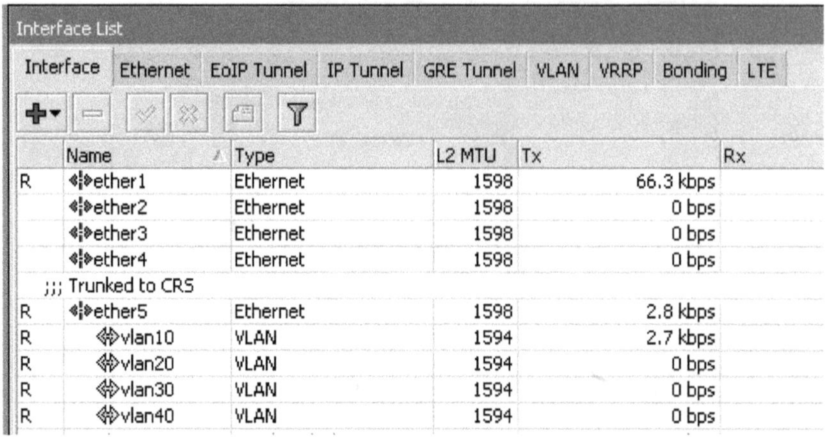

Interface List

Interface | Ethernet | EoIP Tunnel | IP Tunnel | GRE Tunnel | VLAN | VRRP | Bonding | LTE

	Name	Type	L2 MTU	Tx	Rx
R	ether1	Ethernet	1598	66.3 kbps	
	ether2	Ethernet	1598	0 bps	
	ether3	Ethernet	1598	0 bps	
	ether4	Ethernet	1598	0 bps	
	;;; Trunked to CRS				
R	ether5	Ethernet	1598	2.8 kbps	
R	vlan10	VLAN	1594	2.7 kbps	
R	vlan20	VLAN	1594	0 bps	
R	vlan30	VLAN	1594	0 bps	
R	vlan40	VLAN	1594	0 bps	

DHCP Server:

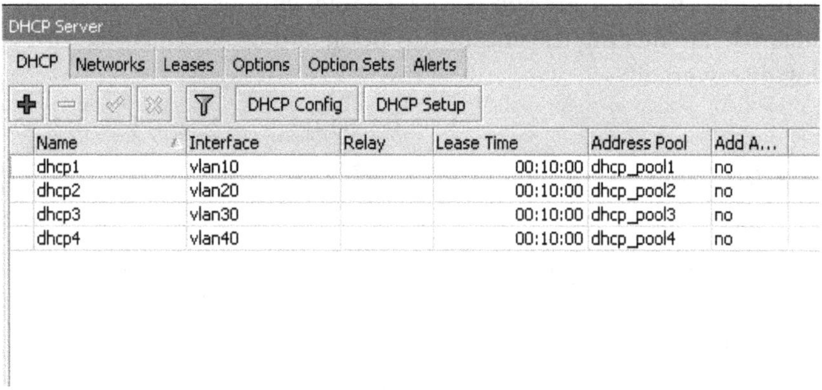

DHCP Server

DHCP | Networks | Leases | Options | Option Sets | Alerts

DHCP Config | DHCP Setup

Name	Interface	Relay	Lease Time	Address Pool	Add A...
dhcp1	vlan10		00:10:00	dhcp_pool1	no
dhcp2	vlan20		00:10:00	dhcp_pool2	no
dhcp3	vlan30		00:10:00	dhcp_pool3	no
dhcp4	vlan40		00:10:00	dhcp_pool4	no

Use this example to create LAN port groups where each grouping shares a single broadcast domain and all the separate broadcast domains are separated from one another.

Example – One Trunk, Multiple Access Ports, Same VLAN

In this example, we will configure a router on a stick using ether1 as our trunk port (connected to a router) and ether2-24 as our access ports with ether2-12 on VLAN 10 and ether13-23 on VLAN20.

1. Begin creating a bridge by clicking Bridge, the Plus sign, and naming the bridge.

2. Next, add all ports you want to switch together to the bridge interface as ports. A simple way to do this is to use the Set Ports script previously described.

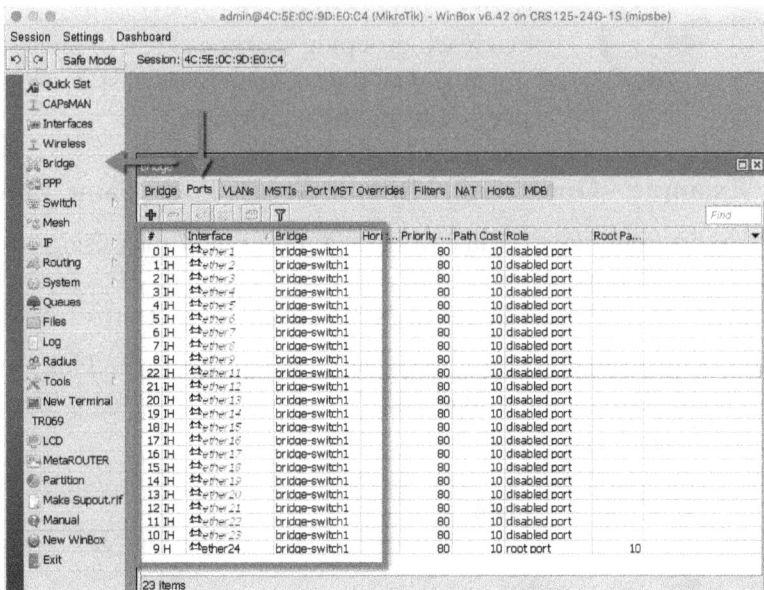

When you are done, the access ports, ether1-24, should have an "H" next to them in the Bridge Ports list, indicating that they are being offloaded to the hardware switch chip.

3. The next step will be to configure the VLANs. Click the Switch button and select VLAN. On the VLAN tab, click the plus sign, configure the VLAN number to 10, and select the VLAN 10 trunk port, ether1, and the access ports, ether2-ether12. Repeat for VLAN20 with ether1 and ether13-ether24. Add the VLAN, Ethernet ports, and accept defaults for everything else as shown. Basically, this tells the switch on which ports to expect these tags.

(Continued on next page)

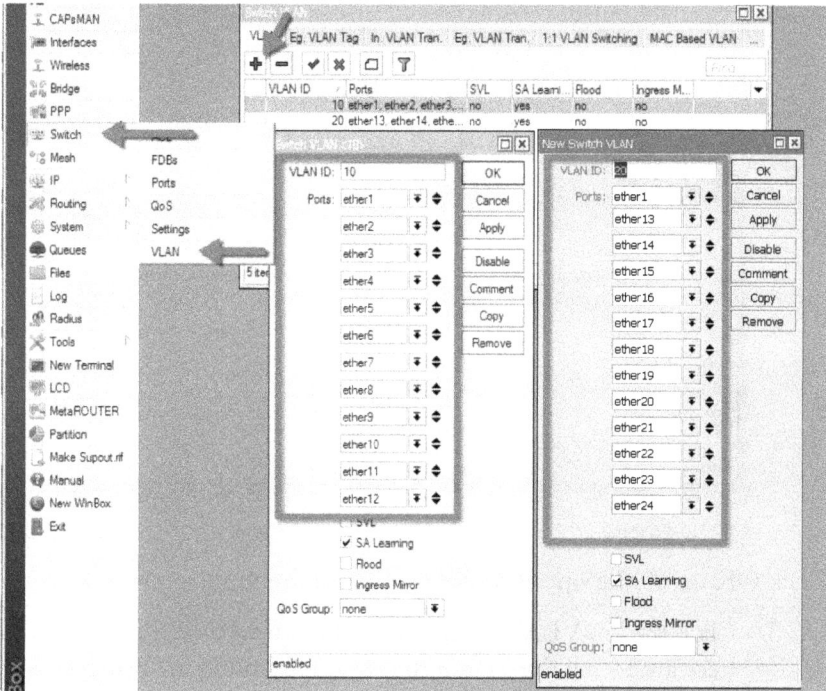

Note: Remember that if you want to manage the switch through any access ports, please follow the instructions on page 377.

Click OK on each of these windows.

4. Next, click the Eg. VLAN Tag tab. On this tab, we will establish the trunk port for each VLAN.

Click the plus sign and set each VLAN that will be present on the trunk port (ether1), including VLAN10, and VLAN20, making one entry for each as follows:

(Continued on next page)

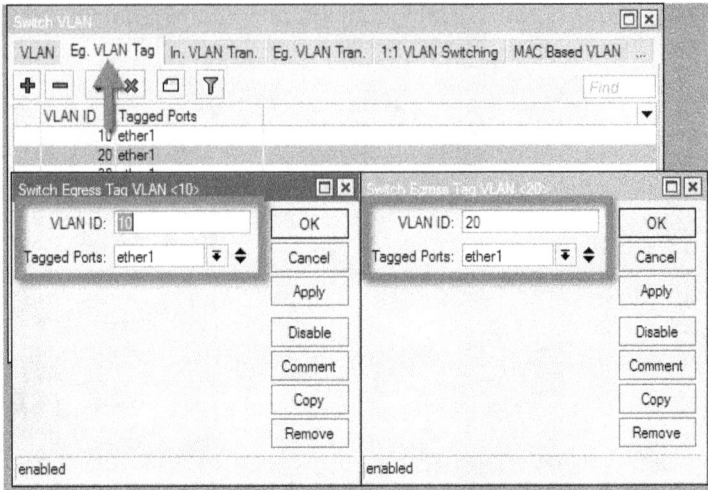

Click OK on all the open windows to close them.

5. Click the In. VLAN Tran. tab. The purpose of the entries here are to tell the switch that frames coming in each access port need to be tagged with the proper VLAN before they are sent on their way. For each port, you will need one entry. That entry contains the Ingress port and the VLAN ID. Everything else is left at defaults. Repeat for all VLANs.

(Continued on next page)

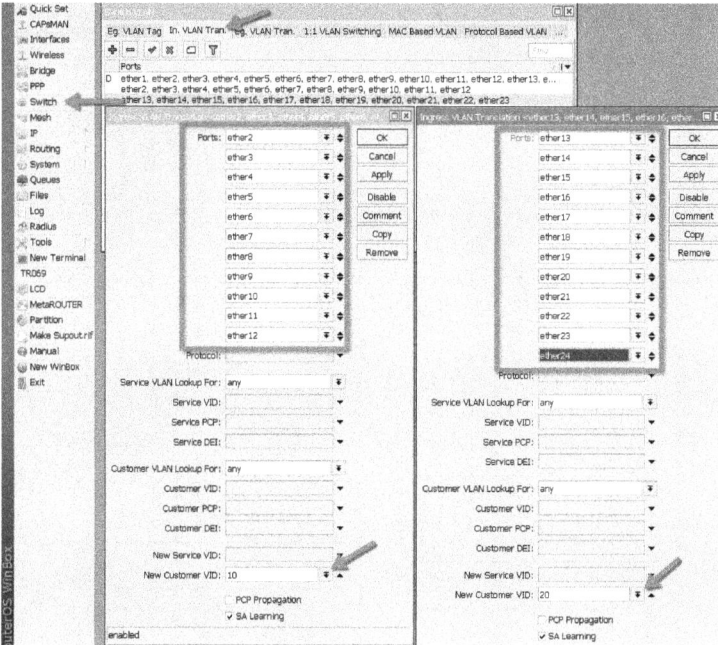

6. I described the next step in the previous example, but just in case you skipped it and went directly to this one, I will include it here as well. If you read the example on the wiki, they suggest locking the configuration down a bit by dropping invalid VLANs on all ports. This is done by clicking the Switch Settings VLAN tab and enabling "Drop if Invalid VLAN" on all the ports we will be using as access ports. In the wiki, they also show the trunk port in that list. However, if you are managing the switch using an untagged IP address, this will cause you to lose access to the switch, so I do not recommend adding the management port to this list. That being said, set "Drop If Invalid VLAN on Ports" for all non-trunk ports:

(Continued on next page)

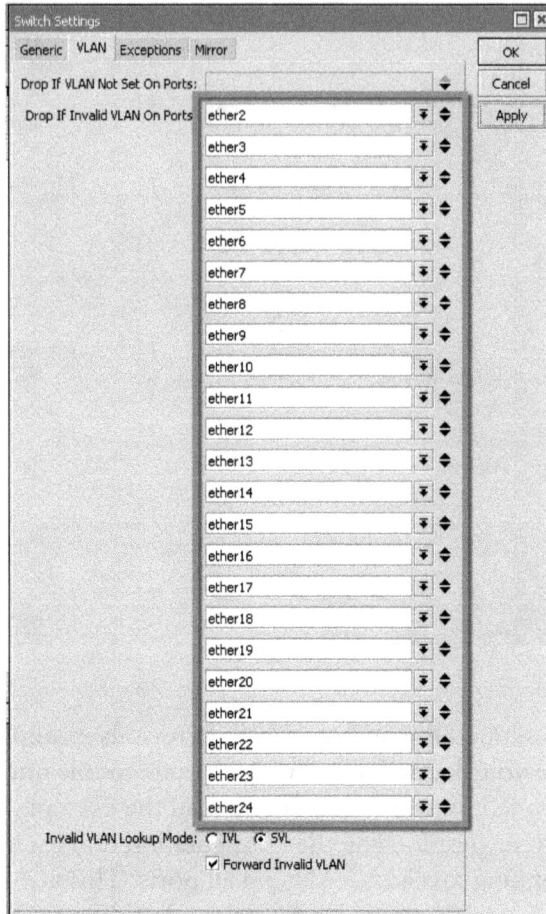

The switch is now configured. At this point, you could do the
Router on a Stick configuration (described previously) by
connecting a router to ether1.

Use this example when you want to make a port both trunk and access port simultaneously, a hybrid port(s). One application might be to extend VLANS through one switch to a second switch for distribution, but you want to manage that second switch using a management VLAN.

Example - Hybrid Topology, Trunk and Access Ports on the Same Physical Port

In this example, we want to connect two switches together and trunk traffic between them, but on the port that connects the two switches, we also want to untag one VLAN. One application for this setup might be to extend all VLANs from Switch 1 to Switch 2. Next, untag VLAN10 before entering Switch 2, since Switch 2 is managed through an untagged interface. Then, we pass VLANS 20, 30, and 40 into Switch 2 for untagging on access ports.

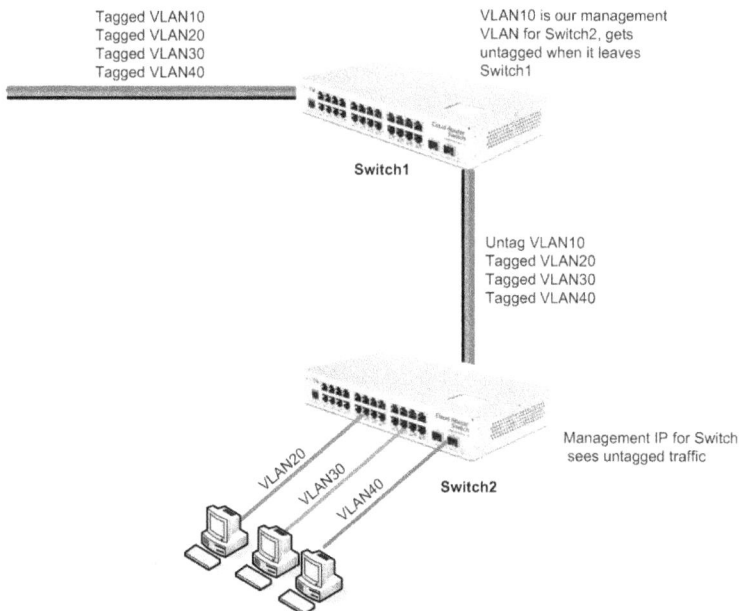

Figure 33 - Hybrid Topology, Trunk and Access Port on the Same Physical Port

Another application example could be both VLAN-aware and non-VLAN-aware devices on the same port. In this example, the VOIP phone is plugged into the switch port, it untags VLAN 20, and the PC sees untagged traffic because it is not VLAN-aware.

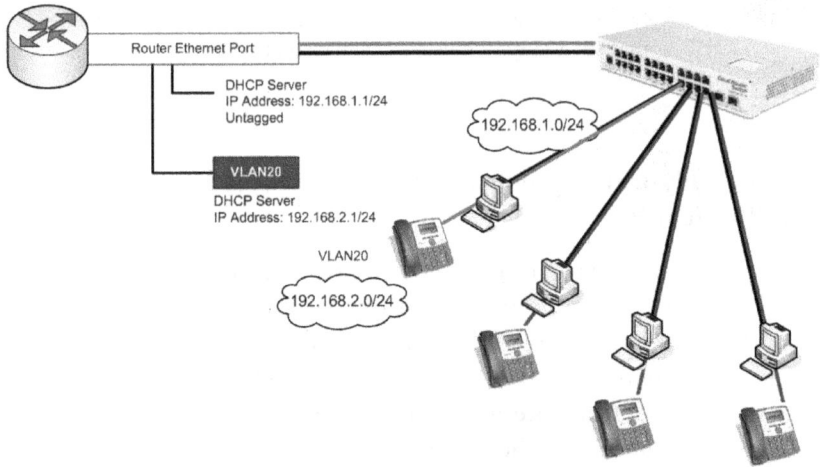

Figure 34 – VLAN-Aware and Non-VLAN-Aware Devices on the Same Port

The configuration is the same for either example. Here we will follow the Router on a Stick example closely with a few modifications.

- In this configuration, ether1 on the switch is a pure trunk port.
- Ether20 is a trunk port and access port for VLAN10.
- Ether21 is a trunk port and access port for VLAN20.
- Ether22 is a trunk port and access port for VLAN30.
- Ether23 is a trunk port and access port for VLAN40.

1. Click the Bridge button and the Plus sign to create a bridge and name the bridge switch-bridge1 or whatever you like. Click OK.

(Continued on next page)

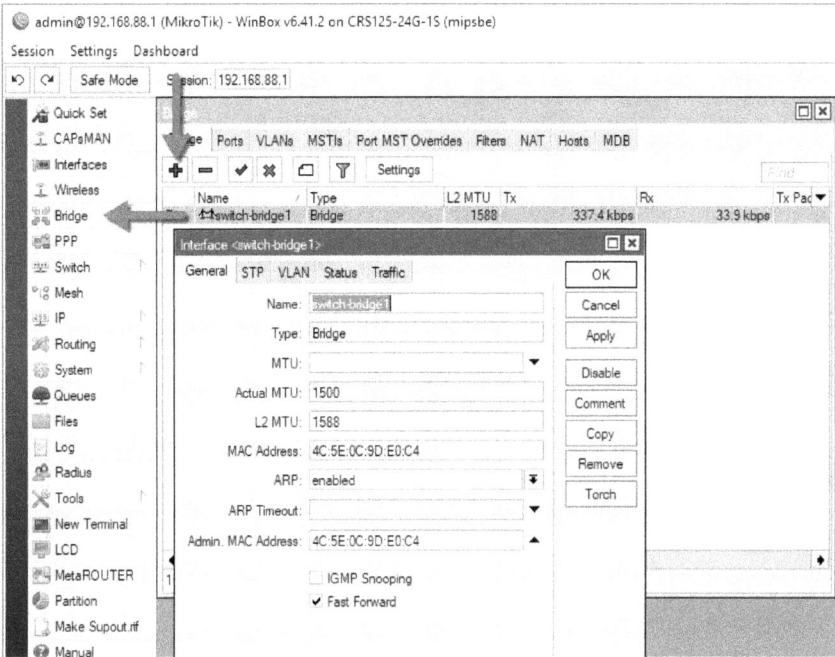

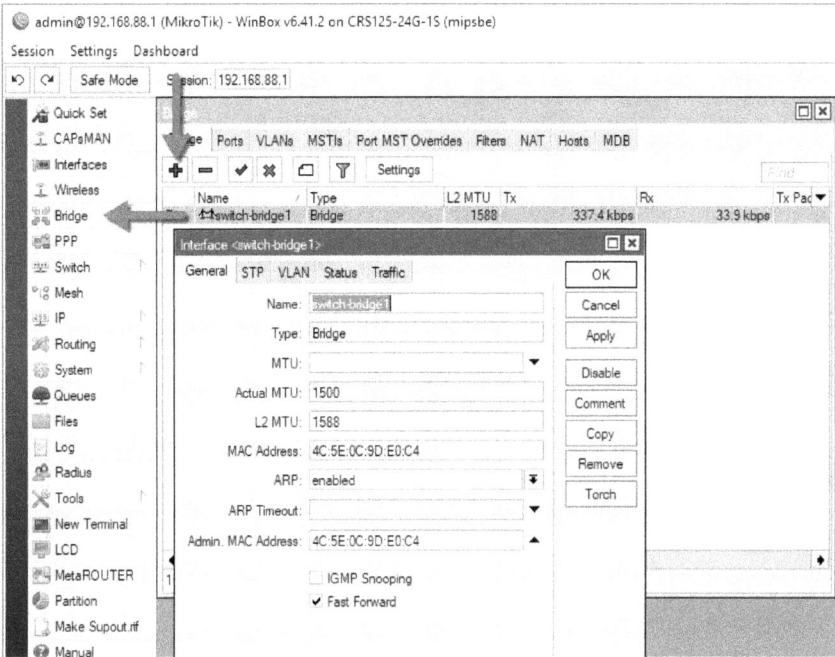

2. Click the Ports tab and add ports ether1 and ether20-ether23 to that bridge. The router will now bridge ether1 and 20-23 together like a switch and offload traffic to the hardware switch chip.

(Continued on next page)

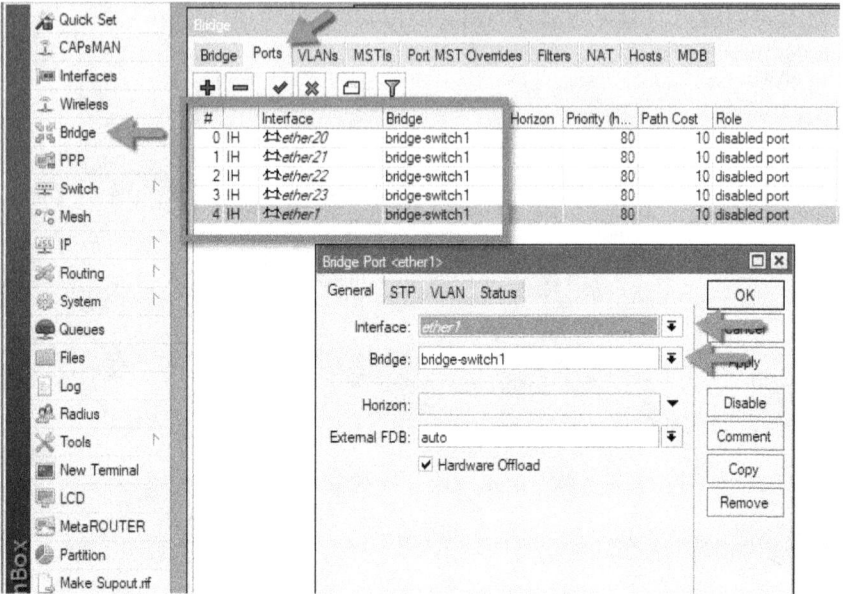

3. The next step will configure the VLANs. Click the Switch button and select VLAN.

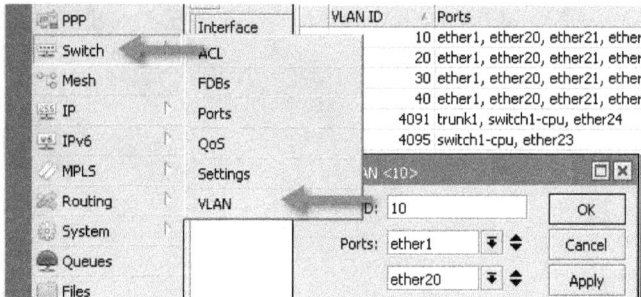

On the VLAN tab, click the plus sign, configure the VLAN number to 10, and select all ports that will see VLAN10 as a trunk or access port. In this case, that is ether1, our trunk port, and the four hybrid ports, 20, 21, 22, and 23. Repeat for VLAN20, 30, and 40. You can simply copy the entry for VLAN 10, and just change the VLAN ID in each successive entry.

(Continued on next page)

Basically, this tells the switch on which ports to expect these tags.

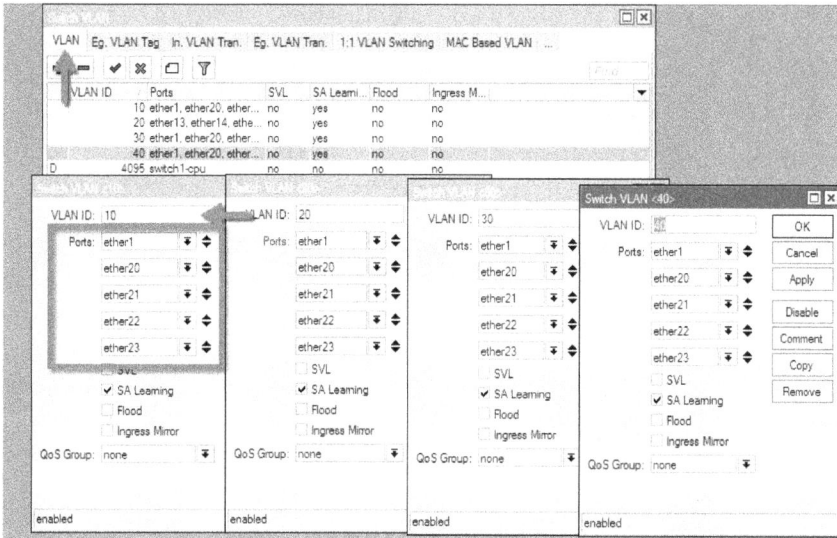

Note: Remember that if you want to manage the switch through any access ports, please follow the instructions on page 377 in this step.

4. Click OK on each of these windows, then click the Eg. VLAN Tag tab. On this tab, we will establish the trunk ports, the one pure trunk, and the four hybrid ports. Click the plus sign and set each VLAN on the ports where tags will be left intact on egress. Remember, if we don't let the tag egress, it will be stripped, and that port becomes an access port for that VLAN.

(Continued on next page)

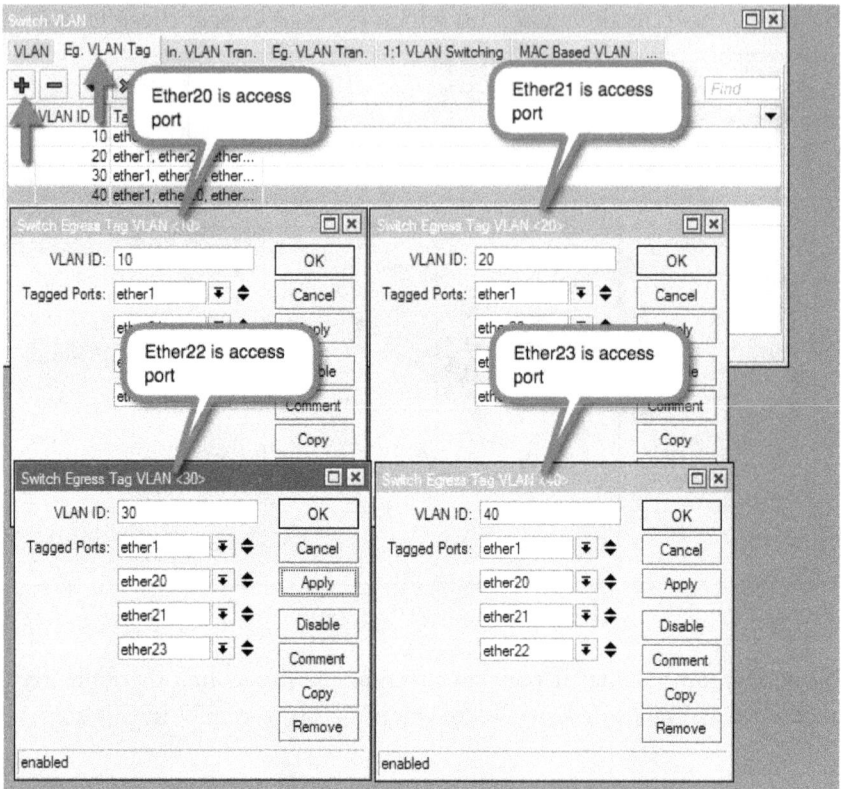

Click OK on all the open windows.

    5.   Click the In. VLAN Tran. tab. The purpose of the entries here is to tell the switch that frames coming in each access port need to be tagged with the proper VLAN before they are sent on their way. For each port, you will need one entry. That entry contains the Ingress port and the VLAN ID. Everything else is left at the default settings. Repeat for all VLANs.

Note: In some versions, SA Learning is not enabled by default and should be. MikroTik engineers told me they could not think of any useful scenarios where you would want it disabled. For each entry, set the New Customer VID as shown below. Everything else is left at the default settings . Repeat for all four VLANs.

(Continued on next page)

Eg. VLAN Tag   In. VLAN Tran.   Eg. VLAN Tran.   1:1 VLAN Switching   MAC Based VLAN   Protocol Based VLAN   ...

	Ports	Protocol	Service VLAN...	Service VID	Customer VLA...	Customer VID	New Service ...	N
D			any		any			
	ether20		any		any			
	ether21		any		any			
	ether22		any		any			
	ether23		any		any			

ether20

Ports: ether20   OK
Protocol: Cancel
Service VLAN Lookup For: any   Apply
Service VID: Disable
Service PCP: Comment
Service DEI: Copy
  Remove
Customer VLAN Lookup For: any
Customer VID:
Customer PCP:
Customer DEI:
New Service VID:
New Customer VID: 10
☐ PCP Propagation
☑ SA Learning

ether21

Ports: ether21   OK
Protocol: Cancel
Service VLAN Lookup For: any   Apply
Service VID: Disable
Service PCP: Comment
Service DEI: Copy
  Remove
Customer VLAN Lookup For: any
Customer VID:
Customer PCP:
Customer DEI:
New Service VID:
New Customer VID: 20
☐ PCP Propagation
☑ SA Learning

Ingress VLAN Translation <ether22>

Ports: ether22   OK
Protocol: Cancel
Service VLAN Lookup For: any   Apply
Service VID: Disable
Service PCP: Comment
Service DEI: Copy
  Remove
Customer VLAN Lookup For: any
Customer VID:
Customer PCP:
Customer DEI:
New Service VID:
New Customer VID: 30
☐ PCP Propagation
☑ SA Learning
enabled

ether23

Ports: ether23   OK
Protocol: Cancel
Service VLAN Lookup For: any   Apply
Service VID: Disable
Service PCP: Comment
Service DEI: Copy
  Remove
Customer VLAN Lookup For: any
Customer VID:
Customer PCP:
Customer DEI:
New Service VID:
New Customer VID: 40
☐ PCP Propagation
☑ SA Learning
enabled

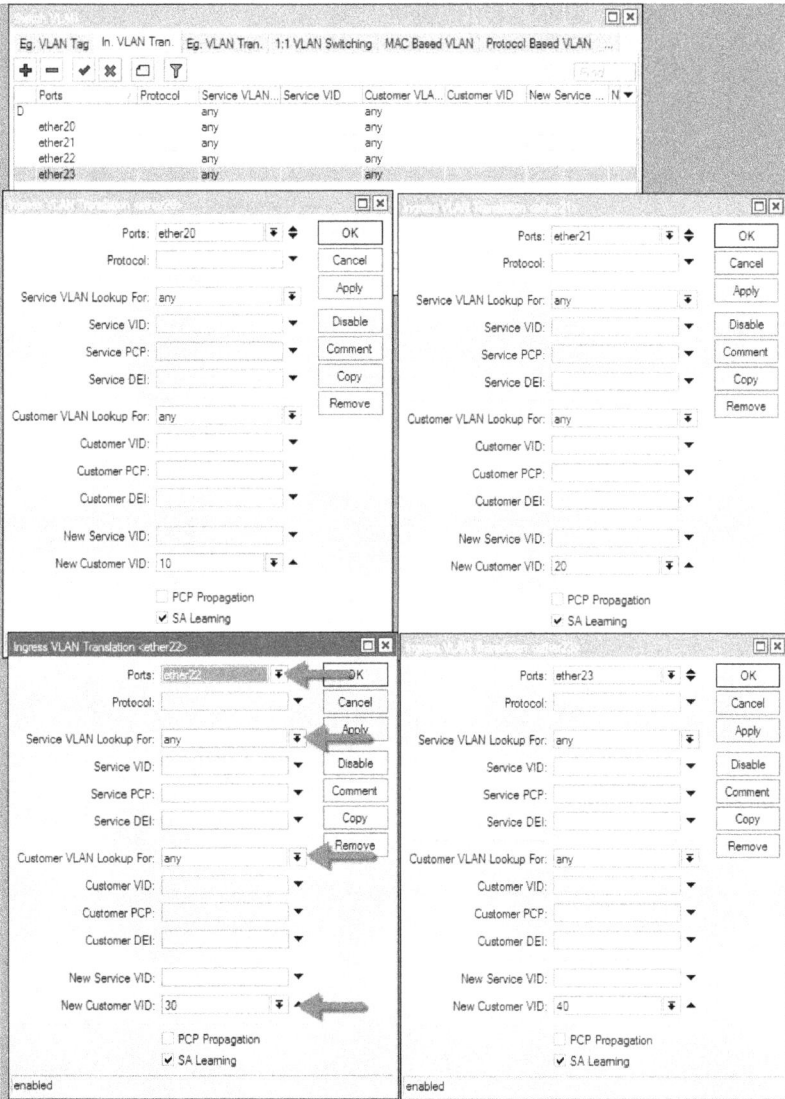

Note: If you read the example on the wiki, they suggest locking the configuration down a bit by dropping invalid VLANs on all ports. This is done by clicking the Switch Settings VLAN tab and enabling "Drop if Invalid VLAN" on all the ports we will be using as access ports. In the wiki, they also show the trunk port in that list; however, if you are managing the switch using an untagged IP address on that port, this will cause you to lose access to the switch. Leave the management trunk port out of that list.

6. Click the Switch Settings VLAN tab and enable all the ports we will be using as access ports.

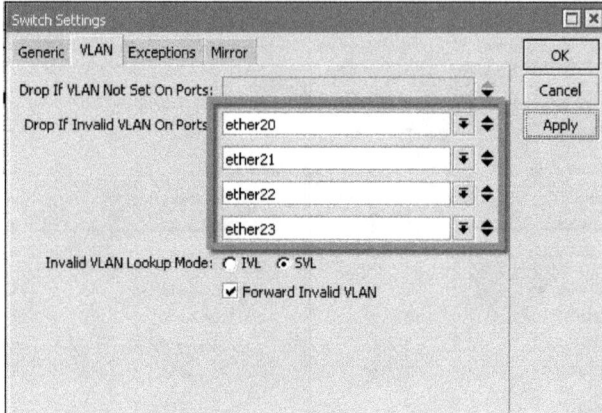

The switch is now configured.

Use this example to set multiple ports as trunk ports that can trunk VLANs to other VLAN-aware devices like switches or routers. This setup works well as a service provider because you can "drop off" customer VLANs as a location, trunk them to other locations, and "drop them" there as well, preserving the VLAN tags throughout the network.

Example – Multiple Trunk Ports

In this example, the switch will support one VLAN-aware router, providing Layer 3 functionality through a trunk port to Switch 1, where we will provide VLAN access to some PC's. Then, through a second trunk port on Switch 1, we will continue sending these VLANs to Switch 2 and untag them on access ports to a second group of PC's.

In summary, this is the Router on a Stick example from page 374 with the addition of a second trunk port on the switch feeding a second switch with a configuration similar to the first switch. The result will look like this:

(Continued on next page)

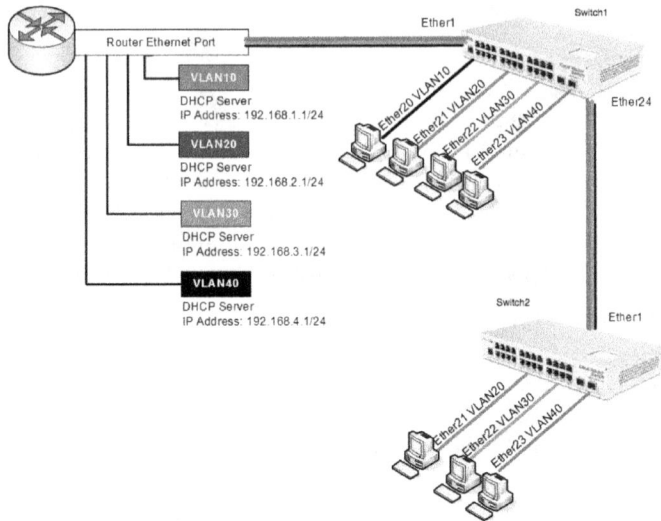

Figure 35 –Multiple Trunk Ports

1. Begin by configuring the router and Switch1, using the Router on a Stick example from page 374. After both devices (I will refer to them as Switch1 and Switch2) are configured, we will add additional configuration to ether24 on Switch1 and will configure Switch2 from scratch.

2. Begin by adding the second trunk port to Switch1, which will be ether24. Do this by adding ether24 to the same bridge as ether1, 20, 21, 22, and giving it a comment "Trunk":

(Continued on next page)

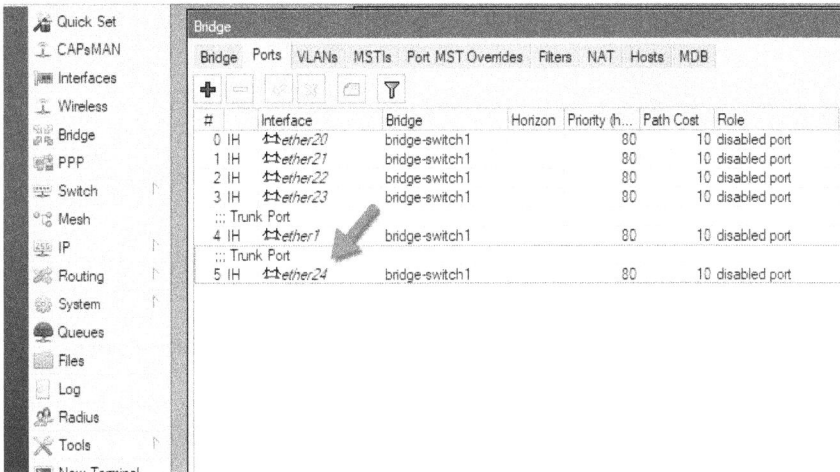

3. If you have properly configured the switch according to the Router on a Stick example from page 374, your Switch VLAN list should look like this:

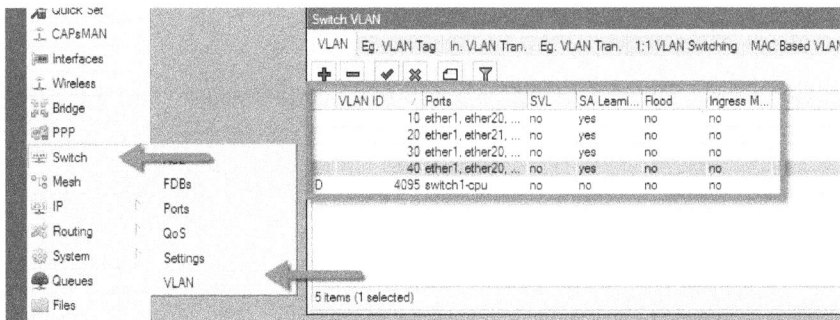

To complete Switch1 and create the second trunk port, interface ether24, edit each entry in the Switch VLAN list as follows, adding ether24 to each VLAN ID:

(Continued on next page)

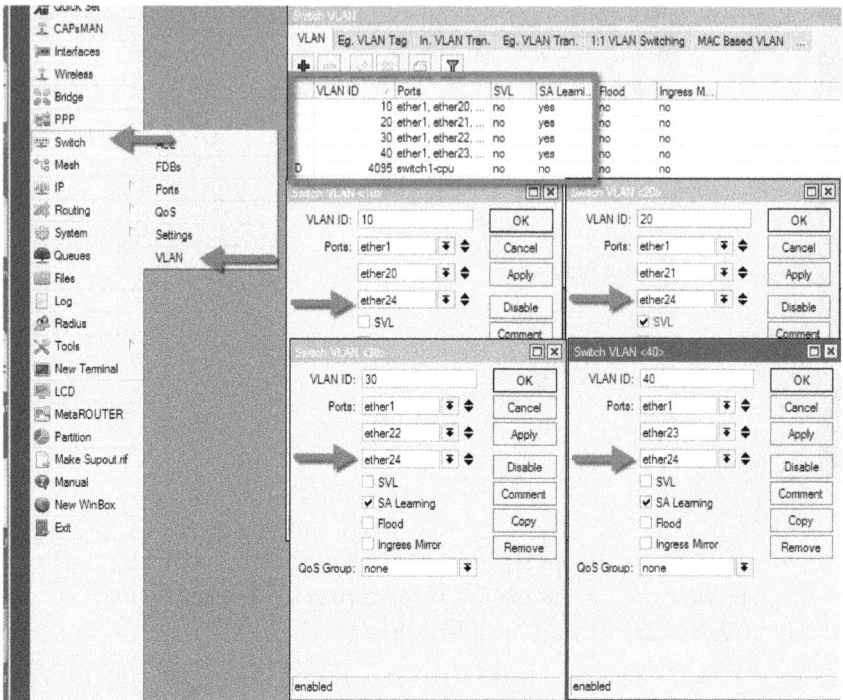

Note: Remember that if you want to manage the switch through any access ports, please follow the instructions on page 377 in this step.

Switch1 is now complete. Let's move to Switch2. Configure exactly the same as Switch1 as outlined on page 398. Duplicating the Switch1 to Switch2 configuration will make ether24 a trunk port on Switch2 (although it will be unused in this example) so that you could continue daisy-chaining these switches together, thereby extending this configuration.

Use a cable to connect ether24 on Switch1 to ether1 on Switch2 and your setup will be complete and operate as shown in the diagram.

Use this example to create QoS policies that will compliment your Layer 3 queues. Per-port QoS for example, will ensure a virus-infected client doesn't saturate the switch.

Example – Create QoS Policies for Individual Ports

Creating a rate limit on each port ensures that the connected device never exceeds a rate that would saturate an uplink and thereby threaten the health of the network. I typically recommend it as a stop gap measure or a "do not exceed" limit and use something like PCQ queuing farther upstream.

Creating a port-based rate limit is done in two pieces: ingress and egress. In terms of a client on an edge switch, ingress means how much the client can upload, and egress means how much they can download. This example assumes we have already configured the basic switch as shown on page 359 and are now applying the per port rate limits.

1. First, we will create the Ingress policy for client upload. Simply click Switch and click the Ingress Port Policer tab. Click the plus sign and set the port you want to impose the limit on and the rate limit you want to impose. In this example, we use 10M. The limit is now set for ingress.

    (Continued on next page)

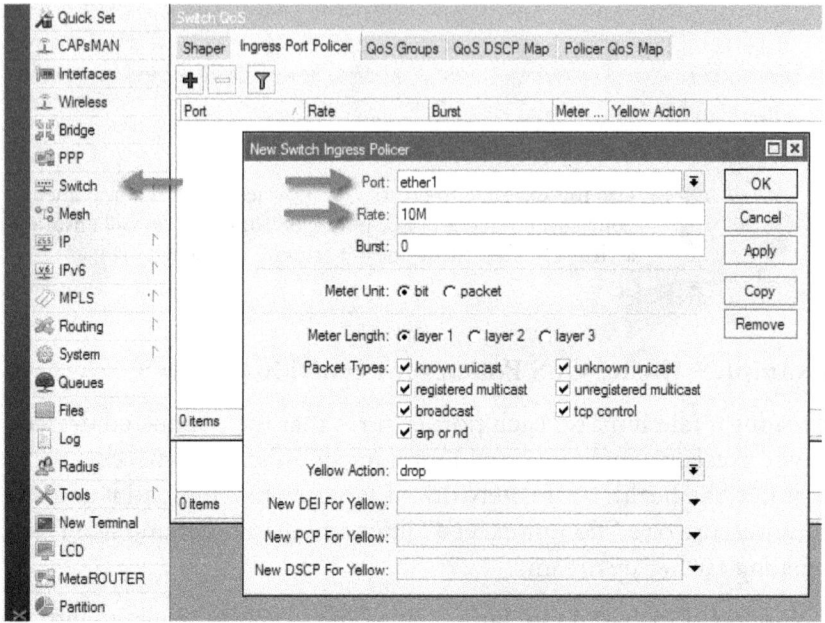

2. Next, we can create an Egress policy to limit the clients' download speeds. Click Switch, the Shaper tab, and the plus sign. Set the port on which you want to impose the limit, set the Target to port, and set the rate to the rate limit you want to impose. In this example, we will use 10M.

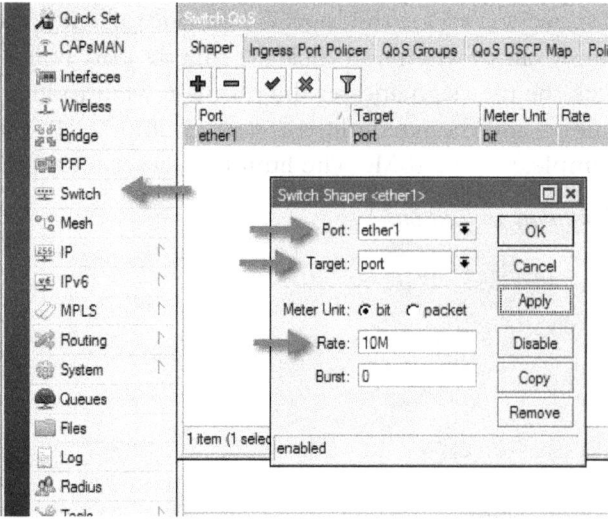

(Continued on next page)

3. Repeat this process for each port on which you want to impose a limit. For many ports, you will likely want to copy and paste the terminal commands into a text file and script this process.

Use this example to create a Link Aggregation Group, a grouping of ports that can aggregate link capacity. One application is to connect a router with three Gigabit ports to a switch with three Gigabit ports to create an aggregate of 3 Gigabits of throughput between the two devices.

APPLICATION

Example – Create a LAG Group

1. Begin by creating a switch group on the switch with ether1, ether2, and ether3. Click the Bridge button and the Plus sign to create a bridge and name the bridge switch-bridge1 or whatever you like. Click OK.

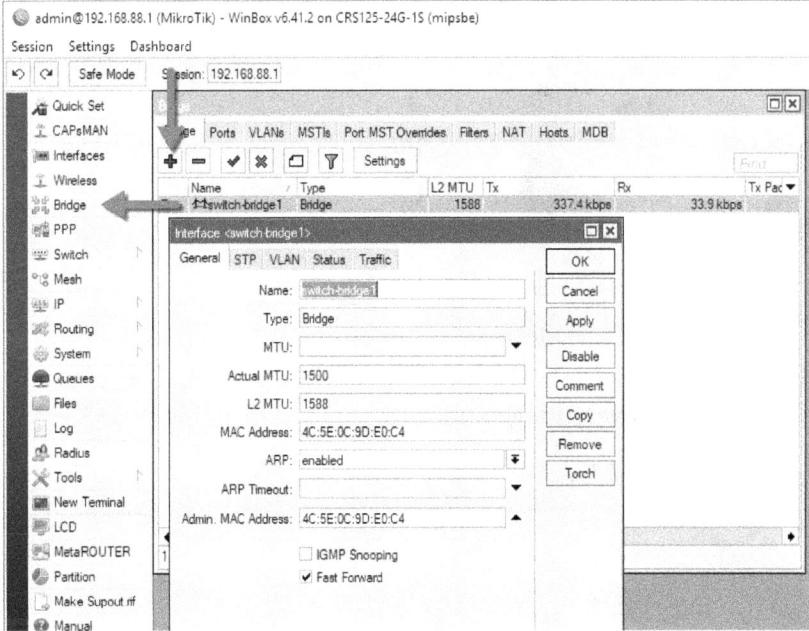

Click the Ports tab and add ports ether1, ether2, and ether3 to that bridge. The router will now bridge ether1, ether2, and ether3 together like a switch and offload traffic to the hardware switch chip.

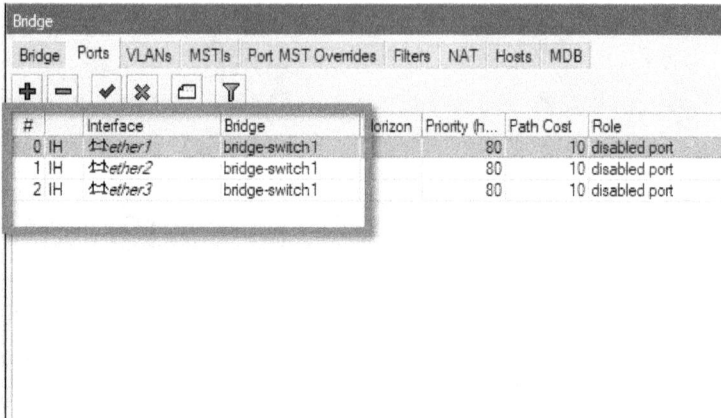

2. Next, create the trunk group by adding ether1 through ether3 to a new trunk, trunk1.

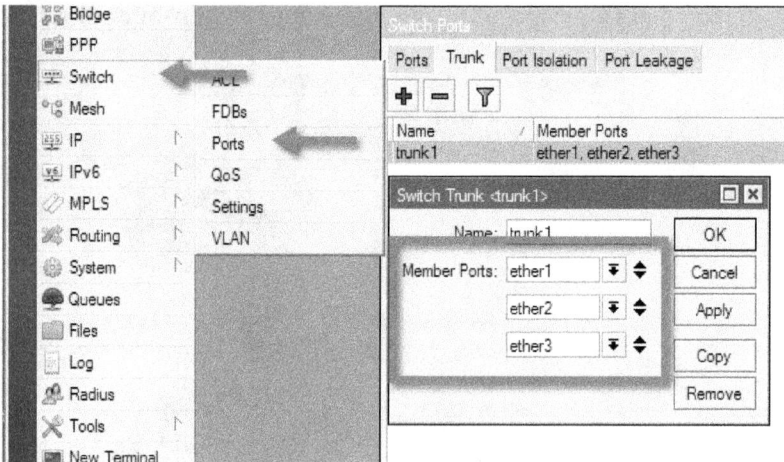

That is it for the switch. On the router, create a bonding interface as follows, setting everything as shown:

(Continued on next page)

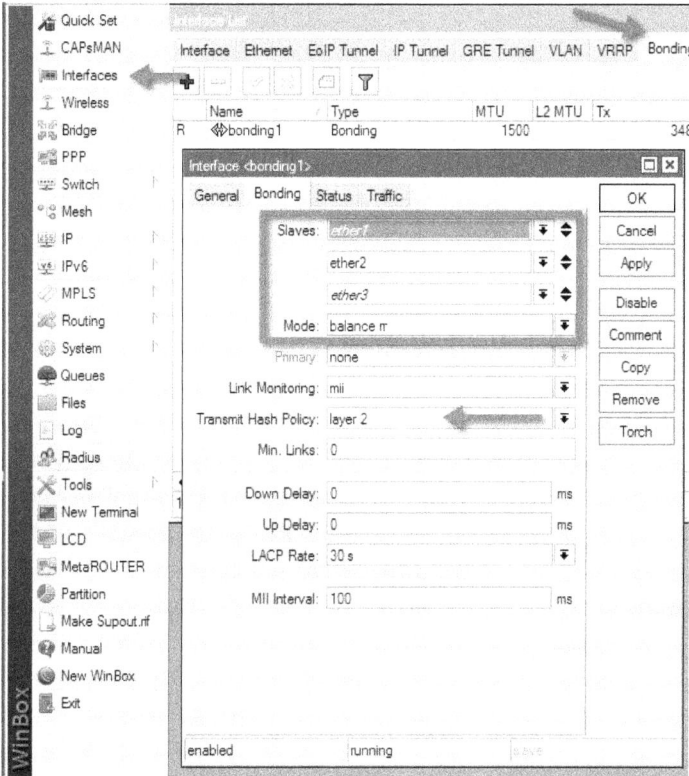

Then, connect a Gigabit cable between ether1 on the router to ether1 on the switch. Repeat for ether2 and 3. You have now successfully completed a Link Aggregation Group.

Use this example to create a policy that will only allow clients to receive DHCP provisioning from a trusted host on one or more switch ports. Rogue DHCP servers can wreak havoc in a Layer 2 network and should be eliminated by using this example and method.

Example – Create Port Isolation to Prevent Rogue DHCP Servers

In this example, we are going to assume you have already configured the switch for your application. Ether24 and ports ether1 through ether9 are ports on a bridge with hardware offload to a switch. Ether24 is connected to our network, likely a router with a DHCP server, and our clients are connected to ports ether1 through ether9. Assuming a customer has mistakenly connected a home router to one of the client ports, we want to block those DHCP server replies and only allow clients to hear DHCP server replies if they come through the trusted port, ether24. This will prevent rogue DHCP servers from passing out IP addresses on your network. Here is the diagram:

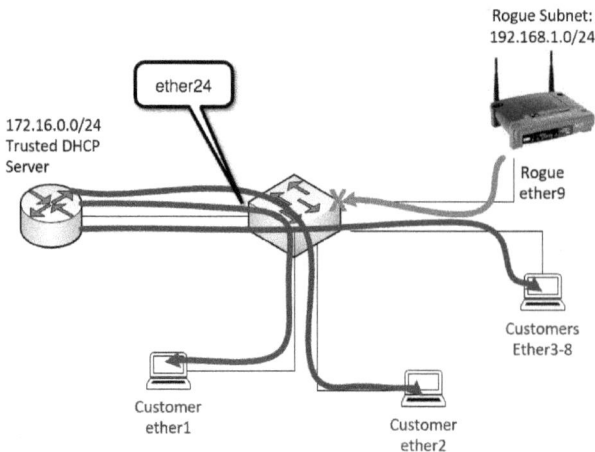

Figure 36 – Rogue DHCP Server

1. Begin by configuring the switch as described in the other examples. Click the Bridge button and the Plus sign to create a bridge and name the bridge switch-bridge1 or whatever you like. Click OK.

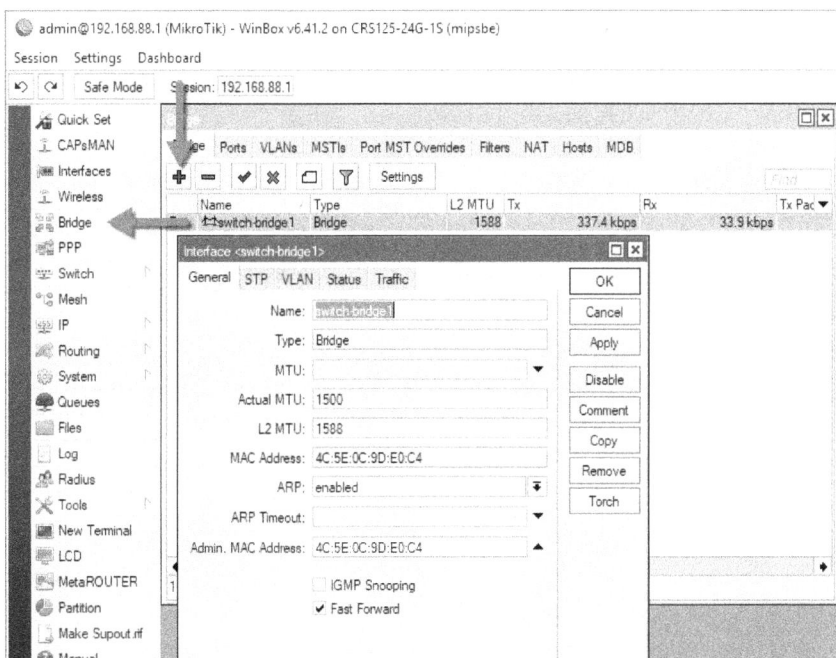

2. Click the Ports tab and add ports ether24 and ether1-ether9 to that bridge. The router will now join ether24 and ether1-ether9 together like a switch and offload traffic to the hardware switch chip.

(Continued on next page)

#	Interface	Bridge	Horiz...	Priority ...	Path Cost
0 IH	ether1	bridge		80	10
1 IH	ether2	bridge		80	10
2 IH	ether3	bridge		80	10
3 IH	ether4	bridge		80	10
4 IH	ether5	bridge		80	10
5 IH	ether6	bridge		80	10
6 IH	ether7	bridge		80	10
7 IH	ether8	bridge		80	10
8 IH	ether9	bridge		80	10
9 H	ether24	bridge		80	10

3. On all ports connecting to customers, ether1-9, set the Switch
    Port Isolation Profile Override to the Community value of 2.
    This will represent the new Isolation Profile we will create
    next. Note that there is nothing magic about the number 2; it
    is just what we picked to name the new profile.

4. Next, we create the Community Profile that will define the direction that DHCP server responses can propagate, that is, from ether24 to ether1-9, but not between ether1 through ether9. Set it exactly as shown below:

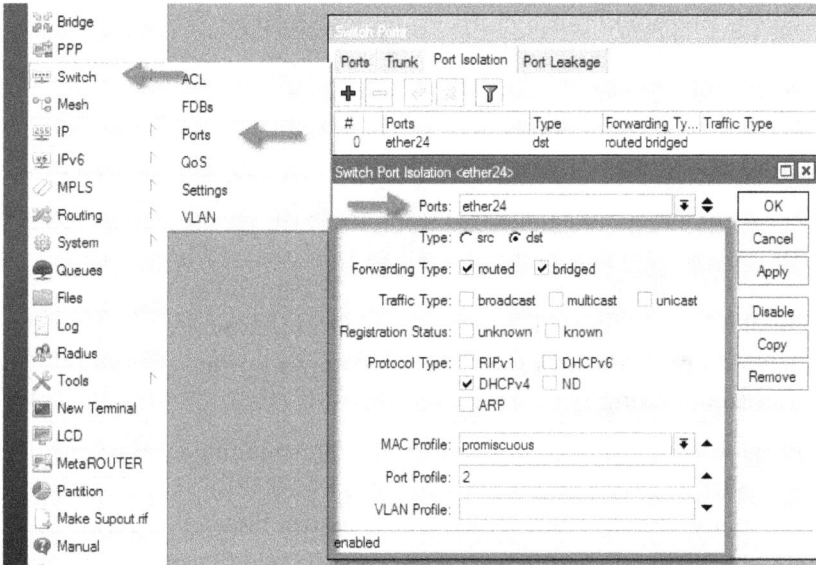

The configuration is now complete and only DHCP Server responses from ether24 will be received by clients on ether1 through 9.

Chapter 19 - Conclusion

I hope that you have enjoyed this book and have learned the concepts presented through my examples. RouterOS is a powerful routing system with many configurable options and capabilities. Fully learning it requires both book knowledge and hands-on experience. Through study, practice, and trial and error, you will learn to master this powerful tool.

After some time and experience using the basics presented in this book, you should challenge yourself by obtaining a MikroTik Certified Network Associate certificate. When you are comfortable with all of the concepts learned in the MTCNA course, you should obtain one or more advanced certifications to further explore this powerful operating system.

Writing a technical book with many similar-sounding acronyms is a real challenge. With protocols like PPP, PPTP, PPPoE, L2TP, and the like, it is easy to make a mistake no matter how many times your work is proofread. For this reason, I invite you to email any errors you may find to info@learnmikrotik.com. I welcome your corrections and suggestions and will incorporate them as well as any updates in future printings.

To my loyal readers, thank you for your suggestions and for supporting my training and my books. I hope to see you in one of my classes soon!

Keep on 'Tiking!

Steve Discher
http://www.LearnMikroTik.com

About the Author

Stephen Discher is a serial entrepreneur and a 1987 graduate of Texas A&M University. He makes his home in College Station, Texas with his wife and three children.

A native of Southern California, transplanted to Texas, he has been in the technology field since 1980.

He formally entered the telecommunications industry in 1999 by joining as a partner in American Cable Services, a telecommunications service company. In 2005, he worked as the Director of Operations for FIBERTOWN, a technology campus and Tier IV data center in Bryan, Texas. Simultaneously, he started Wickson Wireless, a WISP (Wireless Internet Service Provider) in Bryan, Texas.

Today, he works full-time managing a wireless distribution company, ISP Supplies, and leading MikroTik training with LearnMikroTik.com.

In his spare time, he enjoys flying his 1941 Piper J3 Cub, fly fishing, traveling, and RV camping with his family.

References

1. © MikroTik, www.mikrotik.com, wiki.mikrotik.com, routerboard.com. All rights reserved. Reprinted with permission when used for training.

2. E.W. Dijkstra. "A Note on Two Problems in Connection with Graphs." *Numerische Mathematic* 1:269-271, 1959.

3. Stephen A. Thomas. "IP Switching and Routing Essentials." *Wiley Computer Publishing* 103, 2002.

4. "Traceroute." *Wikipedia, The Free Encyclopedia.* Wikimedia Foundation, Inc. Web, 22, September 2011.

5. Cisco Networking Academy. "Routing and Switching Essentials Companion Guide." 10-12, *Cisco Press*, 2014.

Appendix 1

Official MikroTik Certified Network Associate Training Syllabus

Last edited on January 22, 2016

MikroTik

Certified Network Associate (MTCNA)
Training outline

Duration:	3 days
Outcomes:	By the end of this training session, the student will be familiar with RouterOS software and RouterBOARD products and be able to connect the client to the Internet. He will also be able to configure, manage, do basic troubleshooting of a MikroTik router and provide basic services to clients.
Target audience:	Network engineers and technicians wanting to deploy and support:
	• Corporate networks
	• Client CPEs (WISPs and ISPs)
Course prerequisites:	The student must have a good understanding of TCP/IP and subnetting.
Suggested reading:	Search for "ipv4 tutorial"
	Test yourself with 'Example Test' on https://www.mikrotik.com/client/training

Title	Objective
Module 1 Introduction	• About MikroTik 　• What is RouterOS 　• What is RouterBoard • First time accessing the router 　• WinBox and MAC-WinBox 　• WebFig and Quick Set 　• Default configuration • RouterOS command line interface (CLI) 　• Null Modem cable 　• SSH and Telnet 　• New terminal in WinBox/WebFig • RouterOS CLI principles 　• <tab>, double <tab>, "?", navigation 　• command history and its benefits • Initial configuration (Internet access) 　• WAN DHCP-client 　• LAN IP address and default gateway 　• Basic Firewall - NAT masquerade • Upgrading RouterOS 　• Package types 　• Ways of upgrading 　• RouterBOOT firmware upgrade • Router identity • Manage RouterOS logins • Manage RouterOS services • Managing configuration backups 　• Saving and restoring the backup 　• Difference between a backup and an export (.rsc) file 　• Editing an export file • Resetting a RouterOS device • Reinstalling a RouterOS device (Netinstall) • RouterOS license levels • Sources of additional information 　• wiki.mikrotik.com 　• forum.mikrotik.com 　• mum.mikrotik.com 　• Distributor and consultant support 　• support@mikrotik.com • **Module 1 laboratory**

Module 2
DHCP
	• DHCP server and client
	    • DHCP client
	    • DHCP server setup
	    • Leases management
	    • DHCP server network configuration
	• Address Resolution Protocol (ARP)
	    • ARP modes
	    • RouterOS ARP table
	• **Module 2 laboratory**

Module 3
Bridging
	• Bridging overview
	    • Bridge concepts and settings
	    • Creating bridges
	    • Adding ports to bridges
	• Bridge wireless networks
	    • Station bridge
	• **Module 3 laboratory**

Module 4
Routing
	• Routing overview
	    • Routing concepts
	    • Route flags
	• Static routing
	    • Creating routes
	    • Setting default route
	    • Managing dynamic routes
	    • Implementing static routing in a simple network
	• **Module 4 laboratory**

Module 5
Wireless
	• 802.11a/b/g/n/ac Concepts
	    • Frequencies (bands, channels) data-rates / chains (tx power, rx sensitivity, country regulations)
	• Setup a simple wireless link
	    • Access Point configuration
	    • Station configuration
	• Wireless Security and Encryption
	    • Access List
	    • Connect List
	    • Default Authenticate
	    • Default Forward
	    • WPA-PSK, WPA2-PSK
	    • WPS accept, WPS client
	• Monitoring Tools
	    • Snooper
	    • Registration table
	• **Module 5 laboratory**

Module 6
Firewall
	• Firewall principles
	    • Connection tracking and states
	    • Structure, chains and actions
	• Firewall Filter in action
	    • Filter actions
	    • Protecting your router (input)
	    • Protection your customers (forward)
	• Basic Address-List
	• Source NAT
	    • Masquerade and src-nat action
	• Destination NAT
	    • dst-nat and redirect action
	• FastTrack
	• **Module 6 laboratory**

Module 7
QoS
	• Simple Queue
	   • Target
	   • Destinations
	   • Max-limit and limit-at
	   • Bursting
	• One Simple queue for the whole network (PCQ)
	   • pcq-rate configuration
	   • pcq-limit configuration
	• **Module 7 laboratory**

Module 8
Tunnels
	• PPP settings
	   • PPP profile
	   • PPP secret
	   • PPP status
	• IP pool
	   • Creating pool
	   • Managing ranges
	   • Assigning to a service
	• Secure local network
	   • PPPoE service-name
	   • PPPoE client
	   • PPPoE server
	• Point-to-point addresses
	• Secure remote networks communication
	   • PPTP client and PPTP server (Quick Set)
	   • SSTP client
	• **Module 8 laboratory**

Module 9
Misc
	• RouterOS tools
	    • E-mail
	    • Netwatch
	    • Ping
	    • Traceroute
	    • Profiler (CPU load)
	• Monitoring
	    • Interface traffic monitor
	    • Torch
	    • Graphs
	    • SNMP
	    • The Dude
	• Contacting support@mikrotik.com
	    • supout.rif, autosupout.rif and viewer
	    • System logs, enabling debug logs
	    • readable configuration (item comments and names)
	    • network diagrams
	• **Module 9 laboratory**

Table of Figures

Index

www.ingramcontent.com/pod-product-compliance
Lightning Source LLC
Chambersburg PA
CBHW060748220326
41598CB00022B/2360